THE STABLE BOOK;

BEING A TREATISE ON THE

MANAGEMENT OF HORSES,

IN RELATION TO

STABLING, GROOMING, FEEDING, WATERING AND WORKING.
CONSTRUCTION OF STABLES, VENTILATION, STABLE
APPENDAGES, MANAGEMENT OF THE FEET.

MANAGEMENT OF DISEASED AND DEFECTIVE HORSES.

BY

JOHN STEWART,

VETERINARY SURGEON, PROFESSOR OF VETERINARY MEDICINE, IN THE
ANDERSONIAN UNIVERSITY, GLASGOW.

WITH NOTES AND ADDITIONS,

ADAPTING IT TO

AMERICAN FOOD AND CLIMATE,

BY A. B. ALLEN,

EDITOR OF THE AMERICAN AGRICULTURIST.

WITH ILLUSTRATIONS.

NEW YORK:

C. M. SAXTON & CO.,

AGRICULTURAL BOOK PUBLISHERS.

1856.

CONTENTS.

SIXTH CHAPTER.

WATER—P. 281 to 289.

SEVENTH CHAPTER.

SERVICE—P. 290 to 361.

EIGHTH CHAPTER.

MANAGEMENT OF DISEASED AND DEFECTIVE
HORSES—P. 362 to 369.

LIST OF ENGRAVINGS.

For the drawings from which these engravings were engraved, I am indebted to the kindness of my friend, Mr. Robert Hart. [Those of Mr. Gibbons' stables and Mr. Pell's stalls, are furnished by the editor of the American edition.]

STABLE ECONOMY

FIRST CHAPTER.

STABLING.

I. CONSTRUCTION OF STABLES.—II. VENTILATION OF
STABLES.—III. APPENDAGES OF STABLES.

CONSTRUCTION OF STABLES.

STABLES have been in use for several hundred years. It
might be expected that the experience of so many genera-
tions would have rendered them perfect. They are better
than they were some years ago. Many of modern erection
have few faults. They are spacious, light, well-aired, dry,
and comfortable. This, however, is not the character of
stables in general. The majority have been built with little
regard to the comfort and health of the horse. Most of them
are too small, too dark, and too close, or too open. Some
are mere dungeons, so destitute of every convenience that no
man of respectability [or ordinary humanity] would willingly
make them the abode of his horses.

Stable architects have not much to boast of. When left
to themselves they seem to think of little beyond shelter and
confinement. If the weather be kept out, and the horse kept
in, the stable is sufficient. If light and air be demanded, the
doorway will admit them, and other apertures are superfluous;
if the horse have room to stand, it matters little though he have
none to lie; and if he get into the stable, it is of no consequence though his loins be sprained, or his haunches broken,
in going out of it.

Bad stables, it is true, are not equally pernicious to all
kinds of horses. Those that have little work suffer much

2

mismanagement before they are injured. But those in constant and laborious employment must have good lodgings.
Where the stables are bad, the management is seldom good,
and it can not be of the best kind. It is no exaggeration to
say, that hundreds of coaching-horses, and others employed
at similar work, are destroyed every year by the combined
influence of bad stables and bad stable management. Excessive toil and bad food have much to do in the work of de-
struction; but every hostile agent operates with most force
where the stables are of the worst kind; and several causes
of disease can operate nowhere else.

SITUATION OF STABLES.—Few have much choice of situation. When any exists, that should be selected which will
admit of draining, shelter from the coldest winds, and easy
access. The aspect should be southern. Training stables
should be near the exercising ground. The surface should
be sloping, and the soil dry. Stables built in a hollow, or in
a marsh, are always damp. When the foundation is sunk in
clay, no draining will keep the walls dry. Some of the means
usually employed against dampness in dwelling-houses, might
be adopted in the construction of stables. These, as every
builder knows, consist in a contrivance for preventing the
wall from absorbing the moisture of the soil. In some places
a course of whin, or other stone, impenetrable to water, joined
by cement, is laid level with the ground; in other places, a
sheet of lead, laid upon a deal board, is employed; and in
the neighborhood of coal-pits, the foundation is sometimes
laid in coal-dust, which does not absorb water, and is much
less expensive than either lead or stone. It is not right to
suppose that precautions of this kind are superfluous.

A DAMP STABLE produces more evil than a damp house.
It is there we expect to find horses with bad eyes, coughs,
greasy heels, swelled legs, mange, and a long, rough, dry,
staring coat, which no grooming can cure. The French
attribute glanders and farcy to a humid atmosphere; and in
a damp situation we find these diseases most prevalent;
though, in this country, excess of moisture is reckoned as
only a subordinate cause. In London, and in other towns,
there are several stables under the surface; they are never
dry, and never healthy. The bad condition, and the disease,
so common and so constantly among their ill-fated inhabitants,
may undoubtedly arise from a combination of causes; but
there is every reason to believe that humidity is not the least
potent.

When horses are first lodged in a damp stable, they soon show how much they feel the change. They become dull, languid, feeble ; the coat stares ; they refuse to feed ; at fast-work they cut their legs in spite of all care to prevent them. This arises from weakness. Some of the horses catch cold, others are attacked by inflammations of the throat, the lungs, or the eyes. Most of them lose flesh very rapidly. The change produces most mischief when it is made in the winter-time.

All New Stables are Damp.—It is a long time ere the walls get rid of the moisture introduced by the mortar. Entry to a new stable should be delayed till it is dry, or as long as possible. If, as often happens, the stable be wanted for immediate occupation, the walls had better be left unplastered, unless there be sufficient time for the plaster to dry. The doors or windows should be kept off or wide open till the day of entry. A few fires of charcoal, judiciously planted, and often shifted, will assist the drying process. White-washing the walls with a solution of quick-lime, seems to have some influence in removing moisture. When ready for entry, the stable should be filled. A horse should go into every stall. One helps to keep another warm. In the winter they should be clothed, have boiled warm food every night [if convenient to cook it] and be deeply littered.

Damp stables may be rendered less uncomfortable by strewing the floor with sand or sawdust; by thorough draining and ventilation. In some cases, a stove-pipe might be made to pass through the stable, near to the floor.

SIZE OF STABLES.—They are seldom too large in proportion to the number of stalls ; but they are often made to hold too many horses. Those employed in public conveyances in coaches and boats, are frequently crowded into an apartment containing twenty or thirty. It is not right to have so many horses, particularly hard-working horses, in one place. Such stables are liable to frequent and great alterations of temperature. When several of the horses are out, those which remain are rendered uncomfortably cold, and when full, the whole are fevered or excited by excess of heat. These transitions are very pernicious, and generally neglected. The owner wonders why so many of his horses catch cold ; there are always some of them coughing. If he were to make the stable his abode for twenty-four hours, and mark the number and degree of alterations which occur in its temperature, he would have little to wonder at.

Besides these transitions, so unavoidable in large stables, there are other evils. A very large stable is not easily ven-tilated; it requires a lofty roof to give any degree of purity; it is not easily kept in order; contagious diseases once in-troduced, spread rapidly, and do extensive mischief before they can be checked; and a large stable seldom affords a hard-working horse all the repose he requires. His rest is disturbed by the entrance and exit of other horses, or of the persons employed in stable operations. It sometimes happens that one mischievous or restless horse disturbs all his fellows. He would do so in a small stable; but there he can not an-noy so many. All these objections are not applicable to every large stable. In some the horses go out and return all together. In that case, they are not exposed to such vicissi-tudes of temperature, nor so liable to have their rest broken. But the other evils are not insignificant. A very large stable has nothing to recommend it that I know of. The expense of erection may be something less, and one or two additional stalls may be obtained by lodging the horses all in one large stable, rather than in several small stables. When it is more important to have a cheap than a healthy stable, the large one may be preferred. The saving, however, may ultimately be a great loss, if the builder of the stable be the owner of the horses.

For hunters and other valuable horses, the stables should not have more than four stalls. These should be on only one side. Nimrod recommends that only three horses be kept in these four-stalled stables, and that the inner partition be moveable, in order that two of the stalls may be converted into a loose box, whenever such an appendage is required. For a pair of carriage-horses, the stable should have three stalls. The odd one is often useful. Should a horse fall sick or lame, another can be taken in to do his work till he get better; or, the inner partition being made to move, two of the stalls can be thrown into one.

Hunters, carriage-horses, and others of equal size and value, require a good deal of room. In width, the stable may vary from sixteen to eighteen feet; and in length it must have six feet for every stall. Some are not above fourteen or fif-teen feet wide, but these are too narrow. Others are twenty feet, which I think is rather wide. There is no need for so much room; when too wide, the stable is too cold. It is sufficiently wide at sixteen feet, and roomy at eighteen. Coach-horses, and others employed at similar work, usually stand in a double row. The number of stalls should never exceed sixteen. It would be better if there were only eight, or a separate stable for each team. For these stables the width may be from twenty-two to twenty-four feet. If the horses do not exceed the average height, the stalls may be only five and a half feet wide; but they are better to be the full width, six feet. Single-headed stables for coach-horses may be sixteen and a half feet wide, and seventeen is quite sufficient. Large cart-horses require a little more room, both in the length and breadth of the stable.

. ARRANGEMENT OF THE STALLS.—In this there is little variety. In a square or circular apartment, the stalls may be ranged on each side, or all round. There is one at Edinburgh in a circular form. When full and lighted from the roof, it looks well, but no particular advantage is gained by this arrangement. The circular and the equilateral form leave a good deal of unoccupied room in the centre. An oblong is the best, and the general form for a stable. The stalls may be arranged on both sides or on one only. Each mode has its advantages and disadvantages.

Double-headed [double-rowed] stables, as those are called in which the stalls occupy each side, require the least space. When the gangway between the horses is not too narrow, they are sufficiently suitable for coach or boat-horses, or any others kept at full work. But many accidents arise from the horses kicking at each other when they grow playful, as they are apt to do while half idle. For this reason, a livery stable should not be double-headed, without a very wide gangway, perhaps of eight or ten feet; they are quite unfit for valuable hunters or carriage-horses. Indeed, no width of gangway is sufficient to prevent some horses from attempting to strike when another is placed directly behind. Those that are disposed to mischief have frequent opportunities, as others are leaving or entering the stables; mares especially are generally very troublesome in these stables. For all kinds of horses, that stable is decidedly the best in which the stalls are ranged on one side only. These are termed single-headed.

THE WALLS may be composed of wood, stone, or brick. In this country they are seldom made of wood. Stone is the most permanent material, and is usually employed wherever it can be cheaply procured, or the building likely to be long required. Stone walls are said by some to be apt to sweat, to keep the stable damp and cold; but this objection, I appre-

2*

hend, is applicable only to a new stone wall, to one composed
of particular kinds of stone, or to that which is sunk in clay.
Brick walls, however, are most esteemed. [Dampness of
stone or brick walls may be entirely obviated in the drier
climate of America, and warmth gained in winter, and coolness in summer, by running the roof over the gable ends and
sides of the building about two feet, as in the Italian or old
French style. Dampness may also be prevented inside,
by furrowing out from the walls, and lath and plastering;
but this is too expensive for stables; nor does it accomplish
the same objects as jutting roofs; and, moreover, the hollow
space makes a harbor for vermin, which is a very great objection to it.] In towns or other places where the ground is
likely in a short time to become too valuable for stables, brick
is the least expensive material, and it brings the highest price
when pulled down. A brick wall is usually recommended to
be hollow, and thirteen and a half, or eighteen inches thick.
Thus built, it is said to exclude the heat of summer and the
cold of winter. Few, however, are made thicker than nine
inches, and none hollow. It is a long time ere either cold
or heat pierces a nine-inch wall; but a thick wall affords recesses for racks, cupboards, and shelves, and, in exposed
situations, it certainly keeps the stable comfortable through a
severe winter.

The inside of the walls is sometimes left bare, but most
frequently it is either plastered or boarded. All the stalls
ought to be lined with wood, boarded at the head for about
three feet above the manger; and the wall forming one side
of the end stall should be boarded as high as the partitions.
Sometimes the back wall is boarded all round to the height
of four or five feet. A few of the more costly kind, which
are built of freestone, are polished on the inside as on the
out. As far as the horse is concerned, it is sufficient to have
the wall neatly and smoothly dressed off. Plaster is apt to
break, to blister, and fall away. The wooden lining round
the lower part of the wall is more durable, and when the
upper part is plastered, the stable has a cleaner, more finished,
and more comfortable appearance. The parts against which
the horse is likely to come in contact when rising, lying down,
or turning, ought to be smooth and soft, not calculated to
bruise or ruffle his skin.

Doors.—A stable should have only one door. [This is
not enough. They should have a door at each end, for the
sake of a draught of air when necessary. The stables are

of an old usage, merely to avoid open conviction of ignorance.
.Dark stables were introduced, not because men thought them
the best, but because they had no inclination to purchase light,
or because they thought the horse had no use for it.

A horse was never known to thrive better for being kept in
a dark stable. The dealer may hide his horse in darkness,
and perhaps he may believe that they fatten sooner there than
in the light of day. But he might as well tell the truth at
once, and say that he wants to keep them out of sight till they
are ready for the market. When a horse is brought from a
dark stable to the open air he sees very indistinctly; he stares
about him, and carries his head high, and he steps high.
The horse looks as if he had a good deal of action and animation. Dark stables may thus suit the purposes of dealers, but
they are certainly not the most suitable for horses. They
are said to injure the eyes. There is not perhaps another
animal on the earth so liable to blindness as the horse. It
can not be said with certainty that darkness is the cause ; but
it is well known that the eyes suffer most frequently where
there is no light.

Whether a dark stable be pernicious to the eyes or not, it
is always a bad stable. It has too many invisible holes and
corners about it ever to be thoroughly cleaned. The gloomy
dungeons in which coach and boat horses are so often im-
mured, are always foul. The horses are attended by men
who will not do their duty if they can neglect it. The dung
and the urine lie rotting for weeks together, and contaminating
the air till it is unfit for use. The horses are never properly
groomed. They can not be seen. One may fall lame, another
sick, and no one know anything about them till they are
brought to the door to commence a journey. Accidents,
choking, getting cast in the stall, tearing open a vein and such
like, sometimes happen when the horse's life may depend
upon immediate assistance, which can not be rendered in
the dark, or which darkness may conceal till assistance is too
late. I speak not of what might occur, but of that which is
common.

All these things considered, it is evident that the stable
ought to be well lighted, and that the expense attending it is
a prudent outlay. When side-windows can not be conveniently introduced, a portion of the hay-loft must be sacrificed, and light obtained from the roof. This in ordinary
cases will not be greatly missed. Let it be well done if done
at all. It is almost as expensive to put in a small window as

a large one; and I believe it is more expensive to light a double-headed stable properly from the sides than from the roof. When the stalls are all on one side the case is different, especially if the back wall be unconnected with any other building. Windows above the horses' head generally light the wrong side of the stable, and those at the ends can hardly be made to light more than one or two stalls.

Windows may or may not be made to open. Some of them should open, in order that the stable may, upon certain occasions, receive an extraordinary airing. But for constant and necessary ventilation there must be apertures which can never be wholly closed.

WINDOW-SHUTTERS, in some situations, are useful for three purposes. By darkening the stable they encourage a fatigued horse to rest through the day; they keep out the flies in the hot days of summer; and in winter they help to keep the stable warm. They may be made of wood, of basket-work, or of matting, according to the purpose for which they are wanted. In some stables the windows are removable, so that in summer they can be taken out and their place filled by a piece of basket-work or framed canvass, which may be wet in hot weather. The stables are thus kept cool; the flies and the heat of the sun are excluded. Some horses are sadly annoyed by flies. They do not enter a dark stable.

THE ROOF of the stable usually forms the floor of the hay-loft. In some of the farm stables there is no hay-loft. The outer roof is the roof of the stable, and is of thatch or tile, plastered or unplastered. "The most wholesome stables," says a popular, though a very superficial author, "are those where nothing intervenes between the roof of the building and the floor, and I have had occasion to observe that roofs made of unplastered tile, form the best mode of ventilation."* In the country, where it is impossible to have the litter removed as it is soiled, and where the horses are not the worse of having a long coat, a roof of tile, plastered or unplastered, may afford all the shelter they require, while it favors the escape of effluvia from the rotting litter, upon which the horses of a slovenly farmer are compelled to seek repose. But stables of this kind are not for horses of fast and laborious work. They are too cold.

If the loft be above the stable, the ceiling must be nine feet from the ground, and if the stable contains more than four horses, the ceiling must be higher. A height of from

* White.

twelve to fourteen feet is sufficient for the largest stable ; and the smallest ought not to be less than eight feet high. When too lofty the stable is cold ; when too low, it requires large ventilators, which create a current, not at all times safe or pleasant to the horses. Professor Coleman used to recommend a very low roof, about seven feet I think from the ground. I forget his reason. His own stable is so low that medicine can not be given to a horse in it without driving the crown of his head through the ceiling. It certainly is not right to have the roof so low. The height must vary from eight to fourteen feet, according to the number of horses. When there is no loft above, the height should be rather greater ; in summer the slates or the tiles become hot, and make the stable like an oven ; and in winter when snow lies on the roof, the stable is like an ice-house. The hay-loft, when over the stable, should have no communication with it.

THE FLOOR.—In Scotland the floor of the stable is almost universally laid either with whinstone or freestone, or partly with the one and partly with the other. Very often, the gangway and about one half of the stall are paved, while the other half of the stall is causewayed. In a few cases hard bricks are employed, and arranged on edge ; the first expense is less, but bricks, even when well selected and properly laid, are not sufficiently durable, especially under heavy horses. So long as they remain in order, however, they make a very good floor, which always affords firm foot-hold, but I do not recommend it.

Pavement is apt to get slippery and make the horses fall when rising, or when leaving the stable. I once saw a horse break his thighbone in rising from a paved stall, but there was no fixed partition between the stalls, and very little litter on the ground, otherwise it is probable the accident would not have happened. In the same stable several other horses have been lamed in the same way and from the same causes.

A *Paved Floor*, however, when properly grooved, is the best both for gangway and stalls ; it is durable and easily kept clean. To prevent the horse from slipping, it ought to be furrowed by concave grooves about three inches wide and one deep. At the gangway these should run across the stable, and in the stall they should run parallel with the partitions. Both should slope to the gutter. In some stables these grooves have others running directly or obliquely across them. They are rarely three inches wide in any stable ; most frequently they do not exceed one inch. When narrow they require to

be numerous. They need not be so wide at bottom as at top
When too narrow they are always full of dirt.   The grooves
may be four inches apart.

A *Causewayed Floor* is the next best : and, when properly
laid, it is more durable than a freestone floor.   Instead of the
usual blocks of stone, of all shapes and all sizes, some rising
and some sinking from the general level, the stones ought to
be square, and neatly joined, having no large intervals filled
with sand, which alternately receives and rejects the urine,
keeping the air constantly saturated with its unwholesome
vapors.   Causeway, however, is never so cleanly as freestone
flags, and it is difficult to get it sufficiently grooved.   When
laid in the ordinary, anyhow way, a causewayed floor is
dirty, uneven, slippery, and easily torn up by the horses' feet,
or undermined by rats.   Pebbles or Dutch clinkers are often
employed as stable flooring ; but I can say nothing about
them, for in this country their place is supplied by whinstone.

In former times the stalls were laid with planks of oak, in
which holes were bored that led the urine into underground
drains.   This mode of flooring has gone entirely out of use,
and there appears no reason for reviving it.   The ancient
writers complain that it produced many accidents from the
horse slipping, and from the planks starting out of place.

[The climate in Great Britain is so much damper than
that of America, that the objections there to a plank floor
will not hold good here.   Lumber is also very much dearer
there than here, which is another serious objection with the
English to wooden floors.

Earth Floors.—One of the best kinds of stable-floors,
where the soil is a dry one, is made of a composition of lime,
ashes, and clay, mixed up in equal parts into a mortar, and
spread twelve to fifteen inches deep over the surface of the
ground forming the bottom of the stables.   It will dry in a
week or ten days, and makes a very smooth fine flooring,
particularly safe, easy, and agreeable for horses to stand on,
and free from all the objections of stone, brick, and wood ;
and were it not that a sharp-shod horse is apt to cut it up,
we should consider it as quite perfect.   When the corks on
the shoes are sharp, more pains should be taken in littering
the floor to a greater depth, which would tend to its preservation.   When much cut and worn, the flooring is easily broken
up with a pick-axe, softened with water, and again relaid.
The stables of Mr. Gibbons of New Jersey, are floored with

the above composition, and he informs us that he highly approves of them on his dry soil. Indian-rubber has been used in England for floors and found to answer well. It has been in use at the royal stables at Woolwich for two years past. It is soft to the feet, comfortable to lie on, and from its yielding nature never injures the knees, hocks, or pasterns. It is easily cleaned, the urine runs off freely, and suffers no collection underneath the floor to taint the air.]

DRAINS.—These are seldom thought of. But, in some situations, to have a dry and sweet stable, they are absolutely necessary. In short stables, having only four or five horses in a row, underground drains are useful only for draining the foundations. On a stable not exceeding twenty-four or thirty feet in length, sufficient declivity can be obtained on the surface for removing the urine. But in a stable fifty or sixty feet long, a gutter is not so easily procured. The declivity necessary for carrying off the water, raises one end of the stable to an inconvenient height. A drain should be sunk. This may receive the water either from each stall, or from a grating placed near the centre of the stable, which, in the latter case, must slope from each end. Goodwin recommends a cast-iron grating near the centre, or rather toward the entrance of each stall, which should incline a little from all sides. The grate is in four pieces, resting upon ridges of stone, and having the bars so close that the calkins of the shoes can not pass between them. They have something like this at the Veterinary College, the only place in which I remember to have seen anything of the kind. The contrivance answers the purpose very well; it carries off the urine by sunk drains, and at once, and it saves the litter. The object of this plan is to get rid of the inclination usually given to the floor of the stall. The cost, however, is greater than the mischief it is supposed to prevent.

When the urine is to be saved, it may be carried to the manure-pit, or to a cess-pool outside the stable, and emptied occasionally by a pump. The end of the drain should never be exposed to the air. It ought to have a trap-door, which will open by the pressure of the water, and shut when the water has passed. When this is neglected, cold air rushes through the gratings and blows upon the horses' heels, or noxious vapors arise from the cess-pool.

In some stables there is no contrivance for carrying off the water. Part is soaked up by the litter, part sinks into the floor, and the remainder, which is the most acrimonious,

evaporates and mingles with the air. These stables of course
are always damp and foul. Their inhabitants are liable to
more than their share of disease at all times, and especially
when an unhealthy season prevails.

Fig. 2.

Fig. 2 gives a view of the stable erected by the late Mr.
James Donaldson. The breadth excepted, it is a perfect
model for a stable of two stalls. One half of the stall floor
is laid with brick; the other half is covered by a single slab
of freestone, which is grooved longitudinally and transversely,
and perforated at each intersection of the grooves. The perforations conduct the urine to an under-ground drain, which
can be cleaned in its whole extent by lifting the channel-
grating. This seems to be a much better contrivance than
the iron-grating, since it is more extensive, less costly, less
likely to give or to receive injury, and requiring no declivity
on any part of the stall. In other respects this stable is very
neat. It has a boiler behind the inside stall; a cupboard, a
window well placed, the mangers and travis moveable. It
is only twelve feet wide; if copied, the gangway should be
three feet broader. In this cut, the manger is shown too low
and the rack too high.

Declivity of the Stall.—The ordinary mode of draining the
stall is to make it slope from the head to a gutter, about ten
feet from the manger. The inclination varies from two to
three inches on the ten feet. This has been objected to, but,

as it appears to me, without any good reason. It is said that the flexor muscles and back sinews are put upon the stretch, to such a degree that they are injured. It is not easy to believe this. As far as I have been able to ascertain, no one has ever seen a horse lamed in this way. The matter might be decided by experiment. By making a horse stand for a week or two upon a declivity somewhat greater than that required for draining the stall, it would be seen whether or not it is possible to make him lame in this way. My own stable has a fall of four inches on the ten feet, but it has never produced any injury to the back sinews. That these parts are put upon the stretch when the horse is standing on a declivity, need not be denied; but the tension is never in an injurious degree. In proof of the contrary, it is urged that we feel pain in the back of our limbs when standing with the toes elevated; and that the horse, feeling the same uneasiness, endeavors to relieve himself by standing as far in the gangway as his collar will permit. It need only be mentioned that pain is not produced in our limbs by standing in any stall, however much it slopes. The horse stands back merely to look around him, or to avoid the foul vapor rising from the litter which lies under his manger. He does the same when there is no declivity in his stall.

White objects to a sloping stall, and concludes by recommending that the inclination be no greater than one inch or the yard. Not one stable in ten has more, and few have quite so much.

The contrivances to avoid inclination are useless; there is no need for them. It may be safely concluded that the ordinary declivity is not in the least pernicious. Some old and tender-footed horses, indeed, would be all the better of having the stall more than usually elevated in front. It would save the fore feet in a slight degree, and enable the horse to rise with more ease. Dealers' stables are often raised in front to a greater elevation than draining requires. The horses look taller and higher in the withers when viewed in these stalls.

PRECAUTIONS AGAINST RATS.—In laying the floor, some measures should be adopted to prevent or check the inroads of these vermin. They are very destructive about stables. They undermine the pavement, eat the wood-work, choke the drains, and rob the horse of his food. Where they abound in great numbers they know the feeding hours, and they watch the departure of the man after food is placed in the manger, which they enter in a drove and manage to eat as much as

the horse, who seems to care little about them. Hellebore
or arsenic, it is said, will kill them in great numbers when
mingled with a warm malt mash and placed in the manger.
The horse of course must not partake of this. He must be
in the stall with his head tied securely to the rack. Soap
waste is sometimes laid around the foundations of the outside
walls. They are unwilling to burrow through this, but they
will, if very anxious to get in. Some rough or sharp material
should be laid under the pavement, and around the walls on
the outside.

PARTITIONS BETWEEN THE HORSES.—In some parts of
England horses are permitted to stand two and two, without
any partition between them. This rarely happens in Scotland. He is " poor indeed" who can not afford a stall to
each horse. When two are standing together, the one is
always doing the other some mischief, either accidentally or
intentionally. The strongest robs the weakest both of his
food and of his rest; while one is lying the other will tram-
ple or lie down on his companion; and mares, while standing
double, seldom or never urinate till one is removed. Two
that have toiled together for many a day, have fed from the
same manger, and crouched under the lash of the same driver,
are generally good friends, forbearing, and sympathizing.
Still accidents will happen in the dark, or when strangers are
put together, or one will fall off, become dull or irritable when
separated from an old companion. Each ought to have a
stall to himself. Cows do well enough in pairs, or in rows
without any separation. But they have no work demanding
full and uninterrupted repose. They lie straight, upon their
breast, with their legs bent under them; not like the horse,
who seeks repose in various positions, often lying on his side
with his legs stretched, and his body across the stall, keeping
his neighbor standing, lest he should do an injury in lying
down.

Separation is effected by means of standing bales, gangway bales, and travises. The latter form the best, the most
complete partition, but in certain situations bales are to be
preferred.

Standing Bales are round bars or posts of wood, about three
inches in diameter, and eight feet long. Each extremity is
furnished with a few iron links, by which the bale is suspended to the head and to the heel-posts.

Sometimes the bales are of cast-iron. They are more
durable, but they are costly, easily broken, and apt to do in-

Fig. 3.

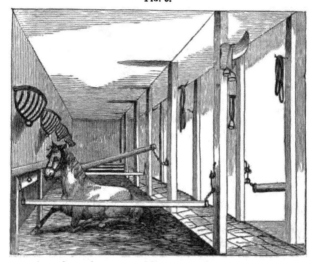

jury when they chance to fall upon a horse's legs or back. Well-seasoned oak forms a bale of sufficient durability. Two or three of cast-iron may be kept and placed beside those horses that are much disposed to bite and destroy the wooden bale.

One is placed between each pair of horses. It should be three feet or three feet and a half from the ground. The suspending chains should be about three or four inches long, so that the bale may yield as the horse comes against it in turning round. Bales are employed in almost all the cavalry stables. There, they are furnished with a contrivance which merits notice. It prevents accidents, which are very common in baled stables. The extremity next the manger is not, or need not, be removable; the other, next the heel-post, is attached in such a way that when a horse gets under the bale, and attempts to rise, he pushes it upward, and it loses its connexion with the post; or when he happens to cast his leg over the bale, it can instantly be lowered to the ground without lifting the horse.

Fig. 4 represents the means by which this is effected; *a* is the bale; *b* a curved bolt by which it is attached to the post. This turns round upon the post, like the hand of a clock. It is retained in its usual place by the ring c, which

3*

FIG. 4.

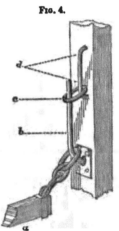

slides upon the bracket *d*. When the bale is to be let down, the ring is raised, and the bolt *b* turns and frees the bale. The engraving, Fig. 3, shows the manner in which the bale is released when a horse gets under it. An iron bale, when thrown off in this way, is likely to be broken, or to injure the next horse. This engraving, I may mention, was taken from one of the cavalry stables at Glasgow barracks.

There are Objections to Bales.—They permit the horses to bite, and to strike each other, whether in play or in mischief, and some harm is often done in this way. Horses that are idle, playful, or vicious, are constantly doing each other some injury ; and those that are at full work, and in want of rest, can not fully obtain it in a baled stable. Then, accidents will occur from the horses getting under or over the bales, and one will rob another of his corn, and infectious diseases will spread rapidly and generally. These evils are sufficient to forbid bales whenever it is possible to have the horses more perfectly separated. Baled stables are not at all fit for valuable horses, and they are the worst of all for a sick horse. It is nothing in their favor that the cavalry horses stand in them. There, a man is in almost constant attendance upon each horse, to watch him while feeding, and to correct him when mischievous, or to assist him in difficulty. There are plenty of spare stalls and loose boxes for the sick, the lame, and the vicious, and the veterinary surgeon is always at hand to remedy or prevent the worst consequences of accidents ; and the horses do not require the undisturbed repose so necessary to horses in full work. They have nothing to do.

In Favor of Bales, it is urged that they are less costly than travises, and that, in a large stable, one or two more standings may be obtained. They have no other advantage. The original cost of fitting up the stable is considerably less. The saving, however, is that of a man alive only to the outlay of the present moment. In two or three years the evils of a baled stable may produce the loss of twice, or, it may be, ten times the sum required for travises. When a space of five and a half or six feet can not be allowed to each horse, bales are to be preferred to travises. They give the tired horse some chance of stretching his legs. He would have none if he were confined to such a narrow stall by a fixed travis. All the additional room that can be thus obtained is just one stall upon every ten. An apartment that would easily hold ten horses is rendered unsafe, uncomfortable to the whole number, merely that it may hold one more. This is sufficiently absurd. Where horses are expected to retain the vigor of perfect health, and perform their work with ease, they must have room to obtain complete repose. They are worth very little if they can not work for this much, and the owner must be in miserable circumstances if he can not afford it.

Gangway Bales are employed only in the stables of very valuable horses. They are merely bars of wood stretching from the heel-post to the back wall. Two and sometimes three are placed between every two horses. They prevent a horse from leaving his stall, though he should break loose. He can not wander over the stable and injure his neighbors. They are removeable. They are, or ought always to be, in place when the stables are shut up, even for a single hour, and when the groom is dressing the horse with his head free. Some horses never break loose, and never attempt it. Stablemen are apt to trust them too much. They make no use of the gangway bales ; it ought to be a standing rule of the stable, that these bales be always in their place. On the eve of an engagement, a racehorse may break loose and receive an injury sufficient to throw him aside. The men are sufficiently attentive and vigilant at these times ; but they ought to be equally so at all times.

Travises are fixed partitions made of wood, and separating the horses so completely that one is not permitted to injure or annoy another. It is the kind of partition generally em ployed in Scotland. We have few baled stables. The travis has been made of stone, of Arbroath pavement, with what intention I can not guess. They are very often too slight and too low, sometimes too short and sometimes too long. When oak wood is employed, the travis need not exceed one inch in thickness, the edges being feathered with iron. Made of fir, it is usually one and a half inch thick; but this is too little. When two or two and a half, the travis is stout and durable. Like all the woodwork of stables, it ought to be of the best Memel timber, well seasoned. In length it may vary from four to nine feet; the latter is the usual measure for a full-sized horse in a roomy stable. Under eight or nine feet, the longer the travis, the less likely is the horse to strike his neighbor.

But room must be left in the gangway for turning horses out, and for passing those which are in. In a narrow, and especially in a double-headed stable, it is a great error to make the travis too long. Horses always like to see what is going on around them; and when the travis is so long and high that they can not see about them, they stand into the gangway and block up the passage. When less than seven feet, the travis is rather short, but a short stall is not so inconvenient as a narrow gangway. Nine feet is the greatest length required for any horse, but this may be abridged if the stable be narrow. In general, a double-headed stable should have the travises only one third the breadth of the stable; in single-headed stables they may be one half of the whole breadth. In other words, the gangway should be as broad as the stall is long. If the stable be much above the ordinary breadth, of course the travis need not exceed nine feet.

What is called the quarter travis, is a short partition about four feet long. It prevents the horses from biting, and from stealing each other's food, but it affords no protection against the heels, nor does it permit the horse to enjoy his rest It is better than none, and better than a longer one, if the stable be no more than twelve feet broad.

In height the travis should be about seven feet at the head and five at the heels. When lower. it permits the horses to bite and tease each other, and to cast their hind-legs over it. About four feet is the usual height behind; but I have seen a horse throw his leg over one that was four feet six inches. Many serious accidents happen in this way. There is no objection to having the travis high. The upper edge of the travis should be bound with iron, to prevent the horses eating it. Plate-iron answers the purpose well enough. It should cover the edge to the depth of two or three inches.

THE STALL-POSTS, that is, the posts by which the partition is bound, are usually made of wood, but sometimes of cast-iron. Those next the manger, termed the head-posts, rise five or six inches above the travis, or up to the ceiling. That at the entrance, termed the heel-post, should be round, or octagonal, not square. The corners injure the legs of a kicking horse, and are easily knocked off. These posts are often no higher than the travis, and surmounted by a ball, or some other figure, intended for ornament. But in many stables the heel-post rises to the roof, its extremities being square, the lower sunk in a stone, and the upper attached to the joists. These are better than the short posts; they keep the travis firmer, and they admit of pillar reins at the proper heights. They are useful for hanging harness, and they afford convenience for slinging a horse, should that ever be necessary. The short posts should be round at top, and not more than two inches above the level of the travis. The surmounting ornament is merely an encumbrance; it is in the horse's way when he is turning round. When made of wood, these short posts require to be sunk about three feet in the ground, charred at the ends, and surrounded by masonry three feet in diameter. When made of cast-iron, they are attached by means of screw-bolts to a large stone below the surface. Short posts, whether of wood or iron, are never so firm as those which rise to the roof of the stable.

In stables intended for valuable fast-working horses each side of the post should have a ring for pillar-reins. These are used when the horse is required to stand reversed in his stall. Coach-horses are reversed, turned with their heads out, for half-an-hour before taking the road. They are turned that they may not go out with a full stomach; they are turned when the groom is cleaning the head and neck. The pillar-reins, one on each side, confine the horse, prevent him from turning, or leaving his stall, and prevent him from biting while under stable operations. The rings should be about six feet from the ground. When short heel-posts are employed, the ring must be on the top of them.

THE WIDTH OF THE STALL, I have already said, should vary from five and a half to six feet. For small ponies five feet, or less, may be sufficient; and for very large dray-horses, the stall may be six feet six inches. The stall is roomy at

six feet, and for horses about fifteen, or fifteen and a half
hands high, it may be two or three inches narrower. When
too broad, the horse stands across it, or turns round with his
head out and his tail in.   When too narrow, he can not lie in
that position which is most favorable to repose, and he is apt
to have his loins injured when rashly or improperly turned
round.   The horse should always be backed out, not turned,
when the stall is too little for him.

Rest, in the recumbent position, is of more importance to
working-horses than many stablemen appear to be aware of.
They seem not to regard a narrow stall as a great evil. Some
even lodge two horses all night, after a day of hard work, in
one stall, only six feet wide ; and, as if it were a matter of
indifference whether the horse stand or lie, they expect to
find him in condition for work next day. It should always
be remembered that a horse can not do full work, unless he
have a good bed.   He may be cramped in a narrow stall,
where he is never permitted to stretch his limbs, or he may
be compelled to stand all night, and still he may continue to
do a good deal of work ; but sooner or later, abuse of this kind
tells its own tale.   It ruins the legs and the feet, it shortens
the horse's pace by at least a mile in the hour ; and though
he may do his work, yet that work would be done with more
ease were he better treated in the stable.   In addition to all
this, much standing produces gourdy legs and greasy heels.

HAY-RACKS.—Ordinary hay-racks are made of wood ; they
are wide as the stall, have the front sloping, and the back
perpendicular.   Racks of this kind are giving way to others
made of cast-iron, and much smaller.   As far as the horse is
concerned, it matters little whether iron or wood be used. It
is said that his lips are apt to receive injury from splinters
which occasionally start on the wood ; but this happens very
rarely.   Iron racks are at first more costly ; but in the end
they are the cheapest.   They require no repairs ; at the expiration of ten years they are nearly as valuable as at the
beginning, and they are easily made clean, a matter of considerable importance when infectious diseases prevail.   They
are never well made.   The spars are placed too far apart, and
they all slope too much in the front.   It would be easy to
make them closer and of a more suitable form.

The face of the rack ought to be perpendicular ; in order
that the hay may always lie within the horse's reach, the
back of the rack ought to form an inclined plane.   The spars
ought to be round, and two inches apart.   For fast-working

horses, the rack is large enough if it hold seven pounds of hay. The largest size need not hold more than double or treble this quantity. The bottom of the rack should be eighteen or twenty inches from the top of the manger. The best situation is midway between the partitions. But in this place, a perpendicular front, flush with the head wall, can not be obtained without recesses.

In reference to situation, hay-racks may be termed front, side, and under racks. The first is that which is elevated on the wall in front of the horse; the second, that which is placed in one corner; and the third is on a level with the manger.

The Front-Rack usually has a sloping face; and sometimes the inclination is so great, and the rack so high, that the horse has to turn his head almost upside down every time he applies to it. When the stable is not sufficiently wide, or the walls sufficiently thick, to admit of a perpendicular face, the front of the rack must be inclined; but the inclination need not be great. A rack having the face upright and the back sloping, is shown in Fig. 10. When the spars are of iron, this is the best rack. The next best is represented in Fig. 2. It answers perfectly well for all kind of horses. It is thirty inches wide, twenty-four deep, and nineteen from front to back. The spars are round, one and a quarter inches thick, and two and a half inches apart. Each rack should have a ring at bottom for securing the horse's head. When tied to the spars he is apt to bend or break them. Another very good front-rack is shown in Fig. 3; but it is too small for large horses, though suitable enough for fast-workers.

The Side-Rack may be placed in either corner, on the right or on the left; but when filled from the stable, it is most convenient on the left side. When made of wood, the side-rack usually has upright round spars, arranged in a semi-circular form. (See Fig. 11.) The back is an inclined plane. The bottom on the outside is boarded up, so that the horse may not injure his head against the corner. This is the best kind of rack for narrow and low stables. It takes nothing off the width of the stable and allows the horse to stand quite within the stall when eating his hay. The front might easily be made of cast iron; the back and bottom of wood; or the inclined back might be dispensed with, and it would thus be both cheap and durable. As usually made (see Fig. 6), it has all the awkwardness of the old-fashioned sloping front, and it is generally too small.

The Under-Rack is sometimes nothing but a large deep manger, having a few spars across the top, placed so far apart that the horse's head can pass between them, and let his muzzle to the bottom. This is used when the stable is too low to admit an elevated rack. It is a poor substitute, troublesome to fill, and permitting the horse to waste his hay by scattering it among his litter, and spoiling it with his breath. Sometimes the under-rack differs not in form from the ordinary wooden one. It is three feet long, occupying half the breadth of the stall, and having its upper border level with the manger, which occupies the other half of the stall. It is sometimes sparred across the top, but most usually open; its front is sparred, sloping, and reaching to within a foot of the ground. The object of this is to permit the horse to eat while lying. Few appear much inclined to take advantage of the contrivance. Some do; but most horses eat what they want before lying down. It allows the horse to breathe upon his hay, and to throw it on the ground; and when sparred at top, he can not get to the bottom of the rack, except from the front, and the front he can hardly apply to without lying down. The under-rack, though generally made of wood, and with an inclined face, is sometimes of cast-iron, and upright.

Fig. 5.

Fig. 5 represents a low rack and two iron mangers, one for grain, another for water. It is taken from the stables of Mr. Johnstone, of Blair Lodge, near Falkirk. He has about ten stalls fitted up in this manner. The bottom of the rack, I think, comes too near the ground. The upper border ought to stand at the height of three feet eight inches ; when lower, these under-racks, particularly in a lofty stable, are very dangerous. The horses may get their fore-feet into them.

In some stables there are no racks. The hay is thrown on the ground, or it is cut and placed in the manger. The first is a wasteful practice, and not common ; the horse destroys more hay than he eats. The second, that of cutting the hay into chaff, is advisable only under certain circumstances. At times hay is so cheap, that the quantity saved does not pay the cost of converting it into chaff. Whether that be the case or not, it is proper in large establishments to have racks in *some* of the stalls. This will be understood by referring to the article on Preparing Food.

The usual mode of filling the hay-rack is none of the best. When the loft is over the stable, as it always is in towns, the hay is put into the rack by a hole directly over it communicating with the loft. For certain reasons these holes ought to be abolished, and in a great many stables they are. The moist foul air of the stable passes through them ; it mingles with the hay and contaminates it. The dust and the seed which are thrown down with the hay, fall upon the mane, into the ears and the eyes, and annoy the horse as well as soil him. Hence, he learns a trick of standing back, or breaking his halter ; and horses have been seriously injured by the hay-fork slipping from the hand of a careless groom and falling upon the head or neck. There should be no communication between the loft and the stable. The hay can be rolled into a bundle and put into the rack from the stable. It can be thrown in at the top. The upper spars of low racks, when they have any, should be fixed to a frame opening on hinges ; it saves the time consumed in thrusting it through the spars. The other racks are all quite open at top, and the hay is thrown in by a fork.

[The most common method in America is, to construct the barns with a space or hall of about fourteen feet in width between the stalls which face each other, and running through the whole width of the building. The hay is then thrown from the loft on to the hall floor, and thence into the racks. This space acts as an admirable ventilator, and is otherwise

4

useful for a variety of purposes. The floors of the lofts over the stables are made so close, either by double layers of boards or a single layer grooved and tongued, as to prevent the seed and dust falling on to the horses below. We think this arrangement better than any we saw in England. In cities, however, in consequence of the high price of building lots, this plan can not so well be adopted. Yet this need not prevent stables being made much higher between joints than is usually practised, and giving windows and cross gauze-wire holes sufficient for ventilation, constructed on the same principle as the respirator for the human subject.]

MANGERS.—The trough in which the horse receives his grain is termed a manger. It is made of wood, or of cast-iron. Stone has been employed, but it forms a bulky clumsy manger, and is not in any respect superior to iron. In Scotland the mangers are usually made of wood, and extend the whole breadth of the stall. In many places these are giving place to others made of cast-iron, which are durable, and, when properly made, more suitable. Wooden mangers are in constant want of repairs, and they are never perfectly sweet and clean. Greater durability is given to them by covering the breast with thick plate-iron ; but no contrivance nor any care can keep them always clean, especially where the food is often boiled. The wood imbibes the moisture, and the manger becomes musty ; it has a sour, fetid smell, which prevents many delicate feeders from eating, and disgusts all horses. The iron manger lasts for ever. A little care keeps it clean, and it is never sour when empty. The short iron manger is not much dearer than the long wooden one, and its superior durability renders it ultimately much cheaper.

There is no occasion for having it so long as the stall is broad. Wooden mangers, I believe, are generally made of this length in order that they may be securely fixed. The horses are tied to them, and their ends are supported by the travises. Iron mangers are usually about thirty or thirty-six inches long, and there is no need for having them longer. In many stables, however, they are six feet long, which adds greatly to their cost, without rendering them more useful. They are seldom sufficiently deep, particularly for horses that receive chaff or roots. Nine or ten inches in the ordinary depth ; two or three inches more would improve them. In breadth they should be twelve inches, which is about one inch wider than usual. All this is inside measure. The smaller-sized iron manger answers well enough for small horses, or indeed for any kind of horses, so long as they receive no manger food, but grain and beans. When bulkier articles are to be eaten from the manger, the usual size is found to be rather inconvenient. It holds the food, but the horse throws it out when turning it over in search of that which he likes best. There is no objection to a manger of greater depth and width. Shallow mangers require two or three spars across them, to prevent the horse from scattering his grain. In general two are sufficient. They should be placed near the ends, and across the top, or just within the manger. Round iron bars, one inch thick, are better than wooden spars. If these have been omitted in the original construction of an iron manger, substitutes of hardwood may be wedged in so firmly, that the horse can not extract them with his teeth. When placed in front of the horse, the manger should be provided with a ring for the collar rein. A long manger, whether of wood or iron, may have two rings, each fourteen inches from the travis. The edge of the manger should be thick, that it may be strong, and blunt, not doing much injury when the horse strikes it with his head. Neither a wooden nor an iron manger should be flat at bottom. It should be concave within, convex without. The sharp corner of a flat-bottomed manger injures the horse about the head when rising, and about the legs or knees when he is pawing, and, in proportion to its size and weight, it holds less than the concave manger.

Some mangers are made to remove. This is particularly desirable with wooden mangers. They can be taken out, cleaned, and exposed to the air. But all the cleaning an iron manger requires can be given without shifting it. It is safest when fixed. Iron mangers are easily secured against a stone wall, by means of cramps and lead; but they are not so firm on a wall of brick. Care must be taken to have them fast; they are very weighty, and when the horse is attached to them, it is not a little matter that holds them. They will be broken, and the horse injured should they fall. On a brick wall, an iron bolt passing completely through, and secured by a screw-nut, affords the greatest security. The iron racks are sometimes attached in the same way. They have as much need to be strongly fixed as the mangers, for the horse is often tied to them.

The manger is always placed too low. Professor Coleman, and some others, direct that it be put upon the ground. Nature, they say, intended the horse to gather his food from the surface of the soil, and for this reason he ought not to have it elevated. With as much force they might object to the use of chairs, tables, and beds, in our own dwelling-houses. They do not attempt to show that the horse suffers any inconvenience by feeding from a high manger, or that he likes better to eat off the ground. God made it easy but not necessary for him to do so. Before domestication he may be indifferent about the situation of his food ; but every groom knows that a stabled horse likes to have both his grain and his water held to a level with his head. There is no reason whatever for having the mangers low, but there is reason for having them high. When too low, the horse can not feed so easily, and he is apt to receive injury by stepping into the manger, or by setting his feet on its edge, and, when lying, it is in his way.

The top of the manger ought to stand between three feet six inches and four feet from the ground. For horses about fifteen hands it may be three feet six or eight inches ; for ponies it must be lower in proportion to their height ; for the very tallest horse it does not require to be more than four feet high. When too high, the horse can not get his muzzle to the bottom ; when too low, he is very apt to get his fore-feet into it. This last accident happens so often, and so frequently lames the horse, that it is rather surprising a low manger should be so common. The manger, indeed, is not blamed so often as the horse, who is chastised and tied down, or sold off as incurably mischievous. It would surely be an easy matter to raise the manger to its proper height. Horses that like to see about them, are most prone to the trick of jumping into it.

A short manger may be placed either directly in front of the horse, or in one corner. It is better to have it in the latter situation, on the right side, supposing the rack to be placed on the left. When in front, it is apt to incommode the horse as he is lying down or rising up. Iron mangers (see Fig. 6), of small dimensions, are sometimes made of a triangular form to fit into corners. They do well enough to hold a feed of oats, out they are all a great deal too small for the mixed food which is now given to many horses.

A long manger, long as the stall is broad, has a space below it unoccupied, save by litter, which, when not perfectly free from moisture, ought never to be placed in this situation. To prevent a careless groom from putting the litter here, and to prevent the horse from getting his head below the manger and hurting himself when rising, this vacancy ought to be boarded up. The boarding may slope from the top of the manger down-

Fig. 6.

ward to the ground, near or close to the wall. This also pre
vents the horse from cutting his knees against the manger,
should it have a flat bottom. Short, or corner mangers have
less space below them, but it is as well to have them enclosed.

In some stables a drawer serves the purposes of a manger.
It is made of wood; it holds little more than one measure of
oats; and it slides into a recess in the wall, exactly like a
table-drawer. It has springs or catches, which keep it in or
out. It is pulled out only when the horse is to eat, and it is
shut up whenever he has done. It is said that horses never
learn to crib-bite when fed in this way. The drawer-man-
ger, however, is little patronised. I have seen only one. It
is doubtful whether it answers the intention with which it has
been invented.

Water-Manger.—Sometimes two mangers are placed in
each stall—one for water, and another for grain. It is said
that a horse drinks least when he has water constantly before
him; and, if this be true, it is certainly desirable that he
should never want it. But, I think, we are still in need of
more experiments to decide this point It is beyond doubt

4*

that a horse who has water always within reach, will never take so much as to hurt himself; but it is doubtful whether he can be ready at all times to work.

When a water-trough is introduced, it ought to be so contrived that it can be easily filled and easily emptied. After standing a certain time, it becomes nauseously warm; the horse plays with it, washing his muzzle; and the vegetable matter which falls into it is soon decomposed, and the water becomes unfit for use. The trough ought to be connected with a pipe at the bottom, which will carry off the water when opened, by lifting the plug or turning the stopcock. This is important. If the groom have to carry the manger or its contents to the door, the supply of fresh water will be often neglected. The stables first built by Mr. Laing at Edinburgh, have water-mangers in each stall. The water is supplied by a pipe running into the manger, and covered with an iron slide to keep the horse's teeth off the stopcock. As far as I remember, there is no means of emptying the trough, without lifting out its contents, or carrying away the manger. The new stable wants the water-trough—so that, I suppose, it has not been found of much service. I believe they are worse than useless—unless provided with a pipe to take away the soiled water, and another to bring the fresh.

Water-mangers must be made of iron. Lead is too soft, and wood is altogether unfit for the purpose. They should be cleaned every day; not merely emptied, but well scrubbed. Vegetable matter falls into the water and covers the manger with a glutinous slime, which soils every fresh supply, and which can be removed only by a good deal of rubbing with a brush or hard wisp. Loose boxes or other places intended for sick horses, should be furnished with these water-troughs whether the stables are or are not. They should be deeper, and may be shorter than the grain-manger, but of the same width, and placed at the same elevation.

VENTILATION OF STABLES.

IT is upward of eight-and-forty years since James Clarke of Edinburgh protested against close stables. He insisted that they were hot and foul, to a degree incompatible with health; and he strongly recommended that they should be aired in such a manner as to have them always cool and sweet. Previous to the publication of Clarke's work, people never thought of admitting fresh air into a stable; they had no notion

of its use. In fact, they regarded it as highly pernicious, and
did all they could to exclude it. In those times, the groom
shut up his stable at night, and was careful to close every
aperture by which a breath of fresh air might find admission.
The keyhole and the threshold of the door were not forgotten.
The horse was confined all night in a sort of hothouse, and
in the morning the groom was delighted to find his stable
warm as an oven. He did not perceive, or he did not notice,
that the air was bad, charged with moisture, and with vapors
more pernicious than moisture. It was oppressively warm,
and that was enough for him. He knew nothing about its
vitiation, or about its influence upon the horse's health. In a
large crowded stable, where the horses were in constant and
laborious work, there would be much disease. Glanders,
grease, mange, blindness, coughs, and broken wind, would
prevail, varied occasionally by fatal inflammations. In
another stable, containing fewer horses, and those doing little
work, the principal diseases would be sore throats, bad eyes,
swelled legs, and inflamed lungs, or frequent invasions of the
influenza. But everything on earth would be blamed for
these before a close stable.

Since 1788, when Clarke's work was published, there has
been a constant outcry against hot, foul stables. Every
veterinary writer who has had to treat of diseases, has blamed
the hot stables for producing at least one half of them. So
far as the influence of these writers has extended, they have
produced some effect. A ventilated stable is not now a wonder ; many are properly aired, and many more bear witness
that ventilation has been attempted though not effected. Farm
stables are, in general, pretty well aired, and it is probable
they always were so. Carelessness is to be thanked for that.
Apertures which admit air are there by accident. The cavalry
stables used to be shamefully close. Before veterinary surgeons were appointed to the army, ignorance had leave to
practise all its tricks. Professor Coleman introduced a system
of ventilation which must have saved the government many
thousands of pounds every year. Like many other salutary
innovations, it was at first strongly resisted. Much evil was
predicted ; but diseases which used to destroy whole troops
are now scarcely known in the army.

Much has been said and written about ventilation, and a
good deal has been done to produce it in places where till
lately it was never thought of. But still very many stables
continue to be badly ventilated. The blame belongs chiefly

to the architect. Few stable-builders think of providing apertures for the express purpose of ventilation. When reminded that the horse is a breathing animal, and that some
provision must be made for letting him have fresh air, they
display as much ignorance as if they had not learned their
business. Mr. Lyon's new stables were ventilated from the
beginning. Each stable contains sixteen horses, and two
apertures were placed at the highest part of the building.
They were very well placed, indeed just where they should
be, for carrying off the heated and foul air. But their size?
Each pipe was exactly three inches and a half square!
These two holes would hardly ventilate a stage-coach, or an
omnibus, and yet they were intended for sixteen horses.
There was no other opening whatever; the windows would
not move, and the doors were as closely fitted as they could
be.

The architect may be ignorant, but the owner of the horse
ought to know better. The wealthy and well-informed proprietors of large coaching and posting studs, are sufficiently
alive to the importance of ventilation. Those by whom it is
neglected are soon taught, and in a way that is not easily
forgotten. But there are many who still oppose ventilation;
some are indifferent about it, and very few know how it ought
to be produced.

Much of the opposition to ventilation has arisen from an
error, very common among those who recommend it. They
invariably confound a hot stable with a foul one. The two
words, *hot* and *foul*, are seldom separated. The stable is
spoken of as if it could not be hot without being foul; and
the evils which spring only from foulness are attributed to
heat. Hence, those who happen to have a stable warm, or
it may be hot, and at the same time clean, are very apt to
oppose the practice of ventilation. Their horses do as well
as those in colder stables, and, it may be, they do much better. One will say, I find the practice of airing stables does
no good; it is founded upon theory, it won't stand the test
of experience. My horses look as well again as those of
my neighbor over the way, and my stable is like an oven
compared to his. This may be quite true. To look well a
horse must be kept warm; but to be well, fit to do all the
work a horse can be made to do, he must have pure air. We
are not contending, or we should not be contending, against
a *warm*, but against a *foul* stable. In general, it so happens
that the air in becoming warm also becomes impure. But

this is not a necessary consequence. Air may be cold and at the same time quite unfit for breathing, or it may be hot and yet perfectly free from impurity. There may be stables in which the atmosphere is perniciously hot; but I do not think I have ever seen them. I have not been able to trace a disease arising from warm or hot stabling. [This is a great error, for nothing is more easily susceptible of proof, than that horses housed in very warm stables are much more liable to take cold when out in a raw wind or during the winter season, than those kept in a lower atmosphere. Dangerous inflammatory complaints are also more likely to follow colds take by horses when too warmly stabled or clothed.] But every year affords innumerable examples of what mischief can be done by a foul stable. Of course these foul stables are always hot; but, in my belief, it is the impure, not the heated air, from which disease arises. Many stables remarkably warm are remarkably healthy. It is important to make this distinction. The horse can be kept warm without being poisoned with foul air. And, among stablemen, it is so well known that warmth is congenial to the horse, that it improves his appearance, and gives him greater vigor, that it is perfectly useless to offer any opposition to it. Practice will always prevail over theory. We ought not to oppose warmth, but the means by which warmth is given. The horse should be kept comfortably warm, but he must have pure air. A cold stable is not so dangerous as a foul one.

Then there are many people who are indifferent about ventilation. They dislike trouble; they can suffer much, but they can do nothing. They will bear all the evils, all the loss, and all the vexations of a bad stable, rather than make any effort to improve it. If an offer were made to ventilate their stables, without cost and without trouble, they would permit it to be done. When advised, for the sake of their horses, to get the stables properly aired, one will reply, " Ah, it is very true what you say, but you may see the thing can not be done!"

Stables are often constructed in such a manner that it is very difficult to ventilate them. The process may be both troublesome and expensive; there ought to be some good reason for suffering the one and incurring the other. Opposition has been excited by magnifying the evils of a close stable; but, divested of all exaggeration, it will be seen that they are not insignificant.

The Object of Ventilation is to procure a constant supply of air in sufficient purity to meet the demands of the animal economy. Sufficient purity is not perfect purity. Neither the horse nor any other animal requires air absolutely pure. In towns and in stables there is no such thing; and that is proof strong enough that it is not essential.

The Composition of Pure Air has been repeatedly ascertained by chemical research. The atmosphere consists of two simple gases. According to Lavoisier, 100 measures of *pure* air contain 73 of nitrogen and 27 of oxygen. [According to later authorities, within a fraction of 21 of oxygen and 79 of nitrogen, and about $\frac{1}{2500}$ of carbonic acid.] It has been proved that a breathing animal consumes the oxygen, and that death ensues when the supply falls below the demand. When a small animal is enclosed in an air-tight vessel, it soon dies. The air suffers no apparent diminution in bulk, yet it undergoes a change in composition. The oxygen is consumed, or a large portion of it is consumed, and its place is occupied by another gas, termed carbonic acid, which is given out from the lungs. This kind of air is rather heavier than that of which the atmosphere is composed. In certain situations it mingles with the air in the proportion of about 1 to 100. When an animal is completely immersed in it, he dies immediately. Some contend that carbonic acid is poisonous; others that it destroys life merely by excluding the common air, without which no breathing animal can live. The carbonic acid is an evacuation; it exists in the system, but it must not accumulate there. It must be thrown out almost as rapidly as it is formed. As it is evacuated, it contaminates the external air with which it mingles. Hence, in the neighborhood of all animals, the air is more or less impure.

The Use of Air, in the animal economy, is to purify the blood. This fluid is in a state of constant change. As it circulates through the various parts of the body, it performs functions innumerable; these operations change its composition, and render it unfit to repeat them unless it be duly renovated. In the lungs the air and the blood come in contact, and both are changed. The air loses a certain portion of oxygen and acquires carbon. It becomes of a brighter red; from a dark purple hue it is changed to bright scarlet. The process is briefly described by the word purification. But it must be remembered that, besides parting with some noxious ingredient, the blood is altered in some other way, probably by the addition of oxygen, and certainly by the agency of oxygen. If the air be destitute of this constituent, or if it do not contain a certain quantity, the blood can not undergo the change by which it maintains life.

The Composition of Impure Air is not always the same. By impurity is here meant any alteration which renders the air less fit for breathing. The impurity varies according to the quantity, the number, and the kind of foreign matters which mingle with the air, and according to the degree in which one of its constituents is deficient in quantity. Air may be bad, merely because it is deprived of part of its oxygen. It is probable, indeed it is certain, that in particular situations the air does not contain its full proportion of oxygen, and that the animals who breathe it do not experience any serious inconvenience. Though there is not the usual quantity, there is sufficient. When the air contains so little oxygen that it can not meet the demand of those animals by whom it is breathed, it may very well be called bad. It has power to do mischief; the animal suffers, not from the presence of a pernicious agent, but from the absence of that which enables the blood to perform its functions. The air, however, may be rendered actively injurious or poisonous, by the addition of foreign ingredients. These are of various kinds, many of which can not be discovered by the chymist. They are known to exist only from their effects upon the health of the living animal.

The Impure Air of a Close Stable is deficient in oxygen, and mingled with carbonic acid, ammoniacal gas, and some other matters. The deficiency of oxygen in stables has never been proved by actual experiment. But there can be no doubt but it occurs wherever the air is confined around a breathing animal. Repeated investigations have shown a deficiency in theatres, hospitals, churches, and other places crowded by human beings. A French chymist analyzed the air of a large theatre, that of the Tuileries, before and after the play. He found it of the usual composition, 100 parts containing 27 of oxygen and 73 of nitrogen, before the performance; at the conclusion, there were 76½ of nitrogen, 2½ of carbonic acid, and only 21 of oxygen. There is every reason to believe that the air of a close stable is deficient in oxygen to a much greater extent. Stables are often as closely packed as a theatre; the animals are much larger, the building much lower, containing less air in proportion to the demand closer, and closed for a longer time, than the habitations of man, and the deficiency of oxygen must be so much the greater.

The deterioration of air by consumption of oxygen, and addition of carbon, is produced entirely by breathing; and when carried beyond a certain point, debility, or disease, or death, one or all, must be the result. But the air of a close stable is vitiated by other means. There are emanations from the surface of the body, from the dung, and from the urine. The effluvia, arising from these, mingle with the air, and contaminate it, till it acquires the power of exciting disease When the dung and urine are allowed to accumulate day after day, till the horse lies upon a bed of rotting litter, the air becomes still more seriously tainted. When first entered in the morning, the pungent vapors of these close stables are almost suffocating. Even after the doors have been open all day, there are many corners where the air is always foul. The acrid odor which irritates the eyes and nostrils, is chiefly or entirely composed of ammonia. It is given out by the evacuations, particularly after they have begun to ferment, to rot. [The best substance to sweeten and purify the atmosphere in stables, and for fixing the ammonia arising so strongly from horse urine in particular, as well as from all animal evacuation, is charcoal-dust scattered over the floors, among the litter, and on the dung-heap. Plaster of Paris is an excellent thing; also sulphuric acid diluted with about fifty per cent. of water, and sprinkled on the litter. All these substances add to the value of the manure, more especially the charcoal-dust, and it has the further advantage of being cheapest, and usually the most easily obtained.]

The chymist can discover the carbonic acid and the ammoniacal vapor which mingle with the air of a close stable. By examining the air after a certain manner, he not only ascertains the presence of these gases, but he also measures their quantity. It has, however, been supposed that the air often contains foreign matters, whose existence can not be shown by any chymical process. There is reason to believe, that whenever a large number of animals are crowded together, and compelled to breathe and rebreathe the same air several times, an aerial poison is generated, having power to produce certain diseases. Professor Coleman is of opinion, that glanders in the horse, rot in sheep, husk in swine, typhus fever, and some other diseases of the human species, are all occasionally produced in this way. It is certain that health can not be maintained in an atmosphere greatly vitiated; but whether the disease arise merely from a deficient supply of oxygen, or from some peculiar poison generated during respiration and perspiration, can not be positively known Chymists, indeed, deny the existence of this animal poison They can not find it; but it does not, therefore, follow that there is none. To their tests the matter of glanders and that of strangles appear to be perfectly similar. That they are not the same, however, is proved by applying them to a living being. The air may contain a poison which no test merely chymical can detect.

The Evils of an Impure Atmosphere, vary according to several circumstances. The ammoniacal vapor is injurious to the eyes, to the nostrils, and the throat. Stables that are both close and 'filthy, are notorious for producing blindness, coughs, and inflammation of the nostrils; these arise from acrid vapors alone. They are most common in those dirty hovels where the dung and the urine are allowed to accumulate for weeks together. The air of a stable may be contaminated by union with ammoniacal vapor, and yet be tolerably pure in other respects. It may never be greatly deficient in oxygen; but when the stable is so close that the supply of oxygen is deficient, other evils are added to those arising from acrid vapors. Disease, in a visible form, may not be the immediate result. The horses may perform their work and take their food, but they do not look well, and they have not the vigor of robust health. Some are lean, hidebound, having a dead dry coat; some have swelled legs, some mange, and some grease. All are spiritless, lazy at work, and soon fatigued. They may have the best of food, and plenty of it, and their work may not be very laborious; yet they always look as if half-starved, or shamefully overwrought. When the influenza comes among them, it spreads fast, and is difficult to treat. Every now and then one or two of the horses becomes glandered and farcied.

Stables are close in various degrees, and it is only in the closest that their worst evils are experienced. But bad air is most pernicious when the horses stand long in the stable, when the food is bad, and when the work is laborious. Hence it is chiefly in the stables occupied by coaching and boat-horses, that the effects of a foul atmosphere are most decisively announced. Other stables, such as those used for carriage-horses, hunters, racers, and roadsters, may be equally ill-ventilated; yet the evils are not so visible, nor of the same kind; coughs, inflamed lungs, a marked liability to in-

fluenza, and general delicacy of constitution, are among the
most serious consequences.   But the two cases are different.
These valuable horses have not so much need for fresh air;
they are not required to perform half the work of a stage-coach
horse; they are much better attended to, particularly after
work.   The stable is kept cleaner; the air is not contaminated by rotting litter, and, in general, the food of these horses
is of the best quality.   Many farm and cart-horse stables are
destitute of efficient ventilation, but the horses do not suffer
so much as might be expected.   Their slow work does
not demand a constant supply of the purest air; and, compared with the fast-working coach-horse, they are but a very
short time in the stable.   A coach-horse who does his work
in one hour, must suffer more than the other, who is in the
open air perhaps ten hours out of the twenty-four.

When a deficient supply of air, hard work, and bad food,
happen to operate in combination, the ravages of disease are
dreadful.   Glanders and the influenza burst among the horses;
and they make brief work of it.   For a long time the horses
may appear to suffer little inconvenience.   They may be lean,
shamefully lean, unfit for full work, and many may become
unable to continue at any work.   Several may have diabetes,
and many be troubled with bad coughs.   But until a sickly
season prevails, or until some other circumstance occurs to
render the horses more than usually susceptible of the evils
arising from the combined influence of bad air, bad food, and
hard work, there is nothing to excite any alarm.   They manage, with some difficulty, to perform their allotted task, though
they never look as if they were fit for it.   At last the influenza appears, or a horse suddenly displays all the symptoms
of glanders.   One after another is taken ill in rapid succession, and death follows death until the stables are half emptied, or until the entire stud is swept away.   The proprietor
begins to look about him.   It is time for him to know that
God has not given him absolute and unconditional control
over his fellow-tenants of the earth.   Oppression has wide
dominions, but there are limits which can not be passed.
Continued suffering terminates in death.

Under circumstances like these, death reveals the operation
of a wise and beneficent law.   Man, in the pride of his ignorance, may regard the result as a great evil, and to him it truly
is such; but a little reflection will show, that it is the unavoidable result of a law designed to prevent evils still greater.   Among other provisions intended for the preservation

of every existing species, it has been ordained, that, when placed under certain conditions, some shall die that others may live. When a class of animals become so excessively numerous that something essential to its existence, such as air, food, or water, is in danger of being exhausted, a disease quickly arises, which carries off a certain number, perhaps a majority of the claimants. Those which survive have sufficient, though it may be a scanty subsistence; while, had all lingered on, all must have perished, and the race would be extinguished. In relation, however, to animals which are spread over the earth so extensively as the horse, this law is probably intended to prevent excessive multiplication, rather than to preserve the species, which could hardly be all endangered in so many different places at the same time. As yet, the existence of such a law has been little observed, and numerous examples of its operation can not be cited. " On some of the dry and sultry plains of South America," says an excellent writer, "the supply of water is often scanty, and then a species of madness seizes the horses, and their generous and docile qualities are no longer recognised. They rush violently into every pond and lake, savagely mangling and trampling upon one another, and the carcasses of many thousands of them destroyed by their fellows [and by the disease ?] have occasionally been seen in and around a considerable pool. This is one of the means by which the too rapid increase of this quadruped is, by the ordinance of nature, here prevented."* When a scarcity of food prevails among wild animals, it is very likely that some cause arises to diminish the demand. Among domestic animals, frequent abortions and barrenness may in many instances be traced to the famine of a severe winter. It is difficult to conceive how any deficiency of air can occur to the free dwellers of the forest and the desert. Yet such an event is possible; I see no absurdity in supposing that animals might congregate in such extraordinary multitudes, that the air would be contaminated and become destructive of those by whom it is breathed. It is said that horses have been seen in droves of ten thousand. Were several of these herds by any chance thrown into one, no place could afford sufficient nutriment to maintain them; and it is probable that the air would then receive power to destroy a few, lest famine should destroy all. It may be true that nothing of this kind has ever been observed to take place among any mass of untamed animals. There

* Mr. Youatt—The Horse. Lib. Use. Knowledge, p. 8.

are other agents which vigilantly guard against excessive multiplication. The contamination of the air may be the last and most potent resource. But though rarely, or it may be never, occurring in the wilderness, the event is frequent in domesticity. The number of horses confined together even in the largest and most crowded stable, bears no proportion to the multitudes which compose a wild drove ; yet, considered in relation to the small quantity of air by which they are surrounded, the number is excessive. The difference between the number of the horses and the quantity of air, is greater than it is ever known to be among wild horses. Hence, stabling has introduced a disease that falls very rarely, perhaps not at all, upon the untamed portion of the species. I allude to glanders. This disease has never been seen among wild horses, and it is hardly known where the European mode of stabling has not been tried. That it can be produced by bad air, or by the want of pure air, is generally admitted. "In the expedition to Quiberon, the horses had not been long on board the transports when it became necessary to shut down the hatchways (we believe for a few hours only) ; the consequence of this was that some of them were suffocated, and all the rest were disembarked either glandered or farcied."[*]

[We have no doubt that these horses were diseased when shipped, and that the confinement was merely the occasion of a quicker development of the disease.]

Stables are never so perfectly close as to suffocate the horses, and they are very rarely so close as to be the sole cause of glanders or farcy. When these diseases appear in a stable, bad air may possibly be the only cause ; but in general the air is assisted by excessive work, or bad food, or by both. Setting these destructive diseases out of the question, chronic cough, blindness, and common colds, form the principal evils of a stable in which the air is mingled with effluvia arising from the dung and the urine. And loss of vigor, imperfect health, and imperfect strength, are, in ordinary cases, the principal consequences of breathing air which is deficient in oxygen. Where the air is still more impure, and still more deficient, the evils are more numerous, and more serious.

When a stable is opened in the morning, if the walls or the woodwork be moist and perspiring, the stable is too close. If the air irritates the eyes and the nostrils, the stable is dirty as well as close. If the air is not comfortably warm, the stable is too open.

* Percivall's Lectures, vol. iii., p. 405.

Modes of Ventilating Stables.—Many people are perfectly aware that their stables ought to be aired ; but they are igno rant of the mode in which it should be done. The owner or groom is told that the stable is too close ; and he replies, " The stable is not so close as you think ; indeed, it is rather cold if anything. This window is generally open all day, and that hole is never closed. I got it made on purpose to air the stable, for it was too hot before." Now, it frequently happens that the stable is not too warm, and that the hole and the window do keep it cool. But this is not to the purpose. These people can not be made to understand the difference between warm air and foul air. They are always thinking and talking of the *temperature,* when it is the *purity* of the atmosphere that ought to engage their attention. Ventilation may be managed in such a way as to preserve the air in toler-able purity, without making it uncomfortably cold. There must be apertures for taking away that which has been vitiated, and apertures for admitting a fresh supply ; and these must be properly placed. Their situation is of some consequence, particularly when it is desirable to keep the stable warm. In general they are placed too far from the roof, too near the ground, perhaps about a foot above the horse's head. In this place, they must be so large, in order to air the stable, that they must also cool it.

When the impure air escapes from the horse's lungs, it is warmer than the surrounding air, and it is lighter. In con-sequence, it rises upward. It ascends to the highest part of the building ; if permitted to escape there, it does no harm. When there is no aperture so high up, the air remains at the roof till it becomes cooler, or cold. When cool as that which occupies the lower part of the stable, or when cooler—and it soon loses its heat—the air descends, and is rebreathed a second, a third, or an indefinite number of times, until it be-comes perfectly saturated with impurities, or exhausted of its oxygen—at least comparatively exhausted—unable to supply the demand. Then a part of the blood must pass through the lungs without undergoing the usual change, and the horse becomes less vigorous, and consumes more food and more water than he would if the air were purer. There may be large openings in the stable capable of admitting fresh air, yet they are of no use unless there be others for letting out the impure air before it cools.

Apertures for the Escape of the Impure Air, ought to be at the highest part of the building, or as near to it as possible.

5*

There should be one for each stall, and when the stall is empty, the hole may, in winter time, be closed. It should be from eight to ten inches square, and placed midway between the travises. When the stable is surrounded by other buildings in such a manner that the air-holes can not be made in the head wall, they should run through the roof. When a loft is over the stable, the air may be let out by small chimneys running up the walls ; and if these have been neglected in the original construction, the air should be conducted through ceiling and roof by square wooden tubes, in order that it may not mingle with the hay. In this case, instead of an aperture to each stall, one, two, or three, of larger size, may be sufficient for the whole number, and much less expensive and inconvenient than a separate tube to each horse ; whether few or many, they should be of sufficient size : taken altogether, the whole should afford an opening equal to ten inches square for every horse ; and when the stable is low-roofed, this size may be too small. When two or three large ventilators are to supply the place of many smaller openings, they should be so constructed that their size may be regulated according to the number of the horses. When the stable is only half filled, the ventilators, except in hot weather, need not be more than half open. But yet they should never be made to close entirely, lest an ignorant groom take it into his head to shut them all, or a careless fellow to neglect them. In a double-headed stable, two or three may be placed on each side, directly over the horses' heads ; or they may be directly above the gangway : the first plan is the best, but the second is the cheapest. In the one case it may require four apertures, two on each side with as many wooden tubes to run through the loft ; in the other case, only two of double the size may be placed in the gangway. Mr. Lyon's stables are thus ventilated.

The same tubes serve for air and for light. Whether large or small, the air-holes should be defended on the outside by a cap to exclude rain and wind. In some situations an iron-grating may be necessary to exclude vermin, thieves, and persons maliciously disposed. When this is used, the apertures must be much larger.

In addition to the usual ventilating apertures, there ought to be one or two others for airing the stables more completely upon certain occasions. After washing, fumigating, or other purifying processes, or when the horses are all out, or when the weather is very hot, it may be convenient to produce a

Fig. 7.

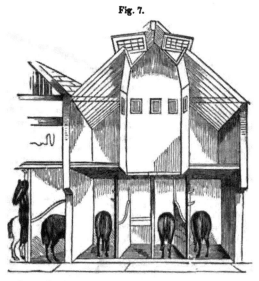

current through the stable capable of carrying off moisture
and impure or noxious air, more rapidly and more perfectly
than the ordinary ventilators will allow. When the litter is
not wholly removed as soon as soiled, these extra apertures
are particularly necessary during the time the stable is being
cleaned. The door at the one end, and a window in the
other, answer the purpose very well; better than a window
in the roof, when the air is not heated. In cold weather, a
large and strong current is not quite harmless when the
horses are at home, but it may be freely permitted while they
are out.

Apertures for the Admission of Pure Air.—Most people do
not imagine that one set of apertures are required to carry
away the foul, and another to admit the pure air. Even those
who know that one set can not answer both purposes in a
perfect manner, are apt to disregard any provision for admitting fresh air. They say there is no fear but sufficient will
find its way in somehow, and the bottom of the door is usually pointed to as a very good inlet. It is clear enough that
while air is going out, some also must be coming in; and
that if none go in, little or none can go out. To make an
outlet without any inlet, betrays ignorance of the circum-

stances which produce motion in the air. To leave the inlet to chance, is just as much as to say that it is of no consequence in what direction the fresh air is admitted, or whether any be admitted. The outlets may also serve as inlets; but then, they must be much larger than I have mentioned, and the stable, without having purer air, must be cool, or cold. When the external atmosphere is colder than that in the stable, it enters at the bottom of the door, or it passes through the lowest apertures to supply and fill the place of that which is escaping from the high apertures. If there be no low openings the cooler air will enter from above; it will form a current inward at the sides, while the warmer air forms another current, setting outward at the centre of each aperture. But when the upper apertures are of small size, this will not take place till the air inside becomes very warm or hot.

The stables at the Veterinary College are all single-headed. Each stall has an aperture at top of the head wall for carrying off the foul air, and in the back wall there is another of the same size, level with the ground, for admitting pure air. These are covered with iron-grating to exclude vermin. This, I think, is not the best place to have these inletting apertures. In order to reach the nostrils, or head of the stall, where the impure air is rising upward, the fresh air must pass over the horse's heels while he is standing, and over a great part of his body while lying. The same thing happens when it passes from the bottom of the door. A current of cold air is established, and constantly flowing from the point where it enters, to the point where it escapes, and the horse, or some part of him, stands in its path. Possibly a current so small and so feeble may do no harm, but possibly also it may have something to do in the production of cold legs, cracked heels, or an attack of inflammation. If it have any effect it can not be of a beneficial tendency, and ought therefore to be prevented if it can be prevented. It is easy to break the current and diffuse the cold air over the stable, by placing a board or some other obstacle opposite the inletting apertures. It would be better, however, if they could be placed nearer the points where the air is wanted.

In Mr. Lyon's stables (Fig. 7) there are no apertures purposely contrived for admitting fresh air. The windows serve both as outlets and as inlets. They are very large. While the warm and impure air is ascending the sides of the tunnel, the external air is descending the centre of the same passage, and spreading over all the stable. This keeps it cool, cooler than would be proper where a fine coat is of more importance Still, by lowering the windows these stables can be kept very comfortable, and without rendering the air unwholesome. From the manner in which they are arranged, low apertures can not be obtained except to four stalls, without considerable expense, and I am not sure that they would be a great improvement though they were introduced.

Admitting that it is better for the sake of warmth to have small outlets with corresponding inlets, than to have large outlets and no inlets, I think the inlets ought to be placed near the horse's nostrils. To keep him warm, the air which surrounds his body should be warm and stagnant, or at least as warm and still as ventilation will permit. When the fresh air enters at some distance, it must traverse the stable to reach the place where it is consumed, and in its passage it cools the stable and plays upon some part of the horse. By admitting the fresh air at the head wall, below the manger, or near the ground, the current would be short; it would not be intercepted by the horse, and it would not cool the air which surrounds his body, and keeps him warm. A stable free at both ends, whether single or double, might have a wooden tube running below all the mangers, and at each extremity open to the external air. As it passed through each stall, a number of small perforations, widely spread and sufficient to admit the air, would be better than a single aperture. If the stable were not very long, perhaps it might be sufficient to have only one end of the tube open; and whether open at one end or at both, the extremity should be turned downward or defended by a cap, to prevent the wind from blowing into it. I do not think that the air would ever enter with such force as to cool the horse's head or his legs. But as the plan has not been tried, whoever thinks well of it had better put it to experiment on a small scale. When the stable abuts against other buildings, this is the only mode by which fresh air can be brought to the head of the stall, without passing over the horse. When the head wall is free, an aperture can be made right through it; but this, though it might be better than having it placed opposite the horse's heels, would be objectionable. The air might come in too strongly, and blow upon the head when the horse is lying. The small sieve-like perforations spread over a considerable surface, the whole forming a space equal to about six inches square, would render a current upon the head almost impossible.

The only use of low apertures is to admit fresh air. In

former times, it was supposed that they were necessary for
taking out the carbonic acid gas formed during respiration. It
was found that this gas is much heavier than common air, and
it was imagined that it fell to the ground, like water when
dropped among oil. But it is now known that, though heavier, the gas unites with the atmosphere, or gravitates in very
small quantities, and only till the air can absorb it.

When the floor of the stable is bad, retaining the urine and
then rejecting it by evaporation, the inlets and the outlets require to be much larger than I have mentioned. A low roof
also renders large apertures very necessary.

Objections urged against Ventilation.—These, as I have
already hinted, often have their origin in ignorance, which
attempts ventilation without knowing its intention or the mode
of producing it; and in indifference, which thinks it does
well while it follows as others have led. The cost of ventilating a stable is very trifling, yet some are so awkwardly
arranged that the process may demand more than the owner
is willing to give. It is the most foolish of all objections;
the evils produced by bad air may be attended with more loss
in six months than would pay the cost of ventilating the
stables six times. Even where there is no actual disease, the
horses, if doing work, require more corn to maintain their
condition than those who have more air.

The cold currents of a ventilated stable, to which people
so often object, are injurious only when the apertures are too
large or improperly placed. If there be a large aperture behind the horse's heels, and another above his head, the cold
air must pass over him, and in force proportioned to its volume. But this is easily avoided, either by having a number
of very small apertures, or by placing the outlets and the inlets in such relation to each other, that the horse can not
stand in the way of the current. The cold air is always
flowing by the nearest road from the point at which it enters
to the point at which it is consumed, that is, at the horse's
nostrils. With a knowledge of this simple fact, to which I
have already alluded more fully, ventilation may be so regulated that the current need not traverse much of the stable, to
cool the air, nor to fall on any particular part of the horse.
When the fresh air must pass over the horse, before it can
reach his nostrils, its force can be broken by admitting it
through numerous and wide-spread perforations, each perhaps
not exceeding half an inch in diameter, but taken altogether,
nearly equal in size to the aperture by which the foul air
escapes.

STABLE APPENDAGES.

These consist of loose boxes; of apartments for provender and litter; of a sleeping chamber for the stable-man; a harness-room; a yard, or shed, for grooming and exercise; and a water-pond. Of the construction, size, situation, and arrangement of these, I have little to say. My principal object is to consider them in relation to the health, vigor, safety, and convenience of the horse.

Loose Boxes are merely large stalls, or apartments for one horse, in which he is shut up without being confined by the head. The horse is loose, and hence the name given to these places. They form a very necessary appendage to all stables whether large or small, yet they are too often forgotten in the construction of these buildings. Their utility is unquestionable. In the sickness of inflamed lungs, the madness of brain-fever, and the agony of colic, they confer quietness, repose, and safety. They permit the lame horse to lie down, and to rise easily and often, without the risk of inflicting further injury. For a fatigued horse, there is no place like a loose box. There he can stretch his wearied limbs in ease and quietness. An overtasked hunter will recover his vigor and activity a full day sooner in a loose box than in a stall. Some horses will not lie down when tied by the head, and they soon injure their legs and become unfit for full work. A loose box is the proper place for such a horse. Then a loose box, when properly contrived, separated from the stable, is a convenient place for a horse having an infectious disease; and it is the safest place for those that obstinately persist in breaking loose.

Loose boxes vary in size from ten to sixteen feet square. They are too small at ten feet, and rather cold at sixteen. It is a very convenient loose box at fourteen feet square. It is better larger than smaller. It should be well paved, the floor inclining a little from all sides toward a grating in the centre. [It is better to have the floor slightly inclining to the back of the stable, and a gutter running its whole length two inches deep and six inches wide, to carry off the urine to a cess-pool under cover outside. All the effluvia may be retained in this by throwing charcoal or peat earth into the cess-pool, to the depth of two feet or so, and removing it with the urine when wanted for manure.] The walls should be boarded; the roof should be eight feet from the ground, neither more

nor less.   There should be a manger for grain or mash, and
another for water; and a hay-rack.   All these may be rather
smaller than those in the stable.   They have been objected
to in a loose box, as likely to injure the horse.   Except when
mad with pain or brain-fever, he will take care of himself.
The mangers, however, may be made to remove when they
are likely to be in the horse's way.   There should be abundance of air and light, admitted by windows and apertures
which can be closed, or their size regulated according to circumstances.   The windows may have shutters, for light is
sometimes objectionable.   They may be placed in the roof,
or high in the wall, out of the horse's reach.   There should
also be a small shelf, near the roof, for holding a light, a
brush, bandages, or any other little article.   A cupboard for
clothes, food, medicines, or articles belonging to the sick
horse, is convenient, and may help to keep disease from the
other horses.   The door should be in two pieces, cut across,
the largest half at bottom; it should open inward, and be
secured by bolts.   The entrance may be five feet wide; it
need not be wider, and it should not be narrower.

The number of loose boxes required in a large stud, varies
greatly according to the kind of work and the kind of management.   In well-ordered coaching studs, one to every thir-
tieth horse is sufficient.   In some, double or treble this number could be in constant use; but on such establishments
there are seldom more than two for a hundred stalls, and very
often not one.   In hunting and in racing stables, one for
every third or fourth horse is almost indispensable.   They
are employed for wintering the racer and summering the
hunter.

Their situation in relation to the stables is a matter of some
consequence, particularly in large studs.   When ranged in a
row, one side should abut against the stable or some other
building.   The boxes are very cold when exposed all round.
But they ought, at least some of them ought, to be perfectly
separate from the stables, having no communication by which
the air may pass from the sick to the sound.   The influenza
appears almost every year at certain seasons; and there is
good reason for believing that, in some of its forms, or in
some seasons, it is infectious.   The owner of a large stud
ought to be prepared for it.   If he had a number of loose
boxes, or a number of small stables for two horses, he might
avert much loss and inconvenience.   These small stables or
loose boxes need not be unoccupied at any time; and when

disease does come, they would afford a quiet place for the sick, where they could not infect the sound. In some stables the loose boxes and the stalls are all under one roof. The loose box may be at one end of the stable. When there are four stalls, one of the travises may be made to remove, so that two of the stalls can be thrown into one. This plan answers very well, and it is almost the only plan by which a loose box can be obtained where ground is valuable. It does well enough for a lame or tired horse, or for one whose work in summer or in winter, demands a month or more of repose. It is also a very good loose box for a sick horse whose sickness has no tendency to spread. But besides this, there ought to be another, quite unconnected with the stable. To that, glanders or influenza may be confined ; and having an entrance of its own, it serves for dressing a horse that comes in after stable hours, without disturbing the others.

Some horses are fond of company. They are restless, and do not thrive in solitude. The isolated loose box is not for them, unless the safety of others demand absolute separation. When lame, fatigued, or laid up for rest, their box may be in the stable.`

THE HAY-CHAMBER, in towns, and indeed in most parts of the country, is placed above the stable. All the authors who have written on these matters, think that the hay should be kept somewhere else. They say that the horse's breath mingles with the hay and spoils it ; that dust and seeds fall through the chinks and openings, and soil the horse or injure his eyes. This is quite true. But it is possible, and very easy to have the hay-loft over the stable, without any danger to the hay or annoyance to the horse. It is only necessary to make the roof of the stable air-tight. It may be lathed and plastered ; but it harbors vermin, and that is a strong objection to ceiling. The boards, however, forming the floor of the loft, may be so closely jointed as to be impervious, and a coat of paint or pitch will prevent the moist air from acting on the wood. The openings for putting down hay, and the trap-door for entering the loft, may be abolished, or furnished with close-fitting covers. Upon these conditions the loft may remain where it usually is. In large towns, ground is so valuable that it is hardly possible to have the hay-chamber in any other place, and indeed no better place is required. The hay can be kept dry and clean. The stable effluvia can not reach it, if there be no communication : when the loft can be entered from the outside, there is no need

6

either for rack-holes or a trap-door. A hay-crib, if the stable afford room for it, may be placed in one corner, and the daily allowance of hay can be put into it every morning. In the country a hay-loft is of little use when the hay can be cut from the stack every day in such quantities as to serve for twenty-four hours. In this way it is always cleaner and fresher than when kept in a loft.

In towns, the only fault I can find with hay-lofts, besides their communication with the stable, is their size. They are always too small. The length and breadth are limited, but the height seldom is. There should always be some spare room for shaking the dust out of the hay, for taking in an extra supply, for turning it over when in danger of heating, or for storing straw or grain. However roomy, the hay-loft is to contain nothing but food and litter, and not litter unless it be sound and dry. A corner may be boarded up to preserve the hay-seed for use or for sale. The practice of cutting the hay is becoming pretty common, and it would be more so if people had room. The hay-loft should afford space for the machine and the process. But in large establishments, an apartment adjoining the hay-loft is required. In that the hay is cut, the grain bruised, mixed, weighed, and measured. The loft has little need for windows, but it should have a ventilator, and the door may be so placed as to give all the light required. The cutting or bruising apartment requires both light and air.

THE STRAW is sometimes kept in the hay-loft, sometimes in a spare stall. It should not be open to dogs, swine, or poultry ; these animals often leave vermin among it, which find their way to the horses.

THE GRANARY is merely a cool and well-aired apartment. And if placed over a stable, the floor should be perfectly close, that the moist air may not pass through. But it is better to have it over a shed or coach-house. Vermin should be carefully excluded.

THE GRAIN-CHEST supplies the place of a granary, where only two or three horses are kept. No more grain is purchased at one time than will be consumed in a few weeks, and that is placed in a box, which usually stands in a corner or recess in the stable. In a small stable the grain-chest takes up too much room. It is constantly in the way ; and in all stables it is occasionally left open or insecurely closed. A horse breaks loose and gorges himself till he is foundered or colicked. It ought to be out of the stable altogether. If placed in the loft, a wooden tube can bring the grain to the stable. The chest may be fixed, and have its bottom sloping like a hopper to the tube by which the grain runs down to the stable. The lower extremity of the pipe may be enclosed in a cupboard, or it may lie against the wall. The grain is obtained by drawing out an iron slide

The chest may be divided into four compartments; one for oats, one for [shorts or bran, one for Indian corn, one for barley, and one for meal of different kinds.]

BOILER-HOUSE.—A copper for heating water or cooking food, is a very necessary appendage to all stables. Hot water is frequently required for numerous operations, which are not performed if the water can not be easily procured. But this is not the principal use of a boiler. It is wanted so often for cooking food, that in town as well as country it ought to form a permanent appendage. [When hay and grain are cheap, it is no object to cut the one or cook the other.] The boiler is usually made of cast-iron, and placed in some corner of the yard. On large establishments it would be an advantage, a saving, to have the boiler of malleable iron. It is in almost constant use, and intrusted to so many different persons, most of them sufficiently careless, that it is generally broken once or twice a year. Mr. Mein has one of plate-iron, oval in form; and it is not injured by the worst of usage.

The boiler should be placed in a house which will afford convenience for keeping all the cooking implements, coals, coolers, and pails. There should be an iron ladle for mixing or measuring the food; a water-pipe, with the stopcock running into the boiler. The door should have a good lock upon it. The entrance should be wide enough to admit a wheelbarrow, or the cooler, which is just a long wooden trough, sometimes placed upon wheels. A part of the boiler-house may be allotted to roots intended for cooking.

When the food is steamed, there is still more need for shelter from the weather, convenience for carrying on the processes, and security from the intrusion of thievery and mischief.

WATER-POND.—At the seats of country gentlemen, this is rather a common appendage to the stables. It is employed for washing, and for watering the horses. They, and sometimes the carriage, are dragged through it twice or thrice to remove the road-mud. The horses are allowed to drink from it, the ducks and geese to swim in it, and the place appears to be useful for drowning supernumerary pups and kittens.

As a bath for water-fowl the pond has its use; but as a place
for watering and washing the horses, it is useless and pernicious. The groom or the coachman, if lazy, may consider
it a great convenience. He does not know, or he is not very
willing to know, that it is not proper to drive the horses through
this cold water; that it makes them subject to swelled legs,
to grease, to colic, and to cold; and perhaps he never considers that this dirty stagnant water is not very pleasant or
wholesome to drink. It is not the place nor the way in
which horses should be either watered or washed. If there
be no other reservoir for the stables, the water should be
taken to the horse, not the horse to the water. To take him
there for washing his legs, is a true sloven's expedient.
Water for drinking should be as near to the stable as possible; when it has to be carried any distance, the horse is
often neglected.

STABLE-YARD OR SHED.—Few, besides the large proprietor and the country gentleman, can have a stable-yard for his
own use. In towns, the only place in the shape of a yard
is the lane. In this the horses must be groomed and the
carriage washed. When the stables are ranged in a square
or circle, the coaches ought to be washed near the centre, or
at some distance from the stables. The practice of doing all
the wet work close to the stable-door, keeps the air always
cold and damp, and the entrance dirty. In some large establishments there is a covered shed, in front of, or around
the stables, or at one side of the yard. There the horses are
groomed, and exercised in dirty weather, or walked till cool,
dry, and ready for grooming. For this latter purpose it is of
great importance. Every coachmaster knows how necessary
it is to keep the horses moving until they be nearly dry and
cool. Without a covered shed this can not be managed in
bad weather. Such a place answers many purposes. It
allows all the horses to be groomed out of the stable, thus
saving litter, and avoiding annoyance to the other horses.
The groom, too, can see better what he is about, and can
handle the horse better here than in the stable. When litter
is dear, that which has merely been wet with urine can be
dried, and made as good as ever, under the shed; and at
night, when not otherwise wanted, it can be converted into a
coach-house.

Such a shed need not be costly. In fact it is nothing but
a roof supported on one side by a few pillars, and projecting
from a dead wall, or the front of the stables. The width and

length must vary. Fourteen feet will make it sufficiently wide, and in length it may be forty or sixty, or as long as possible. The roof may be of unplastered tile. The floor may be causewayed or pitched with pebbles. At one end, about twelve feet may have a soft bottom for those horses that beat the ground very much when under the groom's operations. The soft floor saves the feet, prevents the horse from striking off his shoes. It may be all alike, but if wet be admitted such a floor is never in order.

HARNESS-ROOM.—In some large stables, where a saddler is kept, his workshop forms the harness-room. In others there is an apartment for the spare and old harness. In posting establishments there is usually a dry room, with a fireplace in it. Each set of harness is numbered, or named, according to the horses it belongs to, and hung always in the same place. In stage-coach stables and others of a similar kind, the harness in use is commonly hung in the stable, each horse's being placed on his stall-post. This encumbers the stable very much; but it appears to be the most convenient way of disposing of the harness. In gentlemen's stables, the saddles and harness are generally placed in the groom's sleeping-room, or in the coach-house. The stable is a bad place to keep them in. They get damp, soiled, and knocked about a good deal. In coaching stables, the harness is not so easily injured, and it is in constant use. Besides being dry and well aired, the room should have plenty of light; there should be racks for the harness, whips, and boots; stools or brackets for the saddles; pegs for the bridles; a shelf for miscellaneous articles; and a cupboard for brushes, sponges, bandages, bits, clothes, and other things of this kind, not in constant use.

STABLE CUPBOARD.—In those stables where the men are often changed, or where several are working together, each should have a small cupboard furnished with a good lock. In this the man may deposite his working implements, such as combs, scissors, sponge, brushes, or whatever he receives from the master. They are safe from thieves, and he can have no excuse for losing them. In some cart-stables the driver receives his horse's daily allowance of grain every morning; but unless each can keep his own, one will steal from another. This cupboard should have a box for holding the grain too.

GROOM'S BEDROOM.—Wherever a number of horses are kept together in stables, accidents will frequently happen

6*

through the night. One will break loose, one will cast himself over the travis, one will get halter-cast, some fall to kicking, and some are taken ill. In any of these cases much mischief may be done before the groom appears in the morning. Among draught horses, it is not uncommon to find one dead that was in perfect health, and ate his supper the night before. He dies from a disease that, at the beginning, can be cured with infallible certainty; and he is in such torture that he struggles, and makes noise enough to waken any one sleeping in the stable. But nobody is there, and the poor horse dies for want of help.

In large studs, a man is usually appointed to watch the stables all night, and to give the alarm should fire break out, or should he hear any unusual stir in the stables. In some cases he has instructions to enter the stables occasionally, and see that all be right. This, of course, must be done without disturbing the horses. This man often requires watching himself: he may slumber at his post, or he may desert it. The owner, or some other for him, should pay him a secret visit now and then. The first breach of duty should be his last. An excuse is never wanting, but it is folly to admit any.

In smaller studs, a sleeping-room for one or two of the grooms is usually regarded as sufficient security against nocturnal danger. The place should be comfortable, that there may be the less inducement to leave it. In coaching-stables there is sometimes a dwelling-house for the head ostler and his family. It should be in a central situation, within hearing of all the stables; and when that can not be managed, a bed may be placed in the most remote for an additional man. In racing establishments there is a settle-bed in each stable for two of the boys; and the groom's house is close adjoining.

[STABLES OF MR. GIBBONS.—The most complete stables which we have seen in the United States, or indeed anywhere else, when we take into consideration their cost, comfort, and convenience, are in Madison, New Jersey, at the Forest—the beautiful estate of William Gibbons, Esq.; plans of which he has kindly permitted us to take, to embellish the American edition of the Stable Economy.

The building comprising the stables stands upon the edge of a piece of broad table-land, gently declining to the south. The foundation, and walls of the lower story, are of stone; the walls of the upper stories are of brick. The whole building is strong and massive, and finished in the most thorough and complete manner.

Fig. 8.

D, *Fig.* 8, *Perspective View* of the elevation of the stables on the north or upper side. They are two stories high on the front, D, and three stories on the lower or south side, opposite D. The building is 90 feet long, 50 wide, and 24 high on this front. The architecture is neat and appropriate. There is a good Macadam carriage-way in front of the side D ; *a* and *b* are large windows, alongside of which the hay-carts drive to unload.

Fig. 9.   Fig. 10.

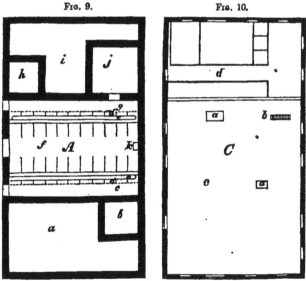

A, *Fig.* 9, *Basement Story*, laid up of thick stone walls.

a, Solid earth.—*b, h*, Cisterns 12 feet square, and 7 feet deep.

c, g, Passage-ways from which the cattle are fed under the water-troughs, *e, e.*

d, d, Racks for receiving hay from above.

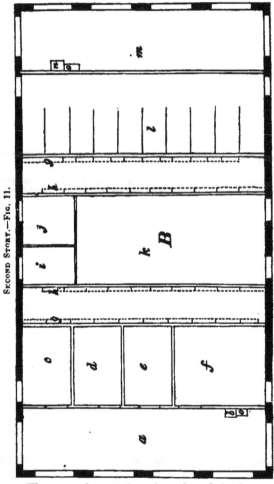

SECOND STORY.—FIG. 11.

e, e, Water-troughs running along the whole front of the cattle-stalls.

f, Passage-way for the cattle, with rows of open stalls on each side, 4 feet 3 inches wide.

i, Solid earth.—*j*, Cellar for roots, 16 feet square.

k, Pump which draws water from the cistern, and delivers *it into the* troughs, *e, e.*

C, *Fig.* 10, *Third Story or Loft.*

a, a, Openings in the floor to put down hay for the stock.

b, Stairway.—*c,* Hay-loft.

d, Granary, partitioned into separate divisions as designated by the lines, for different kinds of grain.

B, *Fig.* 11, *Second Story,* on a level with the broad table-land on the front of D, *fig.* 8, north side.

a, m, Sheds 50 feet long and 13 feet wide. The loft or third story, C, *fig.* 10, forms their ceiling or roof, by projecting over them at each end. The open spaces along the outside lines are arches; the black spots are brick walls to support the ends of the upper story. These sheds are very convenient for taking out the horses to dress, and for other purposes.

b, n, Pumps.

c, d, e, f, Box-stalls for horses, 14 feet, 6 inches deep, by 9 feet 8 inches, 9 feet 7 inches, 9 feet 6 inches, and 19 feet wide.

g, g, Rows of feed-boxes for the horses.

h, h, Rows of openings through which to put down hay into the racks for the cattle in the basement story (see *d, d,* in A, *fig.* 9).

i, Farmer's room for utensils, 11 by 7 feet 6 inches.

j, Harness-room, 11 by 12 feet 6 inches. *k,* Coach-room.

l, Horse-stalls 4 feet 9 inches, by 14 feet 6 inches.

o, o, Water-troughs.

Mr. Gibbons has a very fine stud of thorough-bred horses, among which are the famous Bonnets-of-Blue, Fashion, and Mariner. His Durham cattle are superb, and all his farm arrangements and farm buildings are in excellent style.

STALLS OF MR. PELL.—Fig. 12 is a perspective view of two stalls in the stables of R. L. Pell, Esq., of Pelham, N. Y.

a, Hay-loft. Behind the hoppers *b, b,* are holes in the floor through which the hay is put down into the racks *e, e, e.*

b, b, Hoppers.—*c,* Floor-beam.

d, d, Conductors which lead from the hoppers to the manger. Close behind *b, b,* are the grain-bins, so that in feeding the horses, it is only necessary to take the requisite quantity of oats from them, and pour into the hoppers. The groom will thus feed a large number of horses in a short time without the necessity of leaving the hay-loft.

e, e, e, Hay-racks, with oak rollers 4 feet long and 2 inches in diameter, standing perpendicularly 3 feet from the wall. They have round gudgeons at each end fitted into round holes in the bottom and top pieces of the rack. As the horse pulls on the hay to eat it these rollers revolve easily, and he thus gets just what *he wants.* The bottom of the racks are lat-

Fig. 12.

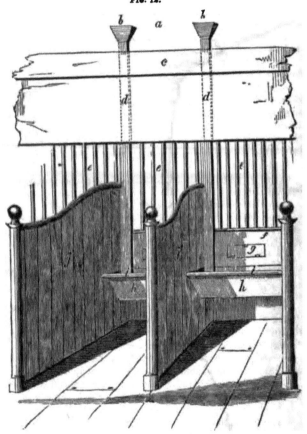

ticed, so that the hay-seeds can fall below into the seed-box *f*.—*f*, Seed-box.

g, Door of seed-box to empty it of the hay-seed.

h, h, Trough running the whole length of the stalls.

i, i, Oak rollers over the edges of the troughs, 3 inches in diameter. The horse will not gnaw this; for the moment he attempts to take hold of it with his teeth, it revolves, and he can not hold it.

j, j, Stall divisions 5 feet wide. The posts at the end of *these are of* turned oak.]

/

SECOND CHAPTER.

STABLE OPERATIONS.

I. STABLEMEN.—II. GROOMING.—III. OPERATIONS OF DECORA-
TION.—IV. MANAGEMENT OF THE FEET.—V. OPERATIONS
ON THE STABLE.

To many people the stable operations may appear to be
few and simple, requiring little dexterity and almost no experience. A great many horses do not demand much care;
their work is easy, and their personal appearance is not a
matter of much consequence. They are horses of small price,
and they are attended by men whose services would not be
accepted where the value, and work, and appearance of the
horse, demand more skilful management. In hunting and in
racing studs, the stable operations are more numerous, and
performed in a different manner. There, nobody can groom
a horse but a groom; one who has learned his business as a
man learns a trade.

It is impossible to have the stable operations performed
well, nor even decently, without good tools, and good hands
to use them. There should be no want of the necessary implements. A bad groom may do without many of them, because he does not know their use; but a good groom requires
brushes, combs, sponges, towels, skins, rubbers, scissors,
bandages, cloths, pails, forks, brooms, and some other little
articles, all which he should have, if the horse is to receive
all the care and decoration a groom can bestow.

The stable operations are learned by imitation and by practice. But there is no one to teach, and no one desirous of
learning them in a systematic manner. A boy, intending to become a groom, goes into the stable of a person not very particular about his horses, or he goes sometimes under a senior.
At first the boy can do almost nothing. After a while he is
able to do some things, perhaps, tolerably well. He can go

about the horse, and manage some of the stable operations better than he could at the beginning. In a few years he may be an excellent groom. But, is it not singular ? he has never in all that time made any effort to learn his business. He has had work to do, and it was done, not because he desired to learn how to do it, but because it could not be left undone. The horse was to clean, and when cleaned, the boy was thankful that his task was finished, and he never did it when he could avoid it. If he had been anxious to learn his business quickly and well, he ought to have done a great deal more. Instead of contriving expedients to escape work, he ought to have done the work ten times for once. He never brushed a horse when he did not need brushing, nor made a bed twice when once would serve.

If the boy has any desire to learn, or if any desire can be excited, let him see the stable and the stable-work of a good groom. Show him the horse's skin, how beautiful and pure it is ; the stable, how clean and orderly ; and the bed, how neatly and comfortably it is made. Let him see the man at work, and make him understand that his dexterity was acquired by practice. For the operations, after seeing them once or twice performed, practice is everything. Two dressings every day may be all the horse requires, but four will do him no harm. The bed may be made twenty times a-day ; and everything which practice teaches should be done often, if it is ever to be done well. In the ordinary course of things the boy may become an expert groom in four or five years. By systematic and persevering efforts, he may be as expert in six or eight months. There are many businesses, and a groom's is one of them, in which it is difficult to get skilful workmen. There are loiterers of all kinds in the world ; and every large town furnishes thousands of men who have arrived at old age in the pursuit or practice of a business which they never made a serious effort to learn. There are few who have *studied* to learn or to improve. Everything is left to chance ; and if much were not acquired by chance, a good workman, among working men, would be a wonder. Even among professional men, there is more anxiety to appear skilful than diligence to be so.

STABLEMEN.

THERE are several kinds of stable servants. There are coachmen, grooms, hunting-grooms, training-grooms, head-grooms, head-lads, boys, strappers, ostlers, carters, and many more of smaller note. Taken altogether, they form a class which can not be easily described. Some of them are very decent men, filling their station with respectability ; and often at the close of a long and useful servitude, receiving the approbation and reward which their conduct deserves. Some are humane to their horses, dutiful, careful, and vigilant ; many know their business well, and are able to teach it so admirably, that I have often thought it a pity there should be no school where these men might practically instruct others.

In our books it has been too long and too much the custom to speak of stablemen as if they were all alike ; as if they were all ignorant, and something worse than ignorant. Their very employment has been treated with contempt by men from whom something better might be expected. There is surely nothing degrading in tending the horse whether well or sick. To throw odium on the employment, is to deprive the horse of many men whose services might make his life more tolerable ; and to degrade all, because a few deserve degradation, is work fit only for a fool. Society, composed as it is of so much pride, and folly, and ignorance, will continue to do this, and to associate the duty with the men who perform it. But in the solitude of his study a writer ought to be more precise. His wisdom is not of much worth if he mingle it with the dogmas of those to whom the distinctions of pride and pomp are more than the distinctions of truth.

It depends upon the man himself. There is no reason why he should not be respectable and respected. He fills a useful place in society. There are many in it shrewd and intelligent above their station.

But then there is much to be said on the other side. The great fault of stablemen in general is want of skill. Only a few have all the qualifications their work demands. Some are inexperienced, perfectly unacquainted with their duties ; some are stupid, awkward, inexpert, incapable of learning anything ; some are lazy, dirty, shuffling ragamuffins, useless as weeds, and more pernicious ; some are abominably ill-tempered, cruel, and even ferocious, frequently laming the horses, overdriving, or abusing them in a variety of ways ; some are dishonest, pilfering and selling the provender ; some are tipplers ; a great many are altogether given over to drunkenness ; some are so mightily puffed up with a notion of their own wisdom and abilities, that there is no bearing with them. These are always intractable. Directions are of no use to them. They
7

will do things their own way, without even attempting any.
other. They know everything, and everybody's business
·but their own. Others are so desperately vain of their swee.
persons, that for one hour they spend upon the horses, they
spend two in letting people see themselves, or in preparing to
be seen. Some are careless, wasteful, indifferent to their
master's interests. Others are insinuating hypocrites, mere
eye-servants ; never doing their duty, yet always busy ; never
grumbling, but often ostentatiously exhibiting some trait of
superfluous obedience, deference, or care. Some are slovenly,
always in disorder. Many are indifferent to the welfare and
comfort of the horses. They may not be ill-tempered nor
violent ; but they are negligent, and that often amounts to
cruelty. They never sympathize with the suffering. They
will stand round a horse in the pangs of death, and, if moved
at all, it is to utter some foul jest, or to bestow a curse or a
kick. These fellows are rarely to be trusted as stablemen,
and never as drivers. Indeed, they are unworthy of all trust.
They are always heartless, selfish vagabonds, indifferent to
everything but their own animal wants, and never doing any
good but what the law compels. A good stableman should
love horses ; while they are ill he should not be quite at
ease.

Some stablemen have the speaking-evil. They are never
right but when they are talking with somebody. While they
are gossipping the work is standing. In general these are
sad boasters and tale-bearers. They must have something to
prate about, and if there is nothing to be said about the master
or his lady, nor any secret to be carried from the stables or the
house, new stories must be laid upon the old foundation, and
with fiction, and truth, and says-he and says-I, some sort of a
story *is* trumped up to afford the talking gentleman a little
merriment or consolation. In most stables this vice is of no
consequence ; but such a man is not to be trusted in a racing
stud. These great talkers are mostly always great liars.

The Gentleman's Coachman is not the same being in the
city that he appears in the country. In the crowded streets
of large towns he should have nothing to learn. Skill in
driving is his most essential qualification. Sobriety stands
next, and after that, experience in the stable management of
his horses. He should be careful at all times ; cool when
accidents happen ; kind to his horses ; active, robust, good-
looking ; of a mature age ; not disposed to sleep on the box,
nor too fond of company. He should be punctual to a

moment ; always ready, indeed, an hour before he is wanted. He should have a religious regard to cleanliness. It should be his pride to excel others, and to have everything in the most exact order. Nothing looks worse than a slovenly, ill-appointed coachman. He should have none of the indecent slang so common among worthless stablemen.

It is not easy to procure men with all these qualifications ; and it very often happens that a man who has most of them, or possibly the whole of them, and some others to boot, has some fault which greatly counterbalances, or neutralizes his good properties. A good servant is very apt to take it into his head that there is nobody like him. He begins to give himself airs, as if he were an indispensable personage, whose loss could not be supplied. He will sometimes forget himself so far as to do things which he knows would procure the discharge of any other servant. The longer a man of this kind is suffered, the worse he grows. He encroaches here and there, till he has privileges sufficient to excite rebellion in all the rest of the household. At last he becomes quite a fool, and there is no longer any managing of him, and he has to be sent about his business. A man who ventures to do wrong, or to forget his duty, merely because he knows that he is highly esteemed, must have little foresight. It is the very way to forfeit all he has gained, and estimation of this kind once lost, is always lost. It is a greater evil to lose a good name, than never to obtain it.

In the country coachman skilful driving is not of the first importance. He need not, like his brother of the town, serve an apprenticeship for it. He may go from the stable or the plough, and a few lessons on a quiet road, with a pair of steady horses, will soon give him all the proficiency he requires. The more of the other qualities he possesses, the better. The principal fault of a country coachman is slovenliness. He sits on the box as if he were driving a cart, his hands resting on his knees, elbows projecting like the paddles of a steamboat, his body bent nearly double, his head hanging low, or his eyes following everything but the horses ; the reins slack, whip pointing to the ground, its handle spliced, and thong curtailed. Then the horses are something like the man ; their coats are long, rough, dim, and their actions sluggish. The harness and the carriage are not much better, looking rusty, tarnished, sun-burned. The stable is always in disorder, presenting an assemblage of things useless and useful, fragments of this and of that, nothing where it should be, and nothing complete ; the whole very much resembling that compilation entitled " The Field-Book."

Slovenly servants always have very particular masters. There is almost no curing of them. Habits of order and despatch must commence in boyhood, or not at all.

The work of a coachman usually consists in taking care of the horses, harness, and carriage, and in driving. Sometimes he has also a saddle or gig horse to look after.'. Where three or more horses are necessary to do the work, he must have a boy or man under him.

THE GROOM.—A good groom should have been among horses from his boyhood. He should have learned his business under a senior. He should have all the regularity, sobriety, activity, and cleanliness of the thorough-bred coachman. In general, he is not such a solid character. He is somewhat flippant, talkative, fond of company, and much disposed to make medicinal experiments upon the horses.

Grooms are of two or three kinds. The word groom, though often applied to any man who looks after a horse, is most usually confined to a man who has been trained to groom and manage horses in the best style. Hence it does not belong to those who work in livery or coaching-stables. In a gentleman's stud the groom looks after the saddle-horses employed on the road or in the field. Where one is kept for the road and another for the field horses, the former is usually only the groom, the latter the hunting-groom. Those who superintend the management of racehorses, are termed train ers or training grooms.

The work of a groom is very variable. In some places he has the charge of only two horses, one for himself and one for his master, whom he accompanies on his rides. In others he has two horses and a gig ; in some he has three horses, or two and a breeding mare with her foal. Two are considered full work, but three can be managed very well, two being out every day.

UNTRAINED GROOMS are those who diet, dress, and exercise the horses employed at ordinary work. They can not put horses into hunting condition, nor do they know how to maintain them in that condition. The thorough-bred groom is, or ought to be, able to do both. But it is not everybody who requires, or who can afford to keep, a thorough-bred groom. His wages are high, and he can always find employment from those who need his services. People who keep only two or three inferior horses, or perhaps only one, for pleasure or business, content themselves with an indifferent groom, one, it may be, who is partly employed about the warehouse, the garden, or the dwelling-house. The horse or horses can not, of course, be so well tended. They may be very well cleaned, but such men can not put the horses into hunting condition, nor maintain them in it, nor bestow all the care that hunters require after a day of severe exertion. For the horses kept by merchants about town, who seldom ride more than ten or twelve miles a-day at a gentle pace, nothing of this kind is required, and a groom who would make a sorry figure in the hunting stable may serve them perfectly well. The man only requires some little dexterity in going about a horse, and a little experience of his habits in reference to food, drink, and work. These he may acquire without a long apprenticeship. He may obtain them in farm, livery, or posting stables. The thorough-bred groom can learn his business completely only under an experienced senior, who may have the charge of racing, hunting, or carriage horses.

In the racing-stables a boy is appointed to each horse, and these are superintended by the head-groom, or trainer, and his assistant, who is termed head-lad.

Boys.—Under the direction and discipline of a good groom, boys of from fourteen to seventeen are soon taught to perform the duties of the stable. But until they have been well trained, and they must be trained while flexible, they are good for very little. It is only in a stable where the discipline never relaxes that they can learn their business well, and acquire those orderly habits which in a manner distinguish the taught from the untaught.

The boys employed about towns to look after a horse, or a horse and gig, generally come from the country, where they have seen some service among the cart-horses. Some of these boys are quiet, attentive, able to do something, and to learn more without much instruction; but a great many of them are awkward, thoughtless, and mischievous, not to be depended upon. It is not that their work is difficult to learn or to perform, but there is no keeping them at it. They are so fond of play, and so little accustomed to restraint, that one half of their work is always neglected, and the other half is never done in proper times. Everything is to seek when it is wanted, and when found not fit for use. Some are much worse than others. Many can attend to nothing. Their work is made subservient to their play. One will be sent to walk a heated horse till cool, and he must ride the beast as if he were riding for a wager. Send him to exercise the horse, and he will gallop till he break its knees. Send by him a message, and he will forget one half of it, and take at least an hour more than he should to deliver the other half. The master has more to do for the servant than the servant for the master. The boy may not, perhaps, be so much to blame as his parents. They have taught him nothing. He has sprung up like the wild weeds of the earth. If he has learned any-thing, good or bad, it is the result of chance, not of foresight on the part of his parents, whom he has scarcely learned even to obey. Instead of coming into the world with orderly and decent behavior, and a knowledge of what is due to those he serves, he has to learn those things from the master. It is natural and right that he should be a stern teacher. He has to deal with those who are little improved by gentleness. He may be severe, and he must, if he would make a good servant, and a useful member of society. Order in time and in place ought to be learned at home; but since it is not, that should be taught in the first place, as forming a groundwork upon which anything may be laid. "A place for everything, and everything in its place," is a golden rule. After that, kind-ness to the horse should be insisted on. *Boys are cruel from want of reflection.* Until hardened by habit, remonstrance, if properly managed, awakens their generous feelings, or ex-cites that kind of consideration which saves the defenceless from abuse.

Livery and coaching stables about town are often infested by idle boys who want to ride. They hang about the stables from morning to night, and contrive to be of some little ser-vice to the men, and their reward is a horse to water or to exercise. These boys are always doing some mischief, either in play or in abuse. It is not for their own good to hang about stables in such a disorderly way, and their attendance is certainly injurious to the horses. The work should all be done by the men who are paid for it. Last year one propri-etor lost two horses entirely, and had a third injured by boys, whom the proper stablemen had employed. Such accidents are very common.

STRAPPERS.—The men who look after horses at livery, and those employed in public conveyances, are termed strap-pers. They have nothing to do with the working of the horses. Their business is to dress, harness, water, and bed them. They also have to keep the harness in order. In some places they have to feed and exercise the horses; in others, these duties are performed by a head-man and his assistant. A strapper should be expert, able, and orderly at his work. He usually looks after eight horses, four of which are out every day. Some have more, but, with the harness, eight is about as many as he can be expected to keep in good order, especially during the winter months, and this number he may manage in the best style which coaching requires. In livery stables the horses need more grooming, and three saddle horses may be sufficient work for one man. In some places, however, he has four or five, and occasionally more.

The strappers employed at out-stages should be picked men, better paid, and better qualified than those who work at headquarters, under the eye of the master or his foreman. But the best are not to be much trusted. They should be visited often, at irregular intervals, without warning, and not at one time of the day more than another. The horses should be examined in reference to their condition for work, the state of the skin, the heels, and the feet. The harness, the stable, every part of it, and everything belonging to it, should pass under review every now and then.

The Head-Ostler or Foreman.—On large establishments a head-man superintends the strappers, and the general management of the horses. His work varies according to the size of the stud, and to the time and attention which the owner himself can bestow upon it. In some places the owner is in constant attendance, and then the head-man is just the master's assistant, having no fixed and regular task. But in general it is his business to feed the horses, or at least to keep the provender, give it out as wanted, and see that it be properly distributed. He has to keep the men at their duty, taking care that everything be done in its own time, and examining the work when it is done. He has to regulate the work of the horses, dividing it in such a manner that each shall have as much as he is fit for, and no more. In small establishments the foreman sometimes has a stable of his own to look after, which may contain the strange, the spare, the lame, or the sick horses. When these exceed two or three, he must have an assistant. When properly qualified, the foreman ought to be, and usually is, empowered to hire and discharge the strappers. Sometimes he pays their wages, but that belongs more properly to the clerk.

For a situation of this kind a man requires to have considerable experience. To maintain order among the strappers, and manage the horses with skill, he must be inflexible, just, sober, vigilant, careful, well acquainted with the habits of horses, and the tricks of the men he has to superintend. He should be a discreet tyrant, always enforcing a rigid adherence to established rules. A man of timid or weak character has little chance of maintaining his authority among a host of unruly strappers; and though he have power to discharge them, he is easily awed or misled by the bold and the cunning. He should know his own place, giving no favors and receiving none. If he frequent the public-house, to mingle with those who are under him, his power is lost. He should not be old, yet well up in years, and perhaps married, having his family upon the premises. A man with these qualifications is worth liberal wages.

Sometimes the duties of this man involve more responsibility. Occasionally he purchases the provender, employs the necessary tradesmen, such as the saddler, shoeing-smith, and veterinarian, and has to do with the sale and purchase of the horses. Very few men are fit for these things. Provender is sometimes to be had below the market price, when the owner is not at hand to purchase it; in such a case, the foreman might have power to take it. But it is only upon certain occasions that this, or anything like it, should be in his power. Knavery is apt to creep into such transactions, and the master can know little of his business if he is not able to manage them better himself. They lay the man open to suspicion, whether he deserves it or not. The shoeing-smith and saddler always make some deduction from their usual charges where there is a great deal of work to be done. What men are to serve him, and what deductions are to be made, should be settled by the master himself. Their work is entered in the pass-book, which is paid up at short intervals. The veterinarian should be, and generally is, allowed a fixed salary for medicines, operations, and attendance. In the disposal of wornout, and the purchase of new horses, the foreman and the veterinarian may be both consulted, the one regarding work, and the other regarding unsoundness; but where the old go or the new come from, is the business of the master only.

The foreman, perhaps, with the assistance of the shoeing-smith, sometimes supplies the place of the veterinarian. In this there is more folly than economy. If the work is to be well done, it must be performed by men who perfectly understand it, by men who have been bred to it. Many foremen pretend to have skill in the veterinary art. They do not say that they know all about it, for in that case they would not have to take the place and pay of a stableman; yet they think they may render good service, and they say that much very plainly. It is all nonsense and imposition. These pretenders seldom, almost never, know their own business. If they knew that, as they ought to know it, they would be good servants without knowing anything else. If they are good grooms and better doctors, it is clear they ought to be veterinary surgeons If equally skilful in both capacities, they ought to choose that business which will pay best. But where have they learned so much about diseases and their remedies? They have seen much—that is, about as much in all as a veterinarian in tolerable practice will see in a day.

DRIVERS.—These are men who work the horses. Some also have the stable management of them. The gentleman's coachman has already been spoken of. The others are post-boys, hackney-coachmen, cab, omnibus, noddy, and stage drivers, carters, ploughmen, and so forth. It is needless to speak of these in detail. A glance at what has already been said of stablemen will indicate what are the most essential qualifications, and what their most common vices, with the consequences of their vice. It is only necessary to observe farther, that, in addition to sobriety and skill in their employment, *all those who work the horses should be humane.* Every stableman should feel for a feeble horse, and spare him; but in those who drive, kindness is of more importance. I have known horses purposely driven to death, or so overtasked, that debility, and other consequences of severe labor, gave the driver an excuse for demanding exchange. These things have been done, sometimes because the horse was too slow, too fast, or too feeble; sometimes merely because he was awkward to manage, or did not please the eye of the driver. Such things could never happen in the hands of an humane man.

But, though the horses are sometimes purposely abused and destroyed by cruel drivers, they are much oftener injured by bad drivers. They are often lamed by starting, and by stopping them too suddenly. They ought to have some warning in both cases; it always indicates bad driving when a horse is thrown upon his knees at starting, or upon his haunches at stopping, or upon his side at turning. A fall is not always the consequence, but some part is sprained by the violent effort which the horse is compelled to make in obeying the bit. A bad driver is also apt to overwork an unseasoned or a hot horse, especially when driving more than one. He often allows a free-working horse to do more than his share

Drunkenness, through dangerous in every situation, is to be avoided more in the driver than in the stableman. Most frequently he loses all skill in driving, and is liable to all the accidents arising from the want of it. Very often he retains his senses sufficiently to manage the horses, and yet does them a great deal of mischief, though he may not run into a ditch, nor upset the vehicle. The racing madness falls upon him; he challenges all who travel in the same direction, and he must beat all; or, if there be no one with whom he can contend, he will run against time. Hence the horses are lamed or overworked, or injured in various other ways

GROOMING.

In general, the word grooming is confined to those operations which have cleanliness for their object. To made the horse clean, and to keep him clean, form a part, and in many stables the whole of grooming; but the health of the horse is involved, and some care must be taken to preserve that. He comes to the stable, wet with rain, or heated by exertion, as well as soiled by the road mud. While he is cleaned, he must also be cooled and dried. The operations which produce a clean skin, and those which tend to prevent the consequences of exertion and of exposure, are so closely connected that they must be considered together. It is not my intention to describe any of them very minutely; grooming is easily learned by imitation; and oral are better than written instructions.

The duties of the groom considered in relation to time usually commence at half-past five or six in the morning. Sometimes he must be in the stable much earlier, and sometimes he need not be there before seven. It depends upon the time the stable is shut up at night, the work there is to do in the morning, and the hour at which the horse is wanted. When the horse is going out early and to fast work, the man should be in the stable an hour before the horse goes to the road. In general he arrives about six o'clock, gives the horse a little water, and then his morning feed of grain. While the horse is eating his breakfast, the man shakes up the litter, sweeps out the stable, and prepares to dress the horse, or take him to exercise. In summer, the morning exercise is often given before breakfast, the horse getting water in the stable, or out of doors, and his grain upon returning. In winter, the horse is dressed in the morning, and exercised or prepared for work in the forenoon. He is again dressed when he comes in; at mid-day he is fed. The remainder of the day is occupied in much the same way, the horse receiving more exercise and another dressing; his third feed at four, and his fourth, at eight. The hours of feeding vary according to the number of times the horse is fed. Hunters are usually fed five times a-day during the hunting season. The most of saddle-horses are fed only three. The allowance of grain for all working-horses should be given in at least three portions, and when the horse receives as much as he will eat, it ought to be given at five times. These should be distributed at nearly equal intervals. When the groom is not employed in feeding, dressing, and exercising the horse, he has the stable to arrange several times a-day, harness to clean, some of the horses to trim, and there are many minor duties which he must manage at his leisure. The stable is usually shut up at night about eight o'clock, when the horse is eating his supper.

DRESSING BEFORE WORK.—To keep the skin in good order, the horse must be dressed once every day, besides the cleaning, which is made after work. This dressing is usually performed in the morning, or in the forenoon. It varies in character according to the state of the skin and the value of the horse. The operation is performed by means of the brush, the currycomb, and the wisp, which is a kind of duster, made of straw, hay, matting, or horse-hair.

The Brush, composed of bristles, and varying in size to suit the strength of the operator, removes all the dust and furfuraceous matter lodged at the roots of the hair, and adhering to its surface. It also polishes the hair, and when properly applied, the friction probably exerts a beneficial influence upon the skin, conducive to health, and to the horse's personal appearance.

The Currycomb is composed of five or six iron combs, each having short small teeth; these are fixed on an iron back, to which a handle is attached. There is also one blade, sometimes two, without teeth, to prevent the combs from sinking too deep. The currycomb serves to raise and to separate the hairs that are matted together by perspiration and dust, and to remove the loose mud. Like the brush, it may also stimulate the skin, and have some effect upon the secretions of this

organ; but, except among thick, torpid-skinned, long-haired
horses, it is too harsh for this purpose. In grooming thorough-
bred, or fine-skinned horses, its principal use is to clean the
dust from the brush, which is done by drawing the one smartly
across the other.

The Wisp is a kind of duster. It removes the light dust and
the loose hairs not taken away by the brush; it polishes the
hair and makes the coat lie smooth and regular. The brush
penetrates between the hairs and reaches the skin, but the
wisp acts altogether on the surface, cleaning and polishing
only those hairs, and those portions of hairs, which are not
covered by others. Applied with some force, the wisp beats
away loose dust lodged about the roots. It is often employed
to raise the temperature of the skin, and to dry the hair when
the horse is cold and wet. In many stables the currycomb
and the wisp form the principal, or the only instruments of
purification.

Valuable horses are usually dressed in the stable. The
groom tosses the litter to the head of the stall, puts up the
gangway bales, turns round the horse, to have his head to the
light, removes the breast-piece, and hood, when a hood is
worn: he takes away the surcingle and folds back the quarter-
piece, but does not remove it entirely. It keeps the dust off
the horse. With the brush in his left hand, and the currycomb in his right, he commences on the left side of the horse,
and finishes the head, neck, and forequarter; then his hands
change tools, and he performs the like service on the right
side. The head requires a deal of patience to clean it properly; the hairs run in so many different directions, and there
are so many depressions and elevations, and the horse is often
so unwilling to have it dressed, that it is generally much
neglected by bad grooms. The dust about the roots, upon
the inside and the outside of the ears, is removed by a few
strokes of the brush, but the hair is polished by repeatedly
and rapidly drawing the hands over the whole ear. The
process is well enough expressed by the word *stripping*.
Having finished the fore part of the horse, the groom returns
his head to the manger, and prepares to dress the body and
the hind quarters. A little straw is thrown under the hind
feet to keep them off the stones; the clothes are drawn off,
and the horse's head secured. The clothes are taken to the
door, shook, and in dry weather exposed to the air, till the
horse is dressed. After the brushing is over, every part of
the skin having been entirely deprived of dust, and the hair

polished till it glistens like satin, the groom passes over the whole with a wisp, with which, or with a linen rubber, dry or slightly damped, he concludes the most laborious portion of the dressing. The clothes are brought in, and replaced upon the horse. His mane, foretop, and tail, are combed, brushed, and, if not hanging equally, damped. The eyes, nostrils, muzzle, anus, and sheath, are wiped with a damp sponge ; the feet are picked out, and perhaps washed. If the legs be white and soiled with urine, they require washing with warm water and soap, *after which they are rubbed till dry*. When not washed, the legs are polished partly by the brush and the wisp, but chiefly by the hands. The bed and the stable being arranged, the horse is done up for the morning.

It is not an easy matter to dress a horse in the best style. It is a laborious operation, requiring a good deal of time, and with many horses much patience and dexterity. Ignorant and lazy grooms never perform it well. They confine themselves to the surface. They do more with the wisp than with the brush. The horse when thus dressed may not look so far amiss, but upon rubbing the fingers into his skin they receive a white greasy stain, never communicated when the horse has been thoroughly dressed.

All horses, however, can not be groomed in this manner. From strappers, carters, farm-servants, and many grooms, it must not be expected. Such a dressing is not of great service, at least it is not essential to the horses they look after, nor it is practicable if it were. The men have not time to bestow it.

The horse may be dressed in the stable or in the open air. When weather permits, that is, when dry and not too cold, it is better for both the horse and his groom that the operation be performed out of doors. When several dirty horses are dressed in the stable at the same time, the air is quickly loaded with impurities. Upon looking into the nostrils of the horse, they are found quite black, covered with a thick layer of dust. This is bad for the lungs of both the horse and the man. I suppose it is with the intention of blowing it away, that stable-men are in the habit of making a hissing noise with the mouth The dust, besides entering, and probably irritating the nostrils, falls upon the clean horses, the harness, and everything else. Racers and other valuable horses are almost invariable dressed in the stable, and there they are safest. They have little mud about them [and from frequent grooming and constantly being clothed, little dandruff in, or dust on their hair] to soil the stable.

Inferior stablemen sometimes dress a horse very wretchedly. That which they do is not well done, and it is not done in the right way. They are apt to be too harsh with the currycomb. Some thin-skinned horses can not bear it, and they do not always require it. It should be applied only when and where necessary. This instrument loosens the mud, raises and separates the hair; and when the hair is long, the comb cuts much of it away, especially when used with considerable force. It is not at all times proper to thin a horse's coat suddenly, and, when improper, it should be forbidden. Having raised and separated the hair, the comb should be laid aside. To use it afterward is to thin the coat; and in general, if the coat be too long, it should be thinned by degrees, not at two or three, but at ten or twelve thinnings. Then, the currycomb has little to do about the head, legs, flanks, or other parts that are bony, tender, or thinly covered with hair. When used in these places it should be drawn in the direction of the hairs, or obliquely across them, and lightly applied. The comb is often too sharp. For some horses it should always be blunt. The horse soon shows whether or not it is painful to him. If the operation be absolutely necessary, and can not be performed without pain, the pain must be suffered. But it is only in the hand of a rude or unskilful groom that the comb gives any pain. Some never think of what the horse is suffering under their operations. They use the comb as if they wanted to scrape off the skin. They do not apparently know the use of the instrument. Without any regard to the horse's struggles, they persist in scratching and rubbing, and rubbing and scratching, when there is not the slightest occasion for employing the comb. On a tender skin, the comb requires very little pressure; it should be drawn with the hair, or across it, rather than against it, and there should be no rubbing. The pain is greatest when the comb is made to pass rapidly backward and forward several times over the same place. It should describe a sweeping, not a rubbing motion.

For some tender horses even the brush is too hard. In the flank, the groin, on the inside of the thigh, there can be little dust to remove which a soft wisp will not take away, and it is needless to persist in brushing these and similar places when the horse offers much resistance. In using it about the head or legs, care must be taken not to strike the horse with the back of the brush. These bony parts are easily hurt, and after repeated blows the horse becomes suspicious and troublesome. For thin-skinned irritable horses the brush should be soft, or somewhat worn.

Where the currycomb is used too much, the brush is used too little. The expertness of a groom may be known by the manner in which he applies the brush. An experienced operator will do as much with a wisp of straw as a half-made groom will do with the brush. He merely cleans, or at the very most polishes the surface, and nothing but the surface. The brush should penetrate the hair and clean the skin, and to do this it must be applied with some vigor, and pass repeatedly over the same place. It is oftenest drawn along the hair, but sometimes across and against it. To sink deeply, it must fall flatly and with some force, and be drawn with considerable pressure.

When the horse is changing his coat, both the brush and the currycomb should be used as little and lightly as possible. A damp whisp will keep him tolerably decent till the new coat be fairly on, and it will not remove the old one too fast.

The ears and the legs are the parts most neglected by untrained grooms. They should be often inspected, and his attention directed to them. White legs need to be often washed with soap and water [and hand-rubbed], and all legs that have little hair about them require a good deal of hand-rubbing. White horses are the most difficult to keep, and in the hands of a bad groom they are always yellow about the hips and hocks. The dung and urine are allowed so often to dry on the hair that at last it is dyed, and the other parts are permitted to assume a dingy smoky hue, like unbleached linen.

Dressing Vicious Horses.—A few horses have an aversion to the operations of the groom from the earliest period of their domestication. In spite of the best care and management, they continue to resist grooming with all the art and force they can exert. This is particularly the case with stallions, and many thorough-bred horses not doing much work. But a great many horses are rendered vicious to clean by the awkwardness, timidity, or folly of the keeper. An awkward man gives the horse more pain than ought to attend the operation; a timid man allows the horse to master him; and a mischievous fellow is always learning him tricks, teaching him to bite, or to strike in play, which easily passes into malice.

Biting may be prevented by putting on a muzzle, or by tying the head to the rack, or to the ring outside of the stable. When reversed in the stall, the head may be secured by the pillar-reins. A muzzle often deters a horse from attempting to bite, but some will strike a man to the ground though they can not seize him. These must be tied up. Many harness-horses are perfectly quiet while they are bridled, and it is sufficient to let the bridle remain on, or to put it on, till they be dressed. Others again are quite safe when blindfolded. Kicking horses are more dangerous than biters. A great many strike out, and are apt to injure an awkward groom; yet they are not so bad but an expert fellow may manage them, without using any restraint. A switch held always in the hand, in view of the horse, and lightly applied, or threatened when he attempts to strike, will render others comparatively docile. A few permit their hind quarters to be cleaned while their clothes are on. Some there are, however, that can not be managed so easily. They strike out, those especially that lead idle lives, so quickly and so maliciously, that the groom is in great danger, and can not get his work properly performed. There are two remedies—the arm-strap and the twitch. Where another man can not be spared to assist, one of the fore legs is tied up; the knee is bent till the foot almost touches the elbow, and a broad buckling-strap is applied over the forearm and the pastern. The horse then stands upon three legs, and the groom is in no danger of a kick. Until the horse is accustomed to stand in this way, he is apt to throw himself down; for the first two or three times the leg should be held up by a man, rather than tied with a strap. The horse should stand on a thick bed of litter, so that he may not be injured should he fall. In course of time he may perhaps become quieter, and the arm-strap may be thrown aside. It should not be applied always to the same leg, for it produces a tendency to knuckling over of the pastern, which, in a great measure, is avoided by tying up each leg alternately, the right to-day, the left to-morrow. Even the arm-strap will not prevent some horses from kicking; some can stand on two legs, and some will throw themselves down. The man must just coax the horse, and get over the operation with as little irritation as possible. Upon extraordinary occasions the twitch may be employed, but it must not be applied every day, otherwise the lip upon

which it is placed becomes inflamed, or palsied. When restraint must be resorted to, the man should be doubly active
in getting through his work, that the horse may not be kept
for a needless length of time in pain. He may, in some
cases, give the horse a very complete dressing when he is
fatigued, and not disposed to offer much resistance.

Irritable, high-bred horses, often cut and bruise their legs
when under the grooming operations. They should have
boots, similar to those used against speedy cutting.

Utility of Dressing.—It improves the horse's appearance ;
it renders the coat short, fine, glossy, and smooth. The coat
of a horse in blooming condition is always a little oily. The
hair rejects water. The anointing matter which confers this
property is secreted by the skin, and the secretion seems to
be much influenced by good grooming. Slow-working horses
often have skins which a fox-hunter would admire, although
they may be receiving very little care from the groom. But
the food of these horses has a good deal to do with the skin,
and their work is not of that kind which impairs the beauty
of a fine glossy coat. They drink much water, and they get
warm boiled food every night. They do not often perspire
a great deal, but they always perspire a little. Fast-working
horses have hard food, a limited allowance of water ; and
every day, or every other day, they are drenched in perspiration, which forbids constant perspiration, and which carries
off, or washes away the oily matter. Hence, unless a horse
that is often and severely heated, be well groomed, have his
skin stimulated, and his hair polished by the brush, he will
never look well. His coat has a dead, dim appearance, a
dry, soft feel. To the hand the hair feels like a coarse, dead
fur ; the most beautiful coat often assumes this state in one
or two days. Some horses always look ill, and no grooming
will make them look well ; but all may be improved, or rendered tolerably decent, except at moulting time. Dressing
is not the only means by which the coat is beautified. There
are other processes, of which I shall speak presently.

Among stablemen, dressing is performed only for the sake
of the horse's personal appearance. They are not aware that
it has any influence upon health, and therefore they generally
neglect the skin of a horse that is not at work. In the open
fields, the skin is not loaded with the dust and perspiration
which it contracts in the stable, or loose box ; and all the
cleaning it obtains, or needs, is performed by the rain, and
by the friction it receives when the horse rolls upon the

ground, or rubs himself against a tree. He comes home with
a very ugly and a very dirty coat, but the skin is cleaner than
if the horse had been all the time in a stable.   I think I have
observed that colts who have never been stabled, preserve a
cleaner skin at grass than those that have been long accustomed to a daily dressing. It would be foolish to attempt
any explanation of this before it is ascertained to be true. I
am not sure of it.   But it is very well known that an old
horse is very apt to become mangy and lousy if kept long in
the stable without grooming.   I do not know what effect the
friction of a daily dressing may have upon the general health.
Its beneficial influence upon the human body is acknowledged
by all medical men, and, especially in warm countries, it is
duly appreciated.   That friction promotes the secretions of
the horse's skin, is evident from the permanent gloss which it
imparts to the hair; that a disordered state of the skin produces a disordered state of the stomach, the bowels, and the
lungs, can hardly be denied, since it is universally admitted
that a particular state of these latter organs is constantly followed by derangement of the former. If diseases in the
stomach or bowels can produce diseases in the skin, surely
diseases in the skin may produce diseases in the stomach.

Want of Dressing, whether it affect the general health or
not, produces lice and mange.   Mange may arise from causes
independent of a neglected skin, but it very rarely visits a
well-groomed horse.   Bad food or starvation has something
to do in the production of lice; but the want of dressing has
quite as much, or more.   It is the business of the stableman
to prevent mange, so far as prevention is possible.   Its treatment belongs to the veterinarian, and need not be here described.   But it is the groom's duty both to prevent and to
cure lousiness.

Lice may accumulate in great numbers before they are discovered.   Sometimes they are diffused over all the skin; at
other times they are confined to the mane, the tail, and parts
adjacent.   The horse is frequently rubbing himself, and often
the hair falls out in large patches.   There are many lotions,
powders, and ointments, for destroying lice.   Ointments are
not easily applied, and they are seldom effective; but when
the vermin are confined to a little space, the mercurial ointment rubbed well into the skin, is better than any other oily
application.   [This is a dangerous remedy, and after being
applied, the horse's head should be so confined that he can
not touch the anointed parts with his tongue or lips, or be

placed within reach of any other animal, otherwise there is danger of their getting the mercurial ointment into the mouth, and thus cause death. We have known valuable animals occasionally lost in this way. Refuse oil or lard, rubbed on a lousy beast of any kind, immediately destroys the vermin, and there is no danger to be apprehended from this application. It merely occasions the hair being shed earlier in the spring, and requires a little extra attention in housing such animals as have been affected.] A decoction of tobacco is an effectual remedy. A pint of boiling water is poured upon an ounce of twist or shag tobacco, and, when cold, the liquor is applied with a sponge, so as to wet the hair to the root. A solution of corrosive sublimate, in the proportion of one drachm to a pint of water, is also a very good remedy, but not to be employed when much of the skin is raw. [This is likewise a dangerous remedy.] When the lice are very numerous, spread over great part of the body, it is a good plan to use both the decoction and the solution. One half of the body may be dressed with the tobacco liquor, and the other half with the solution of sublimate. Vinegar, mixed with three times its bulk of water, is a good application, and not so dangerous as the other. It is more irritating, but the irritation soon subsides and does not sicken the horse; tobacco often will. Next day the skin should be examined, and wherever there is any sign of living vermin, another application should be made. Two days afterward the horse should be washed with soapy water, warm, and applied with a brush that will reach the skin without irritating it.

In many cases, none of these remedies are necessary. It is sufficient to wash the horse all over with soapy water. Black soap is better than any other. It need not, and should not be rubbed upon the skin. It may be beat into the water till it forms a strong lather, and that should be applied with a brush and washed off with clean warm water. Care must be taken that the horse do not catch cold. He should be thoroughly washed, but dried as quickly as possible, and get a walk afterward if the weather be favorable.

The clothes should be dipped into boiling water, and the inside of the saddle wet with the sublimate lotion. The litter should all be turned out, and burned, or buried where swine, dogs, or poultry, will not get among it. If it can not be easily removed without scattering it across the stable or yard, a solution of quick-lime may be dashed over it, before it is taken from the stall.

DRESSING AFTER WORK.——This operation varies according to many circumstances; it is influenced by the kind of horse, the state and time in which he arrives at the stable. Slow-working horses merely require to be dried and cleaned; those of fast work may require something more, and those which arrive at a late hour are not usually dressed as they would be by coming home earlier. The principal objects in dressing a horse after work are to get him dry, cool, and clean. It is only, however, in stables tolerably well regulated, that these three objects are aimed at, or attainable. Carters, and other inferior stablemen, endeavor to remove the mud which adheres to the belly, the feet, and the legs, and they are not often very particular as to the manner in which this is done. If a pond or river be at hand, or on the road home, the horse is driven through it, and his keeper considers that the best, which I suppose means the easiest, way of cleaning him. Others, having no such convenience, are content to throw two or three buckets of water over the legs. Their only way of drying the horse is by sponging the legs, and wisping the body, and this is generally done as if it were a matter of form more than of utility. There are some lazy fellows who give themselves no concern about dressing the horse. They put him in the stable wet and dirty as he comes off the road; and after he is dry, perhaps he gets a scratch with the currycomb, and a rub with the straw-wisp. Fast-working horses require very different treatment. The rate at which they travel renders them particularly liable to all those diseases arising from, or connected with changes of temperature. In winter, the horse comes off the road, heated, wet, and bespattered with mud; in summer, he is hotter, drenched in perspiration, or half dry, his coat matted, and sticking close to the skin. Sometimes he is quite cool, but wet, and clothed in mud. The treatment he receives can not be always the same. In summer, after easy work, his feet and legs may be washed and dried, and his body dressed in nearly the same manner that it is dressed before work. The wisp dries the places that are moist with perspiration, the currycomb removes the mud, and the brush polishes the hair, lays it, and takes away the dust. The dressing in such a case is simple and soon over, but it is all the horse requires. When drenched in rain or perspiration, he must be dried by means of the scraper, the wisp, and evaporation; when heated, he must be walked about till cool, and sometimes he may be bathed, that he may be both cooled and cleaned.

Scraping.—The scraper is sometimes termed a sweat-knife. In some stables it is just a piece of hoop iron, about twenty inches long, by one and a half broad ; in the racing and hunting-stables it is made of wood, sharp only on one edge, and having the back thick and strong. When properly handled, it is a very useful instrument. The groom taking an extremity in each hand, passes over the neck, back, belly, quarters, sides, every place where it can operate ; and with a gentle and steady pressure, he removes the wet mud, the rain, and the perspiration. Fresh horses do not understand this, and are apt to resist it. A little more than the usual care and gentleness at the first two or three dressings, render them familiar with it. The pressure applied must vary at different parts of the body, being lightest where the coat and the skin are thinnest. The scraper must pass over the same places several times, especially the belly, to which the water gravitates from the back and sides. It has little or nothing to do about the legs ; these parts are easily dried by a large sponge, and are apt to be injured by the scraper. This operation finished, the horse, if hot, must be walked about a little, and if cool, he must be dried.

Walking a Heated Horse.—Everybody knows that a horse ought not to be stabled when perspiring very copiously after severe exertion ; he must not stand still. It is known that he is likely to catch cold, or to take inflamed lungs, or to founder. By keeping him in gentle motion till cool, these evils are prevented. This is all that stablemen can say about it, and perhaps little more can be said with certainty We must go a little deeper than the skin, and consider the state of the internal organs at the moment the horse has finished a severe task. The action of the heart, the bloodvessels, the nerves, and perhaps other parts, has been greatly increased, to correspond with the extraordinary action of the muscles, the instruments of motion. The circulation, once excited, does not become tranquil the moment exertion ceases. The heart and other internal organs which act in concert with the heart, continue for a time to perform their functions with all the energy which violent muscular exertion demands, and they do mischief before they are aware that their extraordinary services are no longer required. An irregularity in the distribution of the blood takes place ; some part receives more than it needs, and an inflammation is the result. Motion prevents this, because it keeps up a demand for blood among the muscles. The transition from rapid motion to rest is too sudden, and should be broken by gentle motion. If the heart and nervous system could be restrained as easily as the action of the voluntary muscles, there would be no need for walking a heated horse, since it would be sufficient to render all the organs tranquil at the same time.

This brief analysis of what is going on internally, may be useful to those who would know exactly when it is safe to put a heated horse to perfect rest. It is needless to keep him in motion after the pulse has sunk to nearly its natural number of beats per minute, which is under 40. Stablemen go by the heat of the skin, but on a hot day the skin will often remain above its usual heat, for a good while after the system is quite calm. The state of the skin, however, in general indicates the degree of internal excitement with sufficient accuracy.

The object, then, in walking a heated horse, is to allay the excitement of exertion in *all* parts of the body at the same time and by degrees, to keep the muscles working because the heart is working. The motion should always be slow, and the horse led, not ridden. If wet, and the weather cold, his walk may be faster than summer weather requires.

When the state of the weather, and the want of a covered ride, put walking out of the question, the horse must either go to the stable or he must suffer a little exposure to the rain. When much excited, that is, when very warm, it is better that he should walk for a few minutes in the rain, than that he should stand quite still. But a horse seldom comes in very warm while it is raining. If he must go into the stable it should not be too close. To a horse hot, perspiring, and breathing very quick, a warm stable is particularly distressing. Some faint under it. Till somewhat calm he may stand with his head to the door, but not in a current of cold air, at least not after he begins to cool.

Walking a Wet Horse.—Gentle motion to a heated horse is necessary, to prevent the evils likely to arise from one set of organs doing more than another set requires. But in many cases motion after work is useful when the horse is not heated. He may come in drenched with rain, but quite cool, and there may be no one at hand to dry him, or his coat may be so long that one man can not get him dry before he begins to shiver. In such cases the horse should be walked about. Were he stabled or allowed to stand at rest in this state, he would be very likely to suffer as much injury as if he were suddenly brought to a stand-still when in a high state of perspiration. Evaporation commences : the moisture with which the skin is charged is converted into vapor, and as it assumes this form it robs the horse of a large quantity of heat. If he be kept in motion while this cooling and drying process is going on, an extra quantity of heat is formed, which may very well be spared for converting the water into vapor, while sufficient is retained to keep the skin comfortably warm. Everybody must understand the difference between sitting and walking in wet clothes. If the horse be allowed to stand while wet, evaporation still goes on. Every particle of moisture takes away so much heat, but there is no stimulus to produce the formation of an extra quantity of heat ; in a little while, the skin becomes sensibly cold, the blood circulates slowly, there is no demand for it ôn the surface, nor among the muscles, and it accumulates upon internal organs. By-and-by the horse takes a violent shivering fit ; after this has continued for a time, the system appears to become aware that it has been insidiously deprived of more heat than it can conveniently spare ; then a process is set up for repairing the loss, and for meeting the increased demand. But before this calorifying process is fairly established, the demand for an extra quantity of heat has probably ceased. The skin has become dry, and there is no longer any evaporation. Hence the heat accumulates, and the horse is fevered. I do not pretend to trace events any further. The next thing of which we become aware is generally an inflammation of the feet, the throat, the lungs, or some other part. But we can not tell what is going on between the time that the body becomes hot, and the time that inflammation appears. I am not even certain that the other changes take place in the order in which they are enumerated ; nor am I sure that there is no other change. The analysis may be defective ; something may take place that I have not observed, and possibly the loss of heat by evaporation may not always produce these effects without assistance. It is positively known, however, that there is danger in exposing a horse to cold when he is not in motion ; and, which is the same thing, it is equally, indeed more dangerous to let him stand when he is wet. If he can not be dried by manual labor, he must be moved about till he is dried by evaporation.

Wisping a Wet Horse.—When there is sufficient strength in the stable, the proper way to dry the horse is by rubbing him with wisps. After removing all the water that can be taken away with the scraper, two men commence on each

side. They rub the skin with soft wisps; those which absorb moisture most readily are the best, and should be often
changed.   None but a bred groom can dry a horse expe-
ditiously and well in this way.   The operation requires some
action, and a good deal of strength.   An awkward groom can
not do it, and a lazy fellow will not.   They will wisp the
horse for a couple of hours, and leave him almost as wet as
at the beginning.   They lay the hair, but do not dry it, and
they are sure to neglect the legs and the belly, the very parts
that have most need to be dried quickly.   The man must put
some strength into his arm.   He must rub hard, and in all
directions, across, and against the hair, oftener than over it.
His wisp should be firm yet soft, the straw broken.   Some
can not even make this simple article.   A stout fellow may
take one in each hand, if only two are employed about the
horse ; and a boy must often take one in both his hands.   Two
men may dry a horse in half an hour, a little more or a little
less, according to his condition, the length of his coat, and
the state of the weather.

Clothing a Wet Horse.—When the horse can neither be
dried by the wisp, nor kept in motion, some other means must
be taken to prevent him catching cold.   He may be scraped,
and then clothed, or he may be clothed without scraping.
This is not a good practice, nor a substitute for grooming ;
it is merely an expedient which may be occasionally resorted
to when the horse must be stabled wet as he comes off the
road.   Clothing renders him less likely to catch cold, but it
does not perform the duty that ought to be performed by the
groom.   When the horse is completely and quickly dried by
manual labor, there is not the slightest chance of his suffering
any mischief from cold ; the friction of the wisp keeps the
blood on the surface, and the horse can be put up quite comfortable.   When he is kept in motion till the moisture has all
evaporated, he can suffer no more injury than if he were
brought in quite dry.   When clothing is applied, it is with the
intention of checking evaporation.   It makes this process go
on more slowly than if the horse were naked ; in consequence
he loses less heat in a given time, and he never becomes very
cold.   The clothing also absorbs much of the water, which,
if allowed to evaporate, would take away much heat that is
thus retained.   Of course, the horse remains wet for a longer
time than if he were unclothed.   But it is doubtful if moisture
applied occasionally for an hour or two on the skin is injurious.   It probably has some influence ; but it is well known

that cold has much more. Long-continued moisture injures
the coat, destroys its glossy appearance; but I am not aware
that it does anything else. I am not speaking of moisture
applied for many successive hours, but of that which is retained perhaps an hour longer by clothing than it would remain
if allowed to evaporate without interruption. I am aware that
a horse is apt to perspire if clothed up when his coat is wet
or damp. But this takes place only when the clothing is too
heavy, or the horse too warm. In the case under consideration, the clothing, unless the horse be cold, is not intended to
heat him, but to prevent him from becoming cold. In hot
weather, a wet horse requires less care; he need not be
clothed, for evaporation will not render him too cold; and if
his coat be long, it will, without the assistance of clothing,
keep the skin tolerably warm even in weather that is not hot.
In all cases the cloth should be of woollen, and thrown closely
over the body, not bound by the roller, and in many cases it
should be changed for a drier and a lighter one, as it becomes
charged with moisture.

To many people all this care about a wet horse will appear
to be superfluous. They will observe that horses are frequently exposed to all weathers, and to the worst of stable
treatment, without receiving any apparent injury. This is
true with regard to many horses; their work is not exciting,
not requiring that exertion which agitates the whole frame.
There are horses, too, of less value, but performing work of
the severest kind, upon whom a great deal of care can not be
bestowed. The proprietor may think it is cheaper to let the
horses run considerable risk, than to keep a sufficient number
of men for taking better care of them. These can be right
only when their horses are very worthless, and perhaps not
then. In a valuable stud it is otherwise. The extra expense
of such careful treatment is not to be considered where horses
are worth from fifty pounds to more than five hundred. It is
also true that among stage-coach, and other horses of a similar
kind, there are many who do not receive any injury from a
wet coat. Those that have been gradually inured to exposure, or to stand unheeded till they dry, may feel cold and uncomfortable, and have a long, rough coat, but their health remains unaffected. The power of the system to accommodate
itself to circumstances is very great. These horses are as
easily wet to the skin as other horses; but their skin has
learned to furnish an additional supply of heat so soon and as
often as the evaporating process demands it. Such horses

require little care, though more would make them look better
But stablemen who know this are apt to treat all the horses
alike.   The young and the delicate must have additional care
till they are inured to exposure.

All horses, whatever be their age, condition, and work, are
most easily injured by exposure to cold, after they have been
heated by exertion.   Every man may have proof of this in his
own person.   After perspiring he feels cold and disposed to
shiver, though by this time the skin may be quite dry.   It is
the same with the horse.   Before he has been heated he might
stand in the cold, or with his coat wet for perhaps half an
hour, without any danger; but after he has perspired pretty
freely from exertion, motionless exposure in a cold atmosphere
for fifteen minutes will do him more harm than he would receive in thirty minutes before the exertion; or, in the one
case, he would be none the worse—in the other, he would
have a cough next day.

Therefore, a wet horse requires most care when his work
has heated him.   He must be dried more quickly, or kept in
motion for a longer time than if he had not been excited.

It is continued cold that does the mischief in all cases;
some, from habit, will bear much more than others, but none
seem able to bear it so well after as before perspiring.   The
intolerance of cold seems to remain for an hour or two after
the horse is quite cool, and to increase as the skin loses its
heat.

The first symptom of approaching danger is staring of the
coat; if the horse be immediately put into a warm stable, or
warmly clothed, or put in motion, he may, and probably will,
escape.   The second symptom is shivering, which ought to
be quickly arrested by applying warmth.   There is no danger
in exposure, so long as the skin remains comfortably warm
or hot.

To Remove the Mud.—There are two ways of removing
the mud.   One may be termed the dry, and another the
wet mode.   The first is performed by means of the scraper
and the currycomb, or a kind of brush made of whalebone,
which answers much better than the currycomb.   In most of
the well-regulated coaching-stables, the strappers are never
allowed to apply water to a horse that has come muddy off the
road [and in no stable should the mud be allowed to be re
moved from the horse by washing, except he be hand-rubbed
dry].   The usual practice is to strip off the mud and loose
water by the sweat knife; to walk the horse about for ten

minutes if he be warm or wet and the weather fair, otherwise he stands a little in his stall or in an open shed; then the man begins with the driest of those that have come in together. Much of the surface mud which the scraper has left about the legs is removed by a straw wisp, or a small birch broom, or the whalebone brush; the wisp likewise helps to dry the horse. The whalebone brush is a very useful article when the coat is long. That, and the currycomb, with the aid of a wisp, are almost the only implements coaching-strappers require in the winter season. It clears away the mud and separates the hairs, but it does not polish them. A gloss such as the coat of these horses requires, is given by the wisp. The whalebone brush is sometimes too coarse, and many horses can not bear it at any time, while others can suffer it only in winter. After the mud has been removed with this brush, the matted hair parted by the currycomb, and the horse dusted all over with the wisp, his feet are washed, the soles picked, the shoes examined, the legs and heels well rubbed, partly by the hand and partly by the wisp, and the mane and tail combed. In the best of these stables he is well dressed with the bristle brush before he goes to work. In other stables the usual mode of removing the mud is by

Washing.—When the horse is very dirty he is usually washed outside the stable; his belly is scraped, and the remainder of the mud is washed off at once by the application of water. Some clean the body before they wash the legs; but that is only when there is not much mud about the horse. They do so that he may go into the stable quite clean. He soils his feet and legs by stamping the ground when his body is being cleaned. It matters little whether the dressing commence with the body or with the legs, but when the legs are washed the last thing, they are generally left undried. In washing, a sponge and a water-brush are employed. Some use a mop, and this is called the lazy method: it is truly the trick of a careless sloven; it wets the legs but does not clean them. The brush goes to the roots of the hair, and removes all the sand and mud, without doing which it is worse than useless to apply any water. The sponge is employed for drying the hair, for soaking up and wiping away the loose water. Afterward, the legs and all the parts that have been washed, are rendered completely dry by rubbing with the straw-wisp, the rubber, and the hand. Among valuable horses this is always done; wherever the legs have little hair about them, and that little can not be properly dried after washing, no washing should take place.

Wet Legs.—It is a very common practice, because it is easy, to wash the legs; but none, save the best of stablemen, will be at the trouble of drying them; they are allowed to dry of themselves, and they become excessively cold. Evaporation commences; after a time a process is set up for producing heat sufficient to carry on evaporation, and to maintain the temperature of the skin. Before this process can be fully established, the water has all evaporated; then the heat accumulates; inflammation succeeds, and often runs so far as to produce mortification. When the inflammation is slight and transient, the skin is soon completely restored to health, and no one knows that it had ever been inflamed. When the process runs higher, there is a slight oozing from the skin, which constitutes what is termed grease, or a spot of grease; for when this disease is spread over a large surface, it is the result of repeated neglect. When the inflammation has been still more severe, mortification ensues; the horse is lame, the leg swollen, and in a day or two a crack is visible across the pastern, generally at that part where the motion is greatest. This crack is sometimes a mere rupture of the tumefied skin, but very often it is produced by a dead portion of the skin having fallen out; what is called a core in the heel arises from the same cause; it differs from the crack only in being deeper and wider. The reason why cold produces such local injury of the skin covering the legs, and not of that covering any other part, is sufficiently plain. The legs, in proportion to their size, have a very extensive surface exposed to evaporation, and the cold becomes more intense than it can ever be come on the body. To avoid these evils, the legs must either be dried after washing, or they must not be washed at all.

Among horses that have the fetlocks and the legs well clothed with long and strong hair, it is not necessary to be so particular about drying the legs: the length and the thickness of the hair check evaporation. This process is not permitted to go on so rapidly; the air and the vapor are entangled among the hair, they can not get away, and of course can not carry off the heat so rapidly as from a naked heel. But for all this, it is possible to make the legs, even of those hairy-heeled horses, so cold as to produce inflammation. And when these horses have the legs trimmed bare, they are more liable to grease than the lighter horse of faster work. But the greatest number of patients with grease occur where the legs and heels are trimmed, washed, and never properly dried. There is no grease where there is good grooming, and not much where the legs are well covered with hair. It is true that fat or plethoric horses are very liable to cracks and moisture of the heels; but though it may not be easy, yet it is quite possible for a good groom to prevent grease even in these horses.

The proprietors of coaching-studs, a great many of them, find that the strappers have not time nor inclination to dry the legs after washing, and they prohibit the operation altogether. The men, nevertheless, are very fond of washing; it is easier to wash the legs clean than to brush them clean; and laziness is never without its plea. It is said that washing has nothing to do with grease or cracked heels, and that these diseases will occur where no washing is ever allowed. This is partly true, but the grease arises from the same cause; though the legs are not washed, yet they are not dried when the horses come in with them wet; hence the great number of cases in wet winters. It is also said that if the legs be wet when the horses come in, washing can not make them wetter: though the legs be wet yet they are warm, and if they must be washed, it should be with water warm as the skin.

I am not objecting to washing under all circumstances. It is a bad practice among naked-heeled horses, only when the men will not or can not make the legs dry. In a gentleman's stable the legs ought to be washed, but they ought also to be thoroughly dried before the horse is left. It is the evaporation, or the cold produced by evaporation, that does the mischief. In a cart-horse stable there is less chance of washing doing any harm; the long hair preventing the legs from becoming very cold; still, if grease, swelled legs, or cracked heels, occur often, either washing must be prohibited, or the legs must be dried after it, or the washing must be performed, at other times. In a farm-stable, the man, after working the horse all day, can not be expected to bestow an hour or two upon the legs at night; but he may forbear washing when he finds that grease is the consequence. He may brush off the mud, when it is dry, and a wisp or a sponge will take away the loose water which the horse brings from his work. If the legs become itchy and scurfy under this treatment, they may be washed once or twice a-week with soapy warm water, well applied, by means of a brush that will reach the skin; and this washing, particularly in cold weather, should be performed *before* the horse goes to his work, not after it. While he is in motion the legs will not become cold. The

9*

object of such a washing is not to clean the hair, but to clean the skin, which is apt to become foul and to itch from the mud adhering to it undisturbed. Upon drawing the hand over the pasterns and the legs, when in this state, numerous pimples are felt, some of which are raw. The horse is often stamping violently, and rubbing one leg against another. A solution of salt is a common and useful remedy against the itchiness, but it will not prevent a return.

I am aware that, in many coaching-stables, the men are still permitted to wash the horse's legs, without being compelled to dry them. This is no argument in favor of washing; for unless the legs be well clothed with hair, they will always tell the same tale. The horses that have recently entered these studs have grease, swelled legs, and cracked heels; those that have been a longer time in the service may be free from these, yet they show that they have had them over and over again. Their legs are round and fleshy; the skin thick, bald, seamed, callous. Nature has done much to inure the skin, but not before the horse has given a great deal of trouble, and perhaps not till he is permanently blemished.

Bathing.—This name may be given to the operation of washing the horse all over. Where possible, and not forbidden by the owner, a lazy or ignorant groom always performs it in the neighboring river or pond. Some take the horse into the water till it is up to his belly, and others swim him into the depths, from which man and horse are often borne away with the stream, to the great grief of the newspaper editor, who deplores their melancholy fate; by which, I suppose, he means melancholy ignorance.

These river bathings ought to be entirely prohibited. In this town boys are often sent to the Clyde with horses, and they play themselves in the water, wading here and there, and up and down, till the horse is benumbed and carried off, or hardly able to reach the shore. Besides this risk, he is cooled both without and within, for he is generally permitted to drink at the same time. The running water removes the mud very effectually; but that can be done quite as well, and with less danger to the horse, though with a little more trouble to the keeper, in the stable-yard. There are only certain times in which bathing is proper, and these times are never observed when the men have got into the habit of going to the river.

In cold weather it is an act of madness. During some of

the hottest days in summer, a general bathing is wonderfully refreshing to a horse that has run a stage at the rate of ten miles an hour. It cleans the skin more effectually than any other means, and with less irritation to the horse; it renders him comfortably cool, and, under certain conditions, it does him no harm. Those employed in public conveyances are almost the only horses that require it. During very hot weather they suffer much from the pace at which they travel. They come off the road steeped in perspiration, but in a few minutes they are dry. The coat is thin and short, and the hairs glued together by dirt and sweat; to raise and separate them with the currycomb is productive of much pain, greatly aggravated by the fevered condition of the horse. The best way of cleaning a horse in this state, is by washing him. The operation is performed by the water-brush and the sponge. The horse should stand in the sun. The man, taking a large coarse sponge in his hand, usually commences at the neck, close to the head; he proceeds backward and downward till he has bathed the horse all over. This may be done in two minutes. Then, dipping his brush in the water, he applies it as generally as the sponge, drawing it always in the direction of the hair, without any rubbing. The sponge merely applies the water; the brush loosens and removes the dust and perspiration which adhere to the hair. The sweat-knife is next employed, and the horse being scraped as dry as possible, he is walked about in the sun for half an hour, more or less, till he be perfectly dry. During the time he is in motion the scraper is reapplied several times, especially to the belly, and the horse gets water at twice or thrice. When quite dry he is stabled, and wisped over, perhaps lightly brushed, to lay and polish his coat, and when his legs are well rubbed he is ready for feeding.

To the hackney and the stage-coach horse, a bathing of this kind may often be given with great benefit. It improves the appearance of the skin, and subdues that fevered state of the system in which horses often remain for a long time after severe exertion under a burning sun. It must not be over-done. The horse should be washed and dried as quickly as possible. The object is to render him comfortably cool, not to freeze him. Upon cold, wet, or cloudy days, it is forbidden, and after sunset it is out of the question. For slow working horses it is neither necessary nor proper. The excitement of their work is so moderate, that the circulation becomes tranquil soon after the work is over. They are not

so difficult to clean, and they are not liable to the faint, fevered condition which fast work produces in hot weather. The
men who attend these slow horses are seldom able to bathe
them, even though bathing were beneficial. They have not
sufficient despatch.

OPERATIONS OF DECORATION.

Some of these might very well be termed expurgatory or
deformatory operations. Many of them consist in removing
something supposed to be superfluous or noxious, or something
offensive to taste, which among stablemen is often sufficiently
corrupt. To judge of their propriety or impropriety, it is
necessary to advert briefly to

The Uses and Properties of the Hair.—That which
forms the general covering is intended to keep the horse
warm. It conducts heat very slowly, and is therefore well
adapted for retaining it. It absorbs no moisture, and when
the horse is in good health, every hair is anointed with an
oily sort of fluid which imparts a beautiful gloss, and repels
moisture.

The hair is shed every spring and every autumn. The short
fine coat which suffices for the summer, affords little protection
against the severity of winter; it falls and is replaced by
another of the same material, though longer and coarser. It
is not very obvious why the horse should moult twice every
year. We might suppose that a mere increase in the length
of the summer coat would render it sufficiently warm for the
winter. Without doubt there is some reason why it is otherwise ordered. The hair perhaps is not of the same texture;
that of the winter coat certainly appears to be coarser; it is
thicker, and it requires more care to keep it glossy than the
hair of a summer coat.

The hair is not cast all at once. Before losing its connexion with the skin it assumes a lighter color, and becomes dim
and deadlike. On some warm day a large quantity comes
away which is not missed, though its fall is very evident.
The process seems to stop for several days and to recom-
mence. Though a little is always falling, yet there are times
at which large quantities come out, and it is said that the
whole is shed at thrice. Moulting, and the length and thickness of the coat, are much influenced by stable treatment and
the weather. Horses that are much and for a long time out
of doors, exposed to cold, always have the hair much longer

than those kept in warm stables, or those that are more in the stable than in the open air. If the horse be kept warm and well fed, his winter coat will be very little longer than that of summer, and it will lie nearly as well. Moulting may even be entirely prevented; heavy clothing and warm stabling will keep the summer coat on all winter. The horse, however, must not be often nor long exposed to cold, for though he may be made to retain his summer coat till after the usual period of changing it, yet it will fall even in the middle of winter, if he be much exposed to winter weather. Grooms often hasten the fall of the winter coat by extra dressing and clothing, in order that the horse may have his fine summer coat a little earlier than usual. This, especially when the spring is cold and the horse much exposed, is not right, for it generally makes the summer coat longer than if it had not appeared till the weather was warmer.

The long hair which grows on the legs of some horses is doubtless intended to answer the same purpose as the short hair of the body. It is longer and stronger, because the parts are more exposed to cold and to wet. It is always longest in horses that are reared in damp or marshy situations, where the grass is luxuriant, and the soil charged with moisture. Such pastures are necessary for the large draught-horse, who consumes much food, more than the light racing-horse, to whom the scanty herbage of a dryer situation is sufficient. But, independent of this, length of hair upon the legs is peculiar to particular breeds. It is always long in draught-horses and Highland ponies, and short in blood-horses wherever they are reared. On the legs of thorough-bred horses, the hair is not much longer than that on the body, with the exception of a tuft at the back of the fetlock-joint. This is termed the foot-lock. It defends the parts beneath from external injury, to which they are liable by contact with the ground. When very long, good grooming, good food, and warm stabling, always shorten the hair of the legs.

The hair of the mane has been regarded as ornamental, and it is so; but to say that any part of an animal was conferred for the sole purpose of pleasing the eye of man, is almost as much as to say that all were not created by the same Being. Had the mane been superfluous to the horse, we could have been made to admire him without it. God has made it pleasing to us, because it is useful to him. In a wild state the horse has many battles to fight, and his neck, deprived of the mane, would be a very vulnerable part. It is likewise a part that he can not reach with his teeth, and not easily with his feet. The flies might settle there and satiate themselves without disturbance: if the mane can not altogether exclude those intruders, it can lash them off by a single jerk of the head. I believe that in wild horses the mane falls equally on both sides of the neck.

The long hair of the mane, the tail, and the legs, is not shed in the same manner as that on the body. It is deciduous, but it does not fall so regularly, so rapidly, nor so often as the other. Each hair, from its length, requires a much longer time to grow; if all were shed at once, the parts would be left defenceless for perhaps more than a month. Some of the hairs are constantly losing their attachment and falling out, while others are as constantly growing. It is not possible to say what determines the fall of these hairs in horses not domesticated. It may be some circumstance connected with their age or length more than with the change of season. When brushed and combed many of them are pulled out.

DOCKING.—In this country the horse's tail is regarded as a useless or troublesome appendage. It was given to ward off the attacks of blood-sucking flies. But men choose to remove it without being able to give the horse any other protection from the insects against which it was intended to operate. They say that the long tail conceals the horse's quarters, diminishes his apparent height, heats him at fast work, and soils his rider. It is also supposed that amputation of the tail renders the back stronger. These sage sayings have been promulgated so extensively from one to another, that it seems to be universally decided that all horses must be docked.

These, it will be observed, are very strong objections to a long tail. It is a terrible thing to hide the quarters, and to make the horse look lower by an inch than he really is. Evils of such a nature are not to be suffered. The tail may be very useful in some respects, and in the good old times it was permitted to flourish as it grew, being only bound up when it troubled the horse's rider. But in times like these, when men clamor for freedom, and practise tyranny, it must be cut off.

It is said that the back becomes stronger after the tail is docked; that the back receives the blood which formerly went to the tail. There is no truth in this. The small quantity of blood which is saved can be furnished by one or two additional ounces of grain, and there is not the slightest proof that the back becomes stronger.

Some writers have contended that the tail of the horse, like that of the greyhound or the kangaroo, assists him in turning, in the same way that a helm guides a ship. If this be so, as its action when the horse is running would seem to indicate, cavalry horses and racers, more than others, must lose a great deal of power by docking. But whether this be true or not, there can be no doubt about the utility of the tail in keeping off flies, which to some horses give extreme torment. I have heard or read of a troop of cavalry employed, I think in some, part of India, that was quite useless in consequence of the annoyance the docked horses received from a large species of fly. In this country, for two months of the year, thin-skinned horses suffer excessively, and many accidents happen from their struggles or their fears. At grass they are in a constant fever.

It is surely worth while inquiring, whether all that is gained by docking balances the loss. In comparing the two it ought to be remembered that lockjaw and death are not rare results of the operation.

Docking is usually performed by the veterinarian, or the shoeing-smith, who keeps instruments for the purpose. In some places it is performed when the colt is only two or three months old. At such an early age, a knife will remove the tail, and the bleeding stops of itself. By docking early there is less risk, and the hair grows more strongly upon the remaining part of the tail than when the operation is delayed to a later period.

NICKING.—In England and Scotland this operation appears to be fast and justly getting into disrepute. It is still very common in all parts of Ireland. Its object is to make the horse carry his tail well elevated. Two or three deep incisions are made on the lower surface of the tail; the muscles by which it is depressed are divided, and a portion of them excised. The wounds are kept open for several days, and the tail is kept in elevation by means of pulleys and a weight. It is a surgical operation, but no respectable veterinarian would recommend it. It need not be described here. On the continent, a tail thus mutilated is termed *Queue à l'Anglaise*, in compliment, I suppose, to the English.

There is a safer and more humane method of obtaining the same object. (See Fig. 8.) If the horse do not carry his

FIG. 13.

tail to his rider's satisfaction, it may be put in the pulley, an
hour or two every day for several successive weeks.

A cord is stretched across the stall, near or between the
heel-posts; the hair of the tail is plaited and attached to
another cord, which passes upward over a pulley in the
transverse line, stretches backward, where it passes through
another pulley and descends. To this a weight is secured, a
bag containing sand or shot sufficient to keep the tail at the
proper elevation. A double pulley on the cross cord permits
the horse to move from side to side without twisting the tail.
The weight should vary with the strength of the tail. From
one to two pounds is sufficient to begin with. After a few days
it may be gradually increased, so as to keep the tail a little more
elevated than the horse is wanted to carry it. The time which
he stands in the pulleys need not in the first week exceed
one hour; on the second week he may stand thus for two or
three hours every day, and at last he may be kept up all day
or all night, if the horse be at work during the day. Should
the tail become hot or tender, or should the hair show any
tendency to fall out, the elevating process must be omitted for
a day or two till the tail be well again, when it may be re-
sumed and carried on every day, unless the hair again become
loose, which is a sign that the weight is too great or too long
continued.

From this operation there is no danger of the horse dying of lockjaw, nor of the tail being set awry, nor broken, as sometimes happens after nicking. It requires a much longer period to effect the elevation, but that is of no consequence, since the horse need not be a single day off work. When nicked he must be idle for several weeks.

[The operation of *nicking*, or more properly *pricking*, as given by our author, is barbarous in the extreme. As practised in America, it is much more simple, effectual, and less painful. If the tail is to be docked, let that first be done, and then permitted to heal perfectly. Perhaps this operation may make the horse carry his tail so well as to prevent the necessity of pricking. But if it does not, then let him be pricked.

Operation.—The tail has four cords, two upper and two lower. The upper ones raise the tail, the lower ones depress it, and these last alone are to be cut. Take a sharp penknife with a long slender blade; insert the blade between the bone and under cord, two inches from the body; place the thumb of the hand holding the knife against the under part of the tail, and opposite the blade. Then press the blade toward the thumb against the cord, and cut the cord off, but do not let the knife cut through the skin. The cord is firm and it will easily be known when it is cut off. The thumb will tell when to desist, that the skin may not be cut. Sever the cord twice on each side in the same manner. Let the cuts be two inches apart. The cord is nearly destitute of sensation; yet when the tail is pricked in the old manner, the wound to the skin and flesh is severe, and much fever is induced, and it takes a long time to heal. But with this method, the horse's tail will not bleed, nor will it be sore under ordinary circumstances more than three days; and he will be pulleyed and his tail made in one half of the time required by the old method.]

DRESSING THE TAIL.—Sometimes the hair of the tail grows too bushy. The best way of thinning it is to comb it often with a dry comb, having small but strong teeth. When the hair is short, stiff, almost standing on end, it may be laid by wetting it, and tying the ends together beyond the stump. Sometimes the whole tail is moistened, and surrounded by a hay-rope, which is applied evenly and moderately tight, and kept on all night. It makes the hair lie better during the next day, but seldom longer. Square tails require occasional clipping. The tail is held in a horizontal position by the left hand, while it is squared with scissors. The hair at the

centre is rendered shorter than that at the outside, and the
tail, when elevated, resembles the feathered extremity of a
pen. Horses of the racing kind have long tails with the
points of the hair cut off.

A switch tail is taper at the point, not square. It is of
varying length, according to the taste of the rider. It sometimes requires to be shortened without squaring it. The man
seizes it within his left hand, cuts off the superfluous length
with a knife not very sharp. He does not go slap-dash
through it as a pair of scissors would; but, holding the knife
across, with the edge inclined to the point of the tail, he
draws it up and down as if he were scraping it; the hairs
are cut as the knife approaches the hand that holds the tail;
in this way he carries the knife all round, and reaches the
central hairs as much from one point of the outer circumfer-
ence as from any other. The hairs are thus left of unequal
length, those at the middle being the longest.

The hair of the tail is usually combed and brushed every
day, and when not hanging gracefully, it should be wet and
combed four or five times a day. White tails, especially
when of full length, require often to be washed with soap and
water. On many horses the hair is very thin. When the
hair is wanted exuberant, it should have little combing; in
the studs of equestrian actors, the comb is never, or it is very
little used. When applied to separate the hairs, care is taken
not to pull them out. The operator seizes the hair near the
root with his left hand, while the right uses the comb, which
in this way is not permitted to act on the roots. At other
times the water-brush, a little moistened, keeps the hair
smooth and clean.

Formerly, many years ago, it was the custom to dye the
tail and often the mane. Red was a favorite color. Nothing
of that kind is done now, and the process need not be described. Both mane and tail used to be preserved in a bag
when the horse was not at work.

DRESSING THE MANE.—In general the mane lies to the
right side, but in some horses it is shaded equally to each.
On some carriage horses it is made to lie to the right side on
the one, and to the left on the other, the bare side of the neck
being exposed. From some, especially ponies, it is the custom to have the mane shorn off near to the roots, only a few
stumps being left to stand perpendicularly. This is termed
the hog-mane. It is almost entirely out of fashion. To
make a mane lie, the groom combs and wets it several times

a day; he keeps it almost constantly wet; when thick, short, and bushy, he pulls away some of the hair from the under side, that is, from the side to which the mane inclines, or is wanted to incline. When that is not sufficient, he plaits it into ten or fifteen cords, weaving into each a piece of matting, and loading the extremity with a little lead. After remaining in this state for several days, the plaiting is undone, and the mane lies as it is wanted. When it becomes too long or too bushy, a few of the hairs are pulled out. This is often done too harshly, and some horses have a great aversion to it. The man takes hold of a few hairs, often too many; he clears them by pushing up the others, wraps them round his finger, and with a sudden jerk tears them out. Mr. Blane contrived a kind of fork with three prongs made of iron, which is said to thin the mane more equally and less painfully than the finger. In harness-horses, that part of the mane which lies directly behind the ears is usually cut away, that the head of the bridle may sit fast.

Heavy draught-horses should seldom have either the mane or the tail thinned, and, to hang gracefully, it should be long in proportion to its thickness. These horses have a naked, stiff, and clumsy appearance when deprived of too much hair. Indeed, their mane and tail require nothing but daily combing and brushing to keep them clean and even. A thinner mane and tail are more in keeping with the general appearance of fine-boned, well-bred horses.

In stage-coach and similar stables, the horses are often robbed of both mane and tail by drunken strappers. For the sake of a dram, which they gain by selling the hair, they pull out more than enough. This should be forbidden.

TRIMMING THE EARS.—The inside of the ear is coated with fine hair, which is intended by nature to exclude rain, flies, dirt, and other foreign matters floating in the air. When left to itself, it grows so long as to protrude considerably out of the ear, and to give the horse a neglected, ungroomed-like appearance. It is a common practice to trim all this hair away by the roots. But it is a very stupid practice. The internal ear becomes exposed to the intrusion of rain, dirt, and insects; and though I know of no disease arising from this cause, yet every horseman is aware that it gives the horse much annoyance. Many are very unwilling to face a blast of rain or sleet, and some will not. In the fly-season, they are constantly throwing the head about as if they would throw it off, and this is an inconvenience to

either rider or driver. The hair on the inside should not be
cut from any horse. It is easily cleaned by a gentle application of the brush. When the hair grows too long, the points
may be taken off. This is done by closing the ear, and cutting away the hair that protrudes beyond the edges. Among
heavy horses even this is unnecessary.

CROPPING THE EARS used at one time to be almost as common as docking is now. But the operation is so entirely
abandoned, that no one now speaks of it.

TRIMMING THE MUZZLE AND FACE.—All round the muzzle,
and especially about the nostrils and lips, there are long fine
hairs, scattered wide apart, and standing perpendicular to the
skin. These are feelers. They perform the same functions
as the whiskers of the cat. Their roots are endowed with
peculiar sensibility. They warn the horse of the vicinity of
objects to which he must attend. There are several grouped
together below and above the eyes, which give these delicate
organs notice of approaching insects or matters that might
enter them and do mischief. The slightest touch on the extremity of these hairs is instantly felt by the horse. They
detect even the agitation of the air.

It is usual with grooms to cut all these hairs away as vulgar
excrescences. They can give no reason for doing so. They
see these hairs on all horses that are not well groomed, and
perhaps they are accustomed to associate them with general
want of grooming. They are so fine and so few in number,
that they can not be seen from a little distance, and surely
they can not be regarded as incompatible with beauty, even
though they were more conspicuous.

The operation ought to be forbidden; few horses suffer it
without some resistance, and many have to be restrained by
the twitch. The pain is not great, but it seems to be sufficiently annoying.

The long hair which grows upon the throat channel and
neck of horses that have been much exposed to cold, is partly
pulled out and partly shortened. It has been supposed that
the removal of the hair from about the throat renders the horse
very liable to catch cold after it, and to have a cough. It is
sometimes shortened by clipping, but oftener by singeing it,
and singeing is blamed more than clipping. The operation
certainly does not improve the appearance of heavy draught-
horses; it is never required by blood horses, or others that
are well groomed and comfortably stabled; and saddle, gig, or
post-horses, to whom the operation might be an improvement,

are so seldom in the charge of men who can perform it properly, that in general it is better to leave it undone.

TRIMMING THE HEELS AND LEGS.*—The hair of the fetlock, the hollow of the pastern, and the posterior aspect of the legs, is longer on heavy draught-horses than on those of finer bone. It is intended to keep the legs warm, and perhaps in some degree to defend them from external violence. It becomes much shorter and less abundant after the horse is stabled, kept warm, well fed, and well groomed. The simple act of washing the legs, or rubbing them, tends to make the hair short and thin, and to keep it so. Nevertheless, it is a very common practice, especially in coaching-stables, to clip this hair away almost close to the root. Cart-horses very rarely have the heels trimmed; well-bred horses seldom require it. The hand-rubbing which the legs and heels of these horses receive, keeps the hair short, and it is never very long even without hand-rubbing.

The heels are trimmed in three different ways: the most common and the easiest is to clip away all the long hair, near or close to the roots; another way is to switch the heels, that is, to shorten the hair without leaving any mark of the scissors —the groom seizes the hair and cuts off a certain portion in the same manner that he shortens a switch tail; the third mode is to pull the long hairs out by the roots. Switching and pulling, which is little practised, are generally confined to the foot-lock; some neat operators combine these different modes so well, that the hair is rendered thin and short without presenting any very visible marks of the alteration. By means of an iron comb with small teeth and a pair of good scissors, the hair may be shortened without setting it on end or leaving scissor marks, but every groom can not do this.

There has been considerable difference of opinion as to the propriety of trimming the heels. Some contend that the long hair soaks up the moisture, keeps the skin long wet and cold, producing grease, sores, cracks, and scurfiness; by others this is denied; they affirm that the long hair, far from favoring the production of these evils, has a tendency to prevent them. But there is another circumstance to be taken into consideration, and that accounts sufficiently for the difference of opinion.

When the horse is carefully tended after his work is over, his legs quickly and completely dried, the less hair he has

* The word *heel* is applied to the back and hollow of the pastern. In this place, all that is said of the heels is applicable to the legs.

10*

about them the better. The moisture which that little takes
up can be easily removed : both the skin and the hair can be
made perfectly dry before evaporation begins, or proceeds so
far as to deprive the legs of their heat. It is the cold produced by evaporation that does all the mischief ; and if there
be no moisture to create evaporation, there can be no cold—
no loss of heat, save that which is taken away by the air. If
there were more hair about the heels, they could not be so
soon nor so easily dried. If the man requires ten minutes to
dry one leg, the last will have thirty minutes to cool ; if he
can dry each in two minutes, the last will have only six minutes
to cool, and in that time it can not become so cold as to be
liable to grease. Whenever, therefore, the legs *must* be dried
by manual labor, they should have little hair about them.

But in coaching and posting-studs, and among cart-horses,
the men can not, or will not bestow this care upon the legs ;
they have not time, and they would not do it if they had time.
A team of four horses, perhaps, comes in at once, the legs all
wet, and, it may be, the whole skin drenched in rain. Before
eight of the legs can be rubbed dry, the other eight have become almost dry of themselves, and are nearly as cold as they
can be. These horses should never have the heels trimmed :
they can not have too much hair about them. They do indeed
soak up a great deal of water, and remain wet for a much
longer time than those that are nearly naked ; but still they
never become so soon nor so intensely cold. Evaporation
can not proceed so rapidly ; the vapor is entangled among the
hair, and can not escape all at once. The evaporating process
proceeds for a long time, but so slowly that the skin has time
to furnish the necessary quantity of heat before it becomes
very cold. If these horses had naked heels, there would be
little difficulty in drying them ; but the little trouble it requires
is too much, and then it must be repeated as the water trickles
from the body downward, making the legs as wet as ever ; but
in truth the men *can not* get them all dried before some become cold.

Possibly this explanation may be considered as insufficient.
I can appeal to observation. During two very wet winters I
have paid particular attention to the subject. My practice
has brought it before me whether I would or not ; I have had
opportunity of observing the results of trimming and of no-
trimming, among upward of five hundred horses. Nearly
three hundred of these are employed at coaching and posting,
or work of a similar kind, and about one hundred and fifty are

cart-horses. Grease, and the other skin diseases of the heels, have been of most frequent occurrence where the horses were both trimmed and washed; they have been common where the horses were trimmed but not washed; and there have been very few cases where washing and trimming were forbidden or neglected. I do not include horses that always have the best of grooming; they naturally have little hair about the legs, and some of that is often removed; their legs are always washed after work, but they are always *dried before they have time to cool.*

If, then, the horse have to work often and long upon wet or muddy roads, and can not have his legs completely dried immediately after work, and kept dry in the stable, and not exposed to any current of cold air, he must not have his heels trimmed. In most well-regulated coaching stables, this operation and washing are both forbidden.

HAND-RUBBING THE LEGS.—This is not altogether an ornamental operation, but as it is performed chiefly or only where decoration is attended to, this seems to be the proper place for taking notice of it. I have said that the hair of the body is anointed by an oily kind of matter, which serves in some measure to repel the rain. The long hair of the heels is anointed in the same way, but these parts are more liable to become wet, and the oily or lubricating fluid is secreted in greater abundance here than elsewhere. It is produced by the skin, and has a slightly fetid smell, which becomes intolerable when the skin is the seat of the disease termed grease. This fluid is easily washed off, but it is soon replaced; the greater part of it is removed by brushing and washing the hair, especially with soapy water, and it is some time ere the hair and skin are again bedewed with it. Dry friction with the hand or a soft wisp stimulates the skin to furnish a new or an extra supply. This is one good reason for hand-rubbing, an operation seldom performed by untrained grooms. " Take care of the heels, and the other parts will take care of themselves," is an old saying in the stable, and a very good one, if it mean only that the heels require more care than other parts. In some horses, particularly those that have little hair about the legs, the hollow of the pastern is very apt to crack; the anointing fluid is not secreted in sufficient quantity to keep the skin supple; it is always dry, and whenever the animal is put to a fast pace, the skin cracks and bleeds at the place where motion is greatest. Lotions are applied which dry the sore, but do not prevent the evil from recurring; hand-rubbing

must do this. The legs of some horses are apt to smell or to
itch, particularly when they stand idle for a day or two.
Others, cold-blooded, long-legged horses, are troubled with
cold legs while standing in the stall. These things are
generally disregarded among coarse horses ; if they disappear,
it is well, if not, they are neglected till they become more
formidable. But little evils of this kind often produce much
annoyance to those who own horses of greater value. It is
difficult to avoid them altogether among horses that are not in
good condition, loaded with fat, or plethoric ; yet, frequent
hand-rubbing does much. Some grooms give it five or six
times a-day ; so much is seldom required, indeed never, except under disease : but it does no harm that I know of, if it
do not make the heels too bare. To be of any use, it must
be done in a systematic manner and in good earnest. If the
horse be perfectly quiet, the man will sit down on his knees,
and, with a small soft wisp, or cloth-rubber in each hand, he
will rub upward and downward, or he will use his hands
without the wisp, particularly if the hair be fine and short ;
much force is not necessary, indeed it is pernicious. In
coming down the leg, the pressure should be light ; and in
passing upward, it must not be so great as to raise or break
the hairs.

Many stablemen perform this simple operation always in
the same way ; they pass over the leg as if they merely meant
to smooth or lay the hair. To polish the hair, if that be all
which is required, this is sufficient. But to stimulate the
skin, to clean it, to disperse gourdiness, and to excite the
secretion by which the hair is anointed, there must be some
friction, some rubbing against or across the hair, as well as
along it ; the hollow of the pastern has most need of this, and
there the rubbing should be across the hair, with the palm of
the hand. When the legs are cold, as they generally are in
inflammatory diseases of internal organs, it is usual to raise
some degree of heat in them by hand-rubbing. For effecting
this the friction must be considerable. The hands, one on
each side of the leg, must pass rapidly upward and downward,
and with a moderate degree of pressure. When necessary to
do this, the hair is broken, rubbed out, or raised into curls,
but in such cases this must in general be disregarded ; at other
times the friction need not be so great, and should not.

After a day of severe and protracted exertion, gentle and
frequent friction is very useful for restoring the legs, and for
preventing the cold swelling to which the legs of many horses

are liable after work, but it is improper where there is any swelling hot and painful. The hind always requires more than the fore legs. The friction seldom requires to be carried higher than the hock or knee-joints.

SINGEING.—Stablemen have long been in the nabit of singeing away the long loose hair which grows about the jaws, throat, neck, belly, and quarters of horses that have been much exposed to cold ; a flame is applied and the hair is allowed to blaze for a moment, when it is extinguished by drawing the hand or a damp cloth over it. Sometimes the hair is moistened a little with spirits of wine, in order that it may burn more readily ; the spirit is not rubbed in, it is enough to moisten the points of the hair ; when too wet it lies too smoothly for singeing. Sometimes the horse is singed all over ; the operation is common, I believe, in England and Ireland. There are instruments for the purpose. An article composed of two iron rollers, the one being hot and the other cold, was at one time in use. But singeing is now done by a kind of knife, having a moveable back, which is surrounded with tow moistened with spirit of wine and set on fire. As the knife is drawn over the hairs, their points start and are taken off by the flame. When properly performed, this operation does not disfigure the horse so much as might be expected. He does not look so ill as a clipped horse, and his hair is never so generally shortened.

SHAVING.—I have heard of horses being shaved. It has been done to make the horse wear a summer coat in winter. The operation is rare and difficult ; it is performed after the horse has moulted, and before the winter coat is full grown. I am unable to say whether it be right or wrong, for I have never seen it performed, and am ignorant of its results.

CLIPPING.—This operation has been truly termed, " a bad substitute for good grooming." It is done only on the better kinds of horses, especially upon hunters, and consists in shortening the hair all over the body, by means of the scissors and comb. The object is to make the winter coat as short as that of summer. The time usually chosen is the beginning of winter, just after the horse has moulted, and before his coat has attained its full length ; but it may be done at any later period, greater care being taken to prevent the horse catching cold. Of the mode in which the operation is performed, I need say nothing. There are persons in all considerable towns who make it their business. Private grooms sometimes attempt it ; but they seldom do it neatly.

The horse requires no preparation. For several days after, he must be well clothed both in the stable and at exercise. He may be ridden the next day, but he must not be exposed while naked, wet, or motionless. He should not be clipped when unwell. If he have any cough, sore throat, discharge from the nose, or tendency to shiver after drinking, these should be removed before he is clipped. He should not have any physic immediately before nor after. When he goes to the forge or to exercise after the operation, he should be well clothed. A double blanket, a hood, and breast-piece, are requisite.

Utility of Clipping.—Some people dislike the appearance of a clipped horse ; and it must be confessed that while some are improved by the operation, others look very ill. Nevertheless, it is to please the eye that clipping is performed. So long as nothing was said against the practice, it had no higher pretensions. They that first tried it had no other object. They did not expect it to exercise any influence upon the comfort or health of the horse, and they did not recommend it as contributing to either the one or the other. But at a later period—that is, after the operation had been patronised by those whom it would be sinful not to imitate, attempts were made to show that clipping did something more than to please the eye. It was urged, and with perfect truth, that it diminishes the labor of the groom, and prevents the horse from sweating in the stable. As if this were not sufficient, other arguments were brought forward in favor of clipping. It was said that the horse becomes lighter by a pound, about the weight of the hair he loses ; that the stomach, bowels, liver, and lungs, derive some benefit from the extra dressing which the skin obtains, in consequence of being more easily reached by the brush, and that the horse perspires less at his work.

Much of what I have said upon trimming is applicable to clipping. If the owner can not suffer a long coat of hair, and will have it shortened, he must never allow the horse to be motionless while he is wet, or exposed to a cold blast. He must have a good groom and a good stable. Those who have both, seldom have a horse that requires clipping, but when clipped, he must not want either. A long coat takes up a deal of moisture, and is difficult to dry ; but whether wet or dry, it affords some defence to the skin, which is laid bare to every breath of air when deprived of its natural covering. Every one must know from himself whether wet clothing and a wet skin, or no clothing and a wet skin, is the most disagreeable and dangerous. It is true that clipping saves the groom a great deal of labor. He can dry the horse in half the time, and with less than half of the exertion which a long coat requires; but it makes his attention and activity more necessary, for the horse is almost sure to catch cold, if not dried immediately. When well clothed with hair, he is in less danger, and not so much dependant upon the care of his groom.*

Objections to Clipping.—Some, as I have just observed, dislike the look of a clipped horse. This is no objection to the operation. As a matter of taste, it is needless to say anything either for or against it. There are no arguments for persuading men to admire that which offends the eye. The clipped horse has a different color; the hair is lighter; a black becomes a rusty brown; the hair stares, stands on end, and is never, or very seldom, glossy. But the only real objections to clipping are these: it costs two guineas, or thereabouts; it renders the horse very liable to catch cold; and it exposes the skin so much, that he is apt to refuse a rough fence in fear of thorns. There is not the slightest reason for supposing—as has been supposed—that it produces blindness, or has any tendency to shorten the duration of life. The cost of the operation, and the additional care which the horse requires, are, I believe, the principal objections; and considering how little is gained, they will probably prevent the operation from ever becoming very general. There are some horses which wear a long rough coat all the year. The groom, with all his care and the best of stables, can not keep it within reasonable bounds. For these horses, if a long coat is a great eye-sore, there is no remedy save clipping. But there are very many horses clipped, to whom the operation would be quite unnecessary, were they better groomed and well stabled. Since a fine coat is an object of so much importance, it is well to know by what means it may be obtained. When these are more generally known there will be less clipping.

To give the horse a fine coat all at once, is not possible under any system of management. With horses that have been previously exposed to the weather, it may be the work of six months, and very often the horse must be two winters in the stable before he becomes creditable to his groom. Comfortable stabling of itself exercises considerable influence upon

* [For an excellent article on clipping horses in England, unsound feet, &c., see American Agriculturist, vol. iii., page 78.]

the coat; but horses that have been reared in cold situations may often be two winters in the stable before their coat is very decidedly altered. The hair becomes finer and shorter, and the principal agent in effecting this change is heat. To produce and preserve a fine silken coat, it is absolutely necessary that the horse be kept warm. The stable must be comfortable, and the clothing must be heavy. Good grooming and good food, in liberal allowance, are the next agents. When these three are combined, the coat gradually becomes so fine, and lies so smoothly, that clipping can never be desired, and indeed it is hardly possible to perform the operation upon such a coat. These agents operate slowly. They very soon make a rough coat smooth, and a dull coat glossy; but they can not shorten the hair. If they are to make the winter coat short, they must be in operation before, and at the time of moulting. On many horses they do not produce their full effect till the second winter; but, in the most of cases, a thorough-bred groom will make the horse tolerably decent, for the first winter, if he get him in autumn, a fortnight before moulting.

There are other agents which may co-operate with these, when they do not produce their ordinary effects. Boiled barley, boiled or raw linseed, raw carrots, and boiled turnips, are among the articles of food which influence the skin. They polish and lay the hair, and they soften the skin. These need not be given constantly. It is sufficient to give one or more of them two or three times in the week. A few raw carrots during the day, and perhaps a little barley at night, will answer the purpose, and occasionally these may give place to turnips and linseed.

Drugs are sometimes given, and when not abused, they are useful. Physic is serviceable only when the skin is too rigid, and the dung pale, or when there is reason to suspect worms. When the horse does not eat up his grain, a mild dose of physic may be given, and when that sets, it may be followed by a few cordials, one being given every second or third day. Cordials are rarely required in warm weather [indeed they are frequently highly injurious, and should only be administered for debility]. Physic alone in general succeeds. When there is no apparent need either for physic or cordials, the coat not improving so much nor so rapidly as it should do, the best remedy is a powder composed of antimony, nitre, and sulphur. Take black antimony, eight ounces; flour of sulphur, four ounces; and finely-powdered nitre, four ounces.

Mix these well together; divide the whole into sixteen doses, and give one every night in the last feed. If the weather be moderately warm and dry, or the horse not much exposed, he may, on every second night, have two doses, or he may have one at morning, and another at night—that is, two every day. At the end of ten or twelve days, the coat ought to be much improved, and by the time all the doses have been given, the antimony will be glittering on the skin. If the horse have to *stand* any time out of doors during cold weather, these powders must not be given. They render him very sensitive of vicissitudes of temperature; and they are apt to make him sweat a little in the stable; but this is a matter of little consequence. The night-sweats will disappear as the horse gets into condition.

Besides the physic, the cordials, and the diaphoretic powder, some grooms are in the habit of giving other things. It is a common practice to force whole eggs raw down the throat. The shell is starred, so that it may be crushed as the horse swallows the egg; but sometimes this is not done sufficiently, the egg sticks in the gullet, and chokes the horse. He dies in two or three minutes, if he do not obtain immediate assistance. I do not believe that eggs, either raw or boiled, have any or much influence on the coat. If it be certain that they have, they can be given in the food without danger. Break them into dry bran, and give that after fasting. Linseed oil is not a bad thing. If the owner fancies it, he may give a quart bottle, instead of the ordinary physic-ball. It is most useful when the skin is rigid, sticking to the ribs. Of tobacco, mercury, and several mineral preparations, which are occasionally given to fine the coat, I can give no account. I have had no experience of them. The means I have already recommended seldom fail, and I have never tried any others. [Mercury and most mineral preparations, we know, from sad experience, are extremely injurious. We have had several horses nearly ruined by them; and as other medicines are equally effective, and less dangerous, minerals should be rarely prescribed.]

Drugs are often employed to give a fine coat when there is no need for them. When warmth, good grooming, and good food, or particular kinds of food, will produce the desired effect, drugs should not be used. A lazy man is always fond of those expedients which save his labor. He is apt to make the warmth and drugs do that which should be done with the brush. Instead of dressing the horse frequently and thorough-

11

ly, he increases the warmth of the stable and the weight of the clothing, till the horse is almost fevered; and he gives drugs, so many and so often, that he renders .he constitution exceedingly delicate. Such means are not always injurious; but in many cases they are made to do too much. They are very serviceable in their proper place; they are not to do that which should be done by grooming.

The gloss of a fine coat is easily destroyed, particularly that gloss which is given by warmth and antimony. Exposure to cold, frequent ablutions, extraordinary exertion, and everything that checks the insensible perspiration, or interferes with the daily dressing, produce a change upon the hair. In a single day it will become dull, hard, dead-like, and staring. Gentle exercise to heat the skin, and hard rubbing with the brush, will generally restore the lost polish and smoothness of the hair; and sometimes one of the diaphoretic powders may be given before and after the day of sweating, which must be very gentle.

All slow-working horses, and those that have to bear much exposure to the weather, and especially those that have to *stand* out of doors, or in cold stables, should not have a short coat; good grooming and food will make it glossy; a single rug will make it lie; but drugs, and a high degree of warmth, are forbidden. They render the horse unfit for cold stables, and unfit to suffer, without injury, that exposure which his work demands.

MANAGEMENT OF THE FEET.

The feet of some horses require particular attention. They are liable to injuries and to diseases, of which one or two may be prevented by a little care.

Picking the Feet is among the first things a good stable man attends to when the horse comes off his work. Very often a stone is wedged between the shoe and the frog; if permitted to remain there till next day, or even for a few hours, the foot may be bruised, and the horse lamed. This seldom happens to the hind feet. But both the fore and the hind feet of all horses should be examined after work, to see that no stone, nail, splinter of wood, nor broken glass, be sticking in the sole. The mud and clay may be picked out or washed away, and the feet examined in about three minutes, and this work of three minutes may often prevent a lameness of as many months. All horses that have flat soles,

low and weak heels, are easily lamed by sand and gravel ac-
cumulating between the sole and the shoe. Every time the
horse comes from work this should be entirely removed,
by carrying the picker all round. Strong-footed cart-horses
do not require this care, but in a gentleman's stable, cleanliness demands it, whether the feet be weak or strong.

STOPPING THE FEET.—This operation is performed only
on the fore feet ; it is often neglected altogether, and often it
is overdone. It consists in applying some moist matter to
the sole, for the purpose of keeping it soft and elastic.

Kinds of Stopping.—Clay and cow-dung are the stoppings
in most general use ; each is employed alone, or in combination with the other. Clay is apt to get too soon dry ; it becomes hard as a stone, if not removed in twenty-four hours ;
and if the horse be taken to the road, and put to fast work,
with a hardened cake of clay in his foot, the sole is bruised
before the clay is displaced. Clay answers very well, however, for heavy draught-horses, whose work is slow, and
their heels raised from the ground by high calkins. It is
sometimes mixed with salt-water or herring-brine. As far
as I can see, plain water is quite as good. Cow-dung contains much more moisture than clay. It softens the sole in
less time, and never becomes too hard or dry. For ordinary
feet, that is, feet with neither too much nor too little horn, a
mixture of cow-dung and clay makes the best stopping. To
this some salt may be added ; it prevents the dung from rotting. Hacks, hunters, and racers, are often stopped with tow
or with moss. They are cleanly, and the quantity of moisture which they impart can be varied to suit the condition of
the feet. The tow or the moss is put into the sole when
dry, and water is poured upon it once or twice a day. For
horses that have thrushy feet, or a tendency to thrushes, the
clay or cow-dung is rather too moist; tow answers much
better. It should be neatly introduced, so as to fill the sole,
and be on a level with the shoe ; it is secured by packing it
a little under the edge of the shoe. Moss is used in the same
way, and is fully as good.

Mr. Cherry of London, invented a felt pad, which he intended to supply the place of stopping, by the moisture it
would contain, and support the sole by the resistance it would
afford. These pads are to be obtained of all sizes ; they
cover all the exposed portion of the sole and the frog. The
inventor argues truly that the sole was intended to receive
some pressure from the ground, which becomes rare and

almost impossible when the horse is shod and worked on
hard roads. He can not work in the pads, and it is not
meant that he should ; but perhaps he may receive some
benefit from them in the stable. They may be useful for
soles that have a tendency to become flat. Care must be
taken to have them of the proper size ; when too small, they
fall out and are lost; when too thin, they do not support the
sole. It is only thin, flat soles that require any support. In
general they have little need for moisture ; but the pad is
usually dipped in water before it is inserted. To a concave
foot these pads are useless, the soles have more need for
moisture than for support: and for them damp or wet tow
answers better than felt pads. Nimrod speaks of a groggy
mare in whom Cherry's pads increased the inflammation of
the feet and produced considerable suffering: he must have
been mistaken ; the pads have no such power.

The Times of Stopping must vary according to the state of
the feet. All horses, those with thin flat soles excepted,
should be stopped on the night before the day of shoeing.
Except at these times, farm-horses seldom require any stopping ; their feet receive sufficient moisture in the fields, or
if they do not get much, they do not need much. Cart-horses
used in the town should be stopped every Saturday night till
Monday morning. Fast-going horses have need to be stopped once a week or oftener during winter, and every
second night in the hot weeks of summer. Groggy horses,
all those with high heels, concave soles, and all those with
hot tender feet, and an exuberance of horn, require stopping
almost every night. When neglected, especially in dry
weather, the sole becomes hard and rigid, and the horse goes
lamer, or he becomes lame.

Some Feet should not be Stopped.—When the sole is flat
and thin, the less moisture it receives the better ; it makes
the sole yield too much ; under the pressure of the super-
incumbent weight it descends and often becomes convex, instead of maintaining its original concavity. Stopping alone
will not bring the sole down, but it helps, when there is an
existing tendency to descend. Flat soles are almost invariably thin ; they can not suffer paring ; when softened,
they not only yield to the horse's weight, but they yield when
they come upon a stone. On a newly-metalled road, the
horse is lame, and his sole is easily cut through ; such soles
are always sufficiently elastic without the assistance of
moisture.

Constant stopping will make even a thick sole too soft. When the sole is so soft or so thin as to yield to any degree of pressure which can be exerted by the thumb, no moist stopping should be applied. If it be rendered more yielding, whether by stopping or by paring, the horse will go tenderly over a rough road, and his foot will be very easily bruised. I am aware that a high authority recommends the sole to be kept as elastic as possible. This is not the place to discuss such a subject. The fact is as I state; experience enables me to declare that a yielding sole will lame the soundest horse that ever walked. Excessive stopping also produces

THRUSHES.—A thrush, as every stableman knows, is a disease of the frog. At first there is a slight discharge from the cleft of this wedge-like protuberance. The discharge is produced by the frequent, long-continued, or excessive application of moisture. A plethoric state of the body may be a predisposing, but moisture is the immediate cause of thrushes. They can be purposely produced by stopping the feet always with a moist stopping, or by letting the horse stand always in dung. If a thrush be neglected, it spreads, involving the whole or greater part of the frog, the heels, and even the sole. The horn becomes ragged and irregular in its growth. The frog shrinks in volume, and the foot contracts. The horse is sometimes disposed to go much on his toes, that he may relieve the posterior parts of the foot; but in general he has no lameness, except when the frog comes upon a stone, or receives pressure in rough or deep ground. When in its more serious stages, the disease should be placed under the care of a veterinarian. At the beginning, almost any person may cure it. Let the cleft of the frog and all the moist crevices be thoroughly cleaned, and then fill them with pledgets of tow, dipped in warm tar. This simple remedy, repeated every day, often effects a cure. When a stronger is necessary, the Egyptiacum ointment may be used instead of the tar, or each may be applied alternately. Bad frogs may be greatly improved by shoeing with leather soles.

To prevent thrushes in feet already disposed to them, the frogs must be kept dry. If the sole need moisture, the stopping must not be applied to the frog. This part may be defended by a coat of pitch, or the stopping may be confined to the sole.

ANOINTING THE WALL OF THE HOOF.—Among grooms and coachmen it is a common practice to apply oil or some greasy mixture to the wall, or, as it is sometimes termed, the crust, all that portion of the hoof which is visible when the horse is standing upon it. They suppose that the ointment penetrates the horn and softens it. But in this there is some error. The depth to which any unctuous application penetrates is very insignificant. The only mode in which an ointment can contribute to the elasticity of the hoof, is by preventing its moisture from flying off. It operates like a varnish, protecting the horn from the desiccating effects of an arid atmosphere. A hoof ointment will exclude moisture as well as retain it ; and there are some feet which require an ointment to keep the moisture in, and others to keep the moisture out. Water alone enters the pores of horn very readily, and it never does so without rendering the horn soft and yielding. There are many horses, particularly heavy horses, that have weak feet, the crust thin, the sole flat, and the heels low. The crust is hardly strong enough to support the horse's weight. When softened it yields, the sole sinks lower, and the whole foot becomes worse than it was before. Such a foot should seldom be purposely softened by the application of water. It should have sufficient moisture to prevent brittleness, but no more. When the horse has to work long and often in deep, wet ground, an ointment will prevent it from absorbing too much water. Should this or any other foot become brittle, it may be soaked in water, and then immediately after covered with an ointment to retain the water. I have observed the effects of long-continued application of water to the hoofs of horses that were employed for several days in carting sand from the bed of a river. The horn became excessively soft, the nails lost their hold ; the sole, especially of weak hoofs, sunk a little, and the crust became oblique. Subsequently, when these horses came to their ordinary work on the stones, the horn became brittle, so brittle that it would hardly hold a nail. The surface of the hoof is naturally covered by a varnish which protects it from the air. But after this varnish is rubbed off by working in wet sand, by standing in sponge boots, or by the smith's rasp in shoeing, water enters the hoof very quickly, and leaves it as quickly, taking with it the moisture which the varnish had previously retained.

Then, to make a rigid, strong foot elastic, the horn should be saturated with water, and to keep it elastic, the ointment should be applied before the water evaporates. To keep a thin weak foot as hard and unyielding as possible without making it brittle, an ointment should be applied to prevent the absorption of water.

The times of anointing must vary with the state of the foot, and the state of the road. During wet weather the thin foot should be oiled before the horse goes out, and the strong thick foot after the horse comes in. When the air is hot and dry, or the road deep and sandy, the ointment will generally require to be renewed every second day.

Fish oil is in general use for anointing the hoof; tar, lard, oil, and bees'-wax, melted together in equal proportions, form a better and more durable application. Pitch, applied warm, lasts still longer, but it does not look well. It may be useful when the horse is going to grass. The hind feet are often anointed, but they seldom need it. The hoofs of cart-horses are usually coated with tar when they are shod, and, if they need such an application at all, this is the time to make it. [We have great doubts as to the utility of oiling the horse's hoof, and in any event, it should be done with great caution. Youatt says, that oils and ointments close the pores of the feet, and ultimately increase the dryness and brittleness which they were designed to remedy.]

MOISTURE TO THE WALL, besides softening the horn, has considerable influence upon its growth. In some horses the horn grows very slowly, in others very quickly. A deficiency is common among heavy draught-horses, and is often a serious evil. There are only two ways of increasing the growth: the one is to blister once or twice around the coronet, the other is to keep the foot constantly saturated with water. In both cases the horse must be thrown off work. Moisture might be applied to any extent in the stable, and the horse still kept on duty. But then the horn yields so much that this remedy creates as great an evil as it removes. The horn grows in more abundance, but the sole sinks till the foot is almost or totally ruined. This happens, however, only to horses of great weight. It is necessary, therefore, in applying much moisture to their feet, to turn such horses into a marsh for two or three months with grass plates. There the foot will receive moisture to increase its growth, and the sole will receive sufficient support to prevent its descent. These two, moisture and support, can not be fully obtained while the horse continues in work. The clay-box is a tolerable substitute for a marsh.

When the secretion of horn is deficient in horses of less weight, with soles less flattened, moisture may be applied to the wall without materially interfering with the horse's duty Sponge boots, leather boots lined with sponge, and shod with iron, are too expensive, for they are soon destroyed. A boot of any kind will do if filled with cold bran-marsh, changed every time the boot is applied. The moisture must never be applied so long as to render the foot extremely soft, yet the horn must never be allowed to become very dry. The boot should never be on more than three or four hours in the twenty-four, and the foot should be anointed, both sole and crust, whenever the boot is removed. An ordinary and simple way of applying moisture to the wall, is by means of what is termed a swab, that is, a double or treble fold of woollen cloth, shaped like a crescent, and tied loosely around the top of the hoof, so that it may lie upon and cover all the crust. This is kept constantly wet. It soon dries, and requires more attention than a boot; but many horses stand in the swab that tear off a boot; and by means of a swab, moisture can be applied to the wall without softening the sole or the frog.

The Clay-Box.—In some establishments, the upper half of a stall, or one corner of a loose box, is laid with wet clay. A horse having tender, contracted, or brittle fore-feet, is put into this for one or two hours every day. Sometimes the floor of a loose box is entirely covered with the wet clay, and the horse turned into it all day, being stabled at night, that he may lie dry. The clay-box is good for some feet, and bad for others. It is used with too little discrimination for all defects of the feet, real or supposed. When the clay is very wet, the moisture softens the horn, increases its growth, expands the hoof, and brings down the sole. It also cools the foot, and tends to subdue inflammation. When the horse is of little weight, his feet strong, contracted, rather hot, and the heels high, the clay may be thoroughly soaked with water; the horse's shoes had better be off, and he may stand in the clay all day for eight or ten successive days, if not at work. If working, one or two hours every second day will be sufficient. When the crust and sole are rather thin and weak, the latter tending downward, the growth of horn deficient, the clay should be tougher, having no loose water about it, the horse's shoes should be kept on, and he may stand in the clay two hours every day. In the first case the sole is to be lowered, the foot expanded and cooled; in the second, the growth of horn is to be stimulated, and the sole supported. The horn would grow faster if there were more moisture; but were the clay softer, it would not afford sufficient support. Additional moisture may be given to the crust by means of a swab. The clay-box is not good for thrushy feet, but in trifling cases the frog may be protected by a pitch or other waterproof covering.

SHOEING.—Many stablemen, especially those employed in livery stables, are very careless as to the state of the horse's feet and his shoes. The shoes are often worn till they drop off in the middle of a journey, and time is lost, the foot broken or destroyed, and very likely the horse lamed. This is not the only evil. If the horse be doing little work, or be very light on his shoes, they may remain on too long. Fast-working horses require to have the feet pared down once every month, whether they need new shoes or not. When the horn is permitted to accumulate, the horse's action is fettered; he can not step out; he can not place his foot firmly on the ground, and he is very liable to corns. If he had no shoes, the horn would be worn away faster than it could be replaced, but the shoe prevents nearly all wear, and does not stop the growth. Hence at certain intervals the superfluous horn must be pared away. A month is the usual time. Some horses having a deficiency of horn, may go five weeks or more; while others that wear their shoes very fast, may require a new set every three weeks. Farm-horses often go for six or eight weeks with one set of shoes. If the heels be strong they may not be injured by this. Their work is different, and their feet are different. If the shoes of fast-workers are not worn out at the end of a month, the feet should be pared, and the old shoes can be replaced. When the heels are weak, or the seat of corns, the shoes may require removal every three weeks

The shoe and its mode of application must always vary according to the horse's weight and action, the state of his foot, the rate at which he travels, the state of the road, and the nature of his work in reference to carrying, drawing, and leaping. To shoe horses properly, all or the most of these circumstances have to be considered. But this is not the place to describe either the kind of shoe, or the mode of applying it. In general, both should be left to the smith. He knows little about his business if he requires instructions from his employer. Those who work in large towns and have much to do, know all the books from which an employer derives that which he would teach.

The shoes should be examined when the horse comes from his work, and again when he is going to it. If there be a loose or broken nail, or a clench started, or if the horse be cutting, let the smith be called at once.

THE UNSHOD FEET OF COLTS are often neglected. Some colts contract thrushes before they are stabled; without looking for them occasionally, they may do much mischief before they are discovered by accident. They ought not to be neglected a single day. Others, especially those that do not stand very well on their legs, frequently wear down the inside of the foot so much more than the outside, that the limbs become more and permanently distorted. The feet should be dressed every five or six weeks.

HORSES STANDING IN LOOSE-BOXES, as stallions, hunters, and racers, often are, for several successive weeks, frequently have their shoes taken off. This is seldom a good practice, but much depends upon the floor of the loose-box, if paved, and not completely covered with litter, the bare feet are almost sure to receive injury. Pieces of the horn are broken off, or the toe is worn down by pawing and scraping, to which idle horses are much addicted. If the horse were to stand here for twelve months, his feet in that time would become tougher and more solid; but in the first three or four months they are injured more than improved. The horse is wanted before improvement has begun. If his foot be contracted, it may be expanded a little by letting him stand unshod; but the floor must be soft and damp, or moist. If the sole be thin and flat, yet strong enough to bear the horse's weight, it will receive more support when the shoe is off than when it is on. It will be less likely to descend farther. But the floor must be such that it will press equally upon every part of the sole. If a clay floor be improper, the box may be laid with tanner's bark. Saw-dust, when in sufficient quantity, and frequently changed, answers very well for a thin sole, and fine sand has been employed for the same purpose. Short, soft litter, however, may supply the place of either. All that is wanted is gentle and uniform pressure. A contracted foot may require moisture, which may be given apart, in the clay-box, or by means of swabs. Racers often have the hoof much broken, and with no spare horn at the time they go into loose-boxes. Further injury may be prevented by putting on narrow shoes, like racing-plates, which save the crust, and permit the sole to receive all the benefit of support, which a common shoe in some measure prevents.

IN THE STRAW-YARD, a flat foot is sometimes injured by excess of moisture, and thrushes always spread in this place.

When horses with such feet must go to a straw-yard, they ought previously to be shod with leather soles. All the ground surface of the foot may be covered with a piece of bend-leather, upon the top of which the shoe is nailed. To exclude the dirt and moisture, the sole must be stopped with tow and pitch, composed of tar and rosin melted together, and run in hot. Greasy stopping is never so good. [All this is of more than doubtful utility : and experience shows it to be at least useless in all cases, and dangerous in many.]

OPERATIONS ON THE STABLE.

BEDDING.—To a hard-working horse, a good bed is almost as essential as food. Many stablemen can not make it. It should be as level and equal as a mattress. There should be no lumps in the litter ; it should come well back, and slope from each side, and from the head toward the centre. Farm-servants and carters never give the horse a good bed, although their horses need it fully as much as any other. They generally have the litter all in a heap, or in a number of heaps, upon which the horse can not lie comfortable for more than half an hour. The effort such a bulky animal must make to rise and change his position, completely awakens him. His rest is broken, and his vigor never fairly recruited. Now, it is not difficult to make a good bed ; any body with hands may learn it in a few days. But no one thinks of learning such a thing. Those who become expert at it can not help their expertness. They never tried to obtain it ; practice gave it them before they knew it was of any use. But for all this it may be learned. Show the man how to use the fork, and how to spread the litter ; give him a pattern-bed in one stall, and make him work in the next, two hours every day for a week. If he can not learn it in this time—the operation is really worth such trouble- -the man will never learn anything.

The bed is generally composed of wheat straw ; but there are several other articles which are used occasionally, and might be used oftener. Saw-dust, wood-shavings, dried tanner's bark, and leaves, have been employed where they are easily and cheaply procured. They are not better than straw, nor so good ; but a very good bed may be made out of either of them. In some Eastern countries the dung, after being dried in the sun, is used as bedding ; it is finer than saw-dust. Oat straw is softer, but not better than that of wheat. The

straw of beans or peas never makes a good bed. I believe
these straws might be employed more profitably as fodder, and
on some farms they are.   In some places it is usual to cut the
bundle of straw across into two with a hay-knife.   It spreads
better, and a saving is made, for long straws are often wasted
at only one end.

Some people give the horse no bedding, or almost none.
Whether they have ever been able to show that he prefers
lying on the stones, I have not heard.   But it is well enough
known that the want of litter prevents repose, and blemishes
the knees, the hocks, and the haunches.

Changing the Litter.—In well-managed stables the dung
and soiled litter are removed every morning at the first stable
hour ; or, if the horses are going to work or exercise, this
operation is delayed till they are gone.   The dry litter is
thrown forward, or put into an empty stall.   That which is
soiled is carried to the manure pit, or laid out to dry   The
stalls and gangways are then swept clean ; and sometimes a
pailful or two of water is thrown over them to render the purification more complete.   After the floor is dry, a portion of
the litter is spread out, levelled on the top, and squared behind.
Everything in and about the stable is set in order, and the
whole is clean and neat.   By constant or frequent attendance,
it is kept in this state all day.   At night more litter is laid
down, spread deeper, and farther back.

In farm and many other stables the soiled litter, if removed
at all, is removed at night when the horses come in, and are
being supped.   This is not right.   It fills the stable with
noxious vapors at the very time it has most need to be pure.
When the horses go out in the morning, the litter should be
changed before or immediately after they are gone ; the floor
left bare, and the doors and windows open all day.   At night
the litter may be laid down just before the horses are fed.

Formerly it was customary to let the soiled litter remain
too long below the horse.   Even in racing stables it was not
usual to clean out the stall oftener than once a week.   All,
or most of the wet litter was allowed to remain for several
days.   That which was trampled among the dung was carried
out, but the remainder was covered by fresh straw, and left
till the day of purification arrived.   Now, however, in these
and some other stables, the litter is completely removed every
morning.   It is impossible to have the stable warm, and at
the same time wholesome, without doing so.

This is a great improvement ; but as yet it has not been

generally introduced. In cavalry, hunting, racing, and some of the superior coaching-stables, the stalls are completely emptied every morning; but in very many others, though there may be a general and complete purification once or twice in a month, yet at other times much of the rotten and wet litter is left to form a bed for the new straw. While not in sufficient quantity to produce any sensible impurity of the air, it can only be called a slovenly, not a pernicious practice. But the stables of farmers and carters are in general too bad. Their horses never have a decent bed. There are no fixed times for changing the litter. When it becomes so wet and filthy that the keeper is somewhat ashamed to see it, he throws down some fresh straw to conceal that which ought to be taken away. That is done, perhaps, every day; but it is not till the horse is standing fetlock-deep in a reeking dunghill, that the stall is cleaned to the bottom.

Upon such a bed the horse can never obtain unbroken rest; and the stable can never be comfortable. The noxious vapors arising from the rotting litter are destructive to the eyes, the lungs, and to the general health or strength. When there is a circulation of air sufficient to carry off these vapors, the stable is cold. While the horse is lying, the cold air is blowing over him on the one side, and the dunghill is roasting him on the other.

This is an old practice, and, of course, not to be abandoned without a struggle. The farmer contends that it is the right way to make good manure, and the carter that it saves the consumption of straw. Manure may be made in this way, perhaps, well enough; but horses are surely not kept for that purpose. Visit the stables of those who have been successful farmers. See how they contrive to obtain manure.

Day Bedding.—Among veterinarians it has been a disputed point whether or not the horse should have litter below him during the day, some contending that he should, others that he should not. The straw, it is said, heats the feet, produces constaction, tenderness, and thrushes. It does nothing of the kind, never did, and never will. It does no harm whatever. There is no need for either argument or experiment to decide this matter. It has already been tried on many thousand horses, and thousands more may be seen every day, who stand on straw twenty hours out of the twenty-four without receiving the slightest injury from it. If the straw be rotten dung, hot and wet, thrushes will be produced; but this dung-hill, which some people call bedding, will do the feet no other

12

injury. It is more pernicious to the eyes and the throat, producing coughs and blindness.

Horses that do little work may have no need for day bedding; but there are some who will not urinate upon the bare
stones, and this is sometimes an evil. The water splashes
upon his legs and annoys him, and he retains his urine till it
gives him more uneasiness or annoyance than that produced
by wet legs. This is more particularly the case with horses
having greasy heels, or bare legs. If required to take the
road with a distended bladder, he can not work. He soon
becomes dull and faint, and perspires very profusely. If he
had been standing on straw, his bladder would never have
become so full. Then, there are horses that constantly paw
and stamp the ground; on the bare stones, they slip about,
and sometimes lame themselves; and they often break the
nails by which the shoes are held. Many, too, are disposed
to lie during the day; without litter they can not, or ought not.
The more a horse lies, the better he works. Lame or tender-
footed horses can not lie too much; and a great deal of standing ruins even the best of legs and feet. Except the cost,
there is no objection to day bedding. Some horses do not
need it; many are the better of it; none are the worse of it.

WASHING THE STABLE.—In some places the floor is washed
every morning, in others only once a week; in very many it
is never washed. The water, with the assistance of a broom,
clears the grooves, and prevents the stones from becoming
slippery. In a causewayed stable it removes the dung and
urine which lodge between the stones, and contaminate the
air. But, while water cleans the floor, it renders the stable
cold and damp. On close or cold days the process should be
omitted. If the horses all go out in the morning, the floor
should be washed after they are gone; the doors and windows
being set wide open till they return. After washing, the
floor is sometimes strewed with sand or saw-dust. This
absorbs the water, roughens the stones, and gives an air of
cleanliness and comfort to the whole stable. It is very useful when the floor is naturally damp, or when wet operations
are performed in the stable.

Besides the daily, weekly, or monthly washing, which in
some places is made upon the floor, the whole stable requires
a general purification once or twice a year. All the wood-
work, travises, doors, mangers, and racks should be thoroughly
washed every six or twelve months; and the stall or stable
in which a horse having glanders has stood, should not be oc-

cupied by any other horse till it has undergone purification, which, in such a case, must be performed with great care. Hot water, soft soap, and a hard brush, when properly applied, will loosen and dissolve the dirt, and the whole may be removed by boiling water and a mop, such as is used for washing coaches. The windows may be cleaned often. The walls and ceiling may be whitewashed with a solution of lime. When the stables are well lighted, a white color is rather glaring, and is supposed to injure the eyes. A little clay dissolved along with the lime, produces a fine stone color. The walls and roof, however, can not be too white, if the stable has not sufficient light.

A warm windy day should be chosen for this operation. If the stable contain more than two or three horses, and is never empty, only two stalls should be washed in one day. The whitewashing may be done in one, and this process should precede the wood-washing. When a large stable is all washed on the same day, it remains cold and damp for a week afterward. The woodwork absorbs much moisture, and does not part with it very readily. It is better not to do much at a time, unless the horses can be kept out till the whole is dry.

The underground drains, where there are any, should be examined occasionally before they become clogged, or much injured by rats. Defects in the pavement, breaches in the wood, decay of anything, or of any place, should be repaired at once. Attention to these, and to many other little things, of which a good stableman need not be reminded, saves a deal of trouble and expense. An industrious groom will keep the stable, and all belonging to it, clean and in order; a lazy fellow, at most only puts them in order, and everything goes wrong at the intervals of his working fits.

THIRD CHAPTER.

STABLE RESTRAINTS.—II. ACCIDENTS.—III. HABITS.—
IV. VICES

RESTRAINTS.

By these I mean all those abridgments of the horse's liberty in the stable which prevent him from injuring himself or
others. The twitch, the arm-strap, and the muzzle, are spoken
of in connexion with the dressing of vicious horses. The
partition between the horses is an abridgment of their freedom ; its use and abuse are considered under the construction
of stables. There are, however, some other restraints, of
which tying up is the principal. Those connected with vice,
or peculiar habits, are described in their proper places.

TYING-UP.—In the stable, horses are tied up by collars,
neck-straps, or halters. They are attached to the manger, or
to a ring driven in one corner, or in front, of the stall-head.
The horse's head must have some play, the rein must be long
enough to let him reach the hay-rack, and to let him lie down,
yet so short that he can not turn in the stall, and attached to
the stall in such a way that it can not get entangled among
the feet.

The Halter is made of rope. Sometimes the head-piece
and nose-band are of web, which is better than rope : the nose-
band is a running noose. The halter is seldom used for tying-
up a horse ; by good stablemen never, without casting a knot
upon the nose-piece, to prevent it from running ; but among
inferior or ignorant grooms the halter is in common use ; wanting a throat-lash, it is very easily cast. The horse can throw
it off whenever he chooses. It often injures the mouth and
the muzzle. The nose-band being a running noose, the least
strain upon the rein draws the noose so tightly that it forces
the cheeks between the back teeth, where they are cut, and,

being commonly made of rope, its constant or frequent use
produces a depression across the nose, or baldness, or a sore.
The head-piece being always of the same length, can not be
altered to suit the horse ; it is often too long, it falls back upon
the neck two or three inches behind the ears, and if the horse
happens at this time to hang back, his neck receives a twist
from which it does not always recover. A long head-piece
permits the nose-band to fall upon the nostrils, and if the
shank be strained the horse is choked. The halter is not a
proper article for tying up the horse ; it may be employed to
lead him to the door, to the shoeing forge, or to exercise, or
to tie him to the door while he is being dressed, but it should
have no other uses.

When taken out with a halter, a cinch, that is, a coil of the
halter shank, is sometimes placed in the mouth to act as a
bit, and give the man more command over the horse. He is
often tied up with this cinch in his mouth, and if he happens
to throw any strain upon the shank, his tongue is severely injured ; I have repeatedly seen it cut through, and the horse
thrown off his feed, unable to eat for two or three weeks.
When the cinch remains an hour or two thus tightened around
the tongue and the jaw, a large portion, two or three inches,
of the tongue mortifies and has to be removed, or it falls off.
When the horse must be tied up with a halter, see that the
head-piece be close behind his ears : cast a knot on the shank
to prevent the nose-band from running ; keep it clear of the
nostrils, and never tie the horse with a cinch in his mouth.

The Collar is made of leather. The nose-band should be
sufficiently wide to let the horse open his mouth to more than
its full extent. The head-piece has a buckle, by which it
can be lengthened or shortened according to the size of the
horse's head. When adjusted, the nose-band should be four
inches clear of the nostrils ; among valuable horses this is
the article almost invariably used for tying up ; it is usually
termed a stall collar. [In America the word *collar* is not
used in this sense. Leather head or halter is the term.]

The Neck-Strap is much used in the stables of hard-working horses, those employed in public conveyances. It is
merely a leather band, two inches broad and a yard long, having an iron D or triangle for attaching a rope or chain, and a
buckle for uniting the ends. It is preferred to the halter because it is cheaper, and for many horses more secure : when
sufficiently tight no horse can cast it ; but it permits him to
turn half round in his stall, which is an inconvenience.

12*

Alone, it is not a good binding for biting horses, for it gives the man no control over the head: it ruffles the mane; but where straps are used, this is of no consequence. When on, it should be so tight that it can not pass over the ears, yet loose enough to admit a man's hand under it.

The Rein by which the horse is bound to the stall has several names. In different places it is termed a collar-rein, a collar shank or shaft, and a binding; most usually, shaft and shank are confined to the halter. For ponies it is sometimes made of leather, which is too weak for strong horses: in general it is rope, but a chain is in common use. In a permanent establishment chains are cheaper than ropes, and more secure, since some horses break or bite the ropes to get free; but they are weighty and noisy.

Sometimes two are employed to each horse, but in general one is sufficient for working horses: when two are necessary, the rings through which they pass are usually fixed on the manger breast, and distant, one from another, about three feet six inches. Some horses require a double rein, but not all; when one will serve, it may be attached to the middle of the stall on the manger breast; or, if the manger be in one corner, the rein ring may be in the other corner, or directly in front, on the head wall; it should be three feet three or six inches from the ground. The ring through which the rein runs is attached by an iron staple driven into the wood; it answers the purpose very well in ordinary cases. In the sale stable of Mr. Laing, Edinburgh, a kind of pulley is used; the rope runs easier, and requires less weight to sink it. (See Fig. 6, page 41.)

The Sinker [*or Weight*].—The weight attached to the collar or halter rein, is usually a ball of wood loaded with lead. Where chains are used, the sinker is sometimes a lump of lead or a cast-iron bullet, weighing about four pounds, and attached immovably, so that neither the chain nor its appendages can be taken away. In posting and coaching-stables this is a necessary precaution against loss and theft. Tying the rein to the ring, or loading it with a straw wisp, are both improper, and among restless horses, dangerous.

ACCIDENTS CONNECTED WITH RESTRAINT.

Some of these accidents arise from peculiar habits of the horse, others from carelessness or ignorance on the part of his groom.

GETTING LOOSE.—Some horses are very cunning and persevering in their efforts to get loose; they often succeed during the night, and wander over the stable in quest of food, quarrelling and playing with the other horses, disturbing their rest, and laming them. Some slip the halter over their ears; these must be tied by a neck-strap; or the throat-lash, by being set out from the head-piece, can perform the office of a neck-strap: others bite the rope through; the only remedy for them is a chain. In admitting a strange horse to a large stable, it might be prudent to tie him up as if he were known to be in the habit of getting loose; it will soon be seen whether or not the precaution be necessary.

HANGING IN THE HALTER.—Many horses attempt to get free by falling back upon the haunches, and throwing their weight upon the halter-rein; there they hang for a while till some part of the rein gives way, or till they find it too strong for them. This is the true breaking loose; cutting the rope with the teeth and casting the halter are merely slipping loose. Such a forcible mode of getting free, or attempting to get free, is attended with some danger. If the tie suddenly give way, the horse falls back with such violence that he is generally lamed or injured. The haunch bones are sometimes broken, and the hocks seldom escape a severe contusion; occasionally the head is cut, either by the fall or by the strain of the halter. I know of only two ways in which a cure is attempted; one consists in giving the horse a good fright and a tumble, by freeing the rope at the moment he is trying to break it. This, however, is not a cure: it seldom prevents the horse from repeating the attempt; it only puts him on his guard against the sudden rupture of the tie; he still persists in his efforts to break it, but he takes care not to fall backward. The other way is to tie him so strongly that no force he can exert will free him. After he has made a few unsuccessful trials, he appears to conclude that the thing is not practicable, and he desists. For an experiment of this kind a leather halter is too weak, the head-piece upon which the stress falls, should be of strong rope, sitting close behind the ears. If the manger is not sufficiently firm, the ring should be sunk deep in the wall.

I believe that the use of a neck-strap, instead of the ordinary halter, deters many horses from this trick of breaking loose; I have seen it succeed in several cases. As additional security, the halter may be put on too; it keeps the head straight, so that the neck may not be twisted when the strain is on the strap. The halter-rein should be as long as the strap-rein. Whenever the horse is observed hanging in the halter, with the purpose of breaking loose, he should be well flogged always from behind.

This trick is often the result of bad management. An awkward or rude groom, by the manner in which he approaches a horse or works about the head, often frightens or pains him. The horse should never be struck on the head or neck, nor a blow threatened by a person standing before him; it makes him draw back. The halter already spoken of, and the ordinary mode of filling the hay-rack, may each have something to do in producing the habit.

A few horses of determined temper will not be tied up after they have succeeded several times in breaking loose. They struggle so long and with such violence, that they injure themselves even when they do not get free. A loose box is the proper place for these.

STANDING IN THE GANGWAY.—When first stabled, horses are much disposed to stand as far out of the stall as they can get. They dislike the confinement; they want to see about them, and they dislike the impure air so often found at the head of stalls when damp or soiled litter is thrown below the manger. The habit of standing in the gangway is inconvenient, particularly in double-headed stables, and injury is sometimes done by the efforts to prevent it. The horse may be tied short, close to the rack or to the manger; but hard work, tender feet, or bad legs, may forbid this, since it prevents lying. The only alternative is to hang a bale behind him, upon which a furze-bush may be fastened. By-and-by, when the horse becomes accustomed to stand within the stall, the bale may be removed. It is seldom, however, that the habit is attended with so much inconvenience as to require this. The usual practice of suddenly striking or whipping the horse when he is found in the gangway, is foolish, and often dangerous. The horse makes a violent spring into the stall, and when his feet happen to slip, he receives a severe wrench, producing stifle, or hip lameness, or sprained loins. I have seen the thigh-bone broken in this way, and the horse had to be destroyed.

LYING IN THE GANGWAY is common among those horses that stand in the gangway. They lie so far out of the stall that the halter-rein is put upon the stretch, and the horse's head has not sufficient freedom to let him rise. He must be unbound before he can get up. He has to lie perhaps all night on one side in an awkward position, and next day he is stiff and sore all over, and as unfit for work as if he had rested none all night. The only way of preventing this is by suspending a bale behind him, in the same manner as for preventing the habit of standing in the gangway.

High and long travises are apt to make horses occupy the gangway both for standing and for lying. A horse that is very troublesome in either way, may be tried in a baled stall, or in one having low and short travises.

ROLLING IN THE STALL.—Many horses are much addicted to this, especially during the night. Some practise it the moment they come off the road. They lie down, harness and all, and roll over from one side to another two or three times, and then rise and shake themselves as if much the better of it, and highly delighted with the feat.* It appears to do him good, and ought to be permitted when possible, the harness or saddle, however, being previously removed. Some manage it very clumsily. In the morning they are often found in an awkward or painful position, lying across the stall, or on one side of it, with the fore legs bent upon the chest, and the hind legs out of the stall altogether, projecting into the next. The horse can not stir, and must be righted before he can rise. His head must be liberated. By casting ropes or straps, two or three stirrup-leathers buckled together, over his legs, he may be turned over; or he may be drawn away from the travis by pulling at the mane or tail; or, in the same way, he may be drawn entirely out of the stall. When the horse is lying on his back, it is sufficient to cast a rope or strap across his hind legs, and pull him over.

As long as the horse appears able to take care of himself in his rolling fits, he may be allowed to enjoy them; but, when he is subject to accident, the rolling must be prevented, at least during the night, when there is no one to render assistance. All risk of injury is avoided by putting the horse in a loose box with his head free. In the stall, rolling may be prevented by a short halter-rein. It should be long enough to let the horse lie down, but so short that he can not get his head flat on the ground. Except in the pains of colic, no horse will roll without getting his head as low as his body.

---

* When a horse rolls more than once, or at the most twice, after his work, and lies as if he were in pain, paws the ground, or looks at his flanks, expressing uneasiness, he is unwell; he has colic, and should be put under immediate treatment.

When the manger is too low, this can not be done, for it prevents the horse from reaching the hay-rack. The manger should be raised. This plan interferes in some measure with the horse's rest. If he has to work all day, a wide stall with long travises had better be tried, in preference to shortening the halter-rein. A travis ten, or more than ten feet long, may prevent the hind legs from getting across the next stall, where they are apt to be trampled upon by the neighboring horse.

TURNING IN THE STALL.—Small horses often get into a habit of standing across the stall, or of turning round in it, head out and tail in. Injuries of the back, the head, the neck, and some lamenesses, are occasionally produced by a sudden and violent effort of the horse to right himself. He should be fastened by a halter rather than by a neck-strap, which gives him too much liberty; and he should have two reins to the halter, each of the proper length.

LYING BELOW THE MANGER.—I have spoken of horses that stand out of the stall, and lie so far back that they can not rise till the head is liberated. Others lie too far forward. For some reason which I can not discover, unless it be to lie well upon the litter, they throw themselves so far forward in lying down, that the head goes under the manger, or abuts against the wall. The horse can not obtain complete repose, and when not young and active, or when the manger is too low, he can not rise from this position. He must be drawn back before he can get up. The space below the manger may be boarded up, and the litter should be spread well back. Perhaps the halter-reins might be attached to the travises instead of the manger; placed so far behind the head, they would keep the horse back; but I have never seen this tried.

HALTER-CASTING.—This is the most dangerous accident to which the stabled horse is liable. The horse often scratches his neck, ears, or some part of his head, with a hind-foot. In doing that, or rather in drawing back the foot after that is done, the pastern is sometimes caught by the halter-rein. In a moment the horse is thrown upon his broadside, while his head and the entangled foot are drawn together. The neck is bent at an acute angle, the head lying upon the shoulder, and in this position it is retained by the hind-foot. The injury which the horse receives varies according to the violence of his struggles, and to the time which he lies in this painful situation. The pastern, or some part of the leg, often the thigh, is sometimes deeply cut; but this is not the worst part of the accident. Frequently the neck is bent so much to one side, and so severely twisted, that weeks must elapse before the horse is able to move it freely, and sometimes it remains permanently distorted, the head being carried awry. The neck has been completely broken in this way, and after the horse was liberated, it was discovered that he could not move a limb, nor make the least motion of any kind, with the exception of breathing, swallowing, and a few movements of the ears, eyes, and mouth. The remainder of the body was quite powerless, and the horse died through the course of the day. This fatal result is not common.

When the horse lies long he is always a good deal bruised and very stiff, unable to get up without assistance. Sometimes the back is injured so as to produce partial palsy of the hind-legs. When the horse happens to fall upon the leg that is drawn up, his head is below him, and if not immediately relieved, he is soon suffocated.

In the most of cases this accident may be prevented. All that is necessary is to keep the halter-rein clear of the feet. It should not be needlessly long; it should always be loaded with a sinker, and the ring, through which it runs should be at the proper height. Two reins prevent the horse from getting his head too far round on either side. As greater security, the rein may be made to pass behind the manger, and in that case one rein is sufficient. (See Fig. 2, page 26.) When the manger is low and the rack high, the rein must be long, and can not be kept tense, for the sinker can not descend far enough. The manger should be raised, or the reinring placed higher, by some other contrivance.

Treatment of Stall-cast Horses.—The first thing to be done is to liberate the head by cutting the rope, or the halter, if the horse be bound by a chain. Place him in a favorable position, and urge him to rise. After a horse has lain long in constraint, it is often difficult to get him up. Sometimes he is perfectly unable to rise. His limbs are benumbed; they are, I suppose, in much the same state as our own when we say they are asleep. The horse must have some assistance. Let one stout fellow support the head, another the shoulder, and place two at the tail, by seizing which they may lift the hind-quarters. Draw the fore-legs out, but not too much; the horse rises head first. See that all hands be ready to give their aid at the moment the horse makes an effort to rise, and to this he may be urged by the lash. When on his legs, steady him for a minute or two; encourage him to urinate.

Let his legs and the side upon which he lay, be well rubbed
If able to walk a few paces, it will help to circulate the blood.
If he can not walk at first, try him again after half an hour.
Examine him all over, lest he have received any injury re-
quiring immediate treatment.   He will not be fit to work on
that day, and perhaps not the next.

Sometimes the horse can not be got upon his feet ; he can
not even make an effort to rise.   Turn him over to his other
side, and let that which was undermost be well rubbed with
wisp or brush ; manipulate the skin—that is, pinch it, and
raise it from the flesh, in order to restore the circulation of
blood through it.   With the same intention let the legs be
rubbed, pulled, and the joints alternately bent and straightened.
Give the horse a good bed, and as much room as possible.
If the travis can be removed, take it away.   If the horse have
no sign of fever, give him half a pint of sherry in cold water,
or a cordial-ball ; let him also have some water, and if he will
eat oats, give them.   By these means the horse may recover
his strength and the use of his limbs sufficiently to rise with
assistance.   A trial should be made every half hour ; when
not successful, there is nothing for it but the block and tackle,
which may be fixed to some beam or support across the stall.
Pass a couple of strong ropes round the chest, and attach
them to the pulley ; pad them with straw where they are like
ly to cut the skin.   If the horse can not stand when thus
raised, support him a little in the ropes ; place his legs fair
below him, and let his weight upon them very gradually.   If
he can not use them at all, let him down again, and make
other efforts to restore his activity ; give more wine, rubbing,
food, and water.   Turn him often, and raise him again in an
hour.—In a few cases the horse never recovers the use of
his legs.   He dies, or is destroyed.   This happens from injury of the back, the neck, and the head.   But I have seen
the horse completely paralytic, when there was no appearance
of injury in these parts.

The treatment here recommended for stall-casting, is equally
applicable to horses that have been cast in the field, in a ditch,
or any situation where they have lain long in a position of
constraint.   The wine-cordial some people will object to, but
it is an excellent remedy against exhaustion.

STEPPING OVER THE HALTER-REIN.—This and the last-
mentioned accident arise from the same cause.   The binding
is too long, or tied to the ring unloaded by the sinker, and the
horse is apt to get his fore-feet over it.   If he be a steady

pacific animal, no harm will be done ; he will wait for assistance. But a troublesome or timid horse often injures himself. By attending to the length of the rein, and to the mode of securing it, this accident need never happen. A liberating ring, however, has been invented, and is used in some places to guard against it.

Fig. 14.

The ring, made of malleable iron, is attached to a cast-iron bolt, which slides into a socket of the same material, and is retained by a spring. This socket is fixed to the manger, with its open end down. As long as the ring is pulled up or back, it remains fast ; but when pulled downward, it comes away, and the horse is free. This is useful where the manger is too low, and can not be raised, but it gives little security against halter-casting. When the hind-foot gets over the rein, the strain is rather downward, but chiefly backward ; and a back pull will not free the ring. Still it may possibly be drawn out in the horse's struggles. The bolt should be pulled out occasionally and oiled, that it may not rust, and stick too firmly in the socket.

LEAPING INTO THE MANGER.—Young idle horses sometimes set their fore-feet into the manger, for the purpose, I suppose, of looking about them. This can rarely happen when the manger is at the proper height, and the halter-rein of the proper length. When a horse is observed in this situation, he must not be rashly struck to bring him down. Go to his head, loose the binding, and set the horse back, keeping his head well up, and rather off you. I remember a very troublesome horse that had a trick of leaping into the manger. One

13

day he had been put into a strange stable where the manger was low, deep, narrow, and sparred across the top. He got into it, and resisted all the keeper's efforts to get him out of it. He could not, or would not descend. Two stout pieces of board were procured, and laid across the manger top. By placing first the one foot and then the other upon these boards, he was brought down, merely by pushing him back.

STABLE HABITS.

AMONG stablemen the word habit is applied only to peculiarity of conduct, to some unusual or objectionable action.

KICKING THE STALL-POST.—Many idle horses, and mares during the spring, more than geldings, amuse themselves at night by kicking at the stall-post, the travis, or the wall. They often injure the legs; the point of the hock is generally bruised and tumified, and the horse frequently throws his shoes. Some are much worse than others. I have known them demolish the travis, break down the walls, and injure themselves very severely. In the *Veterinarian*, a horse is spoken of that persisted in kicking till he broke his leg. The habit, I think, is sometimes a species of insanity. There is no accounting for it. The horse may be perfectly peaceable in all other respects. Some seem to intend injury to horses standing next them. But many kick all night, though there should be no other horse in the stable. Few take to the habit while they are in full and constant work, and many give it over partly, or entirely, after their work becomes laborious. If curable, it will be cured by work. Nothing else brings them so effectually to their senses.

Once confirmed, however, the habit is very rarely cured. When first observed, some means should be taken to check it. Most of them kick all to one side. Such should be tried in another stall, having a short travis on the kicking side, and no horse in the next standing. The groom sometimes nails a whin-bush against the post, and that appears to succeed in a few cases, especially with mares that kick only in spring.

Clogs fastened to the legs prevent kicking, and if constantly worn for a long time, perhaps they might cure it. The horse might forget the habit, but in general he has a good memory. The second, if not the first night in which he finds himself unfettered, he recurs to his old trick.

The clogs are applied to different parts of the leg; to the pastern, to the leg directly above the fetlock, or to the ham, above the point of the hock. The clog in most common use is a piece of hard wood, or a wooden bullet, weighing two or three pounds, and attached to a light chain from twelve to twenty-four inches long. The other end of the chain is fastened to the pastern by a strap. This is applied only to the leg with which the horse kicks. When he strikes with both, a clog is required for each. The horse should be fatigued when the clog is put on for the first time. The only objection to a clog of this kind is its liability to be trampled on by the other foot; but the horse soon learns to take care of that. Sometimes the chain, without a bullet, suffices. Sometimes the chain is much shorter, and the strap buckled above the fetlock, not on the pastern, so that the clog lies upon the hoof without touching the ground. In this way the clog should be long or egg-shaped rather than round. The strap requires to be tighter than when it is placed upon the pastern, otherwise it falls down. A broad strong strap, applied very tightly above the hock-joint, with or without a clog, prevents kicking, but it also prevents the horse from lying down; it often marks the leg and makes it swell. The legs are sometimes shackled together. But this is seldom needful or right. The horse is apt to hurt himself, and he can not lie. I have met with cases in which all these means failed to prevent nocturnal kicking.

WEAVING.—This habit consists in darting the head from side to side of the stall. The horse stands in the middle of the stall, with his fore feet somewhat apart; the motion of his head is constant and rapid, as if he were watching something running from end to end of the manger. Sometimes he performs a kind of up-and-down motion, perhaps when he gets tired of the lateral. I am unable to discover the origin or object of this habit. Some horses are fond of playing with the halter-chains. They are of an irritable, restless disposition, desirous of constant employment. They seem to have pleasure in making a noise with the chains, by drawing each alternately and rapidly through the rings. Possibly this may have something to do in the production of weaving. Whatever be the cause, the habit is harmless. A dark stall has been recommended; but at this moment I know a confirmed weaver who is perfectly blind. In general the horse should be tied with only one rein.

PAWING.—Hot-tempered horses are much in the habit of scraping away the litter and digging their fore feet into the ground, as if they meant to tear up the pavement. They wear down their shoes very fast, break the nails, and keep their bed always in disorder. When the horse uses only one foot in pawing, a clog may be put upon it similar to that employed against kicking. It may be fastened to the pastern, to the leg above the fetlock-joint, or above the knee-joint. In general, that is the most successful which is attached to the fetlock. The chain should be just long enough to let the clog hang against the hoof. When the horse paws equally with both feet, a clog may be placed on each, or the two may be shackled together without clogs.

Shackles, or fetters, are two straps, one for each pastern, connected by a light chain ten or twelve inches long. The last link at each extremity of this chain is triangular, for admitting the straps, which should be about twelve or fourteen inches long, lined inside with soft leather or cloth, and so broad that they can not cut the skin, from which the edges are a little raised by the inside lining. These fetters are objectionable; they prevent the horse from lying down. They are sometimes employed for other purposes than that of preventing pawing. In the racing-stables, I believe, they are occasionally applied to keep an irritable horse from striking and wounding his legs while under the operations of his groom, and they are sometimes put on horses when they are turned out, to be retaken in an hour or two.

WASTING THE GRAIN.—Playful, lively horses, sometimes waste a great deal of their oats. They seize a large mouthful, look about while masticating, and suffer much of it to drop among the litter. Often more than half of the feed is lost. This may be partly prevented by giving a small quantity at a time, by spreading it thinly over the bottom of the manger, by shortening the halter-rein, and by placing the horse in a remote stall, where nothing will attract his attention at feeding-time. Some waste the grain in another way. They drive it out of the manger by a jerk of the muzzle. The cross-spars, already spoken of, prevent this habit.

SHYING THE DOOR.—While leaving or entering the stable, the horse frequently gets a fright. The posts catch his hips or some part of the harness, and besides being alarmed he is sometimes seriously injured. After this has happened several times to an irritable horse, he becomes somewhat unmanageable every time he has to go through a doorway. He approaches it with hesitation, and when urged forward he makes a sudden bound, so as to clear the passage at a leap He is repeatedly injured by his own violence, and is ulti mately so terrified and unruly, that he must be backed out. This habit may be prevented by wider doorways, and more care in going through them. When attempted early, it may be so far overcome that it will be unattended with danger or difficulty. The horse ought to be always bridled when led out or in. He should be held short and tight by the head, that he may feel he has not liberty to make a leap, and of itself this is often sufficient to restrain him. Great care must be taken to keep him off the door-posts. Punishment, or a threat of punishment, is improper. It is only timid or high-spirited horses that acquire the habit, and rough usage invariably increases their agitation and terror. The man must be gentle and quiet. After the habit is fairly established, it is seldom entirely cured; the horse may become less unmanageable, but still continue to require precaution. Some are much worse than others. Some may be led out, quite at leisure, when blindfolded; others when they have the harness-bridle on; a few manage best when neither led nor restrained, but allowed to take their own way; and a few may be ridden through the doorway that can not be led. When the horse is very troublesome, each of these ways may be tried. Some shy the door only in going in, others in coming out.

EATING THE LITTER is sometimes regarded as a peculiar habit. It does not, however, deserve this name. If the horse have too little hay he will eat the straw, selecting the cleanest and soundest portions of it. But this is not what is meant. He eats the dirty litter, the straw which has been soiled by the urine. This he does only at times. It indicates a morbid state of the stomach and bowels. Put a lump of rock-salt in the manger. It is the salt contained in the litter that induces the horse to eat it.

LICKING themselves, other horses, the mangers, the ground and the walls, and eating earth or lime, arise from the same cause. The hair of horses often contains a good deal of salt deposited in perspiration, and it is to obtain this that the horses lick the skin of themselves and others. Give a piece of rock-salt, and if the horse eat earth, or lick a lime-wall, let him have a lump of chalk in addition to the salt. Place them in the manger and leave them there. The lick is sometimes connected with fever, and requires other treatment. [Clay is very beneficial occasionally in small quantities, when snow is on the ground, or horses are so confined that they can not get to the ground; or a few roots with the dirt at-

tached to them. But one must be careful not to give so
many as to cause scouring.]

Wind-sucking and Crib-biting are spoken of in connexion
with the management of defective and diseased horses.

STABLE VICES.

HORSES are often termed vicious when they have no vice.
Docile but bold horses may be excited to retaliate upon those
who abuse them. They never strike but when they are
struck; they are obstinate, but should not be called vicious;
they are sullen and often refuse to perform painful exertions;
they require nothing but gentle treatment. Punishment invariably makes them more dangerous, and ultimately quite
vicious, even to ferocity; they learn to give injury when none
is offered. Some, especially mares, often feign that they are
going to bite or strike, yet never do any intentional mischief;
they merely desire to attract attention, and to be made pets
of. The very best of horses often have this peculiarity. A
foolish or timed groom is apt to deal too harshly with them.
They may scowl and grind their teeth; they may present
their quarters, and even lift a foot as if in the act to strike, or
they may fix their teeth in the man's jacket, but it is all in
play. The best way is not to mind them, or at most to give
them warning with the voice. It is a pleasing kind of fa-
miliarity which need not offend nor alarm any one. Good
horsemen generally like it as indicative of energy and endurance; and I think such horses become sooner and more
warmly attached to persons about them than others of a heed
less disposition.

Some horses are perfectly quiet to the groom, but very
quarrelsome in the company of other horses; this is the case
with mares more than with geldings, but it is common enough
in geldings too: they bite or strike a strange horse.the moment he comes in reach, but seem to get reconciled to him
after a little acquaintance. Horses of this kind should always
work with the same companion, and stand in the next stall to
him; they never work well with strangers; and in the stable,
when standing beside strangers, they are so intent upon mischief, that they neither feed nor rest.

All vicious horses are most easily managed by one person.
I have often met with instances of balling, shoeing, and
similar operations, being strenuously resisted when attempted
by a number of persons, and yet easily performed when taken

in hand by one. The horse appears to get alarmed, to expect something painful, when surrounded by a crowd. It is not wonderful that he should, for there are always several assistants at the performance of painful operations.

Some are awed when harshly commanded and boldly approached; some must be soothed and cherished; and some must occasionally be well flogged. There are many that, to be managed at all in safety, must be managed in perfect silence. To horses of this kind, every word increases their suspicion and terror; they must be treated as if they were quite docile; an attempt to bite or strike should pass without the least notice, and this sometimes confounds and tames the horse more than anything that could be said or done to him. Caresses and chastisement are equally pernicious or useless.

Grooms and others often err in their treatment of vicious horses. They punish those that are not to be improved by punishment, and they apply the lash either before the horse has done anything to merit it, or some time after he has forgotten the offence. No horse should ever be chastised without knowing why; the object should be to prevent repetition of the offence; but this is seldom thought of; the horse is flogged merely because the man is angry. There is a very common piece of stupidity which may be cited in illustration of this. By some means the horse gets free and runs off or scampers about, giving the man a great deal of trouble to retake him. While free, he gets kind words, he is called in a soothing tone, and perhaps coaxed to submit himself to the halter by an offer of oats; he is patted and caressed till he is fairly secured, and then he is flogged, kicked, and knocked about, as if he had been caught in the act of committing a great crime. If this is ever to do any good, it should be done directly after the horse deserves it. As it is, he can not understand why he receives this treatment, or he must suppose it is the penalty of submitting himself, and the next time he gets free, he will delay surrender as long as possible. This is but a sample of the way in which a horse, and especially a vicious horse, is often chastised: he is caressed and soothed till it is convenient and safe to punish him, and by that time he has forgotten the crime. If correction can not instantly follow the offence, none should be given. The horse may be injured, and there is not the least chance of his being improved.

BITING.—There are horses who delight in biting. Some are so much addicted to it that it is not possible to enter their stall without obtaining substantial evidence of their prowess in this respect. An experienced biter gives no warning. He knows the extent of his reach, and abstains from all demonstration of hostility until the man comes up to the proper place; then, quick as lightning, he darts at the intruder, and generally succeeds in tearing off some part of his clothing. Many are content with this triumph, and crouch into a corner of the stall, trembling, and expecting the accustomed punishment. Others, however, are not so easily satisfied. A single snatch is not sufficient. A ferocious horse makes repeated efforts to seize the man, and he is not content with a tug at the clothes, even when he can carry off half a yard of fustian. He takes a deeper and firmer hold; he will struggle to seize his enemy; he will shake him, lift him off the ground, and perhaps throw him down, and then attack him with the fore-feet, striking and trampling upon him. There are several instances of men having been killed in this way, generally by stallions.

I have seen biters punished till they trembled in every joint, and were ready to drop; but have never, in any case, known them cured by this treatment, nor by any other. The lash is forgotten in an hour, and the horse is as ready and determined to repeat the offence as before. He appears unable to resist the temptation. In its worst forms biting is a kind of insanity. There are various degrees of the complaint. Constant and laborious work often converts a ferocious into a very tame biter. So far as I know, there are no means of effecting a complete cure; but, by careful management, mischief may be prevented, even in the worst cases. When not very resolute, the horse may be overawed by a bold groom. He may warn the horse by speaking to him; and he may enter the stall with a rod, held in view of the horse, and ready to fall should he attempt to bite. After getting hold of the head, the man is safe. He may then apply a muzzle, or tie the horse's head to the hay-rack, if there be anything to do about him, such as dressing or harnessing. When grain or water is to be delivered, muzzling or tying up is not necessary. The man has only to be upon his guard till he get hold of the head, and retain his hold till he get clear of the horse. That he can easily manage by pushing the horse back till he can clear the stall, by one step, after he lets go the head.

When the rod is not sufficient to intimidate the horse, a long rope must be fastened to his halter. This must run through

FIG. 15.—STALL FOR A BITER.

a ring in the head of the stall, or in the head-post on the left
side, and proceed backward to the heel-post, where it is secured.   This enables the man to draw the head close up to
the ring, and to keep it there, till grain or water is delivered,
till the horse can be bridled, muzzled, harnessed, or dressed.
Of course the head is to be released, after the man leaves the
stall; but the rope remains in place, attached to the halter,
and ready for use.

A muzzle alone is often sufficient to deter some horses from
biting; or attempting to bite.   These do not require to be tied
up when under stable operations.   But some, though muzzled,
will strike a man to the ground; for these there is no remedy
but tying up.

KICKING.—This vice is not so common as that of biting;
but it is much more dangerous, and the mischief is not so
easily avoided.   Some strike only at horses, and never attempt
to injure persons.   These have little chance of doing harm
when placed in the end stall of a single-headed stable, where

other horses will never have occasion to stand or pass behind them. Those that kick at the groom, or persons going about them, are always most dangerous to strangers. A great many can be intimidated by threatening them with the whip. Previous to entering the stall, the man warns the horse by speaking roughly to him ; and by placing him on one side, he may be approached on the other. A drunken, or awkward groom, however, is almost sure to receive injury from a confirmed kicker ; and a timid man is never safe. Vicious, and perhaps all kinds of horses, discover timidity very quickly ; those that are so inclined soon take advantage of the discovery. Many kickers give warning. They whisk the tail, present the quarters, and hang the leg a moment before they throw it out. Others have more cunning, and give no notice. They often let a man enter the stall, when they turn suddenly round and strike out, either with one foot or with both. Some strike only as the man is leaving the stall with his back to the horse ; some are slow, and some so quick that the motion is scarcely seen till the blow is struck. Some strike with the fore-feet but these are easily avoided when the vice is known.

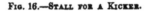

Fig. 16.—Stall for a Kicker.

Timid grooms are always too close, or too far away from a kicker. When the man must come within reach of the heels, he should stand as close to them as possible. A blow thus becomes a push, seldom injurious.

When the horse is a ferocious kicker, so malicious and determined that it is very hazardous to approach him even with a rod—which in such a case, however, oftener irritates than intimidates—he must be placed out of the way in a remote stall, the partitions of which should be high and long. A long rope must be attached to the head, nearly the same as for a savage biter; but this, instead of drawing the horse's head up to a ring at top of the stall, draws him backward so far that the head can be seized before entering the stall. As long as the man keeps well forward with his hand on the head, he is safe from the heels. This rope is not attached at the stall-head; it is supported in front by a ring placed in the travis near its top, and about three feet from the head-post. In some cases, a small door in the partition is requisite, through which the horse is fed and watered. When the door is large enough to admit a man, and the horse not a biter as well as a kicker, it renders a side-line unnecessary.

REFUSING THE GIRTHS.—Some horses are difficult to saddle. When the girths are tightened, or as the man is in the act of tightening them, the horse suddenly drops on his knees as if he were shot. Sometimes he rears up and falls backward. This is a rare occurrence. It is generally termed a vice, but it is difficult to understand it in that light. The horse sometimes cuts his knees to the bone by the violence with which he falls, and I should think he would not do that if he could help it. I am inclined to believe that the fall is involuntary, but how a tight girth should produce it, can not be told. In one horse that often, but not always threw himself down when the girths were tightened, I thought I could discover something like a broken rib, yet it was doubtful; I could not be sure about it.

Whatever be the cause, the horse should stand deep in litter when he is saddled, and the girths should be tightened by degrees. Let him stand a few minutes after the saddle is on, before the girths are full drawn, and never make them needlessly tight.

There are one or two other stable vices so unimportant, that I think they deserve no notice. Refusing the crupper and shying the bridle are among them. These, and similar trifles, can hardly be called vices.   They require a little tact, perhaps, but no particular mode of treatment.

On the Habits and Vices connected with Work, I had written a section of some length; but the press of other matter compels me to exclude this, which belongs to horsemanship more than to Stable Economy.

FOURTH CHAPTER.

WARMTH.

Hot Stables have been condemned by every veterinarian who has had occasion to mention them. They have been blamed for producing debility, inflamed lungs, diseased eyes, chronic cough, and recent cough, distemper, and some other evils, direct or indirect; and a cold stable has been recommended, times out of number, for preventing them. I have elsewhere stated, that a *hot* stable and a *foul* stable have always been confounded one with another, as if they were not different. Mr. Youatt is the only exception that I know of. He seems to regard a heated and an impure atmosphere as two. His distinction is not, indeed, very broadly marked, yet it can be traced. It is not wonderful that it should have been overlooked by others. Heat and impurity, almost uniformly arising from the same source, must as uniformly co-exist and operate in combination. Hence the common error of considering them as inseparable, or as a single agent. It must be obvious, however, that a heated atmosphere is capable of producing one series of effects, and an impure atmosphere another. The evils arising from impurity are described in connexion with the ventilation of stables. This is the proper place to consider the effects of heat. There is some difficulty in ascertaining precisely what they are. Some experiments would almost be necessary to arrive at accurate conclusions. We have ample opportunity of examining hot stables, and of observing the health and condition of their occupants. But these hot stables rarely have a pure atmosphere. The air, as I have elsewhere observed, is never perfectly pure in any oc cupied stable; but by pure I here mean comparatively pure quite wholesome, yet not quite free from extraneous matters An atmosphere of untainted purity can not be obtained in the neighborhood of breathing animals, and it appears quite cer tain that it may suffer deterioration to a certain extent, withou

14

producing any evil. The only mode of learning the effects of a hot atmosphere, would be to place a number of horses in an apartment heated by fire or steam, and so well ventilated that emanations from the lungs, the skin, and the evacuations, would escape before they had time to operate in combination with the heat. The keen advocates for hot stables might try the experiment for a few weeks or months, and such an experiment would tell us at once what heat will, and what it will not do. So far as I have been able to observe, by close attention to a great number of horses confined in all kind of stables, it would appear that

The Effects of Hot Stabling are only three in number. The first is a fine, short, glossy coat; the second, a strong disposition to accumulate flesh; and the third is an extreme susceptibility to the influence of cold. These are the permanent effects. Those produced by sudden removal from a cold to a warm stable are somewhat different. For the first week the horse looks as if he were a little fevered. He does not feed well, but drinks much. Sometimes he is dull, and sometimes restless, fidgety. If somewhat lusty, or if he eat and drink tolerably well, he often sweats in the stable, particularly about the flanks, the groin and quarters. In a few days he seems to become accustomed to the high temperature. His coat lies smoothly; it glitters as if it were anointed; the horse recovers his appetite, and rapidly takes on flesh.

The short glossy coat is not in this country any evil. The accumulation of flesh is not always desirable, but the stables are never cooled for the purpose of preventing it. The third effect, that is, the intolerance of exposure to cold, produced by hot stabling, is a serious evil. If all the diseases, mostly of a dangerous character, which are ascribed to sudden exposure in a cold atmosphere, really have such an origin, a hot stable can hardly be more destructive than a foul one. It is universally acknowledged, that sudden exposure to cold, that is, rapid abstraction of heat, is dangerous, but whether it have all the power which some attribute to it may be doubted. That cold often does mischief can not be denied, and that the hot stabled horse is in greatest danger is, I think, as unquestionable. The least exposure makes him shiver, and everybody knows that this shivering is very often followed by a deadly inflammation.

I do not say that hot stables will produce no other effect. ⸱ speak only from my own observation, and of a stable without apparent impurity. When the air is tolerably pure, the heat can not rise to a great height, unless it be produced by artificial means. I have never seen a stable heated by fire, and can not say what would be the result of excessive heat. Diseased liver, debility, a broken constitution, are said to be the consequences of a long residence in a hot climate, but whether a horse's work and temperance save him from these, or whether an elevated temperature alone will produce them in him, I do not know. There is little analogy between a horse living in a hot stable, and a European living in a hot climate. Other circumstances differ so much that nothing could be learned by contrasting them.

WARM STABLES.—[When exposed to an average temperature of 60 to 65 degrees, to keep up a healthy animal heat, the horse expires every twenty-fours, 97½ ounces of carbon. The food which he eats supplies this carbon, and the oxygen which is respired in the atmosphere, is its consumer. The union of these two, carbon and oxygen, produces heat, and this is all we know of it. The colder the atmosphere the more oxygen it contains ; it follows, therefore, that the lower the temperature to which animals are exposed, the greater the consumption of carbon in their respiration, and the greater the amount of food necessary to supply that carbon ; and this is the reason why a horse in a warm stable fats faster, or is kept in better condition with the same amount of food than in a cold stable. A warmer atmosphere, or warmer clothing, as stated by Liebig, is *merely an equivalent for a certain amount of food*. The warming of stables is unnecessary except for the racer or trotter when in training, and the hunter and stage-coach horse at full work. For horses engaged in the ordinary work of the farm or the road, they are extremely pernicious ; for the moment they are exposed to a raw wind, or to standing in the open air, they are liable to take cold, when inflammation of the lungs, founder, and other diseases, are pretty certain to follow. We are persuaded that roomy, well-ventilated stables, of nearly the same temperature within as the atmosphere is without, are decidedly the most healthy for the horse ; and that he will do more ordinary work during the winter thus lodged, than if kept in a heated atmosphere, and be a hardier and longer-lived animal. If the cold weather makes his hair a little longer, or his coat somewhat the rougher, this is of no consequence, when by it we secure greater hardihood, constitution, and endurance. Our rule is to feed horses well ; keep them dry and clean ; use them fairly within their powers ; walk them cool after being heated ; then take them to their stable, and properly clothe them if the weather requires it. When well-bred, thus treated, horses may attain an average working life of twenty-five years.]

TEMPERATURE OF THE STABLE.—When the stable is properly constructed, and not too large for the number of horses, it need never be heated by fire or steam. These conditions being observed, I know of no case in which it is necessary to produce an artificial supply of heat for healthy horses. The heat which is constantly passing from the horse's body soon warms the air, and judicious ventilation will keep it sufficiently comfortable ; but in no case should a high heat be purchased by sacrificing *ventilation* so far as to produce sensible contamination of the air. It is better either to employ heavier clothing, or to heat the stable by fire.

Slow-work horses, and all those that are much exposed to the weather, and especially those that have to *stand* out of doors, must not have hot stables, yet they should be comfortable.

The temperature of stables is generally regulated by opening or shutting the windows. On very hot days, it may be proper to sprinkle clean water on the floor, or about the ground outside the doors.

Sudden Transitions should be carefully avoided, most especially when the temperature of the stable is habitually very low or very high. Whether the transition from heat to cold, or that from cold to heat, be most pernicious, is still a subject of debate. But it is admitted by all that both are injurious My own experience leads me to believe that cold does much more harm to a horse that has just been severely heated, than heat ever does to a cold horse. Either transition, however, should be effected by slow degrees. To a certain extent the horse may be inured to an alteration either way, without suffering any injury, if time be allowed for the system to adapt itself to the change.

When the horse himself is very hot, he may be refreshed by standing about three minutes in a cool stable, but he must not stand there till he begin to shiver. Neither must a hot horse be put into a hot stable, especially if he have been much exhausted by his work. It makes him sick, and keeps up the perspiration, and some faint outright. A very cold horse should not be put into a very hot stable. If he be wet there is little danger, but if dry he becomes restless and somewhat feverish, and in this state he remains till he begins to perspire.

CLOTHING.—When it is desirable to keep the horse warm without endangering the purity of the air, he may be clothed. Coarse slow-working horses require clothing only when sick. A fine coat is not much wanted in these animals; yet if they have to stand in cold stables, and especially when the stables are not fully occupied, even these would be none the worse of a cover during some of the sharp winter weather. In the hunting and racing stables, clothes are used nearly all the year round, and they should be so wherever it is important to make the coat lie smoothly. The stable may be more completely ventilated when the heat of the horse's body is retained by appropriate clothing. Stage-coach and post-horses are not usually clothed, but a few covers are always kept for the sick and the delicate. The cavalry horses are never clothed.

Clothes are of different Kinds.—There is one suit for winter and another for summer; besides extra-heavy clothing, used in hunting and racing stables for sweating the horses. The last are termed *sweaters*, and consist of one or more sheets of blanket-like stuff. Sometimes when copious sweating is necessary, a single blanket is put on and covered by several old or half-worn quarter-pieces. These require to be frequently washed. That which lies in contact with the skin is apt to become hard and dirty. Unless it be soft and clean it galls the horse, and refuses the perspiration. When soaked in sweat it should be rinsed in cold water before being dried. When two hoods are put on, the outermost alone should have ear-pieces. That below it requires only ear-holes.

A full Winter Suit is composed of a hood, which envelopes the head and neck, a breast-piece for the bosom, and a quarter-piece for the body. This is sometimes termed a kersey-suit. It is made of a stuff so called, and is edged with worsted tape. A woollen rug is often employed as an addition to the ordinary suit, for very cold weather. Hoods are not much used except in hunting or racing-stables; they are useful, however, at times, for sick horses, for sweating, and for exercise under physic, or in severe winter. The clothing in most general use for winter is merely a horse-blanket, or rug of sufficient size to cover all the body. The girth which secures the clothing is termed a roller, or surcingle. It should be broad, that it may be tight without producing uneasiness, and padded, that it may not lie upon the spine. When the horse is narrow-loined, a breast-strap made of web is necessary to keep the cloth and girth from slipping back.

The summer-clothing is composed of white or striped cloth,

14*

linen, or calico. It consists of a single sheet of small dimen
sions. It is almost entirely an ornamental covering, but it is
useful to keep off flies and dust, and to prevent the hair from
staring.

Weather Clothing.—When horses go to exercise, they usually go out in the stable-clothing, to which a hood and a blanket,
or quarter-piece, may be added, if the weather demand them.
But many require some defence while performing their work.
This is particularly the case with carriage horses that have to
stand for two or three hours exposed to the night air. A
small quarter-piece, made of Mackintosh's water-proof cloth,
is getting into use. It is thrown over the harness, to which
it is attached; it keeps the horses dry without heating them.
Heavier clothing would be desirable when the horses are
standing, but it would make them sweat profusely, even at a
slow pace, and is therefore objectionable. A good driver will
endeavor to keep his horses in motion. At night, when a
crowd renders motion impracticable, he might be, and often is,
provided with a pair of rugs, which can be thrown over the
horses till they be ready to start. Long standing in the cold,
however, always benumbs a horse's legs, and should be avoided
as much as possible, by occasional or constant motion. During wet weather, a piece of oil-cloth is sometimes worn across
the loins of cart-horses; it keeps the rain off parts that have
little motion and no natural defence. Some also use a neck-
piece. The owners of horses employed in street-coaches,
are becoming more careful than they were wont. They generally have some sort of covering for the horses when standing in the weather. Water-proof sheets of different sizes, to
cover one, or a pair of horses, are in use to protect them from
rain. This stuff, however, is apt to make them perspire very
much, when they are the least heated. Stage-coach horses
usually have a light quarter-piece put on with the harness,
and withdrawn when the coach is ready to start.

Tearing off the Clothes.—Some horses destroy a great
many clothes. They endeavor to pull them off, and tear them
all to pieces. There are only three modes of preventing this
trick; the hinder portion, or the whole of the quarter-piece,
may be made of hair-cloth, lined by a softer material to lie
next the skin. Few horses like to touch this harsh substance
with their teeth and lips; but some will not rest till they
manage to tear it off. A staff of wood is sometimes used;
one extremity is attached to the collar, the other to the sur-
ingle. This prevents the horse from turning his head round

to get at the clothing, but it also prevents him from lying down. The other mode is to tie the horse's head to the hayrack; of course he must be liberated when he is to lie down or to feed.

In some stables the clothing is removed every night. The clothes last a great deal longer, but the practice of removing them at night, is advisable only when the clothing is light, or when the stables are warmer at night than in the daytime, which is generally the case.

Application and Care of the Clothes.—In putting on the hood, care must be taken that the ears are fairly inserted, the eyes clear, and the strings sufficiently tight to keep the hood in its place without galling the skin. The breast-piece must not be drawn up so much as to press upon the windpipe when the horse's head is directed to the ground. The quarter-piece should be thrown well forward and subsequently adjusted by drawing it back, so as to lay the hairs, not to raise them, by pulling the cloth forward or sidewise. The surcingle is to be placed on the middle of the back, and the pad fairly adjusted. Both the surcingle and the breast-band are to be just tight enough to keep the clothing in place. Sweating-clothes are to be closely and generally applied, but must not descend so far upon the horse's legs as to encumber his action. The breast-band and the breast-piece are to be quite slack. The saddle alone keeps them from shifting backward.

All the clothing is to be shook and dried every morning, after dressing the horse. The loose hair and dust can be removed by beating and brushing. A small birch broom is convenient for taking off loose hair; that which is packed and woven into the cloth does no harm. When soiled by urine, the clothing must be wholly or partially washed with soap and water. The summer clothing is to be repaired, washed, dried, and laid carefully away, on the approach of winter. Now and then it may be examined and aired. The woollen articles, when out of use, are to be kept perfectly dry; they should be examined every month, brushed, and aired in the sun.

FIFTH CHAPTER.

FOOD.

I. ARTICLES OF FOOD—II. COMPOSITION OF FOOD—III. PREP-
ARATION OF FOOD—IV. ASSIMILATION OF THE FOOD—V. IN-
DIGESTION OF THE FOOD—VI. PRINCIPLES OF FEEDING—
VII. PRACTICE OF FEEDING—VIII. PASTURING—IX. SOILING
-X. FEEDING AT STRAW-YARD.

ARTICLES USED AS FOOD.

KINDS OF FOOD.—In this country horses are fed upon oats,
hay, grass, and roots. Many people talk as if they could be
fed on nothing else. But in other parts of the world, where
the productions of the soil are different, the food of the horse
is different. "In some sterile countries, they are forced to
subsist on dried fish, and even on vegetable mould; in Arabia, on milk, flesh-balls, eggs, broth, &c. In India, horses
are variously fed. The native grasses are judged very nutritious. Few, perhaps no oats are grown; barley is rare,
and not commonly given to horses. In Bengal, a vetch,
something like the tare is used. On the western side of India, a sort of pigeon-pea, called gram (*cicer arietinum*), forms
the ordinary food, with grass while in season, and hay all the
year round. Indian-corn or rice is seldom given. In the
West Indies, maize, Guinea-corn, sugar-cane tops, and sometimes molasses, are given. In the Mahratta country, salt,
pepper, and other spices, are made into balls, with flour and
butter, and these are supposed to produce animation, and to
fine the coat. Broth made from sheep's-head, is sometimes
given. In France, Spain, and Italy, besides the grasses, the
leaves of limes, vines, the tops of acacia, and the seeds of
the carab-tree, are given to horses."*
[In the United States many different kinds of natural and
cultivated grasses, green or dried as hay, are used in feeding

* London's Enc. of Agric., p. 1004.

horses ; also Indian, Egyptian, and broom corn, their blades and stalk ; sugar and wild cane tops, and molasses drippings ; rice, wheat, and other straw of different kinds, and their grain and bran ; beans, pease, and their pods and vines ; artichoke and potato tops and their roots, together with many other vegetables : pumpkins, squash, and other vine fruit ; flax and flaxseed ; sunflower seed ; acorns and other nuts ; the twigs, buds, and leaves of trees ; apples and other fruit ; cabbage.]

The articles upon which horses are fed in this country are usually arranged into three classes. That which possesses the least nutriment in proportion to its bulk, is termed *fodder*, and consists of grass, hay, and straw ; that which possesses the most nutriment, in proportion to its bulk, is termed *corn*. This word is often used as if it belonged exclusively to oats ; but it is a general name for all the kinds of grain and pulse upon which horses are fed. In this work it is used only in its general sense. *Roots*, such as carrots, turnips, and potatoes, form the third kind of food. In relation to their bulk, they have less nutriment than grain, and more than fodder. I do not think this classification is of any use, and here it will not be regarded, but it is well to know the meaning usually attached to the terms.

GREEN HERBAGE.—There are several kinds of green food, but the individual properties of each are so little known, that much can not be said about them.

Grass is the natural food of horses. It is provided for him without the interference of art. It is composed of a great number of plants, differing much or little from each other in structure, composition, and duration. Some of the natural grasses are to the horse mere weeds, destitute of nutriment, though not positively injurious. Several are rejected, or eaten only when there is nothing else to eat, and none are sufficiently rich to maintain the horse in condition for constant work, even though the work be moderate. At a gentle pace he may travel a few miles to-day, but he is unfit for a journey to-morrow. By cutting the grass and bringing it to the stable, the horse may be saved the labor of collecting it ; but still he can render very little service.

Grass, however, or green herbage of some kind, is given to almost all horses during a part of the year. The young animals, from the time they are weaned till they are fit for work, receive grass as long as it can be had   Hunting and racing colts excepted, they receive little else.

It is commonly believed that grass has some renovating and purifying properties, not possessed by hay nor by grain. It is true that all the kinds of green herbage, including clover, saintfoin, lucerne, tares, and ryegrass, produce a change upon the horse. But whether the change be for better or for worse, is another question. For the first two or three days, green food relaxes the bowels and increases the secretion of urine and of perspiration. Very often it produces an eruption on the skin, particularly when given along with a large allowance of grain. When the horse is permitted to eat what he pleases, the belly becomes large. These effects may be termed immediate. They are most apparent at the commencement, but are visible so long as the horse receives any considerable quantity of grass. Green food produces other effects not so easily traced. Wounds heal more kindly, inflammatory diseases are not so fatal, and chronic diseases frequently abate, or they entirely disappear under the use of grass. The horse, however, is always soft, when fed much on green food. He sweats a great deal, and is soon exhausted by his work.

Clover, Ryegrass, Tares, Lucerne, Saintfoin, and the *Oat-Plant,* are all used as green food. So far as the horse is concerned, one seems to be as good as any of the others. They appear to produce the same effects as grass. Amid such variety we might expect to find some difference ; but I have not been able to perceive any. Some horses, indeed, like one article better than another, but this seems to be mere taste, for no one of them appears to be generally preferred nor rejected. There are various opinions, however, as to the comparative value of these articles. Some affirm that clover is less nutritious than ryegrass, some that tares are poor watery feeding, and others that lucerne and saintfoin are the best of the whole lot. But opinion on the subject seems to be quite vague. Whatever one affirms, another will be found to deny. In Scotland, lucerne and saintfoin are very little used ; but clover, ryegrass, and tares, are given each in their season, as if one were equal to another.

Beans, wheat, rye, and oats, the whole plant, are sometimes, but very seldom, and never regularly used as food for horses. Cabbage, and some other green articles, are eaten, but they deserve no particular notice. Several, which form the ordinary green food of horses in other countries, are not grown here. The leaves and clippings of the vine are much used in many parts of France.

Whin, Furze, or Gorse. This is an abundant and cheap plant. It is very good green food for horses, and is procured when there is no other. To sick horses it is an excellent substitute for grass, and many will eat it when they will eat nothing else ; but it has been extensively tried as an article of ordinary feeding. It has long been used in many parts of Wales, and of Scotland, and in several of the Irish counties. Mr. Tytler of Balmain was the first, I understand, to publish a useful account of its properties. His essay will be found in the fifth volume of the Highland Society's Transactions. "It appears that, for five successive years, Mr. Tytler fed his farm-horses from the beginning of November to the middle of March, on furze and straw, with a very moderate allowance of oats during only a part of that time. At first oats were given throughout the winter, but afterward only from the beginning of February, and then only at the rate of three pounds two ounces, or about one third of a peck, of average quality, to each ; the daily allowance of furze during the first period being tweny-eight pounds, and during the second, eighteen pounds, with fourteen of straw."

Furze is generally used on the frontiers of France and Spain ; and the British cavalry while in the Pyrenees, under the duke of Wellington, had no other forage.

According to the Mid-Lothian Report (Appendix No. VI., p. 56), it has been found that an acre of whins is sufficient for six horses, during four months ; that they require two years to produce them ; that horses, with whins, and one feed of grain, were in as good order as with two feeds and straw ;[*] that all the straw and one feed of oats were thus saved ; that, valuing these at sevenpence a-day each horse, the saving in seventeen weeks amounted on the six horses, to £17 17s.—from which, deducting five shillings a-week as the expense of cutting and bruising, there would remain £13 12s., as the product of two acres.[†]

DRY HERBAGE.—In this country the dry herbage consists of hay and straw. In France the vine-leaves are collected and stored for winter fodder. In the West Indies the tops of the sugar-cane are deemed highly nutritious, after they are dried and sweated a little in heaps. In a season of abundance, ricks of the cane-tops the but-ends in, are made in a

* The "order," I suspect, would be nothing to boast of.
† British Husbandry, vol. i., p. 135. See also the Annals of Agriculture, vol. xxxv., p. 13. Ency. Brit., art. Agriculture. Farmer's Mag., vol. xx., p. 288. Comp. Grazier, fifth ed., p. 559 ; and Quar. Journal of Agric., No. 3.

corner of each field, to supply the want of pasturage and
other food. These are chopped small, and mixed with common salt, or sprinkled with a solution of molasses. Maize
is sometimes made into hay. " When Guinea or Indian corn
is planted in May, and cut in July, in order to bear seed that
year, that cutting properly tended, makes an excellent hay,
which cattle prefer to meadow hay. In like manner, after
the corn has done bearing seed, the after crop furnishes abundance of that kind of fodder which keeps well in ricks for
two or three years."* " In some places dried ferns, reeds,
flags, small branches, or twigs, are dried and used as substitutes for hay."† Doubtless there are many other plants made
into fodder in different parts of the world. Where Canary
corn is raised, the chaff and straw are given to horses, from
which it is said they derive more nutriment than from hay.

Hay.—In Scotland, most of the hay used for horses is
composed of ryegrass, or ryegrass and clover. The natural
hay, which is not very much used here, contains several
plants. Much of the hay in Scotland is bad. A good deal
is grown on poor land, and this is soft, dwarfish, and destitute of nutriment. But hay in general is not well made. In
the south it is cured with more skill, and preserved with more
care. The best we have in the west of Scotland is procured
from Stirlingshire, and is composed of ryegrass and a little
clover.

In England clover-hay stands in high repute for hard-working draught horses. In the market it brings 20 per cent. more
than meadow or ryegrass hay. Hard upland meadow hay is
preferred for hunters and racers, because, I suppose, they are
apt to eat too much of the clover. In Scotland, ryegrass, or
a mixture of ryegrass and clover, is considered the best for
all horses. Here we have almost no good meadow hay, and
most of that made from the natural grasses is hardly worth
preserving.

Good Hay is about a year old, long and large, hard, tough;
its color inclining to green, rather than to white; it has a
sweet taste and pleasant smell; the seed is abundant; in-
fused in hot water, it produces a rich dark-colored tea. The
less dust it has about it the better; but, from the soil, and the
way in which hay is made here, it is seldom free from dust.
In damp weather hay absorbs much moisture, and weighs a
good deal the heavier. In England, the market weight of

---

* Bracy Clark's Pharmacopœia Equina.
† Blaine's Outlines of Vet. Med.

new hay is sixty pounds per truss till the 4th of September. The truss of old hay contains only fifty-six pounds.

New Hay is purgative and debilitating. It seems to be difficult of digestion. [American hay is drier and better cured than English, and we believe that it contains more saccharine matter; these observations, therefore can hardly apply to it.] The horse is fond of it, and will eat a large quantity, much of which passes through him little altered by the digestive process, and probably retaining a good deal of its nutriment. On the other hand, hay which is very old is dry, tasteless, and brittle. The horse rejects much and eats little. Old hay is much recommended; but by old I suppose is meant not new. In the south, perhaps, stacked hay does not so soon degenerate as in the north, where it is certainly old enough in one year.

Heated Hay, sometimes termed mowburnt, is that which has undergone too much fermentation. In curing hay it is thrown in a heap to sweat, that is, till a slight degree of fermentation takes place, which is arrested by exposing the hay to the air. This, it appears, is necessary for its preservation in the stack. But sometimes the process is carried too far, or, more frequently, it is re-excited, after the hay is stored past. Hay that has been thus injured is not all alike. Some of it acquires a very sweet sugary taste; and this portion is eaten; some of it is changed in color to a dark brown, and has its texture altered; it is short, brittle as rotten wood, and has a disagreeable taste; this portion seems to be rejected; another portion of the same stack is mouldy, stinking, quite rotten, and no horse will eat this. All kinds of hay, however good originally, may suffer this injury. When the damage has been slight, most horses will eat certain portions of the hay very greedily; they seem to be fond of it for the first week, but subsequently it is rejected in disgust. Upon the whole, I believe it is the most unprofitable fodder that horses can receive. When very bad it is dear, though obtained in a gift, for it often does much mischief, particularly to horses of fast-work. Much is wasted, and that which is eaten does little good. It is almost as poisonous as it is nutritious. Slow draught-horses may not, indeed, be greatly injured by it. But good wheat-straw may be better. To fast, hard-working horses, such as those employed in mails, it is a strong diuretic; and its diuretic power does not diminish by use. Hay forms an important part of the horse's food, particularly of those horses that receive no roots nor boiled meat. Bad

15

hay will change the horse's appearance and condition in
two days, when he has an unlimited quantity of corn. By
bad hay I mean that which is unwholesome. It may be
poor, having little nutriment, but sweet and digestible, without being pernicious. But good straw is better than unwholesome hay for all kinds of horses. The kidneys are
excited to extraordinary activity. The urine, which, in this
disease, is always perfectly transparent, is discharged very
frequently and in copious profusion. The horse soon becomes
hidebound, emaciated, and feeble. His thirst is excessive.
He never refuses water, and he drinks it as if he would never
give over. The disease does not produce death, but it renders the horse useless, and ruins the constitution. Should
he catch cold, or take the influenza, which prevailed so much
in Glasgow during the winter of 1836, glanders is seldom far
off.* This worthless hay is always sold at a lower rate, and
much of it enters the coaching-stables, but I am perfectly
sure that it would be cheaper to pay the highest price for the
best. One ton of good hay will, unless the men be excessively careless, go as far as two tons of that which is bad.
To slow-work horses, mowburnt hay may be given with less
detriment, but it is less unprofitable when consumed by cattle.

Musty Hay is known by its bad color, its unpleasant
smell, and bitter taste. It is soft and coated with fungi. Like
all other hay, its smell is most distinct when slightly damped
by breathing upon it. Old hay is often musty, without having
been heated. None but a hungry horse will eat it, and when
eaten in considerable quantity it is said to be "bad for the
wind." In truth, it is bad for every part of the body. In
some places they sprinkle this musty hay with a solution of
salt, which induces the horse to eat it; but even thus it answers better for bedding than for feeding, and to that purpose
the horse applies the most of it.

Weather-beaten Hay is that which has lain in the sward
exposed to the rain and the sun. It is musty, full of dust,
sapless, bleached, or blackened, and destitute of seed. Such,
also, is the state of that which has stood too long uncut. All
hay should be cut a few days before the seed is quite ripe.
After it has lost most of its seed, and its juices, little is left
to afford nutriment.

---

* The influenza I mean, was not at all similar to a disease which went
under the same name at the same time in England. We had almost none
of the English influenza till the last week of May. 1837. In the month of
June it was very prevalent.

Salted Hay, that is, hay with which salt has been mingled at the time of stacking it, is not much used in Scotland. It is not to be had. I can tell nothing about it. Horses are said to prefer it to any other. But the principal motive for salting hay is to preserve it when the weather requires that it be stacked before it is sufficiently dry. Salt prevents or checks fermentation. It darkens the color of the hay and makes it weigh heavier, for salt attracts moisture. Salt, I think, should not be forced on the horse. It may excite too much thirst. Given apart from the food, he may take all that is good for him. Damaged hay is often sprinkled with salt water, which seems to render it less disgusting, and may possibly correct its bad properties. It should be wetted as wanted, for it soon becomes sodden and rotten.

The Daily Quantity of Hay allowed to each horse must vary with its quality and the work. If the grain be limited, the horse will eat a greater weight of poor hay than of that which is more nutritious. If it be damaged, he must consume more than if it were sound, for he rejects some, perhaps a half, and that which he eats does not furnish so much nutriment. When the work is fast, the horse must not have so much as to give him a large belly. Eight pounds of good hay is about the usual allowance to fast-working hor ses, who may receive from twelve to fifteen or eighteer pounds of grain. Large draught-horses will consume from twenty to thirty pounds, but the quantity is seldom limited for these. Much, however, depends upon the allowance of grain. A German agriculturist calculates that eight pounds of meadow hay, or seven of that made from clover, tares, or saintfoin, afford as much nourishment as three pounds of oats. Of the hay raised on poor soils, nine pounds may be required.

A horse can live on hay and water, and when thrown off work for a considerable period, he often receives nothing else. This is not always right. The horse becomes so feeble and so pot-bellied, that it is long ere better food will restore his condition for work. A little grain, some roots, or a bran-mash, though given only once in two days, will help to keep him in flesh. I have heard of the horse being kept almost entirely on hay, receiving grain only when he was to be used. I would recommend the owner to confine himself to bread and water for a week or two, and then try what work a beef-steak will enable him to do. There is a material difference between eating to live and eating to work The stomach and bowels will hardly hold sufficient hay to keep even an idle horse alive.

The only preparation which hay receives before it is given is that of cutting it into chaff, into short pieces. When given uncut, the groom does, or should, shake out the dust before he puts it in the rack.

Hay Tea.—An infusion of hay made by pouring boiling water upon it, and covering it up till cool, has been recommended as an excellent nutritious drink for sick horses, and also for those in health. It might perhaps be a very good substitute for gruel; possibly a quart or two of the tea might not be a bad thing for a racer, given between heats, and toward the end of the day, when the horse is beginning to get exhausted from fasting, but it has not been tried.

Hay-Seed.—In Scotland, and wherever the hay is made chiefly from rye-grass, the seed is often made use of in feeding. It is sometimes mixed with the oats to prevent the horse from swallowing them whole, but most generally it is given along with the boiled food, either to divide it or to soak up the liquor. It contains more nutriment than the hay itself, but probably not a great deal, unless the hay has stood too long uncut. Some people say that hay-seed is bad for the wind, but I have never been able to trace any evil to its use. There is always much dust mingled with it, and this should always be removed by washing. Sometimes the seed is boiled, and sometimes merely added to the boiled food while it is hot. I do not know that boiling improves it, but it is much better liked after boiling or masking than in its raw state.

Straw.—There are five kinds of straw used as fodder. [Of their relative value for food see page 199.] Straw, however, is little used here. In many parts of Europe, wheat, barley, or rye straw forms the whole or greater part of the dried herbage, hay being almost unknown. In some of the towns, wheat and oat straw are occasionally given to cart-horses, and in some cases to coaching-horses. In the country both white and black straw are in common use as winter fodder for the farm-horses. It is very probable that wheat-straw, and perhaps some of the others, may soon be used much more extensively than they are at present. Good straw is certainly better than bad hay, and possibly, by increasing the allowance of grain, and cutting the straw, hay might be almost entirely dispensed with. Though containing much less nutriment, it still contains some, and it serves quite as well as hay to divide the grain and give it a wholesome size. It must be understood that food ought to possess bulk proportioned in some degree to the capacity of the digestive organs. Nutriment can be given in a very concentrated state, yet it is not proper to condense it beyond a certain point. Grain alone will give all the nourishment which any horse can need, but he must also have some fodder to give bulk to the grain, though it need not of necessity yield much nutriment. Straw, therefore, may often be used where hay is used. This has been proved very fairly in this country. The late Mr. Peter Mein, of Glasgow, kept his coaching-horses in excellent order for nearly eight months, without a single stalk of hay. During dear hay seasons it is the custom with many large owners, to make straw form part of the fodder. Wheat-straw is preferred, but few object to that of the oat.

But when horses are living chiefly on hay, as many farm-horses do, during part of the winter, it must not be supposed that an equal quantity, or indeed any quantity of straw, will supply the place of that hay. The stomach and bowels will hardly hold hay enough to nourish even an idle horse, and as straw yields less nutriment in proportion to its bulk, enough can not be eaten to furnish the nutriment required. The deficiency must be made up by roots or grain.

When much straw is used, part or the whole ought to be cut into chaff. It is laborious work to masticate it all, and in time it will tell upon the teeth, which in old horses are often worn to the gums, even by hay and grain.

I had written thus far on straw in previous editions of this work. Yet Nimrod, in the "Veterinarian," for 1839, at page 330, wishes "Mr. Stewart had said something of wheaten straw, the use of which for certain work, he is inclined to think well of." That I *had* said something may be seen by consulting the first and second editions, both published before 1839. Why Nimrod should have a wish implying that I had omitted to notice this article, must be explained by the gentleman himself.

Nimrod's residence in France seems to have given him a very favorable opinion of wheat straw. He says: "I am not only convinced that to the fact of horses in France eating as much straw as hay, is to be attributed their generally healthy condition, and also the non-necessity for physic, even to those who work hard and eat much grain (post and diligence horses for example) ; but I was informed by Lord Henry

15*

Seymour, at Paris, last March twelvemonth, that his race-horses, then of course doing good work, were eating nothing but wheaten straw and grain."—P. 514.

It need not be supposed, from what Nimrod or any other body says, that straw is, in any respect, better for horses than good hay. When straw is given instead of hay, the allowance of grain must be enlarged, and it will depend upon the relative cost of all the three, which of them should be given. It is not every horse, however, that will eat straw.

Bean-straw is tough and woody, and horses soon get tired of it. But I am persuaded that it might be advantageously made into tea. Bean-straw tea is much esteemed as a drink for milch-cows, and if not found equally good for horses, no harm can be done by trying it. Pea-straw also makes very good tea, but the straw itself can be entirely consumed as fodder. The white straws seem to make a very weak infusion. All the kinds of straw soon grow sapless and brittle. They should be fresh.

Barn Chaff.—The shell which is separated from wheat and oats in thrashing is often given to farm-horses. It seems to be very poor stuff. It looks as if it contained no nutriment, yet it may serve to divide the grain, to make the horse masticate it, and to prevent him from swallowing it too hurriedly. In this way it may so far supply the place of cut fodder. But the barn chaff is usually mingled with the boiled food, and if the articles be very soft, the chaff may give them consistence, but it does little more. The coving chaff of beans is said to form a very good manger food.

ROOTS.—Potatoes, carrots, and turnips, are the roots chiefly used for feeding horses. Parsnips, sugar beet, mangel-wurzel, and yams, are occasionally employed.

POTATOES are given both raw and boiled; in either state they are much relished by all horses as a change from other food. They are rather laxative than otherwise, and especially when given uncooked. Given raw and in considerable quantity to a horse not accustomed to them, they are almost sure to produce indigestion and colic; when boiled or steamed they are less apt to ferment in the stomach. For horses that do slow, and perhaps not very hard, or long-continued work, potatoes may, in a great measure, or entirely, supersede grain. They are little used for fast-work horses, yet they may be given, and sometimes they are given, without any harm. On many farms they form, along with straw fodder, the whole of the horse's winter food. In Essex, farm-horses have been kept throughout the winter entirely upon steamed potatoes. Each horse got fifty pounds per day, and did the ordinary work of the farm with the greatest ease. Some salt was mixed with them, and occasionally a little sulphur, which is quite superfluous.

According to Professor Low, fifteen pounds of raw potatoes yield as much nutriment as four and a half pounds of oats. Von Thaer says, that three bushels are equal to 112 lbs. of hay. Curwen, who tried potatoes very extensively in feeding horses, says that an acre goes as far as four acres of hay. He steamed them all, and allowed each horse daily 21 lbs., with a tenth of cut straw, which he preferred to hay for this mode of feeding.

The potatoes should be of a good kind and not frosted. They should always be cooked either by steaming or boiling. They are best when steamed. Horses like them as well raw, but they are excessively flatulent, and this bad property is much corrected by cooking, and by adding some salt. When boiled, the process should be performed with little water, and as quickly as possible. When nearly ready, the water should be altogether withdrawn, and the potatoes allowed to dry, uncovered, on the fire for a few minutes. They should be put on with hot water. They are always overboiled. Horses prefer them when hard at the heart. There is a general prejudice against the liquor in which potatoes are boiled. It is said to be injurious. In small quantities it certainly produces no apparent evil. I often see it given, not as a drink, but along with potatoes, beans, and chaff, which are all boiled together and mixed into a uniform mass, in general too soft. In some places the potatoes are not washed when boiled. If the earth do not relax the bowels, I am not aware that it does any injury, and the horses do not appear to dislike it. When the mass, however, from the addition of chaff, requires much mastication, this sand or earth must wear down the teeth very fast.

TURNIPS are in very general use for farm and cart-horses. Of late they have also been used a good deal in the coaching-stables; in many they have superseded the carrot. The Swedish variety is preferred. Common white and also yellow turnips are almost worthless. According to Von Thaer, 100 pounds of Swedes are equal in nutriment to 22 of hay. For slow horses, turnips to a certain extent supersede grain, but for fast-workers, they save the hay more than the grain. They have a fine odor when boiled, and this seems to make the horse feed more heartily. They fatten the horse very rapidly, and produce a smooth glossy coat and loose skin.

They are sometimes washed, sliced, and given raw, but in general they are boiled, and occasionally steamed. In the raw state they excite indigestion very readily, and are not much liked. Few horses get them oftener than once a day They may be given oftener, but the horse soon begins to refuse them. If they are to be used for several successive weeks, they should not be given oftener than once in twenty-four hours, or at most twice, and then not in very large quantities. When the quantity of food is limited, the horse will be glad to get them at all times, but in that case he must have little work. Straw, or hay, and turnips, will make an idle horse fat; they will enable him to do some slow work, but to perform full work the horse will not, or can not eat enough to keep him in condition: and for fast work he would eat more than he could well carry. Most usually they are given only once a day, and at night after work is over; chaff or hay-seed, and some grain, generally beans, are boiled along with them. They should always be washed. They require much boiling, and when large they may be cut.

CARROTS.—This root is held in much esteem. There is none better, nor perhaps so good. When first given it is slightly diuretic and laxative. But as the horse becomes accustomed to it, these effects are not produced. Carrots also improve the state of the skin. They form a good substitute for grass, and an excellent alterative for horses out of condition. To sick and idle horses they render grain unnecessary. They are beneficial in all chronic diseases of the organs connected with breathing, and have a marked influence upon chronic cough and broken wind. They are serviceable in diseases of the skin. In combination with oats, they restore a wornout horse much sooner than oats alone.

Carrots are usually given raw. Sometimes they are boiled or steamed, but horses seem to like them better raw. They are washed and sliced. They are often mingled with the grain, but I think they ought to form a separate feed. They diminish the consumption of both hay and grain. Some tell me that six, others that eight pounds of carrots, are equal to four pounds of oats. But the calculation can not be much depended upon, for the horse may eat more or less hay without the difference being observed. According to Curwen, a work-horse getting from eight to twelve pounds of grain, may have four pounds deducted for every five he receives of carrots. For fast-working horses, carrots never entirely supersede grain. Mention is made, indeed, of an Essex sportsman who gave his hunters each a bushel of carrots daily with a little hay, but no grain ; the horses are said to have followed a pack of harriers twice a week, but the possibility of doing this needs further proof. For slow-working horses, carrots may supply the place of grain quite well, at least for those employed on the farm. Burrows, an English agriculturist, gave his farm-horses each seventy pounds of carrots per day, along with chaff and barn-door refuse, with which the carrots were sliced and mixed. He gave a little rack-hay at night, but no grain. He fed his horses in this way from the end of October to the beginning of June, giving a little less than seventy pounds in the very shortest days, and a little more in spring. The tops of the carrots have been given to horses, and it is said they were much liked and quite wholesome.

PARSNIPS.—This root is used a good deal in France : in the neighborhood of Brest, parsnips and cabbages are boiled together and given to the horses warm, along with some buckwheat flour. In the island of Jersey the root is much cultivated, and is extensively used for fattening stock, and for the table of all classes. It is said not to be generally given to horses, for it is alleged that their eyes suffer under its use. Arthur Young, however, assures us, that the horses about Morlaix are ordinarily fed upon parsnips, and that they are considered " the best of all foods for a horse, and much exceeding oats." They are eaten both raw and boiled. They are most usually washed, sliced, and mixed with bran or chaff. The leaves, mown while in good condition, are eaten as readily as clover.

Mangel-wurzel, Yams, and the Turnip Cabbage, have each been employed as food for horses, but I have not been able to learn with what effect.

GRAIN.—In this country the grain consists chiefly of oats, beans, and pease, but barley is now in very common use, and wheat is occasionally given. The last two articles, however, are rarely used to the exclusion of oats, but are generally mixed with them in certain proportions. Rye, buckwheat, and maize, are used as grain in various parts of the world, but very little or not at all in this.

OATS.—There are several varieties which need not be described.

Good Oats are about one year old, plump, short, hard, rattling when poured into the manger, sweet, clean, free from chaff and dust, and weighing about forty pounds per bushel

New Oats are slightly purgative, indigestible, and unprofitable. They seem to resist the action of the stomach, and to
retain their nutriment. They make the horse soft ; he sweats
soon and much at work. [Oats, and indeed all kinds of
grain, are less watery, and therefore more nutritious and
sweeter, grown in America than in Great Britain ; so that
these observations will not hold good entirely, applied to this
country.] If they must be used when under three or four
months old, they may be improved by kiln-drying. They are
not good, however, till they are about a year old. They may
be kept till too old, when they become musty and full of insects. The period at which oats begin to degenerate depends
so much upon the manner in which they are harvested and
preserved, that the age alone affords no rule for rejecting them.
They can be kept in good condition for several years.

Fumigated Oats are those which have been exposed to the
vapor of ignited sulphur. They are put through this process
to improve their color. A good deal of the sulphur adheres
to the husk of the oat, which is of a pretty color. A little
sulphur can not do the horse any harm, but light small oats
absorb a considerable quantity. The sulphur is easily de-
tected by rubbing the oats between the hands a little warmed.
When the sulphur is in large quantity, the horses refuse the
oats, or they do not feed heartily. I do not perceive that
fumigated oats are objectionable in other respects.

Kiln-dried Oats are those which have been dried by the
application of fire. They are generally blamed for producing
diabetes ; but though this disease is common enough, it does
not appear wherever kiln-dried oats are used. In many parts
of Russia, oats and all other kinds of grain are kiln-dried in
the straw before they are stored. It is not likely that this
would be the case if it were so prejudicial to the oats as
many people imagine. Most of the kiln-dried oats which are
given to horses have been damaged before they were dried,
and I suspect that the injury received in harvesting or in
storing has more to do with diabetes than kiln-drying has.

Bad Oats.—Some oats are light, containing little nutriment
in proportion to their bulk ; some contain much dust and
chaff, small stones, and earth ; these can hardly be called
good oats, yet there are others which are much worse.
Light, husky, and ill-cleaned oats may be sweet and wholesome ; if they do little good they do no harm, but some oats
are positively injurious to the horse. They may please the
eye tolerably well, but they have a bad smell and a bitter

disagreeable taste. Horses do not like them. After the first day or two they begin to refuse them. That which they eat produces diabetes, a disease which goes under various names, the most common are staling evil and jaw-piss. I do not know how the oats obtain this diuretic property: many, as I have said, attribute it to kiln-drying, many to the oats having been heated, undergone a little fermentation in the stack or in the granary, and a few ascribe it to the oats being ill-harvested, musty, or half-rotten, before they are got off the field. Oats may be frost-bitten, damaged by insects, or in-jured in various other ways, but it seems yet uncertain what condition they are in when they produce diabetes; or what makes them so strongly diuretic. There is no doubt but heated oats will produce diabetes; but whether any other alteration in the oat will have the same effect I do not know. Whatever be the cause, the oats must be changed as soon as it is discovered that they produce

Diabetes.—It is the same disease as that which arises from the use of mowburnt hay. The horses urinate often; the urine is quite colorless, and it is discharged in immense quantities. The horse would drink for ever, and the water is hardly down his throat till it is thrown among his feet in the form of urine. In a day or two his coat stares, he refuses to feed, loses flesh, and becomes excessively weak. He may for a time continue at work; but if he catch cold, and remain at work while he has both the cold and the diabetes upon him, he often becomes glandered.

The horses may not all be alike. In a large stud some are always more affected by these bad oats than others. The worst must go out of work for a while, and some others must be spared as much as possible, while a few may continue at their usual employment. The oats must be changed. Give plenty of beans, some barley, and good hay. Let each horse have a lump of rock-salt, and a piece of chalk in his manger. Put some clay and bean-meal in the water. Carrots, whins, or grass, may be given with benefit. But by changing the oats, and diminishing the work, the disease will generally disappear. If all these means fail, medicine must be tried. A veterinarian will furnish that of the proper kind. But nothing will arrest the disease permanently unless the oats be changed. If not very bad, they do for horses in easy work. But while a horse has diabetes, he can not maintain his con-dition for full work. He would lose flesh though he stood up to the knees in grain.

There is a kind of diabetes which does not proceed from bad food. It is accompanied with a good deal of fever, and requires different treatment; it may be suspected when the food has not been changed; but the eye is red, and the mouth hot, and the horse is dull for a day or two before the staling-evil is upon him.

Preparation of Oats.—Most frequently oats are given raw and whole. But occasionally they are bruised, or coarsely ground. Sometimes they are boiled, and sometimes germinated. There is no objection to bruising but the cost; grinding is never useful, and sometimes it is improper; boiling does not seem to improve oats, and, after the first week, high-fed horses prefer them raw; germination is rarely practised, and only for sick horses. In Lincolnshire oats are malted in salt water, and given for three weeks or a month in spring.

Oats are sometimes given in the straw, either cut or uncut The cost of thrashing is saved, but that is no great gain. It can not be known how much the horse gets. One may be cheated altogether out of a meal and another may be surfeited. There is always some waste, for the horse must be getting very little grain if he eat all the straw he gets along with it, and if he get more, some of the grain is left in the straw.

The Daily Allowance of oats is very variable. Hunters and racers receive almost as much as they will eat during the season of work. The quantity for these horses varies from twelve to sixteen or eighteen pounds per day. Stage and mail horses get about the same allowance. Some will not consume above fourteen pounds, others will manage nearly eighteen. In most stables some other grain is used. For every pound of barley or beans that may be given, rather more than an equal weight is taken off the ordinary allowance of oats. Saddle-horses receive about twelve pounds of oats, cart-horses from ten to fourteen. Those employed on the farm get from four to twelve pounds. The ordinary feeding-measure in Scotland, termed a lippy, holds from three to four pounds of heavy oats.

Substitutes for Oats have been frequently sought. Many experiments have been made to ascertain how far their use might be dispensed with. Roots and bread have both been tried, and the results have shown that horses of moderate work, or even laborious work at a slow pace, can be kept in good condition on carrots or potatoes, with some fodder and no grain. The bread has been made from grain, but it does not seem to have been productive of any economy. Barley beans, peas, and wheat, are partial substitutes for oats. They may form a large portion of the grain; and in Spain barley forms the whole of it. But in this country oats are in general as cheap as any of the other kinds of grain. It has been alleged that oats contain some aromatic, invigorating property, not possessed by other articles; and it does appear that horses fed on roots to the exclusion of grain, are not so gay as grain-fed horses. But whether oats, in equal weight, give the horse more animation than other kinds of grain, is not known with certainty, although common opinion is in their favor.

Oat-Dust is a dirty, brown, useless-like powder, removed from the oat in converting it into meal. It is sometimes mixed with the boiled food. It does not appear to contain any nutriment; and it is blamed for producing balls in the bowels and obstructing them.

Oat-Meal Seeds.—The husk of the oat, as it is sifted from the meal, is sometimes given to horses. This stuff is termed seeds. It always contains a little meal; but is often adulterated by adding what are called the sheeling seeds, the husk without any meal. It does very well as a masticant; and may be mingled with oats, beans, or barley, to make the horse grind them, but it can not yield much nutriment, and many horses will not eat it.

Gruel is made from oat-meal. It is very useful for sick horses: and after a day of severe exertion, when the horse will not take solid food, gruel is the best thing he can have. Few stablemen are able to make it properly. The meal is never sufficiently incorporated with the water. One gallon of good gruel may be made from a pound of meal, which should be thrown into cold water, set on the fire and stirred till boiling, and afterward permitted to simmer over a gentle fire till the water is quite thick. It is not gruel at all if the meal subside and leave the water transparent. Bracy Clark recommends that the meal be well triturated with a little cold water, in a beechen bowl, by a heavy wooden pestle. He thinks the trituration necessary to effect a union between the water and some constituent of the meal. This seems to be one of the " not a few useful and important discoveries" for which Mr. Clarke so clamorously demands our homage.

Oaten Bread is sometimes given to sick horses. It may tempt the appetite and excite a disposition to feed.—*See Bread.*

BARLEY.—There is much difference of opinion concerning this article. Some consider it quite as good as oats in every

16

respect; others allege that it is too laxative; others that it
is heating; some that it is cooling; and some that it is
flatulent. In Spain, and in some other places, horses and
mules receive no grain but barley; in this country it is very
often boiled and given once a day, and sometimes a little is
given raw with every ration of oats; and one or two proprietors have used, and perhaps still use it to the entire exclusion of oats. I can not, from personal observation, tell
what are its effects when given habitually without mixture.
But when given along with a few oats or beans, so as to form
only a part of the feed, I know that barley has none of the
evil properties ascribed to it. I am daily among a large
number of horses, both fast and slow-workers, who receive a
considerable quantity in the course of the twenty-four hours.
At first, it relaxes the bowels a little, and unless it be mingled with chaff the horses swallow the grain whole. They
seem to swallow it more readily than oats. After a week or
two the bowels return to their ordinary state. The skin and
the coat are almost invariably improved by barley, particularly
when boiled and given warm. Like every other kind of
grain, it is somewhat indigestible, until the stomach becomes
accustomed to it. If much be given at first, the horse is
likely to take colic. But by gradually increasing the quantity from day to day, deducting the oats in proportion, the
horse may be safely inured to barley without any other grain.

White tells us of a Southampton postmaster, who fed his
horses entirely on barley and cut straw. They were given together, and the barley was steeped in water twelve hours before
it was given. Two pecks of barley and one bushel of straw
formed the daily allowance. It is said that, upon this, "the
horses did more work, and were in better condition, than
others at the same task upon the ordinary feeding." This
is the usual story whenever any new mode or article is recommended. But nevertheless, it seems sufficiently clear
that barley is not much, if at all inferior to oats. The price
should influence the choice. Spotted or dark-colored barley,
though rejected for malting, may be quite good enough for
food, and it is often to be bought at the price of oats. It
weighs about fifty pounds the bushel. Giving weight for
weight of oats, at forty pounds the bushel, there are only ten
feeds, while barley gives twelve and one half.

Boiled Barley is used chiefly among stage, cart, and road
horses. It is rarely given to the racer or to the hunter, ex-

cept when sick. Boiled to jelly, it is good for a hard dry cough, when there is no fever.

Barley Mash.—Barley steeped or boiled.

Malted Barley is that which has been germinated. It is steeped or moistened, and spread in a layer till it sprout. In that state it is given, though not very often. Horses are very fond of it, and they will take a little of this when they refuse almost everything else. But I do not know how they would do upon it for constant use.

Malt is used a good deal on the continent, and is supposed to be highly nutritious, more so than the raw barley. But in this country the heavy duty upon malt forbids its use for horses; and it is not certain that the process of malting improves the grain so much as to pay its cost. [Malting and cooking are valuable where it is required to lay on flesh; but for working condition the food should be dry.]

Malt Dust, in some places termed *cumins*, is that portion of barley which sprouts in germination. It is generally given to cattle, but horses sometimes get it mixed with the boiled food. They seem to like it very well. I do not know any more about it.

Grains, the refuse of breweries, are sometimes given to horses, and are eaten greedily; but it is alleged that, when given constantly, and so as to form the bulk of the grain, they produce general rottenness, which I suspect in this case means disease of the liver. They are also blamed for producing staggers and founder.

[The cart-horses of the breweries of London are fed on grains. But they are horses largely disposed to fat, and have small lungs and livers. The well-bred horse when in quick work does not take on fat readily; his lungs and liver are large. Grains consist of carbon and fecal matter. In the cart-horse, a part of the carbon of the grains is consumed in breathing, and the balance is deposited in the cellular tissue as fat. In the horse of quick work, the lungs and liver take up all the carbon, which being in excess acts to produce large quantities of bile; this bile is passed off by the bowels, occasioning purging, and by reaction, costiveness. The bowels and the liver sympathize until the liver becomes diseased: and this disease usually is imflammatory in its early stages, ending in death by inflammation immediately or by ulceration ultimately. In the southern country, well-bred horses in quick work, fed on Indian corn (which abounds largely in the fat-forming principle), suffer in the same manner. The well-bred

or blood horse, not in quick work, fats rapidly on corn, and
would doubtless on grains. Where Indian corn is fed exclusively, as in the southern states, diseases of the liver are
very frequent and fatal, and so are inflammation of the bowels
and colic. The mule, in comparison with the blood-horse,
has small lungs and liver, and is slow in his paces. He does
better on Indian corn, especially if ground with the cob on,
and this meal is fed to him. In the training stables of both
the south and the north, in this country, little Indian corn is
fed and this is cracked coarse like hommony.]

Barley Dust is rather better than oat dust, but it is fitter for
cattle or swine than horses.

WHEAT.—There is a general prejudice against wheat as
horse-grain, especially in its raw state. It is supposed to be
poisonous; and without doubt many horses have been destroyed by it. Horses eat it very greedily, and are almost sure to
eat too much, when permitted. Fermentation, colic, and
death, are the consequences; but these are easily avoided.
The grain seems difficult to masticate and also difficult to
digest, and colic may be produced more readily by one measure of wheat than by two of oats. I have never known it
used to the exclusion of oats, but it is sometimes given in
quantities not exceeding four pounds per day, and that divided
among five feeds. Given in this quantity and in this way, it
does no harm that any other grain will not do; and it appears
perfectly to supply the place of the oats which are withheld
for it. For every four pounds of wheat, four pounds, or nearly four and a half, may be deducted from the ordinary allowance of oats.

Still, unless the use of good wheat renders the feeding
cheaper, I do not see that it has any good property to recommend it. If a stone of wheat can be bought for less money
than a stone of oats or beans, it may form a part of the grain,
using it at first very sparingly, and not exceeding the quantity
I mention, four pounds per day. A larger quantity may be
tried on two or three horses, but as I have not seen it tried
to a greater extent, I can not tell what might be the result.

Wheat should never be given alone. Chaff, straw-chaff is
best, serves to divide it, and ensures complete mastication.
The wheat mixes better with the chaff when it is flattened
between a pair of rollers.

Boiled wheat is in common use. It is boiled with beans
and chaff, and generally forms the last feed, or the last but
one, at night. It soon gets sour, and makes the mangers of

wood very foul. No more should be boiled nor given than will be consumed before next morning. It should not be boiled to a jelly. It should always be mixed with chaff.

. *The Husk of Wheat* is very useful, and employed in all town stables. It goes under several names, of which the principal are bran, and pollard, hen-meal, and gudgings. There are two kinds, the one much finer than the other. The coarsest is most usually termed bran ; pollard is supposed to contain and to yield more nutriment; but the difference does not appear to be great.

Bran is seldom give in its dry state, but when beans or peas form the bulk of the grain, some dry bran is added, to make the horse masticate them, and to correct the constipating property of these articles.

Bran-Mash is the usual food of sick horses ; it relaxes the bowels. Its laxative property has been supposed to depend upon mechanical irritation, which can not be true, since bran is constipating to dogs. It contains little nutriment, but supplies the place of grain to an idle or a sick horse, when he must be kept low ; and it helps to keep the bowels in order when the horse is confined to hay without grain. The bran-mash is given either cold or warm. Some horses like it better in one way than another; some will not eat it when mashed, but will take it dry, and a few seem to dislike it altogether. The *cold bran-mash* is usually made with cold water ; as much being poured upon the bran as it will absorb. The *warm mash* is made with boiling water. The mash should be closely covered up till cool enough to be eaten. When oats, beans, and hay, form the ordinary feeding, it is usual to give a large bran-mash, about half a pailful, once a week. It relaxes the bowels, operating upon them very gently, and clearing out their contents. In Scotland, road and canal-horses work none on Sunday. On Saturday night they get a bran-mash instead of their ordinary feed of grain ; but when grass or boiled food is in season, bran is not generally used in this way. When the horses are in high condition, with bowels liable to constipation, the bran-mash prevents any evil that might arise from Sunday's rest ; but when low in flesh, doing all the work they can bear, they can hardly afford to lose a meal, even though they rest on Sunday. [Mashes are laxative, and of course debilitating. They should not be given to lean horses, that are to continue in hard work. But when they are to stand idle, or it is desired to make them fat, mashes act as an alterative and are therefore beneficial.] If the bowels be

16*

costive, the mash may be given, but the grain should be given too; not both together, for a bran-mash almost compels the horse to swallow his corn without mastication.

Many stablemen add bran to the boiled food. They seem to think its use indispensable; they talk as if the food could not be eaten or not boiled without the addition of bran. This is nonsense. The food may be of constipating quality, and bran will be wanted to correct that; or the horse's health or his work may make bran a useful article in his food. But to give bran as nourishment to a horse under ordinary circumstances, is to give him almost the dearest food he can live upon even when his work does not absolutely demand stronger food. A shilling's worth of oats is a great deal more nourishing than a shilling's worth of bran. To the horse, bran is just what gruel is to man; but the relative cost of the two is very different.

Wheaten Bread, either brown or white, is much relished by nearly all horses. Occasionally it may be given to a horse that has been tired off his appetite, or to an invalid. It should never be less than twenty-four hours' old, and it should be given only in small quantity. Bakers sometimes give their horses a good deal of it; but it ought to be mixed with chaff. Some will not eat it till it is mashed by pouring boiling water over it.

Buck-Wheat, or Brank, is hardly known in this country. It is used on the Continent, and the horses are said to thrive on it. Young says that a bushel goes farther than two of oats, and that, mixed with at least four times as much bran, one bushel will be full feed for any horse for a week. The author of the Farmer's Calendar thinks he has seen it produce a stupifying effect; and Bracy Clarke says it appeared to him to be very laxative. In Holland, and many parts of Germany and Norway, it is made into a black bread, with which the horses are fed.

Maize, or Indian-Corn, is much used as a horse-food in America, and in various parts of Europe. Cobbett recommended its introduction, and among its other uses, spoke of horse-feeding. I do not know that it has been tried sufficiently to determine whether it might be used with advantage during a scarcity of other grain. Probably it ought to be boiled and mixed with chaff, but horses eat it greedily when raw. Bracy Clarke says it is apt to clog the stomach and affect the feet in such a singular way, that the hoofs frequently fall off when the horse is on a journey. He alludes to founder, but seems ignorant that any kind of grain, when improperly given, will produce the same effect. Maize does it more readily [perhaps on account of its greater amount of carbon or the fat-forming principle].

RYE is used in Germany, but generally in the shape of bread made from the whole flour and bran ; and it is not unusual, in travelling through some parts of that country, and of Holland, to see the postillions help themselves and their horses from the same loaf.*

BEANS.—There are several varieties of the bean in use as horse-food, but I do not know that one is better than another. The small plump bean is preferred to the large shrivelled kind. Whichever be used, the beans should be old, sweet, and sound. New beans are indigestible and flatulent ; they produce colic, and founder very readily. They should be at least a year old. Beans are often ill-harvested ; and when musty or mouldy, though quite sweet internally, horses do not like them. They are often attacked by an insect which consumes much of the flour, and destroys the vitality of the rest. The ravages of the insect are plain enough. The bean is excavated, light, brittle, and bitter tasted. A few in this state may do no harm ; but when the beans are generally infected, it is not likely that they are eaten with impunity, and very often the horse refuses them altogether. Damp, musty, ill-kept beans, though old, are as flatulent as those which are new. All kinds are constipating.

Though in very general use for horses, beans are not so extensively employed as oats. According to the chymists, they contain more nutriment ; and in practice it is universally allowed that beans are much the stronger of the two. The comparison, however, is almost always made in reference to a measured quantity. A bushel of beans is, beyond all doubt, more nutritious than a bushel of o' .s, but it is questionable whether a pound of beans is stronger than a pound of oats. Beans weigh about sixty-three pounds per bushel, and if given in an oat measure, the horse may be getting nearly double allowance. This, I am persuaded, often happens, and hence arise those complaints about the heating, inflammatory nature of beans ; [they are constipating and their heating quality is secondary, by inducing fever as a consequence of costiveness.] The horse becomes plethoric ; the groom says the humors are flying about him. It is very likely that he would be in

* British Husbandry, vol. i., p. 146.

the very same state if he were getting an equal weight of oats.

If beans do not afford more nutriment, weight for weight of oats, they at least produce more lasting vigor. To use a common expression, they keep the stomach longer. The horse can travel farther; he is not so soon exhausted. " I remember." says Nimrod, " hearing Mr. Warde exclaim, as his hounds were settling to their fox, ' Now we shall see what horses eat old oats, and what eat new.' I am inclined to think that this distinction may be applied to horses that eat beans, and those that eat none, for they help to bring him home at the end of a long day, and support his strength in the run." I believe Nimrod is quite right. In the coaching-stables beans are almost indispensable to horses that have to run long stages. They afford a stronger and more permanent stimulus than oats alone, however good. Washy horses, those of slender carcass, can not perform severe work without a liberal allowance of beans; and old horses need them more than the young. The quantity varies from three to six pounds per day; but in some of the coaching-stables the horses get more, a pound of oats being deducted for every pound of beans. Cart-horses are often fed on beans, to the exclusion of all other grain, but they are always given with dry bran, which is necessary to keep the bowels open, and to ensure mastication. Beans are not in general use for racehorses, but are sometimes given to bad eaters. They are usually split and hulled, which is a superfluous process. For old horses they should be broken or bruised.

The bowels are very apt to become constipated, and dangerously obstructed when the horse is getting a large allowance of beans. They are so constipating that, as they are increased in quantity, bran must be added in proportion. Beans, and bean-straw, which is as constipating as the beans, should not be both used at the same time.

Some horses will not eat beans. The Irish horses, when first brought to this country, always refuse them; they invariably pick out the oats and leave the beans. It does not appear that they dislike them, for after they begin, they feed as well as other horses. Ultimately, they seem to discover that beans are for eating, although it is often a long time ere they make the discovery.

The horse, however, may soon be taught. Let him fast for an hour beyond the feeding-time, and then give him *half* a ration of beans without oats. If he still reject them, offer them split or broken, or moisten them, and sprinkle a little oatmeal over them, sufficient to make the beans white. If he still demur, put another horse, a hungry one, beside him, and he will soon teach his ignorant neighbor; if he do not, I can not tell what will.

Bean meal, or *flour*, is sometimes added to the boiled food; but it is oftener given in the water to cure the staling-evil.

PEAS are seldom used without beans, with which they are mixed in large or small quantities. They may be given without either beans or other grain, but much care is necessary to inure the horse to them. Peas seem to be very indigestible, more so than beans, and perhaps as much so as wheat; but when given very sparingly at first, they may be used with perfect safety. It is often said that peas swell so much in the stomach as to burst it. This is an error. Peas do absorb much water, and swell more perhaps than beans, but they never swell so much as to burst the stomach, for the horse can not or will not eat such a large quantity. When the stomach is burst, it is from fermentation, not from swelling of the peas. All kinds of food will produce the same result when the horse is permitted to gorge himself, or when he is fed in full measure upon food that he has not been accustomed to; but peas seem to be rather more apt to ferment than some other kinds of grain.

Peas should be sound, and a year old. They weigh, on an average, sixty-four pounds per bushel. Pea-meal is sometimes given in the same way, and for the same purposes as that of the bean. Some prefer it for diabetes, and in a few places it is given in the water for baiting on the road.

VETCH SEED has been employed for feeding horses, but I have learned nothing of the result.

BREAD.—In former times it was customary to feed horses with bread, and the statute book is said to contain several acts of parliament relating to the manner of making it. Gervase Markham, a very old author, says, " Horse bread which is made of clean beans, clean peas, or clean fitches, feedeth exceedingly." It is not many years since a bread, composed of wheat, oats, barley, and beans, ground and mixed in varying proportions, was used in the racing-stables. The bread was well baked, and given when sufficiently old to crumble down and mingle with the grain. Eggs and some spices were sometimes introduced in making it. Nothing of the kind, so far as I know, is now used in this country.

In different parts of Europe bread forms the customary

food of the horses. A French periodical of 1828 mentions
an agriculturist " who fed his horses with a bread composed
of thirty bushels of oatmeal, and an equal quantity of rye-
flour, to which he added a portion of yeast, and nine bushels
of potatoes reduced to a pulp. With this bread he kept seven
horses, each having twelve pounds per day in three feeds. It
was broken into small pieces, and mixed with a little moistened chaff." He had fed his horses in this way for four
years. Previously he had used oats, hay, and straw chaff.

The Magazine of Domestic Economy, February number
for 1837, tells us that one ton of oats made into bread yields
more nutriment than six tons of the raw article, and that in
Sweden this has been proved by experience. It has never
been proved in Scotland, and I dare say it never will. It is
true, however, that a bread composed of oatmeal and rye, in
equal quantities, has long been used for horses in Sweden.
It is broken down and mixed with cut straw. It is in common use over different parts of Germany. I can not learn
any particulars as to the mode of making. nor of the quantity
given, nor of the horses' condition. In France, many attempts have been made to produce a bread that would wholly
or partially supersede oats, which seem to be comparatively
precious on the continent. Buckwheat, rye, barley, wheat,
and potatoes, have been tried in varying proportion, and, according to several accounts, with success. But it does not
appear very distinctly why these articles should be converted
into bread, which is a costly process, rather than given raw
or boiled. It is indeed alleged that some of the constituent
principles are not digestible until they have undergone fermentation; and it may be so, but no proof is shown that I
have seen.

LINSEED in small quantities, either whole or ground, raw
or boiled, is sometimes given to sick horses. It is too nutri
tious for a fevered horse, but is very useful for a cough, and
it makes the skin loose and the coat glossy. Half a pint may
be mixed with the usual feed every night. For a cough it
should be boiled, and given in a bran mash, to which two or
three ounces of coarse sugar may be added.

OIL CAKE, ground and given in the boiled food, when not very
rich, consisting chiefly or entirely of roots, is much stronger
than bran, and stronger, perhaps, than oatmeal seeds. Two
to four pounds per day is the usual allowance. It makes the
hair glossy. Horses seem to tire of it soon, but the farmer
will find it useful for helping his horses through the winter.

HEMPSEED used to be given to racers a few days before running. It was supposed to be invigorating and "good for the wind." I believe it is not now employed, except occasionally to stallions, during the travelling season. Some give four or six ounces every night.

SAGO.—In the year 1839, this article was a good deal spoken of as an excellent food for horses. Mr. Ritchie, veterinary surgeon of Edinburgh, made some experiments with it, and detailed them in the Quarterly Journal of Agriculture. He tried it with only one horse. He gave daily three pounds of sago stirred into two gallons of boiling water; and this quantity was divided into three feeds. After a few days he found that this feeding made the horse sweat more at his work. He then gave the sago nearly dry, or just moistened, by adding to it about four ounces of water; and thus fed, the horse perspired no more than he had done upon oats and hay.

I have no doubt but sago might be used partially as a substitute for oats, and possibly it might, under certain circumstances, be used to the exclusion of other grain. But from my own experience of it on several horses, I found,

1. That no horse would eat it unmixed with other grain.

2. That very few would eat it raw, even when mixed with oats.

3. That none refused it when it was boiled with oats or beans.

4. That it is not profitable if it costs more than twelve shillings per cwt., while oats are twenty shillings per boll.

SUGAR.—Mr. Black, veterinary surgeon of the 14th Light Dragoons, informed me that sugar was tried as an article of horses' food during the peninsular war. The experiment was made at the Brighton depôt, upon ten horses, during a period of three months. Each got eight pounds per day at four rations. They took to it very readily, and it was remarked that their coats became fine, smooth, and glossy. They got no grain, and only seven pounds of hay, instead of the ordinary allowance, which is twelve pounds. The sugar seemed to supply the place of grain so well, that it would probably have been given to the horses abroad; but peace came, and the circumstances which rendered the use of sugar for grain desirable ceased. The horses returned to their usual diet; but several of those who were the subjects of this experiment became crib-biters. [Sugar wants nitrogen, but abounds in carbon. It would not, therefore, answer as a horse food. The food must contain nitrogen to form muscle.]

That the sugar might not be appropriated to other purposes, it was slightly scented with assafœtida, which did not produce any apparent effect upon the horses.

"FRUIT, as pumpkins, apples, &c., and sweet potatoes in America, figs and chestnuts in Spain and Italy, apples in some parts of France, and numerous other fructified exotics, are occasionally employed as food for horses."[*] *Horse Chestnuts*, it is said, "would probably form a valuable article of medicinal food for horses. In Turkey the nuts are ground, and mixed with other food; and they are regarded as a remedy for broken wind, and serviceable to horses troubled with coughs."[†] *Haws*, the fruit of the hawthorn, have been employed by West, of Hampshire, as an article of food for farm-horses, with what profit I have not learned. "The people of Medjid feed their horses regularly on dates. At Deyrach, in the country of the Flassæ, dates are mixed with the clover. Barley, however, is the most usual food in all parts of Arabia."[‡]

FLESH.—The structure of the horse does not seem adapted to the assimilation of animal food. But some seem to have no dislike to it; and it is well to know that it may, to a certain extent, supply the place of grain. I have seen them lick blood repeatedly and greedily. Bracy Clark says he has "seen a well-attested account in a magazine, of a colt that was in the habit of visiting a pantry window which looked into his paddock, and of stealing and eating mutton, beef, veal, and poultry. Pork he seemed to reject. In the East Indies, meat boiled to rags, to which is added some kinds of grain and butter, is made into balls and forced down the horse's throat.—*Carpenter's Introduc. to the Wars of India.* Also sheep's heads during a campaign are boiled for horses in that country."[‖]

"While at the stable of Mr. Mellings, of Wakefield, the groom would let me see a flesh-eating horse. He brought about a pound of roasted beef and as much raw bacon, which he warmed. I took away the horse, while the groom put the meat in one corner of the manger, and a feed of oats in the other. I put in the horse and directed his nose to the oats, but he darted from that to the bacon, which he greedily devoured. He then ate his oats. The groom said this horse

* Blaine's Vet. Outlines, p. 94. London, 1832.
† Comp. Grazier, p. 529. 1833.
‡ Past and Present State of the English Racer. Hookham. 1826.
‖ Clarke, Pharmacop. Equina. London, 1833.

would finish the bone of a leg of mutton in a few minutes, and that roasted meat was his favorite dish."* The wealthy people of Medjid frequently give flesh to their horses, raw as well as boiled, together with all the offals of the table. "I knew a man at Hamah, in Syria, who assured me that he had often given his horses washed meat after a journey, to make them endure it with greater facility. The same person related to me, that, apprehensive of the governor of the town taking a liking to his favorite horse, he fed it for a fortnight entirely on roasted pork, which raised its mettle to such a height that it became absolutely unmanageable, and could no longer be an object of desire to the governor."†

Fish.—"In Iceland, it is stated by Buffon, that dried fish is made the food of horses; and my friend William Bullock, senior, lately informed me that he saw them in the same practice in Norway."‡

Eggs are sometimes given to stallions in the travelling season, for exciting desire, and to other horses for producing a smooth coat. They are quite useless for either purpose, at least as they are given, only one or two at a time. If they are to do any good the horse would need a dozen of them, or thereabouts, I should think. One or two, however, can have no good effect. The egg is chipped, *starred*, as they call it, all round, and given raw, like a ball.

Several, many horses have been lost by the egg sticking in the throat, and producing suffocation. If eggs must be given, let them be broken and mixed with a mash, or boiled hard and added to the grain. But I see no need for them in any shape.

Milk.—In this country, milk is not used as an article of food for grown-up horses. Occasionally it is given to stallions in the covering season. A mash is made of milk, bran, and oil-cake, ground; and in Ayrshire, whey is frequently given to stallions as a drink. It is supposed to be " amatory food." The Arabs, in traversing the desert are said to give their horses camel's milk when forage fails. Major Denham, speaking of some horses he met with among the Tiboos, says: " Two of them were very handsome, though small; and on remarking their extreme fatness, I was not a little surprised to learn that they were fed entirely on camel's milk, grain be-

* The Veterinian, vol. v., p. 25. Letter from Mr. Garland, V. S. Wakefield.
† Past and Present State of the English Racer. 1836.
‡ B. Clarke, Pharm. Eq.

17

ing too scarce and valuable an article for the Tiboos to spare them. They drink it both sweet and sour; and animals in higher condition I scarcely ever saw."[*]

Mare's Milk.—For the first six months of the young horse's life, his principal food is mare's milk. He begins to eat much sooner, but few are entirely weaned before this time. Farm mares are usually put to gentle work two or three weeks after parturition. Her work should be moderate, and her diet substantial. She is often treated as if work could have no influence on the milk. When she has much to do, the milk is neither good nor abundant, and the foal is half-starved. The foal is sometimes permitted to follow his dam to the field, where he may occasionally suckle her. This renders the foal familiar, and at an early age reconciles him to subjection, and it prevents engorgement of the udder. Bad weather, or the nature of the mare's work, may forbid the practice. When the mare comes home, the foal is put to suck her. In some places, the milk is previously stripped on to the ground, and the udder bathed with cold water, or vinegar and water. This is not necessary. It is supposed that the milk is injured and pernicious when the mare is overheated; but, in the first place, her work should never be so severe as to overheat her; and, in the second, the milk is not apparently altered when she is. Hard work will diminish the quantity of milk, and render it less nutritious, but it will do no more. [Hard work diminishes the carbonaceous portion of the food; it contains less sugar of milk and less oil.] If the foal be withheld till the udder be gorged and distended, a little inflammation will take place, and the milk will be bad. In such case it is proper to draw off a portion before the foal is put to it; and it may also be proper to bathe the udder with cold water. But to empty it or to bathe it merely because the mare has been perspiring, is absurd; and to neglect both mare and foal till the udder needs such treatment, betrays very bad management.

Sometimes a mare, especially with her first foal, will not permit sucking. She requires to be held, to have the udder rubbed with the hand and stripped. Hold her by the head and keep her steady till the foal is satisfied. Do so five or six times a day. On the third day, or thereabouts, she usually begins to perform her duty without interference. In general, the mare is merely restless; she will not stand quiet till the foal suckles her; but sometimes she is ill-natured or vicious

* Denham's Travels in Africa.

If she strike at the foal, threaten her with the lash, and hold up one of her fore-feet. If she continue obstinate and resists the repeated efforts of the foal so long that he is likely to get exhausted, put the twitch on the mare's nose. But, if possible, she must be managed without this, and every time the foal is to suckle her, she must be patiently tried before applying the twitch. It is not good to meddle with the foal by way of assisting or directing him to the udder. He may be very awkward, but he soon learns. It is sufficient to control the mare, and this often requires a great deal of patience and perseverance. After the foal has been permitted to suckle her, she is reconciled to it in a day or two, and may afterward prove a very good nurse. Confinement in a dark loose box sometimes renders her kinder.

Unless the mare be very obstinate, or the foal very weak and awkward, no cow's milk should be given to it. If its hunger be appeased by drinks, it will make no attempt to suckle, and it is only by constantly persevering with the mother that she can be brought to her duty.

Cow's Milk.—Should the mare die, or become unfit, from sickness or a diseased udder, to suckle her foal, it must be fed with cow's milk. If a week or two old, it may be fed from a pail in the same way as calves. The man puts his hand into a pail of milk, with his fingers projecting above the surface. The calf or foal seizes the fingers, and sucks up the milk, which should always be new and warm from the cow. In a little while the young animal learns to drink it. If so young or stupid that it can not be fed in this way, the milk must be poured into its mouth. Take a teapot, or teakettle with a small spout. Surround the spout with three or four folds of linen cloth, sufficient to make it soft, but not too large. Place this prepared spout in the foal's mouth, and it will suck the milk from the vessel. An article might be made for the purpose, of tin. The aperture in the spout should not be much more than an eighth of an inch in calibre, otherwise the milk will come faster than the foal can swallow it. Let the spout rise from the bottom of the vessel, so that the air can not get into it when the foal is sucking.

I do not know how much milk a foal will consume. It should be given four or five times a day.

Weaning.—When the foal is to be taken from the udder, he is either shut up in a loose house by himself, or turned to pasture; in either case his cry must not be heard by the dam. When within hearing, both become fretful, the one unwilling

to work, and the other refusing to eat. Once or twice a day
they rejoin each other for a short time, in order that the foal
may empty the udder, and not be suddenly deprived of its
natural food. When the foal is removed all at once, as by
death, the mare's udder should be stripped once or twice a
day, for perhaps a week ; but at no time need it be quite
drained. Spare diet, harder work, or milk physic, will diminish the secretion of milk, and one or another should be
employed, if the mare must give up nursing while her milk is
abundant.

In connexion with foals, I will just observe here, though
out of place, that the young animal should be well fed from
the day he is born. A starved foal or colt is almost never
well made when he arrives at maturity. He is always, as
stablemen say, *a weed ;* and though bad shapes, such as light
carcass and spare quarters, are not supposed to have any connexion with the feeding, I am well persuaded that a poor diet
is a common cause of them.   ▲

COMPOSITION OF FOOD.

The articles used as food for horses have been submitted
to chymical examination, with the purpose of ascertaining the
amount of nutritive matter yielded by each in proportion to its
bulk.

The Nutritive Matter of plants consists of starch, sugar,
gluten, and extract. These four substances exist together in
varying proportions. In some vegetables, as carrots, the
sugar is most abundant ; in many, as in the different kinds of
grain, starch predominates. Gluten abounds in grain and
pulse, while it is deficient in the most of grasses. Extract is
wanting in grain and several of the roots, while beans, peas,
herbage, plants, and grasses, possess a considerable quantity.

It is not known whether a certain quantity of any one of
these substances will produce the same effect as an equal
quantity of any other ; starch and sugar, though both nutritive
articles, are very different in many respects, and it is not likely that the one can perform all the functions of the other.
But this subject, so far as I know, has not been put to trial.
I am disposed to believe that each of the nutritive matters
performs its own duty ; that life may be maintained for a time
by any one of them ; that certain combinations will produce
results different from other combinations ; and that it is very
desirable to know the power of each individual substance, and

the power of every possible combination, which must vary according to the number of the nutritive matters, and their relative proportions.

The animal economy exists in very different states at different times. It is almost certain that in all states it demands and consumes more than one of the nutritive articles; but it is probable that in particular states there is a predominating demand for sugar, in another for starch, and so on. From one or two circumstances, it would appear as if sugar were useful or necessary for making fat, while a large quantity may be pernicious if severe labor forbid the formation of fat. Diabetes may perhaps be explained upon this supposition. Mowburnt hay, which contains a large quantity of sugar, may be eaten with impunity by idle or half-worked horses. It is said to make them fat. But in the coaching-stables it is a destructive poison. The sugar enters the circulation, but the system can not appropriate it, and the kidneys have to labor incessantly in order to eject it with the urine, a large quantity of which must be made to carry off the sugar. This is entirely a conjectural explanation, the truth or error of which can not be proved without experiments.

If it were possible to learn what combinations are merely fattening, what invigorating; what producing bone, what flesh, what milk; and what the signs which indicate a demand for one substance more than for another, the feeding of horses and other animals would become a science. It is possible that we often err in giving that which is rejected at the time, but which might be highly acceptable in some other state of the system. If we knew, for instance, what combination of gluten, starch, and sugar, were invigorating and what fattening, it would be absurd to give the former to an ox while preparing for the butcher, or the latter to a racer while preparing for the course. The ox wants no vigor, and the racer wants no fat. That which is not wanted may be inconvenient, or it may be rejected as useless, the system of the animal not demanding it, or his habits forbidding its appropriation. It will be long, however, ere the feeding of live stock becomes a matter of such accuracy, and perhaps it is not attainable. But it may be good to remember that what the chymists term nutritive matter, is composed of four substances, which do not each produce the same effect; that in combination, it is probable the effects vary according to the proportions in which the substances operate together; and that, in particular states

17*

of the system, one or two may be in greater request than the others.

BESIDES THE NUTRITIVE MATTER, food contains other substances. Roots, and herbage undried, contain a large quantity of water; and new grain and new hay have more than the old. In many articles there is much woody fibre, which passes through the stomach and bowels like inert matter, having no nutritious nor any medical property. This, however, is useful; for, to be in health, it is necessary that the stomach and bowels suffer a moderate degree of distention, which is most cheaply, and perhaps most safely produced by the woody fibre. Bean straw, I believe, furnishes more in proportion to its bulk than any other fodder; grains and roots have not much. Hay stands next to straw. It is probable that several kinds of food, possibly all the kinds, contain some ingredients neither inert nor nutritious, but still very useful. To digest the food, the stomach must be in a particular state; the food itself excites that state; but it is not likely that every portion or ingredient of the food is equally able to rouse the digestive process. In some articles a bitter ingredient is found, which is supposed to stimulate the stomach, and other portions of the digestive apparatus to action. It has been termed.

BITTER EXTRACT.—It is distinguished from all other ingredients chiefly by its bitter taste. In some plants it is found in great abundance, in some others, not at all, or only in certain stages of their growth. It maintains some relation to the amount of nutriment. Those plants which have little nutritious matter have much of the bitter principle, and grain has most before it is ripe.

"It seems to be as essential to herbivorous, as salt is to carnivorous animals. It acts as a natural stimulant. Several experiments have proved that it passes through the stomach and bowels without suffering any diminution in quantity, or any change in composition. No cattle will thrive upon food which does not contain a portion of this bitter principle. The researches of the late Mr. Sinclair, gardener to the Duke of Bedford, fully established this fact. As recorded in the Hortus Gramineus Woburnensis, they show that, when sheep are fed exclusively upon yellow turnips, which contain almost no bitter matter, they instinctively seek and devour any provender which does. If unable to find it, they sicken and die."

[A TABLE OF THE COMPARATIVE VALUE OF DIFFERENT KINDS OF FODDER FOR CATTLE has been published by M

Antoine, in France, and is the result of experiments made by the principal agriculturists on the continent, Thaer, Gemerhausen, Petró, Rieder, Weber, Krantz, Andrê, Block, De Dombasle, Boussingault, Meyer, Plotow, Pohl, Smée, Crud, Schwertz, Pabst. It is unnecessary to give the figures which each of these experimentalists have set down, but the mean of their experiments being taken, there is more chance of the result being near the truth. Allowance must be made for the different qualities of the same food on different soils and different seasons. In very dry summers the same weight of any green food will be much more nourishing than in a dripping season. So likewise any fodder raised on a rich dry soil will be more nourishing than on a poor wet one. The standard of comparison is the best upland meadow-hay, cut as the flower expands, and properly made and stacked, without much heating; in short, hay of the best quality. With respect to hay, such is the difference in value, that if 100 lbs. of the best is used, it will require 120 lbs. of a second quality to keep the same stock as well, 140 lbs. of the third, and so on, till very coarse and hard hay, not well made, will only be of half the value, and not so fit for cows or store cattle, even when given in double the quantity. While good hay alone will fatten cattle, inferior hay will not do so without other food.

100 lbs. of good hay is equal in nourishment to
102 " " Lattermath hay
90 " " hay-made Clover, when the blossom is completely developed
86 " " Ditto, before the blossom expands.
96 " " Clover, 2d crop, is equal in nourishment to
98 " " Lucerne hay
80 " " Saintfoin hay
91 " " Tare hay
90 " " Spergula arvensis, dried
146 " " Clover hay, after the seed
410 " " Green clover
457 " " Vetches or tares, green
275 " " Green Indian corn
425 " " Green spergula
335 " " Stems and leaves Jerusalem artichoke
341 " " Cow-cabbage leaves
600 " " Beet-root leaves
300 " " Potato halm
374 " " Shelter wheat-straw
442 " " Rye straw
195 " " Oat straw
153 " " Peas halm
150 " " Vetch halm
140 " " Bean halm
195 " " Buckwheat straw
270 " " Dried stalks of Jerusalem artichokes

400 lbs. of Dried stalks of Indian corn
250 " " Millet straw
201 " " Raw potatoes
175 " " Boiled do.
220 " " White Silesian beet
339 " " Mangel-wurzel
504 " " Turnips
276 " " Carrots
287 " " Cohlkalis
308 " " Swedish turnips
350 " " Do. do. with the leaves on
54 " " Rye
45 " " Wheat
54 " " Barley
59 " " Oats
50 " " Votches
45 " " Peas
45 " " Beans
64 " " Buckwheat
57 " " Indian corn
32 " " French Beans, dried
47 " " Chestnuts
68 " " Acorns
50 " " Horse-chestnuts
62 " " Sun-flower seed
69 " " Linseed cake
105 " " Wheat bran
109 " " Rye bran
167 " " Wheat, peas, and oat chaff
179 " " Rye and Barley chaff
72 " " Dried lime-tree leaves
82 " " " oak leaves
67 " " " Canada poplar leaves.

Lattermath hay is good for cows, not for horses. The second cut is generally considered as inferior in nourishment to the first. New hay is not wholesome. At Paris, when a load of 1,000 kilos is bargained for, the seller must deliver—if between haymaking and October 1, 1,300 kilos—from October 1 to April 1, 1,100 kilos—and after April, only 1,000. This is fair, and allows for loss of weight in drying. In London a load of new hay is 20 cwt., of old hay, only 18 cwt.

The dried halm of the trifolium incarnatum, after the seed is ripe, is little better than straw. Clover, lucerne, and saintfoin, are generally supposed to lose three fourths of their weight in drying; but in general they lose more, especially in moist climates, where the sap is more diluted. When touched by the frost, they become very unwholesome, and should never be given to cattle except quite dry.

Straw is, on the whole, but poor food, and unless cattle have something better with it, they will not keep in any condition; when given with turnips or other roots, straw corrects their watery nature, and is very useful; cut into chaff it is very good for sheep when fed on turnips and oil-cake, and when newly thrashed is as good nearly as hay. By a judicious mixture of different kinds of food, a more economical mode of feeding may be substituted for a more expensive one, and the same result obtained. The value of straw depends much on the soil; a very clean crop will not give so nourishing straw as one containing many succulent weeds. Peas and vetch halm are superior to straw, especially when cut into chaff; it is by some thought equal to hay. The same may be said of bean halm not left too long in the field, and cut before it is completely dry. Buckwheat halm is of little value: it is thought unwholesome if given to sheep.

16 lbs. of raw, or 14 lbs. of boiled potatoes will allow a diminution of 8 lbs of hay.

Turnips will feed store pigs, but they will not fatten on them. Carrots and parsnips are excellent for horses, and, when boiled, will fatten hogs. Ruta-baga is liked by horses: it makes their coats fine, but must not be given in too great quantity, or it will gripe them.

FEEDING.—A certain quantity of food is required to keep an animal alive and in health: this is called his necessary ration of food: if he has more he will gain flesh, or give milk or wool.

A horse usually requires $2\frac{1}{2}$ per cent. of his live weight in hay per day if he has no other food ; if he works, 3 per cent. : an ox, 2 per cent. ; if he works, 2½ per cent. : a milch cow, 3 per cent. : a fatting ox, 5 per cent. at first ; 4½ per cent. when half fat ; and only 4 per cent. when fat ; or 4½ on the an average. Sheep grown up take 3½ per cent. of their weight in hay per day, to keep in store condition.

Growing animals require more food, and should never be stinted.*

The *table* below shows the relative value of different articles of food, as ascertained by practice ; good meadow hay being taken at 100.

Hay	-	-	-	100	Carrots -	-	-	- 250 to 300
Clover hay	-	-	- 80 to 100	Turnips -	-	-	- 500
Green clover -	-	- 450 to 500	Cabbage -	-	-	- 200 to 300
Wheat straw -	-	- 400 to 500	Peas and beans	-	- 30 to 50
Barley straw -	-	- 200 to 400	Wheat -	-	-	- 50 to 60
Oat straw	-	-	- 200 to 400	Barley -	-	-	- 50 to 60
Pea straw	-	-	- 100 to 150	Oats -	-	-	- 40 to 70
Potatoes	-	-	200	Indian corn	-	-	- 50
Old potatoes -	-	-	400	Oil cake -	-	-	- 20 to 40

The above table represents the average results from a number of experiments made in France and Holland.]

PREPARATION OF FOOD.

Some of the articles used as food frequently undergo preparation before they are given : they are dried, boiled, bruised, cut, and so forth.

One object is to economize the consumption ; another to render the food more easily eaten ; a third to correct some unwholesome quality ; a fourth to give it a new property ; a fifth to ensure complete mastication ; a sixth to ensure deliberate ingestion ; and a seventh to preserve the food. These will be best illustrated by considering the processes to which the food is submitted.

Drying need hardly be mentioned. Its principal object is to preserve the food. Besides depriving it of a large quantity of water, it seems, in some cases, to alter the article in other respects. New oats are purgative ; those which are kiln-dried are diuretic. The drying in this case gives a new property, which is not beneficial, but can not, perhaps, be avoided. If the change were effected entirely by taking away water, the food should be restored to its original state by moistening it. This does not happen. Drying renders grain and fodder constipating ; new grain and new hay are always laxative. Grass, when converted into hay, suffers fermentation, and loses more than half its weight. According

* Jour. Roy. Ag. Soc.

:o Sinclair, 7,829 pounds of rye grass lost 4 494 in drying It becomes still drier as it becomes older.

CUTTING THE FODDER.—Hay, straw, and grass, are sometimes cut into short pieces. A portion of this is mixed with grain, and another portion is given by itself, instead of rack hay ; in a few cases the grain is given oftener than usual, and divided among all the allotted quantity of fodder. Chaff-cutting is general on the continent. In this country it prevails only in large establishments, and not in all of these. When the fodder is cut, it is termed chaff, and the cutting-machine is termed a chaff-cutter.

The Chaff-Cutter varies in power and in construction. Some are worked by the hand, others are driven by a horse or an ass, a few by steam, and a few by water. Some have the cutting-knives attached to the fly-wheel, and others have them mounted on a skeleton cylinder. Models are to be seen in most of the agricultural museums ; and the machines themselves are kept at the makers of agricultural implements. With an ordinary chaff-cutter two men may easily cut 200 stones of hay per week, working ten hours per day. One feeds, and another turns the knives ; each changing place with the other as he gets tired. At the same, or less cost, a much larger quantity can be cut by using horse-power. The chaff, whether of hay or straw, is all cut very short, perhaps from a fourth to a half inch ; the shorter the better, if it is to be mixed with grain.

The Utility of Cutting has been much exaggerated. There are five or six advantages alleged to be gained by cutting, two of which are in favor of the horse ; the others in favor of economy. By cutting the hay it is said that waste is prevented ; that mastication of the grain is ensured ; that damaged provender is consumed ; that chaff is easily eaten ; that it is easily and accurately distributed ; and that horses like a mixture of chaff and grain better than grain alone. All this requires some elucidation.

Prevention of Waste.—It has been said that cutting the hay is attended with a saving, according to some, of one fourth ; or, according to others, of a third, and even a half, in the whole consumption : that is to say, a stone of chaff will go as far as two stones of hay. This is very like nonsense. But the accounts, though different, are probably all true. Much may be saved, yet all the saving must not be attributed to cutting, but to greater care of the hay after it is cut. The chaff is no more nutritious than the hay ; the horse needs as much, and will eat as much of the one as of the other; but a smaller quantity being given at a time, the horse has it not in his power to waste so much. The chaff is supplied in limited measure; it is put into the manger; if the horse is not hungry it lies there till he is. But it is different with hay The rack often receives as much at one time as might serve two days. After the horse has appeased his hunger, he amuses himself by pulling the hay among his feet, and, selecting such portions as suit his palled appetite, the remainder is wasted. All this is lost through carelessness. As much chaff might be wasted, but it is not so easy, not so convenient, there is no inducement to give so much at one time; and the horse can not so readily destroy that which he is not disposed to eat. If the hay could be given in measured quantities like the chaff, and the horse prevented from wasting any, cutting, it is obvious, would effect no saving whatever. This can be done well enough. The hay can be weighed and supplied in small quantities; by giving it oftener than usual —no more at a time than the horse will eat—none will be lost. There would be additional trouble in doing so; but the trouble of cutting and serving chaff is greater.

Mastication of the Grain Insured.—By mixing chaff with the oats and beans, these articles must be broken down before they can be swallowed. They can not be entirely separated from the chaff; and the chaff is too sharp to be swallowed without a good deal of mastication. In grinding the chaff, the horse must grind the grain. This is the most important use of chaff. Many horses swallow both oats and beans without chewing them. That which is unbroken passes through the body entire, and, affording no nutriment, is lost. Chaff prevents this. Still, when the grain is bruised before it is given, chaff may be dispensed with. The horse might swallow much of it as he received it, yet it would be digested; we rarely, almost never, see broken beans or broken oats among the evacuations. Once broken, they must be dissolved before they escape. Nevertheless, if mastication and digestion of the grain are to be promoted, it is a better practice to mingle chaff with it than to bruise it.

Deliberate Ingestion Insured.—Many horses swallow their grain in great haste; when much is eaten, this is dangerous. The stomach is filled, overloaded, before it has time to make preparation for acting upon its contents. The food ferments, and the horse takes colic, which is often fatal. By adding chaff to his grain, the horse must take more time to eat it

Satiety takes place before the stomach is overloaded, and time is given for the commencement of digestion, before fermentation can occur.   In this way chaff is very useful, especially where the horses receive large meals after long fasts.

Consumption of Damaged Provender Promoted.—When the hay is not of the best quality, the bad is rejected and lost; but by converting it into chaff, the horse must either eat the whole or leave the whole.   He can make no selection.   This is a favorite argument, and often urged on the side of cutting.

When the fodder is damaged in only a slight degree, the mowburnt or musty hay may be eaten by some horses with impunity; and, to make them eat it, they may have it cut down and mixed with a better article.   But this will not do for horses in constant and laborious employment.   In coaching stables, the hay, if cut into chaff, must all be of the best quality; if bad, it is cheaper to convert it into litter than to make the horses eat it.   If eaten, the horses are in a manner poisoned; if rejected they are starved.   The bad being mixed with the good, the horse has no power of selection.   He eats some, but he does not eat so much as if it were all good; and his work requires all that he can eat of the very best.

Chaff quickly eaten.—It is eaten in less time than an equal quantity of hay.   For old horses, having bad teeth, and for those that work all day, it is desirable that the food be easily eaten, in order that they may have as much rest as possible. When the hay is given long, the horse has to do with his teeth all that is done by the machine when it is made into chaff.   The time and labor saved to him is not a great deal; perhaps half an hour, or, at the most, a whole hour, makes all the difference, supposing the hay easily taken from the rack, and all so good that the horse need lose no time in selection. Horses having bad teeth, particularly heavy draught-horses, seldom eat a large allowance of fodder.   Their teeth are so ineffective that the jaws tire before the horse is satisfied These, under all circumstances, except when out of work should have both grain and fodder broken down.

But for horses that perform their daily work in two hours, and perhaps in less time, it is not an advantage to have the food easily and quickly eaten.   From the long time they stand in the stable, these horses require something to engage their attention.   They are apt to get troublesome, pawing the ground, breaking loose, eating the woodwork and the litter, and teazing their neighbors.   A little hay, in a close-sparred rack, gives them something to do.   As they have plenty of spare time it is needless to cut their food, merely to save their time. To give chaff for the purpose of insuring mastication of the grain, is another affair; all horses should have sufficient for this purpose.

Accurate Distribution obtained.—Chaff is easily weighed or measured. The allotted quantity can be served to within an ounce. Hay also can be given quite as exactly, but it is not so easy. The difference is so insignificant, and there are so very few cases in which a very accurate distribution of fodder is necessary, that it would be folly to cut it merely for this purpose.

The Mixture preferred.—It has been said, that after horses have been accustomed to feeding on grain and chaff mixed, they prefer it to oats or beans without chaff. This is untrue. He who said it must have been misinformed.

Objections to Chaff.—It has been urged that the cost of converting the hay into chaff is greater than the grain; tha. some horses will not thrive without an allowance of rack fodder; that the horse must be often fed, otherwise the chaff will be wasted as much as hay.

The first of these objections may have some truth in it, but the assertion requires limitation. The cost of the cutting machine is always spoken of as a great matter itself. It varies in price from three to six or more pounds. In a small establishment, containing, perhaps, twenty horses, the grain that would be saved by mixing it with chaff, would soon pay the cost of a small machine; and as it is not necessary to bruise the grain, the cost of that process is avoided. The saving of grain, therefore, pays the machine, and the cost of that article should not be included, except where only one or two horses are kept.

But to cut all the fodder may, in many cases, be too costly a practice. Heavy draught-horses consume a great deal. Some may be saved by cutting it, yet, perhaps, not sufficient to pay the cost of cutting. Much depends upon the care of the stablemen. If they will give the hay often, and in such quantities that none will be wasted, there is no need to cut more than enough to mingle with the grain. In such a case it would be a loss to cut all the fodder. But such care can not always be obtained.

The cost of cutting may be calculated. If it be twenty shillings per week, the owner has only to inquire whether good hay to that amount be wasted. He can easily ascertain how long a certain quantity serves a certain number of horses

18

The allowance for horses of different kinds varies from eight
to twenty pounds per day. Some will eat more, but others
will eat less. Taking the whole, he will find how much
more hay is consumed than the horses should eat. When it
is not necessary to employ additional men to cut the hay, that
makes a difference ; some portion of it is always saved by converting it into chaff, but the quantity will depend upon the disposition of the horses to waste, and the care of the stableman
in preventing waste. The cost of cutting that which is to
mingle with the grain is not great. There is always some one
about the place having half an hour to spare for this purpose

Some horses will not thrive without an allowance of rack
fodder. This is positively asserted by men who have tried
cutting very extensively. It may be so ; but I have never met
with any very clear proof of it. They say that horses will
leave the chaff before them, to devour the same hay uncut,
and I have seen them do so, though I can not understand it.
The chaff ought to be as acceptable as the hay. Perhaps the
circumstance might be attributed to the use of damaged hay.
When cut into chaff the horse may refuse it, and yet seem to
eat it uncut. He takes the good and rejects the bad. With
chaff he has no choice. With horses, unaccustomed to this
mode of feeding, and long used to the other, the habit of tearing hay from the rack, and selecting the most esteemed portions, may perhaps have become a source of gratification. If
there be any, however, who will not thrive as well upon chaff
as upon hay, the number must be very small. At first, the
horse may not feed so heartily, but, in general, this happens
for only a short time.

When the fodder is all cut, the horse must be often fed.
If he gets more than he is disposed to eat, he soon learns to
shake it up and turn it over till he extracts all the grain. In
doing so he soils the chaff, makes it wet, and the moisture
spoils it in two or three hours. The horse will not eat this.
At next feeding hour another allowance is added to that which
was left ; and a horse is induced to feed, but he does not feed
heartily. The only remedy lies either in giving less at a time,
or in giving none at the next feeding hour, when it is found
that the preceding allowance has not been finished ; or, after
the horse is done feeding, that which he leaves may be taken
away. All this care is seldom bestowed, especially by strappers. Chaff-feeding does require almost or quite as much
care to prevent waste as hay-feeding. This is not denied even
by the strongest advocates of the system. Without care the

chaff mixture is wasted, and the horses are cloyed, thrown off their feed; having corn always before them, they never obtain a sharp appetite.

Then, to sum up this matter, which seems to be very ill understood, it appears,

That, where the stablemen are careful, waste of fodder is diminished, though not prevented.

That where the racks are good, careful stablemen may prevent nearly all waste of fodder, without cutting it.

That an accurate distribution of fodder is not a very important object.

That no horse seems to like his corn the better for being mingled with chaff.

That, among half-starved horses, chaff-cutting promotes the consumption of damaged fodder.

That full-fed horses, rather than eat the mixture of sound and unsound, will reject the whole, or eat less than their work demands.

That chaff is more easily eaten than hay; that this is an advantage to old horses, and others working all day; a disadvantage when the horses stand long in the stable.

That chaff ensures complete mastication and deliberate ingestion of the grain; that it is of considerable and of most importance in this respect; that all the fodder need not be mingled with the grain, one pound of chaff being sufficient to insure the mastication and slow ingestion of four pounds of grain.

That the cost of cutting *all* the fodder, especially for heavy horses, is repaid only where the hay is dear, and wasted in large quantities.

That, among hard-working horses, bad fodder should never be cut.

MIXING.—When a number of articles having different properties are to be mingled together, some trouble must be taken to mix them equally. I often see beans, barley, bran, and chaff, thrown into a bucket hardly large enough to contain them. An attempt is always made to stir them up and mingle one with another; but either from the laziness of the man, or from the want of proper utensils, the attempt frequently fails. Hence some of the horses are fed on that which is too rich, and they are surfeited, while others receive little but chaff, and are starved. The mixing vessel ought to be large enough to hold double the quantity ever put into it.

The whole of each article ought not to be put in at once. Suppose boiled beans, boiled barley, chaff, and roots, or bran, are to be mixed; the beans, barley, and roots, are boiled together; a measure of chaff is thrown into the tub, then a measure of the boiled food, then a measure of bran, and lastly a measure of the boiled liquor. These are well mingled by means of a wooden spade; another measure of each article is then added, and the whole again incorporated together. In this way the man proceeds, adding the ingredients to each other in small quantities, and mixing them thoroughly at each addition, till a quantity taken from one part of the vessel is quite the same as a quantity taken from any other part of it.

In mixing dry grain with chaff, the same plan is to be followed. If seven bushels of chaff, one of barley, one of beans, and five of oats, are to be mingled together, mix the grain and pulse first, in six or seven layers, and toss them together with a wooden shovel; then mix one bushel of chaff with one of the mixed grain; in another place mix a like quantity, and after all is divided in this manner into seven parcels, each containing an equal quantity of each article, throw the whole into one heap, and toss it over two or three times. Unless the ingredients be thoroughly incorporated, the horses can not be equally served. There is error in mixing very much, and also in mixing very little. The man may soon discover in what quantities he can manage to make the most equal mass.

WASHING.—Turnips, carrots, potatoes, and other roots, are generally washed before they are given. In some places, however, they are given with the mud about them, which I think is not a good practice. It is an unpleasant thing to hear the sand and mud grating on the horse's teeth, and it can not surely be very agreeable to him. When the roots are boiled without washing, a dirty mess is produced having little resemblance to food. It has been alleged that the earth is wholesome: but I rather think this is a discovery made by laziness. On some soils, the mud, when adhering to the roots in considerable quantity, has an effect slightly laxative. It may be desirable that the food should occasionally, but I should think not constantly, possess this property. I have never seen the mud do either good or ill. The horse at first seems soon tired of it, but at last he eats quite heartily. The sand may perhaps wear the teeth a little too fast.

The best machine for washing roots, such as potatoes and small turnips, is a sparred cylinder, set in a trough which is filled with water. A door in the cylinder admits the roots it is placed on axles, and turned by a crank.

Hay seed, when used as food, should always be washed. It contains a great deal of sand and dust, which are easily separated by throwing the seed into a tub of water, and stirring it about with the hand. The seed swims and the impurities fall to the bottom. To get rid of the water, skim off the seed into a sieve, or a tub having a perforated bottom, and let it drain there for ten minutes.

BRUISING.—Grain and pulse are broken, or bruised, by passing them between a pair of metal rollers. The only object of this practice is to insure the digestion of these seeds, which do not resist solution when their husk is broken. If the horse would masticate his food sufficiently, there would be no need to bruise it ; But some have bad teeth, and others feed in haste ; and by both much of the grain is swallowed entire, and passes through the digestive apparatus without yielding any nutriment. The skin which covers oats, beans, and some other seeds, seems to resist the action of the stomach. It will not dissolve, or at least it is evacuated before it is dissolved, and it prevents solution of the meal which it covers. In some horses, the quantity that passes off entire is very considerable : it has been estimated at one sixth of all that is eaten. But the quantity is not certain ; and there is seldom such a loss as this. Still the saving effected by preventing it pays for the cost of preventing it. If the husk of the seed be broken, the farina will be dissolved.

There are hand-mills of different sizes for bruising grain. Beans are seldom submitted to the process. Horses are not so apt to swallow the entire beans ; yet some do, especially those having bad teeth. There are mills for bruising beans, [also for grinding corn with the cob, oats, and other small grain].

In this town the grain is generally bruised at the public mills. But when only three or four horses are kept, it is better to have the bruising performed at home. The bruised grain rapidly absorbs moisture and becomes musty. A hand-mill furnishes it always fresh ; enough for only one or two days should be prepared at a time. [In the drier climate of America, meal will keep sweet for weeks or months.]

Bruised grain mixes readily with chaff, and it saves an old horse some trouble. It has little more to recommend it. If the horses be young, the addition of chaff will compel them to do that which is done by the mill, and they are able enough to do it. But when chaff is not used, the grain should be bruised for all kinds of horses.

18*

GRINDING the grain has been recommended for facilitating its digestion; but whether it be more rapidly digested, or whether it be right to make it so, is yet unknown. When ground grain is given without admixture, the horse appears to have some difficulty in managing it. The meal requires much saliva, but very little mastication. The secretion of saliva is stimulated, and its supply regulated by the act of mastication. Hence the food that requires the most moisture, should also require the most mastication. With ground grain this order is reversed, the horse fills his mouth with flour too dry to swallow, and too fine to produce saliva. He always requires more time to consume a pound of oatmeal than a pound of oats; and many will not, or can not eat a whole feed of it. When put into the manger in a heap, the broken husks run down the sides and accumulate; the portion having most of the husk is eaten before the flour; this shows which the horse likes best. Flour or meal, however, is a useful addition to boiled food; and when given with chaff it may be better than alone.

Grinding, I believe, is always performed at the meal-mills. When the grain is soft or new, it is previously dried or baked. The husks are not separated from the meal.

GERMINATING.—In this process the grain is steeped in water for twelve or twenty-four hours, and afterward exposed to the air till it begins to sprout, when it is ready for use. In the stable this preparation is termed "malting." Barley and oats are occasionally submitted to the process. Other kinds of grain, and perhaps pulse, may be thus treated, but I have not heard of any experiments upon them.

The time required for producing germination varies in different kinds of grain; and it is influenced by the degree of heat, the quantity of moisture, and the access of light. The steeped seed is usually spread upon the floor of a warm and dark apartment; the layer should not exceed an inch thick, and it should occasionally be turned over. The grain swells, becomes warm, bursts, and springs; it is fermenting; in this state it is given to the horse. When germination in barley is checked by a dry heat, the grain is fully malted; but malt is not employed as an article of food for horses. The heavy duty forbids its use, and I do not know that it is wanted. When merely sprouted, it is said to be much relished by horses of defective appetite, and useful to those recovering from sickness. It is supposed to be more easily digested, and less inflammatory than the raw grain.

STEEPING consists in throwing the grain into cold or tepid water for twelve or twenty-four hours. It absorbs much water, it softens, and it is easily eaten; but I know not that anything is gained by such change. If the grain be drier and harder than usual, or the horse's teeth bad, or his mouth sore, steeping may be of some service. The horse drinks less water, but perhaps he receives as much with the grain as he refuses from the pail.

MASKING.—When hay is steeped in boiling water, it is said to be masked. The juice, and perhaps all the nutritive matter, is extracted from the hay and dissolved in the water. This liquor, termed hay-tea, is seldom given to horses, and indeed horses do not appear to be very fond of it. Some, however, have tried it, and they say that it makes a lean horse put up flesh very rapidly. Perhaps it might be useful after a day of extraordinary exertion, when the horse is more disposed to drink than to eat. It might be tried as a substitute for gruel. For this purpose clover hay is better than ryegrass. It should be of the best quality; the water boiling, and the vessel closely covered till the tea be cool enough for use.

MASHING is nearly the same as masking; but both the solid and the fluid are given. A warm bran-mash is made by pouring boiling water upon the bran and covering it up till cool. Tepid water, it is supposed, does not answer so well; does not render the bran so digestible and mucilaginous as it becomes by steeping in boiling water. A cold mash is made at once, by pouring cold water upon the bran; but if it be true that the bran is improved by heat, hot water should be used, and the mash exposed till cold. After all, there may be no difference. Barley and oats are each occasionally made into mashes; that is to say, they are steeped in water, hot or boiling, and the water is given with the grain. When the surgeon orders the horse to be put on mashes, he always means those made of bran.

BOILING.—The articles usually boiled are turnips, potatoes, grain of all kinds, beans, and peas. It is not likely that boiled food has exactly the same properties as that which is raw. To the eye and to the taste it is different, and probably it is different to the stomach also. It may yield more nutriment; it may yield less; possibly it may furnish nutriment of a different kind, or, without any alteration in the quantity or quality of the nutriment, the food may be more or less rapidly or easily digested: but there is no positive proof, no

well-conducted experiments, to decide these conjectures. It
is known, however, that turnips and potatoes are more digestible when boiled than when raw. They are not so liable to
produce colic, a disease arising from fermentation of that
food over which the stomach has little power. Boiled grain
seems to assimilate very quickly with the living solids and
fluids. It restores vigor more rapidly than raw grain; but
that vigor does not last so long. Whatever be the changes
produced upon the food by boiling, it appears probable that
some articles are more improved than others, and that a few
are better in the raw state.

Agricultural and coach horses generally receive one feed
of boiled food every day during about four months of the
year, commencing at the end of autumn. Some horses get
it all the year, except when grass is to be had. This boiled
food is composed of several articles. Barley, beans, and turnips, form a mixture in common use, to which chaff, hay-seed,
and perhaps bran, may be added. Oats often supply the place
of barley; and potatoes that of turnips. Wheat is not a
great favorite; but it is sometimes given for barley. The
mixture is given warm, and is generally the last feed. For
all hard-working horses this is a good system. They are
fond of food thus prepared and mixed. They eat more of it.
They always look better, have a finer skin, carry more flesh,
and perform their work with less fatigue than when fed in
the ordinary way upon raw oats and beans. In cold wet
weather the warm boiled food is particularly beneficial. It
makes the horse comfortable, and sets him soon to rest.

I believe that much of the good ascribed to boiled food may
be attributed to its warmth. [Cooking renders it more digestible, and it is more easily assimilated. The absorbing
vessels are thus enabled more readily and fully to act. Animal heat is necessary for digestion; therefore cooking renders food more nutritious.] No horse likes it when cold,
many refuse it, and most of them prefer the raw article to
that which has been boiled and become cold. The heat
which boiled food should contain is conveyed into the system, or, at least, it saves the expense of producing all the
heat which cold food takes from the system.

There are two other circumstances which probably contribute a good deal to improve the horse's condition. The
boiled food is rarely composed of the same articles. If oats
and beans be given during the day, and barley, or barley and
oats at night, the horse has the advantage of a mixed diet.

which is always better than that into which only one or two
articles enter.   The other circumstance I allude to is an increased consumption of food.   The horse eats a larger quantity of this boiled food, partly because it is boiled, and partly
because it contains articles to which he is less accustomed,
and which are therefore more agreeable, and because he likes
variety.

It is not usual to give boiled food to working horses oftener
than once a day.   Slow, and even fast-workers do, however,
sometimes get it twice or thrice a day.   Heavy draught-
horses may have it thus often without disadvantage.   But it
is complained that those employed at fast-work, and on long
journeys, become *soft* when they get boiled food so frequently.
They perspire a great deal; their vigor is not lasting; they
are sooner exhausted than horses that receive less boiled and
more raw food.   Whether this be true or not, the approach
of hot weather always produces a dislike for boiled food.
The horses, particularly fast horses, may take one feed, but
few are fond of more.   In coaching-stables, the boiling is
discontinued as the weather becomes warm.   It is not discarded all at once.   Instead of giving boiled food every night,
it is given only thrice a week; after a while, only once a
week, and ultimately not at all.   The practice commences in
the same way, about the end of autumn.

In boiling grain, care must be taken to prevent it from adhering to the bottom of the pot, where it gets burned, and becomes nauseous.   It must be often stirred.   As the water
evaporates, more should be added.   Never let the liquor boil
over.   It contains a great deal of nutriment, extracted from
the food.   I often see it running to waste, the vessel being
too small, or the attendant careless.   Give the grain plenty
of water, more than it will take up, and either give the liquor
as a drink, or add chaff or bran to imbibe it.

All the kinds of food are generally over-boiled.   The horse
dislikes slops.   His food should be firm, hard enough to give
the teeth some employment.   Neither roots nor grain should
be boiled to a jelly.   They should be a little hard at the heart.
The skin of grain and pulse, however, should be burst.   When
ready, the mass is emptied into a cooler, which is just a tub
or trough, sometimes placed on wheels.   In this, other articles, such as chaff, bran, and meal, which do not require
boiling, are added, and the whole incorporated into an equal
mass.

Oats require more boiling than beans, beans more than bar-

ley, carrots and turnips more than potatoes. To have none
overdone, the articles which require the most should be put
on some time before the others.

There are some other things connected with boiling which
I have not been able to learn. It would be well to know how
much each article gains or loses in weight and in bulk, and
in what time it may be sufficiently boiled. A few simple and
not costly experiments would decide these, and they may be
made by any person who has time to perform them. The
following table taken from the Quarterly Journal of Agriculture, shows only the increase of bulk which certain grains
suffer in boiling :—

4 measures of oats, boiled to bursting, fill 7 measures.
4 of barley, ... 10 ——
4 of buckwheat or brand, ... 14 ——
4 of maize, rather more than . . · 13 ——
4 of wheat, little more than . . . 10 ——
4 of rye, nearly . . . . 15 ——
4 of beans, ... $8\frac{1}{2}$ ——

STEAMING.—In some places the food is cooked by steam.
Whether it be better to steam it or to boil it, must depend
upon circumstances. In a large establishment, if the food
be very bulky, consisting chiefly of roots, it may require a
vessel inconveniently large to boil it all at one time ; and in
such a case steam is to be preferred. But where roots are
not used, and the number of horses does not exceed fifty, the
ordinary iron boiler answers the purpose well enough.

As far as the food is concerned, I believe it is, with one
exception, a matter of indifference whether it be cooked by
steam or water. This exception refers to potatoes. which
are drier, and according to some people more wholesome
when steamed than when boiled. With the other articles I
do not know that there is any difference.

In favor of the steamer, it may be urged that it does all
that the boiler can do ; that it never burns the food ; [that it·
does not require the labor of stirring ;] that it is more easily
managed than a very large boiler ; and that it admits of the
best mode of cooking potatoes, which the boiler does not.

The apparatus may be very simple ; and after the attendant
has had a little practice, it is easily worked. A steam-tight
boiler is erected, having a funnel and stop-cock for admitting
water ; a pipe for conveying the steam to its destination ; and
a safety-valve to prevent explosion. Sometimes the valve is

FIG. 17.—STEAMING APPARATUS.

wanting; and when the steam-pipe is short and wide, per
haps the valve is of no great use. It is right, however, that
there should be one. In connexion with the boiler there is
a tub for holding the food. This has a false bottom, per
forated with numerous holes, and resting upon steps, within
three or four inches of the true bottom; the steam is admitted
between them; the steam rises upward, is diffused through
the food, and retained by the lid, which should be made to
lift off entirely, so that the food may be the more easily taken
out. After the food is mixed and washed, it is thrown into
the tub. A layer of chaff may previously be spread in the
bottom, to prevent the grain from falling through the perfora
tions; and another thick layer, may, if there be room, spread
on the top of all. As the steam condenses, water accumulates in the space between the true and false bottoms; occasionally this should be drawn off; if it rises on the food it
will be boiled instead of steamed. There is a hole for the
purpose of withdrawing the water. When potatoes alone are
steamed, this fluid is to be thrown away, but that which
comes from other articles is to be given as a drink, or along
with the food; it is rich and palatable. That which comes
from potatoes is said to be unwholesome.

The steaming apparatus varies much in construction; the
simpler it is the better. Those to whom its management is
intrusted are in general sufficiently stupid, not able to comprehend a complex arrangement. Sometimes the boiler is at

a distance from the steam-tub. They are not easily attended when closely connected. Sometimes the tub is adjusted to the rim of an ordinary boiler, and this is the simplest of all methods, but inconvenient when there is much to be cooked. Sometimes a steaming-tub is employed for each horse ; it is just like a stable-pail. Several are arranged in a row, and each has a branch-tube from the steam-pipe. Complication and expense attend this method, without any adequate advan‧tage.

BAKING.—Potatoes are the only article to which this pro‧cess has been applied. I have not seen any detailed account of the practice, nor has it come under my own observation. There is some notice of it in the fourth volume of Communi‧cations to the Board of Agriculture.

SEASONING.—The custom of seasoning the horse's food is of recent origin, and, as yet, it is not general. Stablemen have indeed, from time immemorial, been in the habit of mix‧ing nitre with all boiled food, and occasionally with the raw. but this is not what I mean by seasoning. Nitre, or salt‧petre, as it is commonly called, does not render the food more palatable, nor aid its digestion, nor is it given for such purposes.

Salt is the only article employed in this country. In India, and perhaps in other places, the horse receives, at certain times, a dose of pepper, or some other stimulating and ar‧omatic spice ; and in hot countries, such things may be use‧ful, as to a certain extent, they are in this.

There are two modes of giving salt, and a kind of salt for each mode. Some give one or two ounces of common table‧salt, every night, along with the boiled food, with which it is well mixed ; others give six or eight ounces at a time, and only once a week, generally on Saturday night, if the horses be idle all Sunday. By the former mode it is said to promote digestion, and to render the food more palatable ; by the latter it relaxes the bowels, and increases the flow of urine. In both cases the salt excites considerable thirst, especially at first, before the horse becomes accustomed to it. When given only once a week, he never becomes accustomed to it. The same effects are produced every time the salt is given.

I‧have no reason to approve much of either of these modes. Fast-working horses, either from the laxative property of the salt, or from the quantity of water which it makes them drink, are very apt to purge, and to sweat easily and copiously. Some horses, too, are not partial to salt, at least they do not

always like it. Its effects, when constantly used, are of such
a doubtful nature, that I think every horse should have it in
his power to take or to refuse it as he is disposed. That he
may do so, he should be supplied with

Rock Salt.—The salt which is sold under this name in
Glasgow, is brought from Cheshire, and is employed chiefly
for cattle. It is procured in large masses, of a stony hardness. It is somewhat different from common salt, of which,
however, it contains 983 parts in 1,000; the rest is sulphate
of lime, muriate of lime, muriate of magnesia, and some in-
soluble matter. It is not likely that these make it different
to the horse from common salt. It is better, only, I believe,
because it can be obtained in a solid form. Most of the
coach proprietors in this neighborhood give it to their horses
all the year round, and they give no other. It is not mixed
with the food. A lump, weighing perhaps two or three
pounds, is placed in the manger; when all consumed, it is
replaced by another piece. With few exceptions the horses
seem to be very fond of it; some always refuse it; and
many reject it at one time, who greedily devour it at another.
Those that have not been used to the salt, are apt to eat a
large quantity on the first day, and, in general, these are
slightly purged on the next. Afterward, instead of eating the
salt, the horse contents himself with licking it. The permanent result is not always apparent. In very many cases
I have never been able to trace either good or evil to its use.
In some there has been a remarkable change, the lean and
spiritless becoming plump and animated.

Nitre, I have said, is frequently given in boiled food.
Many foolish stablemen keep it constantly by them as an article of indispensable utility. They say it cools the blood,
and takes away swellings of the legs.

Nitre is a diuretic of considerable power, and like all
others, tends to reduce watery swellings, such as those to
which the legs of horses are subject when they stand much
in the house, when they are too highly fed, and when the
legs are not sufficiently hand-rubbed. It excites the kidneys
to secrete more urine: the urine is a certain portion of the
blood, and, to replace what is lost by the kidneys, that which
is superfluous about the legs or the sheath is taken up. To
speak of nitre cooling the blood is nonsense, very evident to
any body not very ignorant. [It promotes evacuation by the
kidneys and skin, and by reducing the system, it acts to cool,

19

It is anti-febrile. To the human patient it is administered as a febrifuge.]

As an article of constant or frequent use it ought to be abolished. In large quantities, it weakens a working-horse precisely in the same way that heated oats and musty hay weaken him. In smaller, but more frequent doses, it injures the kidneys [by reaction when omitted], and renders them unable to throw off all the superfluous and watery portion of the blood; this, when not evacuated in the shape of urine, is deposited in the legs, the sheath, and other parts; hence the constant use of nitre ultimately produces the evils it is at first given to cure. An occasional dose to a half-worked, full-fed horse may do good, particularly when he is to stand idle on the following day. When the grain or hay is not very good, and is apt to excite diabetes, no diuretic medicines should ever be given but under the directions of a professional man. A veterinarian was once called to examine some horses that were sadly emaciated from the staling evil. The hay was bad; but it was changed, and other measures taken to arrest the disease. They appeared to have the desired effect always till Sunday, when all the horses became nearly as ill as ever. At last it was discovered that the man put two pounds of nitre among the boiled food every Saturday night. This explained the repeated relapse. The fellow pretended to be a foreman—to know, not only his own business, but also something about the veterinarian's.

ASSIMILATION OF THE FOOD.

By the assimilation of the food, I mean its conversion into a part of the living body. This is effected by a series of processes, each of which is preparatory to that which follows it. Most of them have been named.

Prehension is the act by which the food is taken into the mouth. At pasture the grass is seized by the lips, compressed into a little bundle, and placed between the front teeth, which separate it from the ground, by incision, aided by a sudden jerk of the head. In stable-feeding, the lips and teeth are used in nearly the same way. They seize the food and place it within reach of the tongue, but they produce no change upon it. The front teeth have less to do in stable than in field-feeding, but in neither case do they masticate the food. Prehension of fluids is performed by sucking. The lips are dipped in the water, and the cavity of the mouth is enlarged by depressing the tongue, by bringing it into the channel—the space between the sides of the lower jaw. Prehension may be difficult or interrupted by palsy or injury of the lips, soreness of the tongue, or loss of the front teeth. Colts often experience difficulty in grazing while changing the teeth. They lose flesh for a while, and, if they lose much, some rich fluid or salt boiled food may be given till the mouth get well. Horses that have lost one or two of their fore-teeth by falls, become unfit for turning out. Those that have lost a large portion of the tongue can not empty a pail. They can drink none unless the nostrils be under water; but when only a small portion of the tongue has been lost, they have no difficulty. They can empty the pail. No horse can drink freely with a bit, particularly with a double-bit, in his mouth. It confines the tongue, and prevents close contact of the lips at the corners; as much air as water enters the mouth.

MASTICATION, the act of grinding the food, is performed altogether by the back-teeth. The food is placed between them by the tongue. Mastication is the first change which the food undergoes. It is broken into small particles, easily penetrable by the juices in which the food is about to be dissolved. In many old horses, and even in some young ones, mastication is imperfect, from irregularity or disease of the teeth. When the horse feeds slowly, holds his head to one side, drops the food from his mouth half-chewed, and passes a large quantity unaltered, his teeth should be examined. One may be rotten, broken, or projecting into the cheek, or into the gum opposite.

INSALIVATION.—The food suffers mastication and insalivation at the same time. While under the operation of the grinders it is moistened and diluted by a fluid which enters the mouth at many little apertures. This fluid is almost transparent; it is tasteless; it is termed saliva. Much of it is furnished by two large glands, which are situated at that part of the throat where the head joins the neck. These two glands pour their secretions into the mouth by means of two tubes which open near the grinding-teeth. Some have supposed that the only use of this fluid is to dilute the food, and to facilitate mastication and deglutition; others, that it also, in a slight degree, animalizes the food. Hence it has been argued that the food should not be too soft, too easily eaten, lest it be swallowed without insalivation, and without the animalization which saliva ought to produce. It has been urged, as proof, that horses do not thrive so well when fed entirely upon boiled food. The illustration seems to be well established. Horses do not appear to possess lasting vigor and great energy when fed exclusively upon soft food; but whether this proves that insalivation is animalization may be doubted. There is no proof of a positive kind, whether it is or is not. It would be easy to argue on either side, but it would be fruitless.

DEGLUTITION is the act of swallowing. The food, after being ground and moistened, is rolled into a ball by the tongue, and placed at the back of the mouth, where a compressing apparatus forces it into the gullet. The gullet, exerting a contractile power, forces the ball into the stomach. Deglutition may become difficult, or it may be partially suspended by soreness of the throat. When the throat in much inflamed, the horse may be anxious to eat, yet unable to swallow. When great pain attends the effort he forbears further trial; he chews the food and then throws it out of his mouth, being able perhaps to swallow only the juice. In less severe cases, he makes a peculiar motion of the head every time he swallows; and in drinking, he drinks very slowly, and part of the water returns by the nostrils. In this state the horse should be put under medical treatment.

MACERATION.—Many of the articles upon which horses feed are hard and dry. They require to be softened before they can be dissolved, or before they will part with their nutritive matter. One end of the horse's stomach seems designed for macerating these substances. It is lined by a membrane void of sensibility. All the food is first lodged in this macerating corner, from which, when sufficiently softened, it passes into the other extremity. Refractory matters are either detained or returned till they are ready to undergo the digestive process.

DIGESTION consists in the extraction of the nutritious from the inert portion of the food. It is not a simple process, nor is it all conducted in the same place. It begins in the stomach and terminates in the bowels, probably at a considerable distance from the point at which the residue is evacuated. The stomach of the horse is very small. There must be some reason why it is so, but none has ever been discovered.* [In the horse's stomach digestion is very rapid. Hence a small

---

* Inquiry seldom acknowledges defeat. A large stomach, it is said would interfere with the horse's speed. Perhaps it might. But it does not appear that the stomach was made small that he might be swift. Look at the pace of a camel and the size of his paunch.

stomach only is necessary. If it were large, it would diminish the size of the lungs. But large lungs are necessary for rapid and continuous action. Hence the necessity of a small stomach. But food in sufficient quantity is necessary, and thus the rapid digestion of the horse.]

It can not retain the food very long; the horse is almost constantly eating. At grass he eats as much in an hour, perhaps in half-an-hour, as would fully distend the stomach, yet he continues to eat for several hours in succession. The change, therefore, which the food undergoes in the stomach must be rapidly performed. The nature of this change is not precisely known. It is supposed that the gastric juice—that is, a juice or secretion furnished by the stomach—seizes the nutritive matter of the food, and combines with it to form a white milk-like fluid termed chyme. This, accompanied by the food, from which it has been extracted, enters the intestines, and there another change of composition takes place. Juices from the liver, from peculiar glands, and from the intestines itself, are added, and the whole combine to form a compound fluid termed chyle. This adheres to the inner surface of the bowels, from which it is removed by an infinite number of tubes, whose mouths are inconceivably minute, to the eye invisible. These little tubes or pipes, are termed lacteals or absorbents; they converge and run toward the spine, where their contents are received by a tube which empties itself into the left jugular vein. Accompanied by the blood, the chyle proceeds to the lungs, passes through them, and becomes blood. Having undergone sanguification, this chyle, the product of digestion, is as much a constituent of the living animal as any other part of him.

It is not necessary to trace the food further. Its nutritive matter having been extracted, and animalized by combination with animal juices, the product is removed as the mass travels through the intestines. By the time it has arrived at the point of evacuation, the food has lost all or most of the nutritive matter, and the residue is ejected as useless.

The nutritive matter is carried from the intestines to the blood-vessels, where it is mingled with their contents. To follow it further would be to trace the conversion of the blood into the solids and fluids of which the body is composed. In this work such an inquiry is not necessary.

19*

INDIGESTION OF THE FOOD.

MEN, particularly household men, who do not work for what they eat, often have indigestion for several successive years. They are said to have a weak stomach, or to be troubled with bile. They are always complaining, never quite well, yet never very ill. The stomach is truly weak. It wants energy, it acts slowly, often imperfectly; yet it is not wholly inactive. It rarely loses all control over the food. The horse seldom suffers under a similar complaint; when indigestion does occur in him, it is a serious affair, soon cured, or soon producing death. In men the disease usually termed indigestion, ought perhaps to have another name, for all or most of the food does undergo the process of digestion, although it may be performed very slowly. The indigestion I am about to speak of in the horse, has been termed acute. It ought to be called complete; or rather, that in man should be termed difficult. After this explanation, the reader need not confound indigestion in man with indigestion in the horse. They are totally different. The structure of the horse's stomach, and the nature of his food, account to a certain extent for the difference. But in men the digestion is difficult, in the horse it is not performed.

It is very obvious that the stomach in health must exercise a peculiar control over the food, which does not putrefy, or ferment, as it would, were it kept equally warm and moist in any place but the stomach. So long as the stomach is able to digest, the food suffers neither putrefaction nor fermentation. But it sometimes happens that the stomach loses its power. It becomes unable to digest the food, or to exercise any control over its changes.

Now, when the horse's stomach ceases to digest, one of two things usually takes place. Either the food remains in the stomach without undergoing any change, or it runs into fermentation. In the one case the horse is often foundered; in the other he is griped, he takes what I shall here call colic.

Founder is an inflammation of the feet, generally of the fore-feet, but sometimes of them all. It is not apparent why a load of undigested food in the stomach should produce a disease in the feet; yet it is well known that it does so. There seems to be some untraced connexion between the feet and the stomach, and some theories have been made on the subject, but I have heard none worth notice; we do not even *know* why in one case the food remains unchanged, and in another undergoes fermentation. Perhaps it depends a good deal upon the quantity of water that happens to be present with the food. [This is all idle speculation and not to be depended on·; founder never springs from this cause.]

An overloaded stomach is one of the causes of indigestion. If a horse reach the grain-chest, or in any other way obtain a large meal of grain, he will be very likely to take colic in an hour or more after he gets water. If water be withheld, he may founder; but colic will not occur, unless there be much water previously in the stomach or bowels. Those who are experienced in these matters know how to manage a horse after he has been gorged with food. They give him no water all that day, and none on the next till evening. Then they give only a little at a time, and often, till thirst be quenched. If he be a slow horse he goes to work, but if his work be fast he must remain at home, having, however, a good deal of walking exercise. In this way the stablemen prevents what he calls the gripes, colic, or batts. He is ignorant of the mode in which water operates, but experience has taught him that it has something to do with the disease. Founder, it is true, may happen, but that is usually regarded as a more curable malady than the other. It is not so deadly, but I shall presently show that colic can be cured sooner, and with more certainty, than founder.

Staggers.—A kind of apoplexy is sometimes produced by the presence of undigested food in the stomach. In this country the disease is not common, and there is nothing like it when the food ferments. Obstinate constipation, and sometimes complete obstruction of the bowels, are the occasional results of indigestion.

The Process of Fermentation must be familiar to almost everybody. Grain, or other vegetable matter, when thrown into a heap, moistened, and heated to a certain point, soon undergoes a change. The principal phenomenon attending which is the evolution of air in great abundance, more perhaps than twenty or thirty times the bulk of the articles from which it is extricated. When this process takes place in the stomach, the horse's life is in danger, for he has no power like some other animals to belch up the air. Distension of the stomach and bowels rapidly succeeds, and runs so far as to rupture them. If the stomach or bowels do not give way, life may be destroyed by inflammation or strangulation of the bowels, or the mere pain of distension may produce death before there is time either for rupture, inflammation, or strangulation. The disease sometimes cures itself, the air not being very abundant, or being evacuated by passing through the bowels; but very often the horse dies in from four to twelve hours. Sometimes he dies in two, and sometimes not till he has been ill for eighteen or twenty-four. The disease goes under various names. In different places it is termed gripes, the batts, fret, colic, flatulent colic, spasmodic colic, enteritis, inflamed bowels, and acute indigestion. It has been described by only one author with whom I am acquainted, and he speaks of it as a rare disease. All who have written treatises on veterinary medicine, have seen the disease several times, but they mistake it for some other to which they have given names, according to the appearances they have seen on dissecting the horse after death. Thus, one describes the symptoms, and attributes them to inflammation of the bowels; another to spasms of the bowels; a third to strangulation; a fourth to rupture of the diaphragm, and so on, with far too many more. All these, and several others, are the effect of fermentation of the food either in the stomach or in the bowels. The cause has been overlooked, and death traced only to the effects of the cause. The disease which is treated and described by authors and teachers as inflamed bowels, spasmodic colic, strangulation, ruptured stomach, ruptured diaphragm, is in 136 out of 137 cases, neither more nor less at the beginning than a distension of the stomach and bowels by air. I know this from my own practice, of which, in reference to this disease, I have kept a record during 18 months. For the sake of brevity in reference, I shall term it

COLIC.—I go a little out of my limits to speak of this disease. I do so for four reasons. In the first place, the disease is deadly; it destroys more heavy draught-horses than all others put together. In the second place, I can show how it may be cured with infallible certainty, if it be taken in time. In the third place, the disease requires immediate relief; the horse may be dead, or past cure, before the medical assistant can be obtained. And in the fourth place, the nature of the disease and its treatment, are not known, or they are too little known by the veterinarian. These circumstances induce me to digress a little from the proper object of this work; and I think they are of sufficient importance to render apology unnecessary. I will, however, be brief. In another place I will enter into details which would be improper in this.

The Causes of Colic are rather numerous. I have already

said that an overloaded stomach is one, particularly when water is given either immediately before, or immediately after an extraordinary allowance of food ; but water directly after even an ordinary meal is never very safe. [It suspends digestion and occasions fermentation.] Another cause is violent exertion on a full stomach ; a third cause, is a sudden change of diet, from hay, for instance, to grass, or from oats to barley ; but an allowance, particularly a large allowance, of any food to which the horse has not been accustomed, is liable to produce colic. Some articles produce it oftener than others. Raw potatoes, carrots, turnips, green food, seem more susceptible of fermentation than hay or oats, barley more than beans ; wheat and pease more than barley. Such at least they have seemed to me ; but it is probable that in the cases from which I have drawn my conclusions, sudden change and quantity may have had as much to do in producing colic, as the fermentable nature of the food. Haste in feeding is a common cause ; if the horse swallow his food very greedily, without sufficient mastication, he is very liable to colic.

Heavy draught-horses are almost the only subjects of colic, and among the owners of them it is difficult to meet with an old farmer or carter who has not lost more than one. Light, fast-working horses are rarely troubled with it, and few die of it. The difference is easily explained. Heavy, slow-working horses are long in the yoke, they fast till their appetite is like a raven's ; when they come home they get a large quantity of grain all at once, and they devour it in such haste that it is not properly masticated, and the stomach is suddenly overloaded. Possibly the quantity may not be very great, yet it is eaten too fast. The juice by which the food should be digested can not be made in such a hurry, at least not enough of it ; and add to this the rapid distension of the stomach ; more deliberate mastication and deglutition would enable this organ to furnish the requisite quantity of gastric juice, and to dilate sufficiently to contain the food with ease. In fast feeding, the stomach is taken too much by surprise.

Light horses are usually fed oftener, and with more regularity. They receive grain so often that they are not so fond of it ; not disposed to eat too much ; and the nature of their work often destroys the appetite, even when abstinence has been unusually prolonged.

The bulk of the food, however, has a great deal to do with this disease. An overloaded stomach will produce it in any kind of horse, but those who have the bowels and stomach habitually loaded are always in greatest danger. Horses that get little grain must eat a large quantity of roots or of fodder as much as the digestive apparatus can control. The stomach and bowels can not act upon any more, and that which they can not act upon runs speedily into fermentation.

This seems to me the principal reason why slow-work horses are so much more liable to the disease than fast-workers. When the pace reaches seven or eight miles an hour, the belly will not carry a great bulk of food, and so much grain is given that the horse has no inclination to load his bowels with fodder. There is never, or very rarely, more food than the stomach, the bowels, and the juices of these, can act upon.

Symptoms of Colic.—The horse is taken suddenly ill. If at work, he slackens his pace, attempts to stop, and when he stops, he prepares to lie down; sometimes he goes down as if shot, the moment he stands or is allowed to stand; at slow work he sometimes quickens his pace and is unwilling to stand. In the stable he begins to paw the ground with his fore feet, lies down, rolls, sometimes quite over, lies on his back; when the distension is not great he lies tolerably quiet, and for several minutes. But when the distension and pain are greater, he neither stands nor lies a minute; he is no sooner down than he is up. He generally starts all at once, and throws himself down again with great violence. He strikes the belly with his hind feet, and in moments of comparative ease he looks wistfully at his flanks. When standing he makes many and fruitless attempts to urinate; and the keeper always declares there is "something wrong with the water." In a little while the belly swells all round, or it swells most on the right flank. The worst, the most painful cases, are those in which the swelling is general; sometimes it is very inconsiderable, the air being in small quantity, or not finding its way into the bowels. As the disease proceeds, the pain becomes more and more intense. The horse dashes himself about with terrible violence. Every fall threatens to be his last. The perspiration runs off him in streams. His countenance betrays extreme agony, his contortions are frightfully violent, and seldom even for an instant suspended.

After continuing in this state for a brief period, other symptoms appear, indicating rupture or inflammation, or the approach of death without either. These, and the treatment they demand, I need not describe here. The horse may either be cured, or a veterinarian obtained, before inflammation or other consequences of the distension can take place.

Treatment of Colic.—The treatment consists in arresting the fermentation, and in re-establishing the digestive powers. There are many things that will do both. In mild cases a good domestic remedy in common use among oldfashioned people who have never heard of inflamed, spasmed, or strangulated bowels, is whiskey and pepper, or gin and pepper. About half a tumbler of spirits with a teaspoonful of pepper, given in a quart bottle of milk or warm water, will often afford immediate relief. If the pain do not abate in twenty or thirty minutes, the dose may be repeated, and even a third dose is in some cases necessary. Four ounces of spirits of turpentine, with twice as much sweet oil, is much stronger, but if the horse is much averse to the medicine, turpentine is not always quite safe.

There is, however, a better remedy, which should always be in readiness wherever several draught-horses are kept. Take a quart of brandy, add to it four ounces of sweet spirit of nitre, three ounces of whole ginger, and three ounces of cloves. In eight days this mixture or tincture is ready for use ; the cloves and ginger may still remain in the bottle, but they are not to be given. Set the bottle away, and put a lable upon it ; call it the " Colic Mixture." The dose is six ounces, to be given in a quart of milk or warm water every fifteen or twenty minutes till the horse be cured. Keep his head straight, and not too high when it is given. Do not pull out his tongue, as some stupid people do, when giving a drink. If the horse be very violent, get him into a wide open place, where you will have room to go about him. If he will not stand till the drink be given, watch him when down, and give it, though he be lying, whenever you can get him to take a mouthful. But give the dose as quickly as possible. After that, rub the belly with a soft wisp, walk the horse about *very slowly*, or give him a good bed, and room to roll. In eighty cases out of ninety this treatment will succeed, provided the medicine be got down the horse's throat before his bowels become inflamed, or strangulated, or burst. The delay of half an hour may be fatal.

When the second dose does not produce relief, the third may be of double or treble strength. I have given a full quart in about an hour, but the horse was very ill.

In many cases the horse takes ill during the night, and is far gone before he is discovered in the morning. In such a case this remedy may be too late, or it may not be proper; still, if the belly be swelled, let it be given, unless the veterinary surgeon can be procured immediately. In all cases it is proper to send for him at the beginning. You or your servants may not be able to give the medicine, or the disease may have produced some other, which this medicine will not cure. If the veterinarian can be got in a few minutes, do nothing till he comes. But do not wait long.

The horse is sometimes found dead in the morning; his belly is always much swelled, and the owner is suspicious of poisoning. I have known much vexation arise from such suspicion, when a single glance at the belly might have shown from what the horse died. There is no poison that will produce this swelling, which is sometimes so great as to burst the surcingle. On dissection the stomach is frequently burst, the belly full of food, water, and air, and the diaphragm ruptured. When death is slow, the bowels are always intensely inflamed, sometimes burst, and often twisted. But these things will never happen when the treatment I have recommended is adopted at the very beginning.

The horse sometimes takes the disease on the road. If his pace be fast, he should stop at once. To push him on beyond a walk, even for a short distance, is certain death. The bowels are displaced, twisted, and strangulated, partly by the distension, but aided a great deal by the exertion; and no medicine will restore them to their proper position. A *walk after* the medicine is good, and the pace *should not pass* a walk.

PRINCIPLES OF FEEDING.

The principles of feeding are facts which influence and ought to regulate the practice of feeding. The word feeding refers to the manger-food, given at intervals, not to the hay or fodder, which is almost constantly within the horse's reach.

People who are unacquainted with stable affairs make many blunders in the management of their horses, and particularly in feeding them. They reason too much from analogy. The rules which regulate their own diet are applied to that of the horse. Medical men are remarkable for this. A skilful surgeon expressed his conviction, that stablemen are full of error and prejudice regarding the diet of horses. He said: "I order my patients to live on plain food, on that which does not tempt excess ; and I tell them to eat when they are hungry, and to desist when satisfied. It is thus I treat my horse," continued he ; " I give him plain wholesome food, as much as he likes, and when he likes."

This is sufficiently absurd ; it is a common way of speaking only with the ignorant. It might be a very good rule, if there were no food for the horse but grass, and none for man but bread. Horses may eat more grain, and men more beef than their work requires ; or the plain, wholesome nourishment, as it is called, may not suffice for certain kinds of work. It is this, it is the work which renders care and system so necessary in the feeding of horses. Men have to work, too, but very few have labor bearing any resemblance to that of the horse, and those few are compelled to regulate their diet by rules which are not known to the bulk of mankind. The diver, the boxer, the runner, and the wrestler, must not live like other men. The fermentable nature of the horse's food, and the peculiar structure of his stomach which forbids vomition, and the abstinence from food and drink occasionally required by the work, are other circumstances which demand particular attention to the mode of feeding.

SLOW WORK *aids digestion*, empties the bowels, and sharpens the appetite. Hence it happens that on Sunday night and Monday morning there are more cases of colic and founder than during any other part of the week. Horses that never want an appetite ought not to have an unlimited allowance of hay on Sunday ; they have time to eat a great deal more than they need, and the torpid state of the stomach and bowels produced by a day of idleness, renders an additional quantity very dangerous.

By slow work, I mean that which is performed at a walk, not that which hurries the breathing, or produces copious perspiration. The moderate exertion of which I speak does not, as some might suppose, interfere with the digestive process. It is attended with some waste ; there is some expenditure of nutriment, and that seems to excite activity in the digestive apparatus for the purpose of replacing the loss. Farm and cart-horses are fed immediately before commencing their labor, and the appetite with which they return shows that the stomach is not full ; but,

DURING FAST WORK *digestion is suspended.*—In the general commotion excited by violent exertion, the stomach can hardly be in a favorable condition for performing its duty
20

The blood circulates too rapidly to permit the formation of gastric juice, or its combination with the food; and the blood and the nervous influence are so exclusively concentrated and expended upon the muscular system, that none can be spared for carrying on the digestive process.

The Effects of Fast Work on a Full Stomach are well enough known among experienced horsemen. The horse becomes sick, dull, breathless. He is unwilling, or unfit to proceed at his usual pace; and if urged onward, he quickly shows all the systems of over-marking, to which I allude among the accidents of work. The effects are not always the same. Sometimes the horse is simply over-marked, distressed by work that should not produce any distress. Some take colic, some are foundered, some broken-winded. The most frequent result is over-marking in combination with colic. Perhaps the colic, that is, the fermentation of the food, begins before the horse is distressed; but whether or not, his distress is always much aggravated by the colic.

These effects are not entirely produced by indigestion. The difficulty of breathing may be ascribed to mere fulness of the stomach. Pressing upon the diaphragm, and encroaching upon the lungs, it prevents a full inspiration; and its weight, though, not, perhaps, exceeding eight or nine pounds, must have considerable influence upon a horse that has to run at full speed, and even upon one who has to go far, though not so fast.

Some horses commence purging on the road, if fed directly before starting They seem to get rid of the food entirely or partly: for these, which are generally light-bellied horses, do not suffer so much, or so often, from any of the evils connected with a full stomach. The purgation, however, often continues too long, and is rapidly followed by great exhaustion. They should be kept short of water on working days, and they should have a large allowance of beans.

All work, then, which materially hurries the breathing, ought to be performed with an empty stomach, or at least without a full stomach. Coaching-horses are usually fed from one to two hours before starting, and hay is withheld after the grain is eaten. Hunters are fed early in the morning; and racers receive no food on running days till their work be over. Abstinence, however, must not be carried so far as to induce exhaustion before the work commences.

AFTER FAST WORK is concluded, it is a little while ere the stomach is in a condition to digest the food. Until thirst has been allayed, and the system calmed, there is seldom any appetite. If the horse have fasted long, or be tempted by an article of which he is very fond, he may be induced to eat. But it is not right to let him; a little does him no good, and a full feed does him harm. The stomach partaking of the general excitement, is not prepared to receive the food. Fermentation takes place, and the horse's life is endangered; or the food lies in the stomach unchanged, and produces founder.

Food, then, is not to be given after work till the horse be cool, his breathing tranquil, and his pulse reduced to its natural standard. By the time he is dressed and watered, he is generally ready for feeding.

SALT AND SPICES AID DIGESTION.—On a journey, or after a severe day, horses often refuse their food. When fatigued, tired of his feed, a handful of salt may be thrown among the horse's grain. That will often induce him to eat it, and it will assist digestion, or at least render fermentation less likely to occur. Some, however, will not eat even with this inducement. Such may have a cordial ball, which in general produces an appetite in ten minutes. I am speaking of cases in which the horse has become cool, and those in which the work has not fevered him. The horse should always be cool before food is offered; and if his eye be red, and pulse quick, cordials, salt, and the ordinary food, are all forbidden. The horse is fevered.

ABSTINENCE unusually prolonged is connected with indigestion, and it produces debility.

The Indigestion of Abstinence may in some cases arise from an enfeebled condition of the digestive apparatus. The stomach and bowels may partake of the general languor and exhaustion, and be in some measure unable to perform their functions; but of this there is no proof. When a horse has fasted all day, he is very apt to have colic soon after he is fed at night. It happens very often. The voracious manner in which the horse feeds has something to do with it. He devours his food in great haste, without sufficient mastication, and he often eats too much. The sudden and forcible distension of the stomach probably renders it unable to perform its duty. The quantity, the quality, and the hurried ingestion of the food, account for the frequency of colic, after a long fast, without supposing that the stomach is weak. The appetite seems to indicate that it is not.

The result may be prevented. Give the horse food oftener

When prolonged abstinence is unavoidable, give him less than he would eat. Divide the allowance into two feeds, with an interval of at least one hour between each. In this way the appetite dies before the stomach is overloaded. To prevent hurried ingestion, give food that is not easily eaten. Boiled food, after a long fast, is unsafe, and grain should be mixed with chaff.

· *The Debility or Inanition of Abstinence* is denoted by dulness. The horse is languid, feeble, and inoffensive. Want of food tames the very wildest; and sometimes vicious horses are purposely starved to quietness. The time a horse may fast before he lose any portion of his vigor, varies very much in different individuals. In some few, it may depend upon peculiarity of form. Light-bellied narrow-chested horses can not afford to fast so long as those of round and large carcase. But in general the power of fasting depends upon habit, the kind of food, and the condition of the horse. When accustomed to receive his food only twice or thrice a day, he can fast longer by an hour or two, without exhaustion, than when he is in the habit of eating four or five times. As a general rule, liable, however, to many exceptions, it may be held that a horse begins to get weak soon after his usual hour of eating is past. The degree and rapidity with which his vigor fails depend upon his work and condition. If idle, or nearly so, for a day or two previous, he may miss two or three meals before exhaustion is apparent. Languor is probably *felt* sooner. If in low condition, he can not fast long without weakness. He has nothing to spare. If his usual food be all or partly soft, he can not bear abstinence so well as when it is all or partly hard.

Horses in daily and ordinary work should seldom fast more than three or four hours. They generally get grain four or five times a day, and between the feeding hours they are permitted to eat hay; so that, except during work, very few horses fast more than four hours. But some, such as hunters and racers, are often required to fast much longer. Hunters are sometimes out for more than nine hours, and they go out with an empty stomach, or with very little in it. The only evil arising from such prolonged abstinence is exhaustion, and among fast-working horses that can not be avoided. The work and the abstinence together may produce great exhaustion and depression, and the horse may require several days of rest to restore him. But if he had been fed in the middle of this trying work, he would have been unable to complete it. The evils arising from prolonged abstinence are less dangerous than those arising from fast work on a full stomach.

The work which must be performed with an empty stomach, should be finished as quickly as circumstances will permit. In order that the racer or the hunter may have all the vigor he ought to have, his work should be over before abstinence begins to produce debility. How long he must fast before he is fit to commence his task, must depend upon the pace, the distance, and the horse's condition. The stomach, after an ordinary meal of grain, is probably empty in about four hours. For a pace of eight or ten miles an hour, it does not need to be empty; if the food be so far digested that it will not readily ferment, a little may remain in the stomach without rendering the horse unfit for exertion of this kind. Coaching-horses, therefore, go to the road in from one to two hours after feeding. For a hunting-pace, perhaps a digestion of two hours will secure the food from fermentation : and in that time, after a moderate meal, the weight and bulk of the food which remains in the stomach will not encumber the horse nor impede his breathing. For a racing-pace the stomach must be empty, and the bowels must not be full. I do not know exactly how long racers are fed before commencing their work. The time appears to vary, spare feeders not being required to fast so long as those of better appetite. I rather think that they are often, or sometimes, kept too long without food ; but I have little right to venture an opinion on the subject. It appears that racers sometimes receive no food on running days till their work is over. If hay were withheld for twelve hours, and grain for three or four before starting, I should think such restriction would be sufficient. These horses, however, are always in high condition ; they can afford to fast for a long time before fasting produces exhaustion, and the distance they run is so short that the expenditure of nutriment is not great. With horses in lower condition, having less spare nutriment in them, a fast of twelve hours produces a sensible diminution of energy, and in this state he is not fit to perform all that he could perform after abstinence of only four or six hours. In the course of training, either for the course or the field, the groom should learn how long the horse can bear fasting without losing vigor, and that will tell him how to regulate the diet on the day of work.

When the distance is considerable, or the work requiring

several hours of continuous exertion, the waste of nutriment
is greater than when the distance is short, or the work soon
over, and the abstinence must be regulated accordingly. For
a long road, the sooner a horse is fit to begin his task after
feeding, the less will he be exhausted at the end of it.

To prevent, in some degree, the debility of abstinence when
the work forbids food, it is not unusual, I believe, to give a
little spirits of wine. Between the heats of a race a pint of
sherry or two glasses of brandy may be given in a quart of
water. The horse will drink it, and I do not know of any
objection to such a practice. The energy it inspires is over
in about an hour, and it is not developed in less than ten
minutes. From ten to fifteen minutes before running is
therefore the proper time to give it; the horse may run in
five, but in that case the race will be over before the stimulant
operates. [We must discountenance spirituous stimulants to
give temporary energy. If any be necessary, a nervous one
should be used.]

I have said that the only evil arising from prolonged abstinence is exhaustion. There is, however, one more, and
though of little consequence, it deserves notice. When the
stomach is empty, and the bowels containing very little, the
horse is sometimes troubled with flatulence. The bowels
seem to contain a good deal of air. They are noisy: the
horse has slight intermitting colicky pains, which do not last
above a minute, are never violent, and cease as the air is expelled. I have never known this require any particular
treatment; but a little spirits, or half a dose of the colic mixture, or a feed of oats, or a cordial ball, removes it at once.

INABSTINENCE.—It often happens that horses who are much
in the stable, and receiving an unlimited allowance of
food, are never permitted to fast. They get food so often,
and so much at a time, that they always have some before
them. This is not right. A short fast produces an appetite,
and induces the horse to eat more, upon the whole, than
when he is cloyed by a constant supply. If not on full work,
the horse eats too much, although not so much as he would
after short and periodical fasts. Still he eats more than his
work demands. He should not have an unlimited quantity.
The food is wasted, and the horse becomes too fat. But
when the work is so laborious that the digestive apparatus
can not furnish more nutriment than the system consumes,
then the more the horse eats the better; and a short fast
prior to every feeding hour creates an appetite. When grain

is always before him, he never becomes sufficiently hungry to eat heartily. In some places thirty or forty minutes are allowed to feed; and when the time expires, a man goes round the mangers and removes all the grain that is left. In other places the left grain is not taken away, but, if not all eaten before the next feeding hour, no more is given at that time.

THE HOURS OF FEEDING must vary with the work; when that is regular, the hours of feeding should be fixed. After the horse has become accustomed to them, they should not be suddenly changed. When the work is irregular, the horse often called to it without much notice, and when it does not demand an empty stomach, the horse should be fed often. By giving the allowance at four or five services, instead of two or three, the horse is always ready for the road. He can never have so much in his stomach at any time as if he were fed seldomer. On a posting establishment, all the horses that are in should not be fed at the same time; one pair, or two, or more, may be kept in readiness for work, not fed till some others are ready.

It is probable that fixed hours of feeding are favorable to digestion, and it is certain that any sudden and considerable change of hour is attended with disadvantage. When the interval of abstinence is abridged, the horse does not eat so heartily; and when prolonged, he becomes exhausted. But when there are no fixed hours observed, the horse's appetite is the only guide. When the feeding hours are variable, the horse gets hungry only when the system wants nutriment; when the hours are fixed, the stomach demands a supply, whether the system wants it or not.

THE BULK OF THE FOOD is an important consideration in the feeding of horses. When fed entirely, or chiefly, upon hay, grass, or roots, they are not fit for fast work. There are three reasons why they are not. Bulky food distends the stomach and makes it encroach upon the lungs, and impede breathing; its weight encumbers the horse; and it does not yield sufficient nutriment. The horse may be able enough for slow work, because that work does not demand all the energies of the system. But hunting, coaching, and racing, are tasks of such labor, that the least impediment to breathing renders the horse unable to perform them. Hay or grass alone will yield sufficient nourishment to an idle horse; but he must eat a great deal of it; so much that his belly is always very large; the bowels must be constantly full. Such a load is not so easily carried in the belly as on the back

This weight, and the difficulty of breathing, are sufficient to render bulky food unfit for fast-working horses. But even slow work, when exacted in full measure, demands food in a condensed form. The work, though slow, requires more nutriment than a bellyful of hay or grass will yield. The nourishment extracted from hay, straw, or potatoes, may be quite as good as that extracted from oats; but the stomach and the bowels can not hold enough of these bulky articles.

A horse may gallop at the top of his speed for a few moments, even when his bowels are loaded with bulky food; but he soon stops or staggers, over-marked, or broken-winded, or he takes colic; one or all of these evils may be expected when he is put to fast-work with his bowels loaded. Bulky food also renders the horse exceedingly liable to colic; and to me this appears to be the principal reason why the disease is so much more common in draught than in saddle horses.

Condensed Food, for reasons already stated, is necessary for fast-working horses. Their food must be in less compass than that of the farm or cart horse. But to this condensation there are some limits. Grain affords all, and more than all, the nutriment a horse is capable of consuming, even under the most extraordinary exertion. His stomach and bowels can hold more than they are able to digest; [or, if it could be digested, it would furnish more nutriment than could be assimilated; or, if assimilated, than the system demands.] Something more than nutriment is wanted. The bowels must suffer a moderate degree of distension; more than a wholesome allowance of grain can produce. They are very capacious. In the dead subject nearly thirty gallons of water can be put into them. It is evident they were not intended for food in a very condensed form; and it seems that they require a moderate degree of pressure or dilatation to assist their functions. It is not certain that their secretions, sensations, and contractions, are altered by emptiness, but it is probable. They must have something to act upon.

When hay is very dear, and grain cheap, it is customary, in many stables, to give less than the usual allowance of hay, and more grain. The alteration is sometimes carried too far, and it is often made too suddenly. The horses may have as much grain as they will eat, yet it does not suffice without fodder. Having no hay, they will leave the grain to eat the litter. A craving sensation of emptiness seems to arise, and the horse endeavors to relieve it by eating straw The sensation can not be the same as that of hunger, otherwise the horse would devour his grain. While he has plenty of grain, and plenty of litter, the diminished allowance of hay is borne with impunity. [The bowels need distension; hay contains a large amount of woody fibre; this produces distension, and is ejected as fecal matter. Without distension and abundant fecal matter, there can be no health.]

When sufficiency is not obtained in any shape, the horse loses appetite, emaciates; his bowels are confined; his flank sadly tucked up—his belly indeed almost entirely disappears; in general he drinks little water, and when he takes much he is apt to purge. His belly is often noisy, rumbling of the bowels; apparently containing a good deal of air, which occasionally produces slight colicky pains. These horses are said, and I believe truly said, to be very liable to crib-biting and wind-sucking. It is certain that the diseases are exceedingly rare among those that live on bulky food.

When the ordinary fodder, then, is very dear, its place must be supplied by some other which will produce a wholesome distension, though it may not yield so much nutriment. Straw or roots, either or both, may be used in such cases. The excessively tucked-up flank, and the horse's repeated efforts to eat his litter, show when his food is not of sufficient bulk.

When work demands the use of condensed food in a horse that has been accustomed for some time to bulkier articles, the change should be made by degrees. Coming from grass, or the straw-yard, the horse, for a time, requires more fodder than it would be proper to allow him at his work.

HARD FOOD.—For a long time it has been almost universally supposed that the greatest and most lasting vigor could not be obtained without an ample allowance of hard, substantial food, such as raw oats and beans with hay. But within a few years there have been several attempts to show that these articles are improved by cooking. It has been argued that steaming or boiling partially digests the food, or renders it more easy of digestion.

It is nonsense to say that cooking is digestion. The stomach is not a boiler. It does its work in a way of its own, not to be imitated by any culinary process.

Food which has been softened by steaming, maceration, or boiling, may possibly be more quickly digested. The nutritive matter may be more rapidly and more easily extracted from food after this preparation. Granting that it is so, there is still room, I think, for doubting whether it is advantageous to have all the food rapidly digested. Stablemen, who ought to know best, admit the propriety of giving one feed of boiled food every day during cold weather. But they declare that more sickens the horse, and makes him *soft;* he perspires profusely, and his energy is soon exhausted. This refers only to horses of fast work, in constant employment.

The opinions of stablemen on this subject have been much ridiculed. They are too apt to theorize. Instead of telling what they see, they tell what they think. They contend that hard food produces hard flesh, and everybody knows that no horse is at his best when his flesh is soft. This is a fine opening for a mere theorist, who knows anything about anatomy. Instead of seeking the foundation of the theory, he attacks the theory itself. "This notion about hard food," he says, "is all nonsense. All the food, whether hard or soft, must become a fluid before it can form any part of the system. Therefore, the softer it is when given, the sooner is it dissolved."

It is quite true, and easily proved, that no food can afford nourishment till it assumes a fluid form. But this is not the way to settle the question. Some men are such inveterate theorists that they always argue when they ought only to experiment.

Place two or more horses, similar in size, age, condition, power, and breeding, at the same work and in the same stable. To one give the food all soft, to another all hard, and to a third give it partly hard and partly soft. Continue the experiment for a month, and then reverse it, by giving to one the food which was given to another. Observe the condition of the horses from beginning to end, and be careful that the result is not influenced by some circumstances not operating equally upon all. One might catch cold, fall lame or sick, and he would not be a fair subject for comparison. This is the proper way to decide the matter. If conjecture should settle it, conjecture is easily made. Thus, soft food contains a deal of water; probably this water enters the system along with the nutritive matter, and though it may fill up the tissues, and produce plumpness, yet it confers no vigor. The nutritive matter which has been obtained from this soft, watery food, has entered the system too rapidly—before it has been sufficiently animalized to form any durable part of the system. I is, therefore, soon and easily evacuated. Ima-

gine this to be true—it is very like the stuff found in the
treatises on dietetics—and there is no difficulty in seeing the
superiority of hard food. Without any theory, however,
upon the subject, appearances seem in favor of the common
opinion.

The continuous use of Hard Food is supposed to produce
progressive increase of vigor for several months, or, according to some, for several years. Among stablemen it is a com
mon way of recommending a horse, to say that *he has got
year's hard keep in him.* Nimrod has gone much further
Speaking of post-horses, the work they do, sometimes sixty
miles in a day, and the abuse they suffer from exposure to
the weather, from bad stables, and bad grooms, he alludes to
their condition, and asks how it is that, in defiance of such
hard usage, they look so well and do so much. " Is it," he
says, "their natural physical strength ? Is it the goodness
of their nature ? My reasoning faculty tells me it is neither
—they would both fail. No! it is solely to be attributed to
the six, eight, ten, twelve, perhaps fourteen years' *hard meat*
which they have got in them—to that consolidation of flesh,
that invigorating of muscle, that stimulus to their nature,
which this high keep has imparted to them—which give
them, as it were, a preternatural power."

Had Nimrod always written thus, he should never have
been quoted by me. There is not, in all his letters, another
passage so remarkable for bad reasoning and bad writing.
No one ever knew a post-horse twelve or fourteen years on
the road without interruption. If he had occasionally to perform a journey of sixty miles in one day, he would often, in
the course of so many years, require to be thrown off work
for several successive weeks, either for lameness or for sickness ; and every time such a horse is idle for a number of
weeks, he loses all the vigor which previous work and solid
food had conferred.

When horses are well fed, they are generally well worked.
In the course of time they acquire strength and endurance,
which the undomesticated horse can never rival. Solid food
has perhaps a good deal to do in the production of such vigor,
but the work has much more. Without work, no kind nor
quantity of food will make a hunter or a racer. To encounter
extraordinary labor, the horse must be trained to it ; and, while
training, he must be fed on solid food, or at least upon rich
food.

It appears that solid is better than soft food for such work ;

but how long the horse must be accustomed to this hard food before he becomes as vigorous as it can make him, is still an undecided question. The improvement is progressive, but it must have some limits. So far as I have been able to observe, it appears that in one year judicious feeding and work will in all cases render a mature horse as fit for his work as he will ever be. Many can be seasoned in less than three months, and a great number receive all the improvement of which they are susceptible in less than six; I do not believe that any mature horse improves after he has been on solid food and in work for one year, and this period includes the time allotted to training.

A MIXED DIET is, in some cases, better than that composed of only two or three articles. Oats and hay form the ordinary food of stabled horses. In summer, a little grass is frequently added, and in winter, roots. But a great number of horses kept in towns receive nothing but oats and hay all the year round. For those that do only moderate work, these two articles, with a weekly feed of bran, seem to be sufficient. But others, whose work is more laborious, and often performed in stormy weather, are, I think, the better of a more complicated diet, more especially when the ordinary food is not of the best quality. Beans form a third article, and to hardworking horses they are almost indispensable. During the trying months of winter, the diet may be still further varied by barley, or wheat, or rye. These may be boiled, and given only once a day, or they may enter into every feed. The change should be made slowly; the new articles, at first, not exceeding a fourth or fifth part of the whole, and an equal quantity of the ordinary food being withheld. As the horse becomes used to them, the quantity may increase, if a larger quantity be deemed useful.

The horses to whom a mixed diet is most necessary, are those that perform the severest work. The principal advantage derived from the combination of several articles, is that of tempting the horses to feed more heartily. They eat more of this mixed food than of the simple, because one or more of the articles are new to them. The horses, therefore, maintain their condition better. It may also be, that the use of several articles enables the system to obtain that from one which can not be furnished by another.

CHANGES OF DIET.—After the horse has been accustomed to a certain kind or mixture of food, it is not to be suddenly changed. By inattention to this, many errors prevail regarding a horse's food. It is extensively believed that boiled food, barley, carrots, and some other articles, produce purgation—that raw wheat is poisonous—that peas swell so much as to burst the stomach—that potatoes, and many other things, are flatulent.

The truth is, a sudden change of diet produces evils which would not occur were the change made with care. The most frequent result of a change is colic, next to that purgation, and after these come founder, surfeit, weed, constipation, and apoplexy. Some of these, perhaps the whole of them except purgation, may arise as often from the horse eating too much, as from the sudden change. But it appears quite certain that the stomach and bowels require some little time to adapt themselves to articles upon which they have not been accustomed to act. The horse eats too much, because the new article is more palatable than his ordinary food; and the groom often gives too much without knowing it; he gives barley and beans in the same measure that he gives oats. These articles, and wheat, are much heavier in proportion to their bulk. An equal weight of oats might not be eaten, though it were given, and the horse would suffer no evil; but if the horse is not used to beans or barley, he will eat a greater *weight* of those than of his oats; if an equal quantity, by weight, were given, the horse would be in less danger; but still it is not safe suddenly to substitute one article for another.

If it were determined to use a certain portion of barley instead of oats, say an equal quantity of each, the change is not to be made in one day nor in one week. At first give the barley in only one of the daily feeds, and in small quantity, so that, during the first week, one feed will consist of three parts oats, and one part barley—the other feeds will be the same as usual; in the second week, one feed will be half oats and half barley; in the third week, give two of those feeds every day; in the next, three, and so on till the horses receive the allotted quantity.

One dose of physic, perhaps two, may be useful when the diet is altered; but if the horses be seasoned, and in full work, it is seldom necessary. It is most required when the food is richer and more constipating than that to which they have been used.

THE QUANTITY OF FOOD may be insufficient, or it may be in excess. The consumption is influenced by the work, the weather, the horse's condition, age, temper, form, and health:

these circumstances, especially the work, must regulate the allowance.

When the horse has to work as much and as often as he is able, his allowance of food should be unlimited.

When the work is such as to destroy the legs more than it exhausts the system, the food must be given with some restriction, unless the horse be a poor eater.

When the work is moderate, or less than moderate, a good feeder will eat too much.

When the weather is cold, horses that are much exposed to it require more food than when the weather is warm.

When the horse is in good working condition, he needs less food than while he is only getting into condition.

Young, growing horses require a little more food than those of mature age ; but, as they are not fit for full work, the difference is not great.

Old horses, those that have begun to decline in vigor, require more food than the young or the matured.

Hot-tempered, irritable horses seldom feed well ; but those that have good appetites require more food to keep them in condition, than others of quiet and calm disposition.

Small-bellied, narrow-chested horses require more food than those of deep and round carcass ; but few of them eat enough to maintain them in condition for full work.

Lame, greasy-heeled, and harness-galled horses require an extra allowance of food to keep them in working condition.

Sickness, fevers, inflammations, all diseases which influence health so much as to throw the horse off work, demand, with few exceptions, a spare diet, which, in general, consists of bran-mashes, grass, carrots, and hay.

Deficiency of Food.—When the owner can afford to feed his horse, he generally allows him sufficient. He soons discovers that the work can not be done without it. He may grudge the cost of keeping, but he soon finds that it is easier to buy food than to buy horses. Starvation and hard work quickly wear them out. Though nobody who can avoid it will starve his working horses, yet many think it no sin to starve idle horses. Colts, before they come into use, and horses thrown out of work by lameness or other causes, are often very ill fed, or, rather, they are not fed at all. The privations of a farmer's stock during winter may not in every case be avoidable, and when they can not be cured they must be endured. But the allowance of food is often reduced too much, not because there is little to give, but because it is thought unnecessary or wasteful to give more.

Both young and old horses suffer more mischief from want of sufficient food than is generally supposed. The young, however, suffer most. Starvation checks the growth and *destroys the shape.* Horses that have been ill-fed when young, are almost invariably small, long-legged, light-carcassed, and narrow-chested. Some of them have a good deal of energy, but all are soon exhausted, unfit for ·protracted exertion. Grown-up horses, when much reduced by deficient nourishment, require more food to put them into working order than would have kept them for two or three months in the condition they require to possess when going into work. If the horses are to be idle for twelve months, it may perhaps be cheaper to let them get very lean than to keep them plump ; but for a period of three or four months, during which farm and some other horses are idle or nearly so, it is cheaper to keep as much flesh upon them as they will need at the com mencement of their labor.

When the horse is starved, besides losing strength and flesh, his bowels get full of worms, and his skin covered with lice. Very often he takes mange, and sometimes he does no moult, or the hair falls suddenly and entirely off, leaving the skin nearly bald for a long time. The skin of an ill-fed horse is always rigid, sticking to the ribs, and the hair dull, staring, soft, dead-like. I have never seen anything like permanent evil arising from temporary starvation of *mature* horses. If not famished to death, they recover strength and animation upon good and sufficient feeding. But starvation always spoils the shape of a *growing* horse.

Excess of Food.—When the supply of food is greater than the work demands, the horse becomes fat. The superfluous nutriment is not all wasted. The system does not require it at the time, but it may at some other. To provide against an increased demand or a deficient supply, this redundant nutri ment is stored away. It is converted into fat and deposited into various parts of the body ; some is laid under the skin, some among the muscles, but the largest quantity is found among the intestines and inside the belly. When wanted, this fat is reconverted into blood.

Slow-working horses may be fat and yet not unfit for work ; but the weight of the fat is a serious encumbrance to fast-workers, and its situation impedes the action of important organs, particularly the lungs. Horses at full and fast work never accumulate fat ; they can not eat too much. When the work is irregular and fast, the horse sometimes idle and sometimes tasked to the utmost, he may eat too much. He may become fat and unfit to do his work, which is the most ruinous of all work.

To keep a horse in condition for fast work, his work should be regular, and when it can not, his food should be given in such measured quantities that it will not make him fat.

A sudden change from a poor to a rich diet does not at once produce fatness. It is more apt to produce plethora, redundancy of blood. The stomach and bowels, previously accustomed to economize the food, and to extract all the nutriment it was capable of yielding, continue to act upon the rich food with equal vigor. A large quantity of blood is made, more than the system can easily dispose of. Were the horse gradually inured to the rich food, there would be time to make the necessary arrangements for converting the superfluous nutriment into fat. But the sudden change fills the system with blood. This often happens to cattle and sheep, but the horse does not suffer in the same way as these animals. Sheep and young oxen, after entering a luxuriant spring pasture, take what is called the blood. All at once they become very ill ; some part of the body is swelled, puffy as if it con tained air : in two or three hours the beast is dead. Upon dissection, a large quantity of blood, black and decomposed, is found in the cellular tissue, where, in life, the swelling appeared. This, if ever it occur in the horse, is exceedingly rare. In him, plethora seems to create a strong disposition to inflammation in the eyes, the feet, and the lungs. Sometimes an eruption appears on the skin ; this is termed a surfeit heat. The hair often falls off in patches, and the skin beneath is raw or pimpled ; these are termed surfeit blotches. The horse is prone to grease. Those of the heavy-draught breed often have what in some places is termed a weed, in others a shoot of grease, in others still, a stroke of water-farcy. One of the legs, generally a hind-leg, swells suddenly ; it is painful ; it is lame ; pressure inside the thigh in the course of the vein, produces great pain ; the horse is a little fevered. In a few cases, among the same kind of horses, there are numerous puffy, painless tumors all over the body, especially about the eyes, muzzle, belly, and legs. This is most commonly termed water-farcy. The proper name is acute anasarca. The horse may be left well, or apparently well at night ; in the morning he is found with his eyes closed, buried in soft *pitting* tumors, and his muzzle so much swelled that he can not open his mouth. All these evils are sudden in their attack. They may arise from other causes; but plethora suddenly attained is the most common cause; and is the result of feeding beyond the work.

Plethora may be produced without any alteration in the quantity or quality of the diet. If the horse be suddenly thrown out of full work, and receive all the food to which he has been accustomed, the result will be very nearly the same as if he were put upon a richer diet. It must be remembered that excess in the supply is excess only when it is greater than the work demands. An idle horse may be eating no more than a working horse, or he may be eating less, yet it may be too much.

The symptoms of plethora are easily recognised before it has produced or contributed to the production of any cutaneous, anasarcous, or inflammatory disease. For one, two or more days the horse is somewhat dull; he eats his grain, perhaps, but refuses his hay; he drinks much, his coat is dry; on some places, across the loins, the face, and the poll, it is soft and staring; the eye is red, often yellowish; the mouth hot and dry; the bowels costive; the urine high-colored. When the stables are shut, the horse sweats; when open, he shivers, or his coat starts on end. If put to work, he is feeble and without animation; he soon perspires, and he is soon exhausted. In this febrile state he may remain for several days. Perspiration seems to relieve him a little; but as the horse eats little, the natural cure is probably performed by refusing to take more nutriment till the superfluity be consumed. When the digestive organs continue to maintain their power, the appetite is not impaired, and the horse, after pining two or three days, or a longer time, in the plethoric fever, suffers from an attack of inflammation, or some of the other evils already mentioned fall upon him. Swelled legs and thrushy frogs are among the earliest and least serious consequences.

The treatment of plethora is very simple. Starvation alone will effect a cure. Bleeding averts its consequences at once; but, in general, this operation is not imperiously demanded. In ordinary cases, it is enough to diminish or withhold the allowance of grain, to give a little green food, carrots, or bran-mashes; as medicine, a diuretic or an alterative may be given, or a dose of physic, which is better than anything else, and when the horse can be spared, it should be given. A gentle sweat is also a good remedy. As the horse recovers his spirits, let him return by degrees to the diet which his work demands.

To prevent plethora, it is customary, in hunting and other stables where the work is only occasional, yet very severe, and requiring a liberal diet, to give an alterative now and then. Black antimony, nitre and sulphur, four drachms of each, form a useful alterative for blank days. Hunters of keen appetite, and legs which will not stand full work, are not easily kept in order: they may have a ball every week, or twice a week during the working season. It should be given an hour before the last feed, in a little bran-mash. On the day before work, it is forbidden.

Influenza and plethora* are often confounded. The symptoms of plethora are very like those which we have at the beginning of influenza; but the treatment is different, and distinction must be made. If the symptoms of plethora appear without any change in the diet, or work sufficient to account for them, it is very likely the horse is taking the influenza, which, in many stables, is usually called the distemper. A veterinarian ought to be consulted. Influenza is in general accompanied by great weakness, often some soreness of the throat, a little cough, a watery discharge from the nose, swelling of the eyelids, stiffness, a peculiar state of the pulse, and several other symptoms by which the veterinarian can distinguish it from plethora.

Humors.—Everybody has heard of "humors flying about the horse." It is an old stable phrase, and still a great favorite. The horse is not well, yet he is not ill. There is always something wrong with him. One month he has swelled legs, another he has inflamed eyes, another he has some tumors about him, or some eruption on the skin, and so on all the year through. He is hardly cured of one disease till he is attacked by some other; and perhaps he never does any good till he changes hands, when he soon becomes an excellent horse, always ready for his food and for his work. This often happens. Plethora, repeatedly excited, is the cause.

The stabling, or the grooming, may have been bad; the horse unequally fed, or irregularly worked—some weeks half-starved, others surfeited to plethora—sometimes idle for ⌐ month, and sometimes over-worked for a month. He does

---

* I ought sooner to have mentioned, that among stablemen plethora is usually termed foulness. The horse is said to be foul. I have rejected this name, because, in Scotland, a glandered horse is termed foul.

better, indeed quite well, when he is properly worked and properly fed. The humors are blamed. According to the groom there is some bad humor flying about the horse. He gives his drugs to sweeten the blood, puts in rowels to drain off impurities, and plays numberless other tricks, such as ignorance alone could suggest. Little, in truth, is required but to get rid of that which plethora has already produced, and subsequently to give regularity to the work and to the feeding, and to proportion the one to the other.

PRACTICE OF FEEDING.

In well-managed stables the practice of feeding is regulated by the principles, so far, at least, as they are understood. Nevertheless it may be useful to give a short account of the matters and modes of feeding in reference to different kinds of horses. I shall here state the general mode, so far as I have been able to learn it, and give a few examples.

The Farm-Horse is fed on oats, meal-seeds, corn-dust, barley-dust, beans, barley, hay, roots, straw, and grass. The grain is given raw and boiled, whole, bruised, or ground, and with or without a masticant.* Wheat is seldom used, beans only when the work is very laborious, and bran rarely except to sick horses. The fodder varies with the work and the season. In winter it consists of hay, and the different kinds of straw, including that of beans and peas. The quantity is unlimited, and it is rarely cut into chaff. Rye-grass, clover and tares, are given while they are in season, to the exclusion of other fodder. They are given in the stable or in the field, and some horses are partly soiled and partly pastured. The quantity of grain varies with the work and the size of the horse. From fourteen to sixteen pounds is considered a liberal allowance for a large horse in full work. The night feed is usually boiled so soon as grass fails. The quantity diminishes as the days shorten. In some places the grain is altogether withheld during a part of the winter, fodder being given in the day, and some boiled roots at night.

Some farmers never give more than ten pounds of grain per day. It is not possible to state the proper allowance. In all cases the horse himself soon tells whether he is getting too much or too little. He should be kept rather above than

* *Masticant.*—Any article—such as cut fodder, bran-chaff, hay-seeds, or meal-seeds—which ensures mastication of the grain with which it is mingled.

under his work ; and even when idle, or nearly so, he should
not lose flesh. If he be half-starved in winter, the spring
will find him very unfit for the labor which it brings, and it
costs more to put flesh on the horse than to keep it on.

" Mr. Harper of Bank Hill, Lancashire, ploughs seven acres
per week the year through, on strong land, with three horses,
each of which receive two bushels of oats per week, with
hay during the winter six months, and during the remainder
of the year one bushel of oats with green food.

" Mr. Ellam of Glynde, in Sussex, gives two bushels of
oats, with peas-haulm, or straw, during thirty winter weeks ;
and one bushel of oats, with green food, in summer."[*]

In Scotland, farm-horses are usually put upon hard food
by the beginning of October, receiving hay and a medium
allowance of oats, from six to nine pounds. In the months
of December and January, the hay gives place to straw, and
the oats are still farther reduced. In February, hay and a
full allowance of oats are given, and form the most of the
food till the commencement of June, when grass comes in.
The allowance of oats is then reduced, and the grass is either
given in the stable or in the field.[†]

As winter food, Professor Low recommends cut-hay, cut-
straw, bruised or coarsely-ground grain, and cooked potatoes,
in equal proportion *by weight*. Of this mixture he says 30 to
35 pounds, or, on an average, $32\frac{1}{2}$ pounds, will be sufficient
for any horse during the twenty-four hours.

In the Quarterly Journal of Agriculture, No. 21, the following mixture, in which there is no hay, is recommended
for its economy. The horse is fed thrice, receiving at each
time fifteen pounds :—

In the morning he gets	$3\frac{1}{2}$ lbs.	of oat and bean meal mixed with
	$11\frac{1}{2}$ "	cut-straw.
At mid-day, . . .	3 "	oat and bean meal, with
	12 "	cut-straw.
At night	$1\frac{1}{2}$ "	oat and bean meal,
	2 "	cut-straw, and
	$11\frac{1}{2}$ "	steamed potatoes.

It is unnecessary accuracy to speak of straw or potatoes
by half pounds. Two or three pounds, more or less, of
either, produce little actual, and no appreciable difference on
the horse.

In many, or most of the places in this neighborhood, farm
horses are fed four or five times while working nine or ten

---

[*] Complete Grazier, 181. Agricultural Survey of Sussex, pp. 378, 381.
[†] Low's Elements of Agriculture.

hours per day. In the morning, about five o'clock, they are fed with grain; they go to work till eight, when they are fed again, sometimes on boiled roots, to which, corn-dust, light oats, or meal-seeds may be added, and sometimes on raw grain; they work from nine till twelve or one—are fed a third time; return to work till six or seven—are fed a fourth time, generally on boiled food, unless there be grass. Some give a small quantity of grain about nine or ten o'clock, which forms a fifth feed, but this is not common.

The farmers hereabout reserve the light husky oats for home consumption. It is very well to do so, for they answer as well as any others, if given in sufficient quantity. But I often see much of this grain wasted. It is boiled with roots, or it is scattered raw upon the boiled food and given along with it. It does not soon burst in boiling, and the horse swallows it whole. Such oats should either be bruised by the rollers, or given raw, with a little chaff.

[The best food for ordinary working-horses in America, is, as much good hay or grass as they will eat, corn-stalks or blades, or for the want of these, straw. and a mixture of from 16 to 24 quarts per day, of about half and half of oats and the better quality of wheat bran. When the horse is seven years old past, two to four quarts of corn or hommony or meal ground from the corn and cob is preferable to the pure grain. Two to four quarts of wheat, barley, rye, buckwheat, peas, or beans, either whole or ground, may be substituted for the corn. A pint of oil meal or a gill of flax-seed mixed with the other food is very good for a relish, especially in keeping up a healthy system and the bowels open, and in giving the hair a fine glossy appearance. Potatoes and other roots, unless cooked, do not seem to be of much benefit in this climate, especially in winter—they lie cold upon the stomach and subject the horse to scouring; besides they are too watery for a hard-working animal. Corn is fed too much at the south and west. It makes horses fat, but can not give them that hard, muscular flesh which oats do; hence their softness and want of endurance in general work and on the road, in comparison with northern and eastern horses, reared and fed on oats and more nutricious grasses.]

The cost of keeping farm-horses has been variously estimated at from 15 to 40 pounds per year. There is, without doubt, a good deal of difference in different places, dependent upon the size and work of the horse, and also upon the varying price of his food. Some feed at much less cost than others, by employing cheap substitutes during the high price of any article of ordinary consumption. When oats are dear, wheat, barley, beans, or roots, may partly or wholly supply their place, and hay may be entirely withheld if good straw can be procured. It has been boasted that farm-horses may be kept at summer work on cut green food, with almost no grain. What the owner might call work is not known. But in this country grass alone will not produce workable horses. If food is not given, work can not be taken. Every man who has a horse has it in his power to starve the animal; but that, I should think, can afford little matter for exultation.

CART-HORSES.—The cart-horses employed about towns are fed on oats, beans, bran, and hay. Meal seeds, barley, and corn-dusts, hay-seeds, and roots, are also in common use. In winter, one feed is generally boiled and given the last at night. If any be left, it is given the first in the morning. It usually consists of beans and turnips, or barley and beans, to which bran and hay, seed or barn chaff, are added. Straw is almost never used as fodder for these horses. Hay is given in unmeasured quantity, and it is seldom cut into chaff. In summer, cut grass is used instead of hay, without any alteration in the quantity of grain ; but boiled food is abandoned as the grass comes in. Some give boiled food every Sunday, once a day in summer, and twice in winter. It is supposed to be less constipating than raw grain for the day of rest. Raw beans, with dry bran, form the manger food of a great many cart-horses during the winter. The last feed is boiled with turnips and hay seed, and the rack is filled with hay. Meal seeds are often given along with oats or beans, and sometimes alone.

The quantity of fodder is seldom limited. The horse eats as much as he pleases, or as much as his owner can afford. It will probably vary from 15 to 30 pounds in the twenty-four hours. The quantity of grain varies from 12 to 16 pounds. The oats and beans are seldom bruised.

When the work is regular, the horses are usually fed three times in the stable, and not at all in the yoke. When irregular, and having many stoppages, the carter generally takes out a small bundle of hay and a little grain along with the horse. The grain is given in a nose-bag, a little at a time and often, when the horse stands. The hay is carried in a sack, and the carter often gives a little from his hand as the horse travels. When stopping, the sack is thrown before him, or attached to the cart-shaft, and the horse helps himself.

Messrs. Wiggins of London keep upward of 300 cart-horses, which are nearly all of the largest size. The grain consists of oats, barley, beans, pease, and bran. In summer, oats are preferred to beans; and in spring, barley is supposed to be better than either. But the choice is determined by the price. It is all given by weight, and whichever kind of grain be used, no difference is made in the quantity. When beans are used, an extra allowance of bran is necessary to keep the bowels in order. Swedish turnips and carrots are given occasionally. The fodder consists of clover, or saintfoin hay, and straw.

The beans are bruised, the oats sometimes coarsely ground, and the barley germinated. The fodder is all cut into chaff. The bruising and cutting are performed by machinery, which is worked by a single horse. Two lads, one to feed the machine, and one to unbind and deliver the hay, cut a load in three hours. It does not appear that any of the food is boiled.

The daily quantity allowed to each horse varies a little with his size. The largest receive about 18 pounds of grain, 16 of hay, 4 of straw, and 2 of bran; in all, 40 pounds. For some of the horses, 33 or 36 pounds of this mixture is found sufficient. The whole is given as manger-food. There is no rack fodder.[*]

Messrs. Hanbury & Trueman, London, keep above 80 horses, all of large size. They are fed on oats, beans, hay, and straw. In summer, beans are denied. The oats and beans are bruised, the fodder all cut. The daily allowance to each horse consists of oats 14 pounds, beans 1, with 18 of fodder, in which there is one pound of straw to every eight of hay. The food is never cooked. Salt is given every week on Saturday night and Sunday morning, four ounces at a time. In this way it relaxes the bowels.[†]

Mr. John Brown of Glasgow.—The cart-horses are fed three times a day. They receive oats and a few beans in the morning before going to work, which, in summer, is at six o'clock, in winter at seven. They come in at nine and get another feed, also of oats and beans. They return to work at ten, and do not come home till six, often not so soon. The third feed consists of beans, barley, and hay-seed, all boiled

[*] Quarterly Journal of Agriculture, No. 11. British Husbandry, vol. i., p 141.
[†] Quarterly Journal of Agriculture, No. 11

together and given warm. The fodder consists entirely of
hay, except for a short time in summer, when cut grass is
given. The fodder is not limited; each horse is permitted to
consume as much as he pleases. Few in the twenty-four
hours use more than sixteen pounds. In winter, a few Swedish turnips are added to the other boiled articles.

These horses are in excellent condition all the year. They
work from ten to twelve hours per day. I have known them
out occasionally for fourteen. They are employed in carting
goods to short distances. The draught is seldom more than
25 cwt. They receive neither fodder nor grain while in the
yoke. Each driver has the stable management of his own
horse. The whole are superintended by a foreman, who
measures out the grain. The horses' legs and feet are washed
and dried every night after work. The stables are visited
every morning by a veterinary surgeon.

Messrs. J. & W. Harvey, Distillers, near Glasgow.—The
cart-horses are fed on oats, beans; barley, hay-seed, hay, and
cut grass. The grain is not bruised, and the fodder is not
cut. In winter the last feed is boiled, and in summer grass
renders boiling unnecessary.

The allowance per week to each horse is three bushels of
oats and half a bushel of beans, besides the boiled food,
which consists of barley, beans, and hay-seed. One bushel
of each feeds ten horses. Few consume more than half a
stone (7 lbs.) of hay per day, but the quantity of grain is uncommonly large. They are fed four times. They are employed chiefly on the road, travelling from 8 to 10 or 11 hours
per day, at from 3½ to 4 miles an hour, with a draught of 30
to 35 cwt., cart included.

CARRIAGE, GIG, *Post, Noddy, Cab, Omnibus, and Street-
Coach Horses.*—All these, with few exceptions, have for many
years been fed in the same way, and upon the same articles
as at present. In general they receive three or four feeds per
day, consisting of oats and beans, unbroken and uncooked.
The quantity varies from 12 to 16 pounds; and the fodder.
of which hay is the only kind, is rarely limited. It is not cut.
During the summer some grass is given, and in winter it is
customary to give a large bran-mash instead of grain, once
a-week, generally on Saturday night if the horse be idle on
Sunday. The horses that stand in the streets are fed three
times in the stable, and get some grain and hay in the yoke.

In large posting and omnibus studs some alteration has taken place. The horses are fed according to that system

which has been most extensively adopted by large coach proprietors.

MAIL, STAGE, AND FAST-BOAT HORSES.—Many of these horses are fed in the old way. In winter they receive oats, beans, bran, and hay; in summer, oats, beans, hay, and grass, all given without preparation, and only three times a day. But a new mode has been much adopted by the owners of nearly all the large studs. The food consists of more articles; it is often prepared with a degree of care that in the good old times would have been deemed preposterously troublesome; the horses are fed oftener, and articles are used which many still deem unfit for horses, and even poisonous.

Mr. Lyon of Glasgow was the first to introduce the hay-cutting system into the west of Scotland. It has been practised in his establishment for fifteen years back. For a long while he bruised the oats and split the beans, but now both are given entire. The chaff, without a portion of which grain is rarely given, ensures the mastication of these articles.

The ordinary feeding consists of oats, beans, and hay; but barley is often given both raw and boiled. Every horse receives about six or seven pounds of rack hay at night. There are five feeding hours; the first at six, the others at nine, one, five, and eight. At each time the horse receives one half-peck of a mixture which usually contains 5 bushels of oats, one of beans, and 6 of chaff. The last is in heaped measure. In five feeds of this mixture, there are one peck and a quarter of grain, and as much chaff. The daily allowance will therefore be, of fodder, cut and uncut, about 9 or 10 pounds, and of grain about 13 or 14 pounds. The quantity, however, is not precisely limited. Some horses will eat less, and others more. They get what they will take, the feeder being careful not to give more at one time than the horse will eat.

In winter the horses get boiled food every night. It is composed of barley and beans, to which a few turnips are sometimes added. Three measures of barley and one of beans go over as many horses as four of oats and one of beans. Some hay chaff is added, and this mixture forms the fifth feed. Carrots are given raw during the day; but when considerably dearer than turnips, turnips supply their place. Grass is sometimes given in summer, but not generally. A certain quantity is taken in every morning for the sick, the feeble, and the lame; if not all consumed by these, the remainder is given to others.

When there is neither grass, carrots, nor any boiled food, the horses receive a large warm mash of bran on Saturday night. They work none on Sunday. Salt is not generally used; never except for the lick or the staling-evil, and then a lump of rock-salt is placed in the manger.

Barley is sometimes given raw. The mixture then consists of oats six bushels, of beans three, of barley three, and of chaff six. The horses are fed the same number of times, and from the same measure. This mixture is most esteemed when the work is more than usually laborious.

Wheat is sometimes used; six bushels of chaff, six of oats, three of beans, and three of wheat, form the wheat mixture, which is given in the same way as the others.

Mr. Lyon has tried meal-seeds. The feeding contained eight bushels of chaff, six of oats, four of barley, four of beans, and three of meal-seeds. In this mixture, there is a larger proportion of grain; but the work was severe, for there were few spare horses.

In dear hay seasons Mr. Lyon has given straw chaff, but he thinks it is not profitable while good hay is to be obtained at a moderate price. The hay-seed is all sold. The horses are always in excellent condition. Their legs are never washed without permission. They are watered four or five times a day. They stand always on litter, except on working days, when the litter is entirely taken from the stall, until the horse returns from work. Much straw is saved by this arrangement, but horses that will not urinate on the bare stones may be sent to the road with a full bladder. From this, however, I have not observed any injury. The foreman resides in the stable-yard. He is authorized to hire and discharge strappers. The stud is visited every morning by a veterinary surgeon, and a stable, containing three loose boxes, is set apart for sick and lame horses.

Mr. Walker of Glasgow gives his stage-coach horses five feeds per day. They are fed at six, nine, twelve, four, and half-past six, or at seven. In winter the first four feeds consist of oats and beans, which are given by measure. Eleven of the feeds form one imperial bushel. The quantity of beans varies according to the condition of the horses, and the quality of the oats. Sometimes less than a fourth of the feed is beans; at other times the oats and beans are in equal proportions. The last feed is boiled, and generally composed of barley three, and beans two. Straw or hay chaff, and sometimes turnips, are added. Of the beans and barley mixed, forty feeds go as far as fifty of the oat and bean mixture. The fodder, clover, and rye-grass hay, is given in the racks without limitation. Some hay, and occasionally straw, is cut into chaff for mixing with the grain, which is not bruised. In winter, delicate horses get carrots. As summer approaches, the boiled food is given up. For a while it is given every other night, then twice a week, then once, and at last it is abandoned altogether. In autumn it is introduced in the same gradual manner; grass is very little used. It is consumed chiefly by the defective or spare horses, who get a little only while it is good.

Although the grain is given at regular hours, and in measured quantities, the horses receive as much as they will eat. Some do not consume their allowance, and that which is left is given to others of keener appetite, or put into the boiler, and less is given out at the next feeding hour. All the horses have full work, many of them for part of the year running sixteen miles for six days a week at eight miles per hour in two stages. The stables are good, and the stud is visited by a veterinarian every morning. The horses always stand on litter. Their legs are not washed in cold weather. In hot summers the horses are bathed all over after work.

The late Mr. Peter Mein of Glasgow tried several modes of feeding. In winter he employed hay, and oat or wheat-straw, as fodder; oats, beans, barley, wheat, and turnips, as grain. The fodder was all cut, the raw grain all bruised, the beans were given whole; the wheat, barley, and turnips, were usually boiled.

The horses were fed eight times every day; the first feed was given at five in the morning, the last at ten in the evening. The daily allowance to each horse used to be eight pounds of fodder, and sixteen of grain. The fodder was one half straw, another half hay; the grain, three fourths oats, and one fourth beans. They were always mixed, neither grain nor fodder being given alone. During cold weather, one feed of this mixture was withheld, and replaced by an equal quantity of boiled food, which consisted of beans, barley, and chaff; Swedish turnips were also used, but no carrots nor any bran, except to sick horses. The cooked food was given as the first after work; horses that seemed very fond of it got another at night. In general, each horse got only one ration of boiled food in the twenty-four hours. Some grass was used in summer; while young it was given alone; as it got old, hard, and dry, it was cut and mixed with the chaff and grain. When old

and not cut, the horses wasted much of it. Cutting prevent
ed all waste.

In the winter of 1836, the horses got no hay. Mr. Mein's
stock was exhausted by the 20th of September, and at that
time hay was both dear and bad. He used straw instead of
hay, from the 20th of September till the 15th of May. Each
horse got eight pounds, with sixteen pounds of grain, prepared
and served in the same way as the hay. The allowance of
turnips was rather larger. After May, good straw could not
easily be procured, and from that time to July, 1837, one half
of the fodder was given in hay.

Mr. Mein tried raw wheat. He gave three pounds per day
to each horse, deducting three pounds of oats. The horses
worked and looked as well as usual, but their bowels seemed
to be out of order, for the dung was pale, clay-like, and fetid.
There was no other objection to the wheat.

Mr. Croall of Edinburgh gives oats, beans, hay, grass, and
carrots. The hay is all cut, and given along with the grain;
the oats are bruised, and the beans split or broken fresh every
day. The winter allowance of grain is 14 pounds per day.
The beans are one to three of the oats, by weight. In summer only twelve pounds are given.

HUNTERS.—The horses employed in the field vary so much
in size and breeding, and are treated so variously in different
places, that it is difficult to give any useful account of the
mode in which they are fed. Those who follow the hounds
only once or twice a month usually do so upon their hack, an
ordinary road-horse, whose labors as a hunter do not require
any particular difference in his feeding. During the hunting
season he may receive more than his usual allowance of
grain, but in other respects he is treated as a saddle-horse.
He is stabled all the year, and his work, never very great, is
not such in winter as to demand the repose which is given to
hunters for two or three months in summer.

But in all hunting establishments the horses are treated in
a different manner. Their labors for the season generally
commence about the end of October or beginning of November, and terminate in March or April. From this time till the
month of July, when training for the ensuing winter commences, the horses are idle, or nearly so. Hence there is much
difference between the summer and the winter feeding. In
winter the food consists of oats, beans, and hay; carrots and
barley are sometimes, though very seldom, added to these.

But there are two modes of *summering* the hunter: by one

he is turned to pasture, and fed entirely upon grass; by another, he is kept almost constantly within doors, receiving a little grass, some hay, and a small allowance of grain. The last is the mode recommended and introduced by Nimrod. Formerly it was the custom to turn all hunters to grass as soon as hunting was over; but in many parts of England this practice has been abandoned. For a long time it was universal. It was supposed that the horses were as well at grass as they could be in the stable, and they were kept at much less cost. Possibly some people might believe that summer grazing was necessary for the horse's health, but that does not appear to have been insisted on until Nimrod began to deny the propriety of turning out. Numerous scribblers appeared to oppose him. It was contended that a summer's run at grass is absolutely necessary, exclusive of its economy. The labors of the winter, it was said, have shattered the constitution, the legs, and the feet. The horse has been injured by his work. Rest and his natural food alone can restore him to usefulness. The moisture of the ground is good for his hoofs, and the open air for his lungs. Grass is the most salubrious food the horse can have; it is cooling, refreshing, alterative; it allays the excitement produced by work and high keep; it clears away obstructions, sweetens the blood, relaxes the bowels, purges off the humors, renovates the whole body, and puts the inside to rights. Moreover, the repose which a horse obtains at grass, rectifies, braces, and strengthens, all the parts that his hard work had shaken and relaxed. Moreover, again, it would be the very death of a hunter, and very cruel, to keep him stabled all the year.

I dare say it is evident that the most of this is sad nonsense. Grass and fresh air can be given in the stable quite as well as in the field. Moisture is easily applied to the feet; and for rest, if rest be necessary, the stabled horse has decidedly the advantange.

Objections to Grazing Hunters.—There are only two. The horse loses his hunting condition, and he acquires so much flesh that his legs and feet are apt to be injured in taking the superfluous flesh off him. It is true that a pasture may be so bare or so crowded that an accumulation of flesh or fat can not take place. The horse may even be starved to emaciation. Still he would lose his hunting condition, even though he obtained neither more nor less flesh than he might carry at work. Unless the horse have more exercise, a faster kind of exercise than he takes at grass, he can not keep his hunt-

ing condition. He becomes weak and short-winded, whether
he have much or little food.

There are no other real objections, unless it be one that the
horse is liable to receive the bot-worm into his stomach; but
this has never been urged against grazing.

One party has magnified, or rather multiplied, the virtues,
and another the evil of a summer's run. Pastured hunters,
it is said, are liable to kicks, sprains, and other injuries, in
playing or quarrelling with their neighbors; that the feet are
often injured by stamping the ground when it is hard, and the
flies irritating; that splints and ringbones are sometimes produced in the same way; that the act of grazing is pernicious
to the back-tendons; that broken-wind, roaring, and excessive emaciation, have been the results of a summer's run. But
these are not the necessary consequences of turning out; they
are merely accidents arising from mismanagement or want of
care. Some of the alleged evils have no existence. Ring-
bone, if ever produced at grass, is the result of inattention to
the feet, and splints do no more harm by appearing while the
horse is at pasture than if he were stabled. They would
come whether or not. It has never been proved that grazing
injures the back-tendons.

The pages of the sporting periodicals abound with what
are called arguments, or what is meant for argument, for and
against grazing hunters. With the exceptions to which I
have briefly alluded, nothing has come under my notice wor-
thy of particular attention. Enough has been written, if it be
measured by quantity; but writers on stable affairs are, in
general, not very good writers. They tell stories which neither interest nor instruct, neither refute nor confirm. In
truth, they are often entirely destitute of any connexion with
the subject of discussion. There are numerous accounts of
horses going to grass without fault, and returning with disease, or acquiring disease soon afterward. The circumstance
is supposed to be conclusive in favor of the in-door system.
On the other side, similar tales are told of horses not doing
well in the house. They reason like children. If they see
two things at the same time, they immediately believe that
one is the cause of the other. If a horse die, or fall lame,
while getting grass, that, and nothing else, was the cause. If
a hunter die that had got no grass, no physic, nor any alterative medicine, the want of one or other is the reason he dies.

If a horse could be kept in hunting condition while at
grass, or prepared without hazard, and in time to follow

hounds after a summer's run, as well as by keeping him in the stable, there could not, I think, be any reason for keeping him at home. This could be done, but it would require more care, and the cost would be as great as if the horse were kept entirely in the stable.

Nimrod's Mode of Summering Hunters.—This gentleman, whose real name is Apperley, has acquired considerable celebrity in the sporting world by his writings in favor of home summering. He was the first to introduce the system which bears his assumed name. His remarks were originally published in the *Sporting Magazine*, between 1822 and 1828. They formed a series of letters, which have recently been collected into a single volume; from this I extract the following account of the mode in which he kept six hunters during the summer of 1825. The quotation is considerably abridged.

Food.—The horses had received alteratives during the hunting season, and required no physic when it terminated, which was on the 20th of April. They got their usual food, with very gentle exercise, till the 7th of May—seventeen days. From this time till the 19th—that is, for twelve days—they received some grass during the day, and hay at night. They were soiled a second time for ten days, from the 11th to the 20th of June. They were then prepared for physic, which was given on the 22d. Four of the six horses got no more grass. The other two got about an armful of vetches daily, mixed with their hay, till the sixth of July. Each horse had three quarterns* of oats per day, and three had a single handful of beans in every feed.

Care of the Feet.—The shoes were taken from all the horses on the 7th of May; the hoofs were closely pared, the soles thinned, and frogs let down to the ground. The horses stood barefoot till the 6th of July, a period of sixty days. Each stood two hours every day in a clay-box, a building ten feet by twelve, the floor of which was covered with clay, occasionally moistened by dashing water upon it.

Lodging.—Nos. 1 and 2 were in a building sixteen yards by six. It was well littered, and had an outlet to a small green yard, in which there was a running stream. No. 3 was in a covered building, twelve yards long and six broad. One half of the floor was littered, the other half paved with brick. No. 4 was in a loose box, six yards square, kept quite dark to exclude flies, of which the horse was uncommonly terrified. He was turned into a paddock forty yards

* A quartern is the fourth of a peck.

square, about six times in the course of summer, after sun set, but the fence would not confine him. No. 5 was fired, and stood in a stall all day; in the cool of evening and early at morning he went to the paddock. No. 6 was kept in an airy box, but being vicious, was not so often in the paddock as she should have been.

Medicine.—The first dose of physic was given on the 22d of June: on the 18th of July each horse got a second dose, which was mild. In the month of August, each horse received one half pound of antimony, an ounce at a time for eight successive days. More physic, it was expected, would not be required till after Christmas, but some of the horses had got an alterative ball every week.

Comparative Cost.—To avoid fractions, the period may be called nine weeks. During the hunting season the horses consumed three hundred-weight of hay per week; but in these loose places some is wasted, and more is eaten, the horses having less grain. The quantity consumed by the six horses may be calculated at five hundred-weight per week.

Forty-five cwt. of hay, at £4 per ton, - - -	£9 0 0
Seventy-one bushels of oats at 4s. per bushel - -	14 4 0
Beans - - - - - - - - -	1 10 0
	24 14 0
Six horses at grass for 9 weeks, at 4s. each per week	10 16 0
Difference	13 18 0

About three pounds of the stable outlay would return for manure; and if any one of the horses were sold at the commencement of next hunting season, his condition would be such that he would bring at least twenty-five pounds more than if he had been summered at grass.[*]

According to this account, it appears that each horse costs about five shillings more per week in the stable than at grass. I am, however, inclined to think that the difference will be be found considerably greater when other items are taken into consideration. The cost of grass for soiling, of straw for litter, of attendance, of stable-room, and a few other little articles, is omitted. To the proprietor of an established stud the expenditure for these is insignificant; but every charge on both sides should be known before it can be told whether the horses may be stabled or grazed.

Objections to Home Summering.—The expense attending the in-door system is the only objection that can, I think, be

[*] Nimrod on the Condition of Hunters, pp. 258, 260.

justly urged against it. As far as the health and vigor of the hunter are concerned, experience seems to have fully proved which of the two plans is the best for him. Most of those who have opposed the home summering, persist in magnifying and multiplying the good effects of grazing ; but little is said against Nimrod's system, except that it deprives the horse of all the advantages of grazing, and that it is cruel. The cruelty has been much insisted on, but without any reason. If it can be shown that the stabled hunter has more vigor at the commencement of his labors than he that has summered abroad, it is sufficient proof that the horse has not been uncomfortable. He has not, indeed, experienced tho. delight of galloping in freedom with his companions, but neither has he suffered the pains of freedom. On the hot days he has been reposing at ease in the stable, while others were scorched by a burning sun, and persecuted by multitudes of winged enemies. If the horse himself be consulted, it will be found that, though he likes now and then to have a day or two to himself in a good pasture, yet he prefers home. If every horse that has been long stabled had his own will, he would walk from the field to the stall upon the third or fourth day.

I see no objection to let the hunter out for two or three weeks, while the grass is young. In such a short period he would not suffer much loss of condition—none but what might be easily and safely restored before he is wanted for the hounds. Yet I do not think he would derive any benefit from this, if the pleasure it would give him be excepted. There are cases in which a summer's grass may be quite necessary, demanded by the state of the horse's health. But I am not speaking of these, nor of those to whom grazing would be more than usually injurious. There are exceptions, and have nothing to do with the question. Hunters in full work are generally lean, something exhausted, and have their legs a little the worse for wear, at the end of the hunting season. Some may have become very lame, and these are not fit for grass ; others may have been sadly over-marked, and in bad health ; these would be much the better of the young grass, the gentle and regular exercise, and the open air which they would procure at pasture. But in all ordinary cases, it appears that hunters can be better managed at home than abroad.

They are not to be constantly tied in stalls, nor even kept loose boxes. If the legs be good the horses should have walking and trotting exercise every day, or every second day, during the first six weeks. Afterward the exercise must be fast enough to give good wind. If the legs be defective, the horse may need absolute rest, or he may have walking exercise in moderation every day.

The Winter Food of Hunters consists of oats, beans, hay, and bran. The articles are generally of the best quality. The quantity of hay is about 8 pounds per day, the one half given at morning, the other at night. Many hunters would eat more, and some may be allowed about 10 pounds. A greater quantity makes the belly too large, and impedes the breathing. The day before hunting, the horse should not have more than 8 pounds. If he eat his litter, the setting muzzle must be applied about 10 or 11 o'clock at night, or after the allowance of hay is consumed. In such a case the groom must be in the stable by 5 next morning, to remove the muzzle and give the horse his first feed, along with 4 pounds of hay. For horses somewhat thick-winded, those that breathe as if with great labor, even 8 pounds of hay may be rather too much on the day before work. Horses differ much in the quantity of hay they may eat without inconvenience. The size of the belly is perhaps a good guide. If 8 pounds of hay make it too large for work, less must be given. When the flank is tucked up, a larger allowance is necessary. Hunters of light carcass and narrow chest seldom eat too much of anything, and they are always poor hay-feeders. The round-barrelled horse is most apt to overeat himself. By giving more grain, he may have less disposition to gorge himself with hay; but, unless his legs be good enough to stand much work, more grain will make him too fat. These great eaters need physic often, and alteratives almost every week.

Hunters during the season, are generally fed five times a day, consuming from 12 to 16 pounds of grain. The ordinary feed is a quartern, in each of which there may be one or two single handfuls of beans. The oats and beans are rarely bruised, and the hay almost never cut into chaff. Occasionally a few carrots are given. They are better after a severe day than before it. Hunters seldom receive any boiled food. Barley boiled, or germinated, is an excellent and speedy restorative when the horse has been tired off his feed. The quantity in such a case should not exceed half a feed. Bran-mashes are given only when the horse shows some signs of plethora, when under physic, when work has fevered him, when lameness, fatigue, or sickness, require rest. To horses of keen appetite, it is usual to give a bran-mash once in 8 or 10 days, instead of the customary feed of grain. It keeps the bowels open and prevents plethora, but it is purgative and debilitating, if given within 48 hours of going to hounds. Horses that purge on the road or in the field never need it while able for work.

THE SADDLE-HORSE is fed in nearly the same manner as hunters. He generally gets more hay and less grain. Three feeds per day, about 10 pounds, is the usual allowance, with 12 of hay. Those in full work may be fed in the same way as hunters, or stage-coach horses. When the work is moderate, the feeding may be the same as that of cavalry-horses.

The cost of keeping a horse at livery, varies from 17s. to 25s. per week.

THE CAVALRY-HORSES used to be fed on barley and hay. At present they get 10 pounds of oats, and 12 of hay. They are fed thrice. In the morning they get 3 pounds, at mid-day 4, and at night 3. For six or seven weeks in summer they get cut grass. They have no beans, no boiled food, nor chaff. The oats are not bruised. Once a week a bran-mash is given at night instead of oats. Sick horses get bran-mashes, boiled oats, raw potatoes, and hay or grass. Each horse is allowed 8 pounds of straw every day for litter.

RACE-HORSES.—I have never been at Newmarket, and have had so little to do with race-horses that I can not say much about them. The few remarks I here make, are not derived from extensive personal observation, and I am not sure that my authorities know any more about the matter than myself. The account which I offer of what is, and of what should be, in the feeding of racers, can not be the same as if it had been written at the headquarters of racing. I would not have either the theories or the practice much trusted in.

It seems that race-horses, when in work, live chiefly upon oats, beans, and hay. The quantity of oats varies from 15 to 20 pounds per day; nobody can tell me how much hay is allowed. The racer appears, however, to get as much as the hunter, if he choose to eat it. Race-horses must have no superfluous flesh about them, yet they must possess great vigor and endurance. Some of them, many of them, are delicate, irritable animals, always lean, and often not eating sufficient to confer the energy their work requires. These require food that is both tempting and highly nutritious. They may have as much oats as they will eat, and an allowance of beans in each feed. The only danger of giving too much or too often, is that of disgusting the horse and destroying his appetite, for two or three meals. Clover hay may be given to these horses, and in what quantity they like. They should be fed often, yet never till they are hungry ; others of robust constitution, disposed to eat too much, that is, so much as to produce fatness, in spite of all the work the legs will suffer, must be fed somewhat sparingly. For these horses beans are too strong, and clover too tempting. It is true, the more they eat, the more work they will endure ; and the more work they get in training or racing, the more vigor they display on the day of action. But there are limits to this. The legs fail ; they become tumid, tender, and the fetlocks knuckle ; the horse gets stiff, and his stride shortens. The work which a greedy feeder may require to keep him free from superfluous flesh, confers speed, and especially stoutness, but, carried beyond a certain point, it ruins the legs. Hence it is necessary to limit the allowance of food in proportion to the delicacy of the limbs. If they threaten to fail, the work must be diminished, and, as the work decreases, so must the food ; otherwise, stable-sweating or purging must be employed to keep the horse spare.

Grass is sometimes given to racers. They work chiefly in summer, but also in spring and in autumn. Between racing-days they occasionally require to be soiled. If work be concluded before grass is quite out of season, some is given, while it lasts, to horses that are laid up for the winter.

When racing is over, which is generally by the end of September, the horses are put into winter-quarters. Some may have had much work ; they are emaciated ; the legs are swollen out of shape ; some are lame ; some have galled backs ; all have the feet much injured, the hoofs broken and reduced by frequent removal of the shoes. Those that have been much reduced and knocked about, are put into loose boxes, where they remain for two or three months, receiving grass, carrots, hay, and oats. The quantity of food should be sufficient to put flesh on the horse, but not to produce fatness. If the legs or sheath swell, he must have physic, or an alterative, exercise, and less grain, replaced by bran-mashes, more particularly should there be a tendency to surfeit. When bad weather or the state of the horse's legs requires that he stay much in the house, he should have bran-mashes often, and the loose box should be as large as possible, without being cold.

The horse is to be dressed every day ; the loose-box cleaned every morning. If the legs have not been much abused, and the horse have no lameness, he ought to have exercise every day. If the back sinews be much swollen, little or no exercise should be given for the first four or six weeks. If the horse be lame he must rest till sound. The feet should always be defended by light shoes to prevent further injury of the hoofs, and to permit of out-door exercise. Thrushes, if there be any, are to be dressed every second day ; and if very bad, a leather sole may be applied under the shoe. The shoes need removal, and the feet dressing, every five or six weeks. If the hoofs be much broken and of slow growth, the shoes should be strong enough to wear at exercise for six or eight weeks. At the end of four, they may be removed, eased off the heels, and the nails driven in the old holes.

If the horse be rather lusty at the conclusion of his running, he will require less grain, more exercise, and perhaps a dose of physic. If the legs be good, he may have exercise every day, and a sweating gallop once a fortnight. If the legs be much out of order, the horse must rest, and get two or three doses of physic. At first he should have little grain. He must be reduced in flesh before his legs can be restored.

Some racers are stalled all winter, and if fit for daily exercise they are almost as well in stalls as in loose boxes. But when lameness, injured legs, or great emaciation, forbids exercise abroad, the horse, for a while at least, must have a loose box, where he will have motion enough to prevent swelled legs, stiffness, repletion, and the fatigue and wearisomeness produced by long confinement.

Too much physic, I think, is given in the racing stables. If the legs be good, and the horse lean, he needs no physic at the conclusion of his running. Engorgement of the legs demands two or three doses, which, for a lean horse, should be mild, for a lusty horse pretty strong. But it seems to be a common practice to give three doses, whether the legs need them or not. It is said, that the physic prevents the horse from getting foul, that is, too plethoric : and for a time it does so. But if other circumstances do not demand physic, would it not be as well to limit the allowance of food? It is the high feeding, the system of feeding beyond the work, that produces the plethora. It would surely be easier and safer to give less food, than to give physic for preventing or curing the evils arising from too much food.

It appears to me that both hunting and racing grooms feed the idle horses too fast. If lean when laid out of work, it is

23

right to have them plump, well filled-up by the time they are
called into training. Racers are generally altogether out of
work for about three months, many of them for a longer, but
few for a shorter time. The whole of this period may be
necessary to restore the legs, but much less time suffices to
fill up an emaciated horse. If a tolerable feeder, six weeks
of repose on a generous diet will recruit the racer, even when
his work—to use a stable phrase—has drawn him very fine.
But it is not right to hasten flesh upon him so rapidly. If the
horse is to lie off for three months, and, in the first two, acquires all the flesh he can carry in training, the last month
will load him with superfluity, which must be pulled off, at
the hazard of the legs, or by means of bleeding, physic,
sweating, or alteratives. In the first place, all the grain from
which the superfluous flesh is derived, goes to waste ; it is
lost. In the second place, the flesh must be removed at considerable hazard to the horse, and a large expenditure of time,
trouble, and money, to the owner.

There are many racers to whom these remarks are not applicable. Those of light carcass and hot tempers rarely feed
so well as to accumulate fat. They may have what they will
eat and drink. But the others, those of deep chests, broad
loins, and keen stomachs, must have their allowance of grain
regulated by their work. The groom should know with what
flesh the horse can go to training in spring, and he should take
care that the requisite quantity is not required too soon.

PASTURING.

IN another place, I have spoken of grass as an article of
food. Its laxative and alterative properties are well known.
So far as mere health is concerned, grass is the most salubrious food the horse can receive. When eaten where it grows,
the horse is said to be turned out—to be getting a run at grass
—or he is at grass. When cut, and consumed in the stable,
the horse is said to be soiled.

PASTURE FIELDS differ very widely. Some are composed
of only two or three plants ; others of an endless variety. Of
the same field some parts are highly relished, and always
cropped to the root ; while many others, luxuriant, healthy,
and, to the eye, attractive, are never touched, or eaten only
when there is nothing else to eat. The soil is sometimes
hard and injurious to naked feet, sometimes soft and marshy,
favorable to the growth of horn but not to a weak hoof. Pas-

tures on the seashore, and occasionally laid under salt-water, are supposed to be more salubrious than others. They are termed salt-marshes, saltings, or ings. For horses worn down, by bad food, hard work, or disease, they are recommended by several authorities as peculiarly renovating, but their superiority is not unquestionable. Whatever be the nature of the soil and of the herbage, there should be abundance of grass, a supply of water, shelter from the sun and the storm, and fences to enforce confinement.

It is probable that grass eaten in the field produces quite the same effects as that eaten in the stable. But at pasture there are several agents in operation to which the stabled horse is not necessarily exposed. The exercise he must take, and the position his head must assume, in order that he may obtain food; the annoyance he suffers from flies; his exposure to the weather; the influence of the soil upon the feet and legs; and the quantity of food placed at his disposal, appear to me to be all the circumstances which make pasturing different from soiling. They deserve a little notice in detail.

THE EXERCISE which the pastured horse must take as he gathers his food, varies according to the state of the herbage. When the ground is bare, the exercise may amount even to work, but to a sound horse it is never injurious; in cold weather it keeps him warm, or, at least, prevents him from becoming very cold. With a lame horse the case is different. In some lamenesses, the slow but constant exercise which a horse must take at grass is beneficial. It is so in the navicular disease, and in all other chronic diseases of the joints; of which, however, there are not many in the horse. The exertion which a bare pasture demands, is unfavorable to any sprain or lameness arising from disease in the ligaments and tendons. Lameness when very great, no matter where seated, forbids pasturing, even though the herbage be knee-high. The pain of standing, and moving on two or three legs, may be so great that the horse will be compelled to lie before he has obtained half a meal. In a rich pasture he will lose flesh, and in a bare one he will starve. I have seen groggy horses, even where the grass was abundant, so much reduced that they could hardly move. They could not stand till they obtained sufficient food, and they could obtain none when lying.

It is for slight lameness only that horses should be turned out; and the pastures should be such as to afford sufficient nutriment, without giving the horse more exercise than is good for the disease.

The legs of fast-working horses often become tumid, shapeless, tottering, bent at the knee, and straight at the pasterns These always improve at pasture, as, indeed, they do in the stable, or loose box, when the horse is thrown out of work. Grazing exercise does not appear to be unfavorable to their restoration; but when the knees are very much bent, the horse is unfit for turning out; he can not graze; when his head is down he is ready to fall upon his nose, and it costs him much effort to maintain his equipoise.

Young horses in good condition take a good deal of exercise in playing with their companions. I have never known any take too much. Some are sprained or otherwise injured, in galloping or leaping; but these are the accidents of pasturage, not the necessary concomitants.

THE POSITION OF THE HEAD in the act of grazing is unfavorable to the return of blood from the brain, from the eyes, from all parts of the head. Horses that have had staggers* or bad eyes, those that have recently lost a jugular vein, and those that have any disease about the head—strangles, for instance—should not be sent to pasture. The disease becomes worse, or if gone, it is apt to return. Even healthy horses are liable to attacks on the brain when turned to grass, particularly when the weather is hot, and the herbage abundant. I have not met with such cases, but they are somewhere on record.

It has been said that horses prefer feeding from the ground, to feeding from the manger; but that is not true. Colts are indifferent about it. They have always been accustomed to grazing, and the act gives them no uneasiness. But horses that have been more than a year in the stable, and especially those that have been reined up in harness, often experience considerable difficulty in grazing. The neck is rigid, and the muscles which support the head are short. It is often several weeks before an old coach-horse can graze with ease. For the first two or three hours after turning out he seems to manage tolerably well, but subsequently he gets wearied, and may be seen in a ditch, feeding off the banks. He loses flesh during the first two or three weeks, but afterward he acquires greater facility in grazing. Some, however, do not. I have known one or two remain out for a month, and require to be taken home to prevent death by starvation. Very old coach-horses that have short, stiff necks, should not be turned

* Phrenitis or apoplexy.

out when they can be kept in. If they must go, they should be watched, lest they die of want.

Exposure to the Weather.—Wet cold weather always produces emaciation and a long coat. If the horse be put out without preparation, he is apt to have an attack of inflamed lungs, a sore throat, or a common cold, with discharge from the nose. He may sicken and die. Many people seem to think no usage too bad for the horse, if it do not immediately produce some deadly disease ; that is to say, they do not care for consequences, unless they are sure their interest will be materially affected. A fool will often sacrifice his interest to a certain extent, rather than be guilty of kindness to his horse, or give himself any trouble. He may know that cold will make the beast lean for certain, and that it will cost so much grain to restore his flesh ; and he may know that sickness may arise from sudden exposure ; but that is only probable, and he incurs the risk rather than take the trouble of putting his horse under cover when a wet night or a cold day comes. Early in spring, or late in autumn, he is turned out of a warm comfortable stable, and left to battle with the weather as he best can. He crouches to the side of a hedge, shivering and neglected, as if he had no friend in the world ; and of all who pass him, no one seems to think he is suffering any hardship, while those who have imbibed the "manly bravery of British subjects" consider him a fair mark for a stone or a jest.

In time, the horse becomes inured to the weather, if he do not sink under it. But sometimes he comes home with diseased lungs, and very often with a cough which never leaves him, and which produces broken wind.

Shelter is too much neglected, especially in winter pastures. It is easily provided, at the cost of a few rude boards. A hovel, covered on three sides, the fourth open to the south, and just high enough to admit the horse, will answer the purpose. The bottom should be sloping, elevated, and quite dry. When litter can be afforded, it will tempt the horse out of the blast. There may be hay-racks and mangers, strong, though of rude construction. In summer the horse can retire here during the heat of the day, and in winter he can avoid the storm of snow or rain.

Exposure to hot weather is not so pernicious, yet it always produces pain, if the horse be turned out in the middle of summer. For a while he is fevered all day and loses flesh ; but he soon recovers. The parts that are most apt to suffer are

23*

the brain and the eyes. Staggers, that is, an affection of the brain, is not common, and the eyes never suffer permanent mischief. They are inflamed by the flies, but the brain is injured, partly by the heat, and partly by the pendent position of the head, aided perhaps by plethora.

THE FLIES.—The horse is persecuted by at least three kinds of flies. One, the common house-fly, settles on his ears and different parts of his body, tickling and teasing him. Another is a larger fly, termed the gad or cleg; it is a blood-sucker, bites pretty smartly, and irritates some tender-skinned horses almost to madness. They gallop about the field in every direction, stamp their feet, tear up the ground, and often kick as if something were behind them. Sometimes they rush into the water to escape the attacks of these formidable insects. It is this fly, I suppose that produces the bot-worm, so often found in the stomach of a horse that has been at grass. [The bot-fly never bites the horse. He irritates him merely. The gad-fly, which so much annoys the horse, is a different one from the bot-fly.] The female deposites her eggs on the hair about the shoulder, neck, and knees; a glutinous matter in which they are enveloped fastens them to the hair. When the horse or his companion licks these places, he swallows some of the eggs, which are hatched in the stomach. The worms are each furnished with two little hooks, by which they adhere to the surface of the stomach till spring arrives, when they are evacuated, and soon become flies like the parent.

There is a third kind of fly, which annoys the pastured horse a good deal. I do not know its name. It is a small insect, and lives on blood. It attacks those parts where the skin is thinnest; the eyelids, inside and outside, the sheath, and the vagina, are often much bitten by it. The eyelids especially always swell where this fly abounds, and the swelling is sometimes so great as to make the horse nearly blind. The eye is red and weeping. Some suffer much more than others. I have never seen any permanently injured.

The principal defence the horse has against these puny, but tormenting enemies, is his tail. On some parts of the body the horse can remove them with his teeth, and his feet, and that which the feet and the teeth can not do is done by the tail. But in this country, so eminently the seat of freedom and wisdom, the effective instrument with which nature furnishes him is almost invariably removed before the horse has attained maturity; as if the pains of servitude were not sufficiently great and numerous, domesticity is rendered still more intolerable by caprice. The tail, though useful, is not ornamental, and therefore it must suffer amputation. In such works the lords of creation delight to exhibit their pride and their power.

THE SOIL.—The influence of the soil upon the horse's feet and legs has been much spoken of; but it has been much exaggerated. Horses reared in soft marshy pastures have large flat feet, low at the heels, and weak everywhere. On dry ground the hoof is hard, strong, and small, the sole concave, and the heels high. But to confer any peculiar character upon the hoof, or produce any change upon it, a long and continued residence upon the same soil is necessary. A period of six months does, perhaps, produce a change, but in general it is so insignificant that it is not apparent.

The low temperature at which the feet and legs are kept in a moist pasture has probably some influence in abating inflammation in these parts; but the benefit can not be very great. The legs become finer, free from tumor and gourdiness, but they would improve nearly or quite as soon, and as much, in a loose box.

When the pastures are hard, baked by the sun, unshod horses are apt to break away the crust, and they often come home with hardly horn enough to hold a nail. Feet that have never been shod suffer less; others should in general be preserved by light shoes, especially on the fore feet; kicking horses, when shod behind, are rather dangerous among others.

It has been supposed that the act of grazing throws considerable stress upon the tendons of the fore legs, and ultimately impairs them. This has been urged against grazing hunters; but so far as sound legs are concerned, there seems to be no truth in the supposition, and it has certainly never been proved.

QUANTITY OF FOOD.—In the stable a horse's food can be given in measure proportioned to his wants. But at pasture he may get too much, or he may get too little. This is a strong objection to summering hunters in the field. It is difficult to put the horse where he will receive all the nourishment he requires, and no more. In a rich pasture he may acquire an inconvenient load of fat; in a poor one he may be half starved. If he must go out, he may be taken in before he becomes too fat, or he may be placed in a bare pasture, and fed up to the point required, by a daily allowance of grain.

In winter, few pastures afford sufficient nourishment to a
horse that must go to work in spring. A little hay is given,
but in many cases some grain should be added. The horse
will pay for it when he goes into work. His condition, however, will tell what is wanted. He had better be rather lean
than too fat when he commences work, especially if the work
be fast.

TIMES OF TURNING OUT.—Horses are pastured at all
times of the year. Some are out for lameness, some for bad
health, and some that they may be kept at less than the stable
cost. The usual time of turning out is about the end of April
or beginning of May. Then the grass is young, juicy, tender, and more laxative than at a later period. The spring
grass is best for a horse in bad health, worn out by sickness,
hard work, or bad food. The weather is mild, neither too
hot nor too cold; when unsettled and backward, the delicate,
sometimes every horse, should come in at night and on bleak
days. Toward the end of summer, the grass is hard, dry,
coarse, fit enough to afford nutriment, but not to renovate a
shattered constitution. The days are hot, the nights cold and
damp, the flies strong and numerous. This is not the time
for turning out a delicate, nor a thin-skinned horse. Those
that are to be out all winter may be turned off at any time in
September. Winter grazing is better for the legs than that
of spring or summer. The bareness of the pasture keeps
the carcass light, and the coolness of the atmosphere fines
the legs. But if the horse be very lame, the exercise may
be too much for him.

PREPARATION FOR PASTURING.—Grooms are much in the
habit of giving the horse a dose or two of physic before sending him to grass. I do not think that any is necessary, yet
it appears to do no harm. Physic, they say, prevents the grain
from fighting with the grass; but this is a nonsensical theory.
The horse may have tumid legs, or some other thing the matter with him, and for that physic may be useful. It would
be so whether the horse went to grass or remained at home.
But so far as the mere change of diet and lodging is concerned, physic is quite unnecessary.

To prepare the horse for exposure to the weather, the
clothing to which he has been accustomed is lightened, and
then entirely removed, a week or two before turning out.
The temperature of the stable is gradually reduced, till it be
as cool as the external air. These precautions are most
necessary for horses that have been much in the stable, and

particularly in a warm stable. If the horse go out at the end
of summer or in autumn, he should go before his winter coat
is on. If its growth be completed in the stable, its subsequent increase may not be sufficient to keep the horse warm.
In autumn, he should not go out while moulting. For eight
or ten days previous he should not be groomed. The dust
and perspiration which accumulate upon the hair, seem in
some measure to protect the skin from rain and from flies.
The feet should be dressed, and the grass shoes, or plates,
applied a week before turning out. If injured by the nails,
the injury will be apparent before much mischief is done.
At grass it might not be noticed so soon. On the day of
going out, the horse should be fed as usual. If he go to grass
when very hungry he may eat too much. Indigestion will
be the result, and next morning the horse will be found dead.
Weather permitting, night is usually chosen for the time of
turning out. The horse is not so apt to gallop about. Let
loose in the daytime, many are disposed to gallop till they
lame themselves, and to try the fences.

In autumn, or early in spring, the stable preparation for
grass is often insufficient. If the horse be tender, or the
weather unsettled or cold, he may require to be taken home
every night, for perhaps the first week. For eight or ten
days longer, it may be proper to house him on very wet or
stormy nights. If there be no sheds in the field, it is an act
of charity to bring the horse home when there is snow on the
ground. The stable assigned to him should always be cool,
not so cold as the external air, but never so warm as if he
were accustomed to it.

CONFINEMENT.—Some horses are not so easily confined at
pasture. They break or leap the fences, and wander over
the country, or proceed to the stable. The fore feet are
sometimes shackled in order to confine them; but these fetters, if long worn, are apt to alter the horse's action, rendering it short, confined, irregular, at least for a time, till he regain the use of his shoulders. Sometimes the horse is tied
by a rope to a stake driven in the ground. He requires
almost constant watching, for he must be often shifted as he
eats down the grass, and he may get his legs entangled in
the rope. He may cast himself, and receive severe injury,
without he be immediately relieved. Sometimes the horse
is tied to a stake, which he can drag about the field. He
soon finds that he can walk where he pleases, but he can not
run, and seldom attempts to leap. This also is liable how-

ever, to throw the horse down, or injure his legs by getting them entangled in the rope. To prevent the horse from leaping, a board is sometimes suspended round his neck, and reaching to the knees, which it is apt to bruise. None of these clumsy and unsafe restraints should ever be employed when it is possible to dispense with them. Few horses, mares in springs and stallions excepted, require them after the first two days. For horses that are turned out only an hour or two during the day, they are as much used to render the horse easily caught when wanted, as to prevent him from wandering.

ATTENDANCE WHILE OUT.—Horses at grass should be visited at least once every day. If neglected for weeks, as often happens, one may be stolen, and conveyed out of the country before he is missed; the fences may be broken; the water may fail; the horses may be lamed or attacked with sickness; one may roll into a ditch, and die there for want of assistance to extricate him; the shoes may be cast; the heels may crack; thrushes may form; sores may run into sinuses, or get full of maggots; the feet and legs may be injured by stubs, thorns, broken glass, or kicks; the horses may quarrel, fight, and wound each other. That these and similar evils and accidents may be prevented, or soon repaired, the horses should be visited every morning. The man set on this duty should be trustworthy, not a stupid fellow, nor one who will loiter in the tavern, and return without seeing the horses. He should know what he has to look for. It is not enough to stand at the gate and count the horses. He must approach them, examine them one by one, looking to their condition, their action, and their spirits, and not forgetting to cast an eye upon the feet, the pasture, the water, the fences, and the shelter-sheds. Let him take a bridle and some grain with him, that he may catch any horse that seems to require closer examination, and he can at once bring home any horse that needs it.

The grain, hay, either or both, if any be given, should be furnished at regular intervals; when fed with grain, the horses ought to be watched till it be eaten, lest they rob each other, and lest a prowling thief rob the whole. Horses at grass require no dressing. They should have none. It exposes the skin too much. The shoes may be removed, and the feet dressed every four or five weeks.

TREATMENT AFTER GRAZING.—When taken from grass to warm stables, and put upon rich constipating food, horses frequently become diseased. Some catch cold, some suffer inflammation in the eyes, some take swelled legs, cracked heels, grease, thrushes, founder, surfeit, or a kind of mange. These are very common, and physic is often, indeed generally, given to prevent them. They are produced by a combination of circumstances; by sudden transition from gentle exercise to indolence or exciting work; from a temperate to a stimulating diet; from a pure, cool, and moving atmosphere, to an air comparatively corrupt, hot, and stagnant. These changes must be made; they are to a certain extent unavoidable, but it is not in all cases necessary that they be made suddenly. It is the rapid transition from one thing to another and different thing, that does all the mischief. If it were effected by slow degrees, the evils would be avoided, and there would be less need, or no need, for those medicines which are given to prevent them.

During the first week the temperature of the stable ought to be little different from that of the external air. Subsequently it may be raised, by slow degrees, till it is as warm as the work or other circumstances demand. The horse should not at first be clothed, and his first clothing should be light. Grooming may commence on the first day; but it is not good to expose the skin very quickly by a thorough dressing. The food should be laxative, consisting of bran-mashes, oats, and hay, but no beans, or very few. Walking exercise, twice a day, is absolutely necessary for keeping the legs clean, and it assists materially in preventing plethora.

The time required for inuring a horse to stable treatment depends upon several circumstances. If taken home in warm weather, the innovation, so far as the temperature and purity of the air are concerned, may be completed in about two weeks. If not very lean, the horse's skin may be well cleaned in the first week; and to clean it, he must have one or two gentle sweats, sufficient to detach and dissolve the dust, mud, and oily matter, which adhere to the skin, and glue the hairs together. All this, or as much of it as possible, must be scraped off while the horse is warm and perspiring. If allowed to get dry before scraping, he is just where he was. If the weather be cold, there need be no great hurry about cleaning him completely.

The propriety of giving physic after grazing has been often questioned. In the stable its utility is generally acknowledged. In books it is sometimes condemned as pernicious, sometimes as useless. The grooms say that physic prevents swelled legs, bad eyes, and other plethoric affections to which horses are so prone after being stabled. But some people—among whom we often find medical practitioners—who have more science than sense in these matters, declare that they can not understand how physic should do anything of this kind. Perhaps it is no great matter whether they understand it or not. The question is, has the physic the power ascribed to it? It has. There are many cases in which physic is not required; there are some in which it is improper; some in which it is absolutely demanded; and many in which it is useful. It is given too indiscriminately, and generally before it is wanted.

To a lusty horse, one or two doses may be given for the purpose of reducing him, for removing superfluous fat and flesh. The physic may be strong, sufficiently so to produce copious purgation. It empties the bowels, takes up the carcase, and gives freedom to respiration; it promotes absorption, and expels the juices which embarrass exertion. Work, sweating, and a spare diet of condensed food, will produce these effects without the aid of physic. But purgation shortens the time of training, and it saves the legs. If the horses must be rapidly prepared for work, with as little hazard as possible to his legs, he must have physic. The first dose may be given on the day he comes from grass; the others, if more than one be necessary, at intervals of eight or ten clear days.

A lean horse, newly from grass, requires no physic till he has been stabled for several days, and perhaps not then. By the time the horse has acquired flesh sufficient to stand training, his bowels are void of grass, and his belly small enough to permit freedom of respiration. At the end of a fortnight or three weeks, the lean horse ought to be decidedly lustier. If too much so, if acquiring flesh too rapidly, one dose of physic may be given, strong enough to produce smart purgation, and prevent the evils I have spoken of as arising from plethora. If the horse is not taking on flesh so quickly as he should, he may have two, perhaps three *mild* doses of physic, just strong enough to produce one or two watery or semifluid evacuations. If the horse eat a great deal without improving in condition, he is probably troubled with worms, and half a drachm of calomel may be added to each dose of physic. If not feeding well, there is probably a torpid state of the digestive apparatus, produced by a bad or deficient diet. In such a case mild physic is still proper, and in addition, the horse may have a few tonic balls between the setting of one dose, and the administration of another. Four drachms of gentian, two of ginger, and one of tartar emetic, made into a ball with honey, form a very useful tonic. One of these may be given every day, or every second day, for a fortnight. If not improved, or improving under these, the horse requires a veterinary surgeon.

In some places the horse is bled upon coming from grass, with what intention or what effect I can not tell. I should think that the operation can not be very necessary to any horse, and to a lean one it may be pernicious. If required at all, it is probably after the horse is stabled and acquiring flesh too rapidly.

The Mode of Grazing Farm-Horses requires a little notice. Other horses are sent to pasture, and, with few exceptions, remain at it for days or weeks without interruption. But those employed in agriculture are pastured in three different ways. By one the horse is constantly at grass, except during his hours of work; he is put out at night, is brought in next morning, goes to work for two or three hours, and is then returned to pasture for about two hours; in the afternoon he again goes to work, which may be concluded at five or six o'clock, and from that time till he is wanted next morning the horse is kept at grass. By another mode, the horse is turned out only at night. During the day he is soiled in the stable at his resting intervals. When work is over for the day, he is sent out till next morning. By the third mode, which is generally allowed to be the best, the horse is turned to grass only once a week. He is pastured from the time his work is finished on Saturday night till it recommences on Monday morning.

If the horses have anything like work, the first two modes of grazing are, I think, objectionable. There is much expenditure of labor in procuring the food, and there is a great loss of time. It may cost the horse four or five hours' good work to cut down the grass he eats. A man armed with a sythe will do the same work with far less labor, and in a few minutes. If there be nothing else for the horse to do, it is very right to make him gather his own food. But, otherwise, it is absurd to exhaust his strength and time in doing that which a man can do so much more easily and quickly. Besides this expenditure of the horse's time and strength, the loss of manure, and the damage done to pasture by the feet, ought to be considered.

The third mode of grazing appears to be less objectionable. The horses have no field labor on Sunday ; if the pasture be good, the weather favorable, and the horses not fatigued, they are better at grass than in the house.

In Scotland, the road-horses are sometimes put to grass on Sunday. The practice has nothing that I know of to recommend it. The weekly work of these horses in general demands the rest which Sunday brings ; and if they run at a fast pace, as all coach-horses do now, they are apt to eat so much grass, and carry such a load in their belly, that on Monday they are easily over-marked. The breathing is impeded unless the horses purge, which a few do. They often come from grass as haggard and dejected as if they had done twice their ordinary work the day before.

SOILING.

WHEN grass is given in the stable, the horse is said to be soiled. From what the word is derived, or what was its original meaning, I have not been able to learn. At present the term is used as if it denoted purification, or *un*soiling. Grass is often given in the stable, under a vague impression that it removes impurities, or foulness, produced by the continued use of a strong, stimulating diet. By some, soiling is regarded as an incomplete substitute : by others, as an equivalent to pasturing ; while a few hold that it is the best mode of giving green food.

When the horse has to continue at work, or when his allowance of food must not be such as to produce fatness, or when its bulk must not impede the breathing, soiling is to be preferred to grazing. The allowance can be regulated in the stable, but not in the field.

All horses do not require soiling. It is not true that green food is absolutely necessary for any horse in health. In many studs, an allowance of grass is given to each horse every year, not because it is a cheaper or more wholesome diet, nor because the horses are in bad condition, but because it is supposed to be necessary for preventing disease. In all large studs there are generally a few horses that require a change of diet; they may be out of work, or in bad health ; reduced, perhaps, by sickless, lameness, bad food, or hard work. For such, soiling may be highly beneficial. But it does not follow that all should be soiled. They may, without *injury* but it has never been proved that it is absolutely necessary they should. When grass is abundant, and hay scarce, the former may wholly or partly supply the place of the latter. Without other fodder it is too laxative for fast-working horses.

Cart-horses usually receive cut grass so long as it is in season. It is generally cheaper than hay; when dearer it may be dispensed with. I know not how much a draught-horse will consume in twenty-four hours. Professor Low, I think, states it at 200 pounds, which seems to be a very large quantity, and perhaps excludes grain. In the "British Husbandry," the daily consumption, with a little grain, is supposed to vary from 84 to 112 pounds.

In soiling horses upon a small quantity of grass, it is given alone, or mixed with hay. Given by itself, it is apt to make the horses refuse their hay. It is better that the two should be mixed, especially when the hay is not very good. It is usual to do so, but the grass and the hay are seldom well mingled. They are so carelessly thrown together, that the horse is able to pick out the grass, and throw the hay among his feet. To mix them properly, they should be placed in a heap, layer upon layer, pressed together, and allowed to stand for two or three hours, so that the grass may communicate a part of its succulence and flavor to the hay. Afterward they may be incorporated by tossing the heap over two or three times.

When only one or two horses are to be soiled, they should be placed apart, or get the grass when the other horses are out, otherwise they will refuse their food, and be much annoyed to see their neighbors enjoying a luxury of which they can not partake. They neither rest nor feed.

THE STRAW-YARD

HORSES are sometimes turned out all winter to a place called a straw-yard. It is, properly speaking, a manure-yard, a dung-pit, a place fitter for manufacturing manure than for lodging horses. It often contains oxen, calves, colts, and swine, as well as horses. It is generally destitute of shelter, and the food consists of straw and hay, or of straw only. Often there is not even an allowance of water, except when the man finds it convenient and not disagreeable to carry it. People who bargain for a winter's run, or imprisonment, in a straw-yard, do sometimes pay for a small daily allowance of grain, which, however, is not always given.

A winter's keep in the straw-yard is going a good deal out of fashion, at least with people not themselves proprietors of such a place; but it is still too common. The horse is not wanted till spring, or perhaps some lameness requires rest for two or three months, and, as he can be kept in a straw-yard at little cost, to that place he is sent, abandoned to neglect, and frequently to treatment worse than neglect. He returns home a skeleton; he has a cough, which is cured with difficulty, or not at all; his feet are destroyed by thrushes; his skin is covered by lice, and his bowels are full of worms.

When the horse must be sent to such a filthy place, he needs neither physic nor bleeding. However lusty, he will require all the blood and flesh he can carry before winter expires. The only preparation he requires refers to the feet and to temperature. The frogs should be coated with pitch or tar. If very thrushy, they should be covered with leather soles well stopped up. The horse should be well inured to cold. He needs more preparation than when going to grass; a straw-yard does not demand, nor permit, the exercise which a pastured horse must take. When he returns he must be treated in nearly the same way as after a winter's run at grass. More time is necessary to confer working condition; and greater care regarding hot stables. Some treatment will probably be requisite to remove lice, and to expel worms.

Every straw-yard should have a covered shed, dry and clean. It should have a constant supply of water, which should be entirely changed every day, and placed in elevated troughs, that it may not receive the evacuations. The fodder should be placed in racks under cover, and the owner should visit his horse every now and then.

SIXTH CHAPTER.

WATER.

THIRST is a compound sensation. There are pain and a desire for that which is known to remove the pain. The two co-exist, but the pain always precedes the desire. The sensation in ordinary circumstances is governed by the wants of the body. Thirst depends not upon a particular state of any one part, but upon a particular state of all parts, to whose welfare fluid is necessary. Water is consumed in almost every living process. Whenever a new supply is wanted, a painful sensation arises which the animal hastens to relieve. The pain does not cease till water has been taken in sufficient quantity to meet the internal demand. If fluid can not be obtained, the sensation, at first only a slight uneasiness, becomes more vivid, and gradually proceeds to intense torture. Except by accident, the thirst never acquires all the intensity of which it is capable. But water is too often withheld till the desire becomes very strong and painful. It is permitted to exist so long that the thirst can not be allayed at once, and by the ordinary means. It is several minutes, possibly some hours, before all parts of the body can be supplied with that which they have so long and so urgently demanded. Thirst, therefore, continues for a good while after the stomach and bowels have received sufficient to supply all the system. The horse continues to drink, however, until the pain of thirst is somewhat lost in the pain of distension. Very often he takes so much as to hurt himself. When the horse has water always before him he never does this. But it is still doubtful whether all horses should have water as they please to take it.

Thirst makes a horse refuse his food, and makes him sluggish; I am not sure if it produces any actual debility; yet in many cases it comes to the same thing. If he be unwilling to go, a race may be lost as certainly as if he were unable to go. When the pain of thirst becomes very intense, the horse becomes unmanageable at the sight of water. He will bolt

off the road and plunge headlong into a river, clearing every
obstacle in his way with astonishing alacrity.

THE KIND OF WATER perferred for horses is that which is
soft.   Hard water seems to be quite as good after the horse
has become accustomed to it.   At first it disorders the skin
and the bowels a little.   The hair stares and the skin is rigid ;
the bowels are relaxed, and at fast work the horse is apt to
purge.   In two or three works, often in as many days, he regains his usual appearance, and continues to thrive as well on
this hard water, as he previously did on the soft.   How far
the sudden change may affect his speed or his spirit I do not
know.   He may be weak ; and training grooms generally
avoid hard water, in fear of its influence upon the horse's
power.   It is not likely that the skin and the bowels may be
thus disordered without alteration in other parts ; but I have
not been able to perceive any.   Nevertheless a change from
soft to hard water ought, if possible, to be avoided on the eve
of a great performance.   Hunters and racers travel to many
strange places ; and when immense sums are pending upon
their exertions, it is prudent to exclude the operation of every
dubious agent.   Possibly water may be carried with the
horse, or inquiry may discover similar water in the neighborhood of his destination.

Hard water may be softened a little by boiling it, and the
addition of about half on ounce of the carbonate of soda to every
pailful of water, renders it softer, but not, so far as I know,
more fit for drinking.   A change from hard to soft water does
not seem to produce any visible effect upon the horse.

TEMPERATURE OF THE WATER.—In the stables of valuable
horses, considerable attention is paid to the temperature of
the water.   If too cold, or supposed to be too cold, it is warmed, either by adding hot water, or by letting it stand a few
hours in the stable or in the sun before it is given.   Sometimes a handful of meal or bran is thrown into the water, to
take the cold air off it.   Prepared in any of these ways it is
termed chilled water, meaning, I suppose, unchilled.   In the
stable there is a very common, though not a general dread of
cold water.   It is often given in considerable quantity to
horses highly heated by exertion, and the men attempt to
justify the practice by declaring that the horse is not heated
at the heart.   In theory it is always asserted that cold water
is dangerous to a hot horse ; but in practice the theory seems
often forgotten, especially among strappers and post-boys.
Training and hunting all the bred grooms practise in this in-

stance as they preach. They never give cold water when the horse is hot.

The Effects of Cold Water vary according to the quantity given, and according to the state of the horse. Two or three quarts will not do any harm, or at the most it will set the coat on end. If the horse be very hot, this small quantity is very refreshing to him, and may be given with perfect safety. If the day be very warm, and the horse kept in gentle motion, twice or thrice as much will do no harm, however warm the horse may be. Yet none should be given till one or two minutes after the horse is pulled up. Let him recover his wind for a minute before he drinks. A large quantity, say a pailful, of very cold water, to a horse at rest, not heated by exertion, may make him shiver, or it may produce pain in the belly, cramp of the bowels. Both the shivering and the cramp may be prevented by putting the horse in motion; a brisk walk or gentle trot. A horse much heated by exertion, which has produced copious perspiration, will drink more than a pailful, and the colder the water the more he will drink; if *he* shiver, founder may be expected in the course of an hour or two. If the same quantity be given when the horse is getting cool, he is almost sure to take cramp of the bowels. So far as my experience goes, it appears that cold water is most dangerous, not when the skin is at its hottest, but when it is becoming cool after being very warm. I have seen cold water produce a kind of rheumatism. The horse is stiff all over, and on one or more of his legs he is lame and cramped, and it is several days before he recovers. I have never known this happen except when the horse had drunk freely of cold water, and eaten grain at the time he was much heated; and in all the cases he had been permitted to stand at rest. I remember only three cases of this kind, and it is possible the rheumatism might not be altogether due to the treatment, I suspect. This, however, a shivering fit, founder, and spasmodic colic, are all the evils that cold water will produce. I have never seen it produce any other. Their treatment, their symptoms, and results, it would be improper to describe; but it may not be very much out of my province to mention that shivering is prevented and cured by motion and clothing; and that cramp of the bowels may be cured by four ounces of sweet spirits of nitre, given in a pint of warm milk, with about a teaspoonful of ground ginger, mustard or pepper.

To prevent these the water must either be warmed, or it must be given oftener and in smaller quantity. A very thirsty

horse should never be permitted to take so much as he
pleases at one draught.   A little, given at intervals of fifteen
or twenty minutes, till his thirst is quenched, will prevent all
danger, and the horse will take less upon the whole than he
would take at first in one draught.   I do not approve of
chilled water for constant use.   It makes the horse so tender
that a very little cold water has a great effect upon him.   It
does no other harm.   It need not, however, be given as it is
taken from a deep well, or from a frozen pond.   As a general rule, the temperature of the water should not be much
above nor much below that of the air which the horse is
breathing.

THE QUANTITY OF WATER which a horse will consume
in twenty-four hours, is quite uncertain.   It varies so much,
that one will drink as much as other two or three.   It is influenced by the food, the work, the weather, and the number
of services.   While getting grass or soft food, the horse
drinks less than wile his food is all dry ; those that eat much
hay need more than those that eat little.   The demand increases with the perspiration ; horses at fast work, and kept
in hot stables, need a large allowance, which must be still
larger in hot weather.   When water is given only twice a
day, more is taken, or would be taken, than if it were given
three or four times.   Horses of slow, or not very fast work,
may be permitted to take what quantity they please, provided
always that it be given before the horse becomes very thirsty.
For other horses, those of very fast work, occasional restriction is necessary ; and many of these are subject to habitual
restriction.

Occasional Restriction is necessary.   When the horse is
very thirsty, he will take more than he needs, and more than
is safe.   This I have already explained.   Restriction is also
necessary before fast work.   In coaching stables the horses
are watered about an hour before going to work.   Should
they be disposed to drink a great deal at this time, they are
not permitted ; half an ordinary pailful ought to suffice.
Twice as much might do harm.   It might impede the breathing, and produce purgation ; yet, very often, it does neither.
Given, however, immediately before starting, it is almost sure
to do both.   When the horse purges, his breathing becomes
freer as he gets quit of the water.   But especially on a long
stage, the purging is very debilitating, and it makes the horse
very lean in two or three journeys.   Racers, it appears, re-
ceive no water on running days till their work is over, and

they are even stinted the day before running. With hunters, the restriction is carried nearly as far, though not so generally. This practice has always been condemned by veterinarians, and in truth it seems of very doubtful propriety. But, notwithstanding what has been said against it, no proof has been produced to show that it is really a pernicious practice Much, after all, has not been urged against it; but the same thing has been said over and over again. It is always censured as cruel and needless and erroneous. The horse, it is said, must suffer a great deal from thirst, and he must be languid and weak. Now, if the horse be fed on dry food, and receive no water for twelve or eighteen hours before going to work, there can be little doubt but he is very thirsty. If water be offered he will drink it greedily. But this is not the question. Stablemen do not inquire what the horse feels. They are concerned only about what he will do. If it can be shown that his speed, his power, or his endurance, suffers any diminution when he is thirsty, the trainer will doubtless endeavor to prevent thirstiness. But this has never been shown. No experiments have been made to decide the matter either one way or another. It seems certain that the thirsty horse is less willing to work. He may need more of the lash and the spur, but his ability to do the work, does that remain the same? An experiment must answer; and those who are most interested have means and opportunity to make it.

If either racer or hunter were put to work with a bellyful of water, no work like hunting or racing would be done. The weight of the water, and the impediment it offers to breathing, render the horse far less fit for his task than if he were excessively thirsty. This is well enough established, and needs no experiment to confirm it. But is it not possible, by giving water often, and in very small quantity, to bring the horse to his work, without thirst, and without an inconvenient quantity of water in his bowels? If the horse were accustomed to get water every two hours, it is probable that the quantity he would take at one time would be all out of his bowels by the time he received the next. He would take no more than would serve for two hours, and between the watering-hours he could do his work undepressed by thirst. But all this is good for nothing except to suggest inquiry and experiment. [We recently made the experiment of frequent watering, during a journey of 800 miles, in the heat of summer. In addition to what he would take at mealtime, we allowed our horse to drink while on the road, every 4 to 7 miles, as near as convenient, or as opportunity allowed. He would merely rinse his mouth in the water, or drink from one to three quarts, which seemed to refresh him sufficiently, without ever overloading his stomach or making him heavy. He was a superior traveller, and averaged 45 miles per day. From this and other shorter experiments we have made at various times, we think that water every hour or two, and *ad libitum*, is the best for a horse engaged in ordinary hard work.]

Habitual Restriction.—It is Lawrence, I think, who remarks that grooms consider water as at best a necessary evil. Among professional men, I mean among veterinarians, it is the general opinion that horses should not suffer habitual restriction. It is admitted that the horse should not be permitted to drink as much as he pleases when he is very thirsty, nor when he is hot, nor to drink largely when he is just going to fast work. But it is contended that, except under these circumstances, he should have water as much as he pleases, and when he pleases. A great many horses, hunters and racers especially, and some mail-horses, are never indulged with an unlimited quantity of water. I have frequently inquired the reason of this. Some tell me that water in unlimited quantity is dangerous; others say that it would purge the horse; others, that it would break his wind; others, that it would make his belly too large; and a few declare that the horse will neither eat nor work if he be constantly confined to a small allowance of water. I would not speak confidently, but I am disposed to believe that there is no good reason for *constant* restriction, and that the evils which grooms fear are those which arise from a large draught of water given at once, and especially when the horse is going to work. They carry restriction so far that the horse is always thirsty, and if he accidentally reach a large quantity he is almost sure to drink too much. It is not considered that this quantity would never be taken if water were given so often that the horse could not become so thirsty. This appears to me to be the foundation of the groom's fears.

But still there may be some other reason for withholding water. It is quite possible that horses may be disposed to consume more fluid than is good for them. They may be stronger or swifter than if they were permitted to drink as much as they pleased. This has never been proved, but a *few* experiments would set the matter at rest, and a point of

such importance ought not to remain unknown. We want to
know whether a horse acquires more speed, power, or endurance, when his daily allowance of water is limited, than
when he has water always before him, to take in such measure, and in such quantities, as he pleases. Stable usages are
so often founded on ignorance and hypothesis, that we may
well be excused for sometimes doubting their propriety, even
when subsequent investigation proves them correct.

It is certain, however, that a horse can be trained to
dispense with a considerable portion of the water that he
is accustomed to take when left to himself. By giving
the water in four or five services, he will drink a little less
than if it were given only thrice. But the quantity may be
further reduced, so that in the course of two or three weeks
the horse will not desire more than two thirds of the quantity
he formerly consumed. Whether this be right or wrong, is
as I have said, not settled; but it can be done. The quantity
must be diminished by slow degrees, not all at once, and so
much must not be withheld on any day as to make the horse
refuse his grain. At the end of a period varying from two
weeks to four, the horse becomes accustomed to the spare
allowance of water. He drinks less than formerly. The
system, perhaps, learns to be more economical in the consumption of fluid. Less urine and less perspiration may be
made, and less vapor may be exhaled from the lungs.

When the daily supply of water is very materially diminished, the horse refuses to feed. He eats some, but not so
much as he should. He soon loses flesh, and becomes unfit
for work; and he does not recover until he either gets more
water, or until the system learns to do without that which is
denied. A certain quantity must be allowed, for the system
can not carry on its operations without it. When Mr. Lyon
first built his stables at Paisley, the well did not yield sufficient water, and the horses were kept on short allowance. In
eight days they were not like the same animals; they were
lean, dull, and feeble, and did not recover till more water was
obtained.

Modes of Watering.—When the horse is at home, he is
watered either in the stable from a pail, or in the yard from a
trough, which, in racing establishments, is provided with a
stout lockfast cover as security against poisoning. In general the horse seems to care little how he gets the water;
but some will drink only from the trough, except when very
thirsty. I know of no objection to the trough, provided it be

kept clean, and that the horse do not tremble after drinking from it. The water, however, is often very cold, and the man is often so very lazy that he is unwilling to bring the horse to the door, and he makes two services stand for three. When the horse happens to be in the yard, he may get his water before going in; but at other times it is as well to make it a rule that the water be carried to the stable. Coming from a warm stable to the open air, and drinking cold water, the horse is apt to take a shivering fit. Each stable should be provided with water-pails always full, and standing in the stable.

In watering with a pail, the bucket is either placed on the ground, or raised manger-high to the horse's head. Old short-necked horses drink from the ground with difficulty, yet they always manage it. When the throat is sore, and when the horse is stiff after a day of severe exertion, his water should be held up to him. Some horses rarely drink well, and the less they drink the less they eat. They often require a little coaxing, and always a little patience. It is not enough to offer water and run away with it immediately. Hold the pail manger-high, and keep it before the horse for a little; after washing his mouth and muzzle he may take sufficient to create an appetite.

Post-horses are often watered on the road. They usually receive a little at the end of the stage, and also in the middle of it, if exceeding 9 or 10 miles. On the way home the post-boy permits the horse to drink once or twice at watering troughs by the road-side. He has, or should endeavor to have, his horse fully watered and cool by the time they arrive at stables. They are then ready for dressing and feeding without delay.

Horses are often taken to water at a pond or river some distance from the stables. If they need exercise or are passing the water, there is no objection to this practice. But it is not proper to send working horses out of the stable for the mere purpose of watering them. The weather, the state of the ground, and the laziness of stablemen, render this mode of watering extremely irregular. Boys, too, are often employed in this service, and they are never out of mischief.

With many grooms it is a common custom to give the horse some exercise after drinking. Some give him a gallop, while others are content with a trot or canter for a few hundred yards. Exercise after a copious draught of cold water is very useful. It does not warm the water in the horse's

belly, as the groom says; but it prevents the evil effects
which I have adverted to, in connexion with the temperature
of water. Motion generates heat, and that which unites
with the cold water can be better spared than if the horse
were motionless. But the exercise need not be work. It is
sufficient if it produce the least perceptible increase of
warmth on the skin in 8 or 10 minutes. The man sometimes
starts from the water at a gallop, but no good groom is guilty
of this folly. Let the horse walk away for a few yards;
from a walk he may proceed to a trot, and from that to a canter. In warm weather a walk is sufficient, and the pace
need very seldom exceed a slow trot. The object is, not to
heat the horse, but to keep him warm, to prevent shivering.

Water is not often given more than three times a day. But
in hot weather, when the horse sweats much, he often needs
more water than it is safe to give at only three services. He
should have it four or five times, and the oftener he gets it,
the less he will take at once. Under ordinary circumstances two rules will guide the groom. The first is, never to
let the horse get very thirsty; the second, to give him water
so often, and in such quantity, that he will not care to take
any within an hour of going to fast work. Water should
always be given before rather than after grain.

Broken-winded horses are usually much restricted in their
water. I know that in stage-coaching they are not the worse
of having as much as they please at night, provided it be
given at twice or thrice, and not too cold.

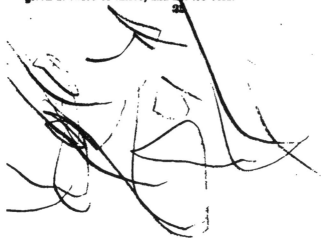

SEVENTH CHAPTER.

SERVICE.

GENERAL PREPARATION FOR WORK.

BREAKING is the first process the horse undergoes to prepare him for work. His education does not, however, come
within the limits of this treatise. It forms a part of horsemanship, and is best performed by men who make it their
business. I am not intimately acquainted with the practical
details, and shall not attempt to describe them. But I would
make a few remarks upon what I consider the principles of
breaking.

The Objects of Breaking are the same in all cases, and they
are only three in number. It should teach the horse to yield
implicit submission to his ruler; it should give him dexterity
in performing his work; and it should confer a graceful carriage. When the horse has learned all these, he has no
more to learn, or at least the breaker has nothing more to
teach him.

The Means employed to teach the horse vary a little, both
in degree and in kind, according to his disposition. There
are punishments to enforce submission, and rewards to encourage it. After that is obtained, the rest is easy. To produce dexterity at work, the horse needs nothing but practice.
In giving his first lesson the breaker has to take certain precautions against awkwardness, timidity, and resistance on the
part of the horse. But, after the novelty of drawing or carrying has worn off, daily practice is all the horse needs. The
difficulty is all in the beginning, and that is often much les-

sened by giving the horse an example. A steady companion may be present at his first two or three lessons. If meant for harness, he may be yoked with a steady horse, already well broke and somewhat stronger than himself. He restrains the colt, and serves as an example to him. Besides learning the horse to work, the breaker has to give him a graceful carriage. He must raise the head, set the horse upon his haunches, and teach him precision in his motions. Before the colt is broke, he carries the head low, leans over his fore legs, and has a slovenly irregular gait. These the breaker must correct. For a certain number of hours every day the head is reined up. In the stable, the bridle-reins are fixed one to each stall-post, and one to a surcingle on the horse's back. While out of the stable, the head is supported by the hand, by the surcingle, or by what is termed a dumb-jockey, an apparatus like a St. Andrew's cross, fixed on the horse's back. After a time, this elevated position of the head becomes easy and habitual. The horse carries it so without support. In old horses the position of the head and neck can not be altered; and when the neck is short, and set very low on the shoulder, it can not be much raised, even in colts By elevating the head and neck, the body is necessarily thrown more upon the hind legs; to use the breaker's phrase, the horse is "set upon his haunches." This requires no separate process. Good action, which is the most important part of a graceful carriage, can not be given to all horses. That of the colt always improves as he becomes accustomed to his work. But a good horseman will produce the same, or greater improvement, in less than half the time that work alone would produce it. He employs the hand, the heel, the voice, and the whip, to restrain, to steady, and to push the horse. I think it is in this part of their business that breakers oftenest fail. Most of them can teach the horse to obey, and to work, and to carry his head, with more or less animation; but few seem able to confer the steady and graceful action which makes a saddle-horse so valuable. Doubtless there are many horses upon whom it can not be conferred; but very often the fault is in the teacher more than in the taught.

I have not said by what means the horse is taught to obey. It is obvious that he can not be taught to work unless he yield obedience to the breaker. Sometimes the colt is so rebellious that he must be mastered by force before he will submit to any instruction. But this does not happen very often. Many colts are obedient from their birth. These have no need either for punishments or for rewards. They may be stupid, awkward, or timid. But these faults are not amended by punishment. If the colt *endeavors* to obey, it is sufficient; and the breaker can not be too gentle. Severity produces stupidity or terror; the colt either stands stock still, or he attempts to run away. He should never be punished for misapprehension, nor for fear, nor for the disobedience which fear sometimes produces.

The temper of a young horse is much influenced by the manner in which he has been reared. If early accustomed to be handled and to have people about him, and to be kindly treated, he is easily subdued, even though his natural temper may be none of the best. For the first two or three months of his domestication, his anger and resentment should not be excited by any painful operation, nor by requiring any painful service from him. He may be haltered, groomed, clothed, led about, over and over again, before he suffers anything alarming or painful. In a short time the colt acquires complete confidence in the people about him; he yields obedience because he fears no evil. Ultimately, by the time he is wanted for breaking, the habit of submission may be so completely established, that the colt will do much that he is not fond of doing, and suffer a great deal before he rebels. But if permitted to run wild till three or four years old, he is sure to offer considerable resistance to the breaker; and if never accustomed to have men about him, except when he must be harshly treated, he will be either a very timid horse or a very savage one. It can not be otherwise. The young animal is thus taught to regard man as his persecutor; the timid fly, and the bold resist or retaliate.

The breaker must modify his treatment according to the temper of the colt. In general, I think he mingles endearment and punishment so much that the colt is at a loss to understand him. A silent breaker succeeds soonest, one who says little or nothing, either to soothe or to threaten. Much bustling and caressing often create suspicion; an angry tone or a touch of the lash rouses alarm or resentment, as often as it produces obedience. When placed in a novel situation, the colt should be allowed a little time to compose himself. For example, when he is first backed, he may stand still for a moment, or he may move on as he pleases: if disposed to plunge about, and attempt to unseat the rider, he must just be restrained, partly by the rider, and partly by

an assistant.   Upon no account should the rider come off, or
be thrown off.   If the colt will not move, if he can be neither
led nor driven forward, the lash must be applied.   At this,
the first struggle, the colt must be compelled to obey.   He
should be punished in good earnest.   If he gain the first
battle he will be sure to make a struggle for the second, and
the third, until he acquires a habit of rebelling wherever and
whenever obedience is demanded.   It is much better, however, if punishment can be dispensed with, especially at an
early stage of the breaking.   Gentle measures are to be fairly
tried, and not abandoned till they have fairly failed.   The
lash should be the last resource, and it ought never to be applied unless the horse can fully understand why.

Very rebellious colts are sometimes worked and starved
till they are a good deal reduced.   It is a certain mode of
subduing the very wildest; but must not be carried so far as
to injure the legs.

[A colt should be halter-broke at three weeks old, and may
be broken in to do very light work in harness at two years
old; but should not be backed, except by a small boy, till
three years old, and a very light man, till four years old.   If
he is backed earlier than this by a heavy man, the weight
upon him is so great, that he can not lift his fore feet sufficiently high in his action, and he is consequently apt to
make a stumbler for life; and he rarely carries himself with
that lightness, ease, and freedom, under the saddle, that he
otherwise would, if not backed by so heavy a weight at this
early age.   It is also liable to injure the spine and make the
horse hollow-backed.

A simple bitting bridle is the best instrument to prepare the
horse for breaking.   After being well bitted, he may be harnessed daily for a week or so, then be taken out and led by
the side of another horse; then driven along some quiet place
with him; then on the road; and finally, hitched in alongside to a light vehicle, for regular work.   After thus driving
him a few weeks, let him stand under the saddle a few days
then mounted and ridden by the side of a well-trained horse.
In learning him to back, commence on descending ground,
where the vehicle will run back of itself, and so gradually
come to ascending ground.   We have broke many horses in
this way, several of which were naturally rather vicious, and
most of them very high-spirited, and yet we never had occasion to strike a blow, or use any harsh means whatever to
accomplish our object.   Horses only want to be properly

taught to do all that can be reasonably required of them.
Their best instructer is one of their own species, who is active, patient, kind in temper, and perfectly broke, to work
alongside of till they have learned what is necessary.   They
are creatures of imitation as well as man ; and they oftener
sin from ignorance, timidity, or fright, than from any other
cause.   Give them a good example and they will generally
follow it.   Something of their grace and ease of movement,
and quickness of walk, trot, and gallop, will depend upon the
person breaking and training them.]

INURING TO THE STABLE AND STABLE TREATMENT.—A
change of lodging, or of diet, is often a cause of disease.
When a fresh horse is procured, it is well to know how he
has been treated during the previous month.   If a valuable
animal, he will be worth this inquiry ; if low-priced he may
not.   Horses that come from a dealer have probably been
standing in a warm stable, well-clothed, well-groomed, highly
fed, and seldom exercised.   They have fine glossy coats,
they are in high spirits, they are lusty ; but their flesh is soft
and flabby.   They are unfit for fast work.   They are easily
heated by exertion, and when the least warm they are very
apt to catch cold.   But wherever the horse come from, or
whatever be his condition, changes in reference to food, temperature, and work, must be effected by slow degrees.   It is
absurd and always pernicious to take a horse from the fields,
or a straw-yard, and put him in a warm stable, and on rich
food all at once ; it is not less erroneous to take him from a
warm to a cold stable, or to demand exertion to which he has
not been trained.

When the horse's history can not be traced, both his work
and his diet should at first be moderate.   More of either than
he has been accustomed to, will do more harm than less of
either.   It may, however, be soon known whether he has
been doing much work.   It is ascertained by trying him.
If fit for work, he may be fed in proportion.   The temperature of the stable had better be warmer than colder.   If too
warm, the horse will perspire ; his coat here and there will
be damp or wet, especially in the morning when the stables
are first opened.   If it be too cold, the coat will stare and become dim ; and the horse will catch cold.   He will cough.

INURING TO THE WEATHER.—The work of some horses
exposes them much to the weather.   Those employed in
street-coaches, in the carriages of medical men, all those that
have to stand in the weather, can never do so with safety till

they have been seasoned. In the cold rainy months, many are destroyed; and many more endangered by injudicious exposure. Wet weather is the most pernicious, yet it is not the rain alone that does the mischief. If the horse be kept in motion, and afterward perfectly and quickly dried, or be kept in motion till dry, he suffers no injury. His coat may be bleached till it is like a dead fur; but the horse does not catch cold. If allowed to stand at rest with his coat drenched in rain, the surface of the body rapidly loses its heat. There is no stimulus to the formation of heat; the blood circulates slowly, accumulates internally, and oppresses vital organs, especially the lungs. The legs become excessively cold and benumbed; the horse can hardly use them, and, when put in motion, he strikes one against another. Exposure, when it deprives the body of heat in this way, is a fertile source of inflamed lungs, of thoracic influenza, catarrh, and founder. When the skin is wet, or the air very cold, the horse should, if possible, be kept in motion, which will preserve him, however little he may have been accustomed to exposure.

Horses that have been kept in warm stables, and never out but in genial weather, are in most danger. If they can not be kept in constant motion, they must be prepared before they are exposed. If they commence work in summer or early in autumn, they will be fully inured to the weather before the worst part of winter arrives. But if they commence at this trying period, they should be out only one or two hours at a time : on good days they may be longer. No precise rule can be given. The length of time for which a horse may be exposed without danger, varies with his condition, the weather, and the work. It should shorten with the wetness or coldness of the weather, and the tenderness of the horse. If he must run rapidly from one place to another, and wait perhaps half an hour at each, he is in more danger than if the pace were slower, and the time of waiting shorter; and if moved about constantly, or every ten minutes, he suffers less injury than if he were standing still. After a time the horse is inured to exposure, and may be safely trusted in the severest weather.

Repeated and continued application of cold to the surface of the body stimulates the skin to produce an extra supply of heat. The exposure of two or three days is not sufficient to rouse the skin to this effort. It is always throwing off a large quantity of heat; but it is several days, with many horses it is several weeks, before the skin can assume activi-

ty sufficient to meet the demands of a cold or wet atmosphere
Ultimately it becomes so vigorous that the application of cold,
whether wet or dry, is almost instantly followed by an in
creased production of heat. To this there are limits. By
exposure, gradually increasing in length and frequency, the
system may become able to maintain the temperature at a
comfortable warmth for three or four successive hours, even
when the horse is standing at rest in wet or cold. But he
can not endure this beyond a certain point. Exhaustion and
emaciation succeed, in spite of all the food the horse can eat.
The formation of so much heat consumes the nutriment that
ought to produce vigor for work. Hence, working horses
kept very much in very cold stables are always lean and dull.

It is chiefly the horses that have to *stand* in the weather
which require preparation for exposure. Bleeding, purging,
and other means, which debilitate or emaciate, are never
necessary in this process. Hunting, stage-coach, and cart
norses, seldom require any preparation for exposure. They
are in motion from the time of leaving till the time of returning to the stable. They just require to be well and
quickly dried when wet.

INURING TO THE HARNESS.—New horses are very liable
to have the skin injured by the harness. The friction of the
saddle, collar, or traces, produces excoriation. In some
horses this is not altogether avoidable, especially when they
are in poor condition. Their skin is tender, and a little matter exposes the quick. In all horses it is some time before
the skin thickens, and becomes sufficiently callous to carry
the harness without injury. The time it requires to undergo
this change is variable, and can not be materially shortened
by any means. But attention to the harness will frequently
prevent excoriation. After every journey the neck should be
closely examined. If there be any spot, however little abra-
ded, hot and tender, when pinched, that part of the collar
which produced it, should be cut out before the next journey.
The guard or safe, is a useful article to prevent galls of this
kind. It is merely a thin slip of soft leather, covering the
seat of the collar. It obviates friction, and prevents injurious
pressure from any little protuberance or hardness in the stuffing of the collar. On the first or second journey a new
horse often comes in with his neck somewhat inflamed ; it is
hot, tender, and covered with pimples. In the stables it is
said to be *fired*. A solution of common salt in water is usually applied, and it serves to allay the inflammation ; it should

De applied whenever the collar is removed. Tumors, containing bloody water, frequently rise on the neck. They should be opened immediately, emptied, and kept open for a few days. The piece must be taken out of the collar, and a safe used. On a hilly road the lower part of the collar often galls the neck very seriously, in spite of every alteration in the stuffing. A broad strap, attached to the top of the collar, and passing over the windpipe, is the only remedy. The strap should be two inches broad, and drawn tight enough to keep the collar steady, and to make it stand nearly upright. It should be adjusted before the head is put on the bearing rein. It should be worn till the neck is quite sound. [A broad breast band may be substituted for the neck collar, till the neck and shoulders get well. A horse will pull about as well in this as in the collar and hames.] When the traces, crupper, or pad, threaten, or produce excoriation, they must be kept off by cushions placed behind, before, or to each side of the part injured.

The back requires nearly as much care as the neck. A new saddle is objectionable for a new horse, particularly when he has to travel far under a heavy rider. A tender back may be hardened by frequent use of the saddle, and a light weight. The horse may stand saddled in the stable, and saddled when he goes to exercise. When the back is hot, and the skin disposed to rise in tumors, the saddle should remain on till the back be cool. Slacken the girths, raise the saddle for a moment, and then replace it. Its weight prevents tumors; excoriation and firing must be treated as on the neck. Always let the pannels of the saddle be dry before it is again used, and put it on half an hour before the horse is to be mounted.

INURING TO EXERTION.—Horses from whom extraordinary exertions are not demanded; those that are never expected nor required to do all that a horse is capable of doing, stand in little need of inurement to work, and it is seldom that any is intentionally given. When a saddle or draught-horse is purchased, he is often put to his work at once without any preparation. He is treated as if he were as able for the work as it is possible to make him. So long as the work is slow, and not very laborious, he may perform it well enough. But this system will not do for full work, whether fast or slow. If the horse have been idle for a month or two, he is weak. It matters little that he is plump and in good spirits. He may be able to draw a load of twenty r thirty hundred weight

with ease, and perhaps to draw it a considerable distance.
But next day he is sore all over, stiff, feeble, dull, almost unable to cr rry his own weight. If the same work be exacted
day after day, the horse loses flesh, and at last becomes unfit
for any work. But if the work be less severe at first, and
gradual'y increase from week to week, the horse at last acquires strength and endurance greater perhaps than he ever
before possessed. He is then able to do with ease as much
in a week as would have completely knocked him up at the
beginning. For slow moderate work this is all the preparation the horse needs. At first let it be very gentle ; and the
weight he is to carry or draw, and the distance he is to travel,
may be increased as he is found able to bear it. In preparing
the horse for work, such as hunting, racing, or coaching, the
treatment must be somewhat different. See the next two
sections.

PHYSIOLOGY OF MUSCULAR EXERTION.

By this I mean an account of what is going on in different
parts of the body during exertion. Motion produces certain
changes, and it is good to know what they are, and for what
reason they occur. All can not be traced ; but it is satisfac-
tory to know all that can be known., A few preliminary remarks are necessary upon

THE CIRCULATION OF THE BLOOD.—This fluid is distributed over every portion of the frame. Without its agency
there is nothing done in any part of the body ; and, in performing its varied duties, it suffers some alteration, which
renders it unfit to reproduce the same effects, or perform the
same functions, until it has acquired something it has lost, and
parted with something it has gained. The purification, or re-
generation, takes place chiefly in the lungs. To these organs,
which almost entirely fill the chest, the blood must be conducted. It is collected from every tissue, by veins infinitely
numerous and small ; too numerous to be counted, and too
small to be traced even with the aid of optical instruments.
These, as they approach the heart, concentrate, become larger and fewer, till they end in two main trunks of very large
size, which pour their contents into a cavity on the right side
of the heart. The heart sends this blood to the lungs, by
one large tube. This, running into the substance of the lungs,
divides and subdivides, till its branches become so numerous
and minute that they can not be distinguished from the tissue

In which they are embedded. Nevertheless these veins form but a small portion of the lungs. There is another set of vessels, equally minute and numerous, for taking the blood back to the heart. In its passage through the lungs, the blood is exposed to the air, which acts upon it, though covered from actual contact. The blood is thus changed in composition. It is purified, losing something or gaining something, and is ready again to perform the duties of which it had previously become incapable. In this state it is collected from the lungs, and taken to the cavity in the left side of the heart, whence it is sent by another set of tubes to be distributed over the body. These are termed arteries; as they pass into the substance of parts, their ultimate arrangement can not be traced. In the hidden recesses, the blood performs its functions. There it produces changes on the tissue, and is itself changed. It suffers some deterioration, or alteration, which can not be rectified till it reaches the lungs, to which the veins collect and carry it.

The blood is in constant motion. It is not all altered at one time, nor at one place At some particular places the alteration may be greater than at others; but the best and the worst are mingled together on their road to the heart. Under ordinary circumstances, the purification keeps pace with the deterioration. Both go on simultaneously, and to an equal degree. But in some cases the equilibrium is deranged.

MUSCULAR EXERTION produces at least four important changes. It quickens the circulation; it quickens the breathing; it increases the formation of heat; and it produces perspiration. The muscles are the active instruments of motion. They act by alternate contraction and relaxation; their active state is that of contraction. They shorten, and their ends being fixed to different bones, motion takes place from the joints. The animal wills to move, and the muscles instantly produce the motion desired. The direction and velocity, the force and duration of the motion, are regulated entirely by the will of the animal. But, in order that the muscles may obey, it is an indispensable condition that they have an abundant supply of pure blood. In action they consume more than at rest.

Quickness of the Circulation is therefore a necessary consequence of muscular exertion. The muscles demand more blood; and the heart hastens to furnish it by performing double, treble, or more than treble its usual number of strokes. When the horse is at rest, the heart contracts from thirty to

forty times in a minute. Every contraction drives a column
of blood through the arteries. At slow work the heart may
beat from fifty to seventy times per minute ; but at fast work
it sometimes makes more than one hundred and forty strokes
in a minute.

Quickness of the Breathing occurs almost simultaneously
with the quickness of the circulation. There is a little time,
however, it may be only a few seconds, between them ; the
circulation has the start. Acceleration of the breathing follows, in order that the blood may be purified as fast as it is
circulated. At rest, the horse respires from six to eight times
per minute ; at slow work he may breathe twice as fast, and
at very fast work, he may respire more than one hundred and
thirty times per minute. The velocity of the blood must
keep pace with the exertion of the muscles, and the respiration must quicken as the circulation quickens. The action
of each is, in a certain measure, influenced by that of the
other, but each is also limited in its individual powers. The
muscles can not act if the heart do not give them sufficient
blood ; the heart can not give the blood if the lungs do not
purify it ; but the muscles may tire, even though well supplied by blood ; or the heart may tire, though the lungs continue vigorous. Deficiency in either deranges the others.

Exertion may raise the pulse to one hundred and forty, and
the breathing to one hundred and thirty ; but at this rate,
neither the heart nor the lungs can work long. After a period,
which varies with the condition of the horse, the blood begins to accumulate in the right side of the heart. It is difficult to say what part is first in fault. The heart may be exhausted, unable to force the blood through the lungs ; or the
lungs may be unable to purify and transmit the blood as fast
as the heart sends it ; or the muscles which produce breathing
may tire, and become unable to expand the chest, sufficiently
to admit the blood and the air into the lungs ; or, possibly,
heart, lungs, and muscles, may all be at fault, some more, some
less : whichever way it happen, the blood begins to accumulate, first in the right side of the heart, and then in the lungs.
After this stagnation commences, the horse is not able to go
much further. The muscles do not receive enough of blood ;
and that which they do receive is not good. The obstruction
in the lungs forbids perfect purification. The horse becomes
feeble, is disposed to slacken his pace, and some stand still
before they are very much distressed. But such is the disposition of certain horses ; one will run on till he is blind,

staggering, and stumbling; at last he falls, and rises no more. He dies suffocated.   Upon dissection, the lungs are found so gorged with blood that almost no air could enter them.

At the first indications of distress the horse should be pulled up, or his pace should be slackened ; half a minute may be sufficient to restore strength to the heart, the lungs, or the muscles, whichever be in fault ; the stagnation or accumulation ceases, and the blood passes on free and pure.

An increased formation of Heat is the third effect of muscular exertion.   The surface of the body becomes warm or hot ; more than the usual quantity of heat is evolved.   It has never been supposed that this is a necessary or useful consequence of exertion.   Acceleration of the blood and of the breathing must take place in order that the muscles may produce progression.   But it is not believed that an extra quantity of heat is useful either as an assistant or as a principal.   It is well known that fast work does least mischief in cool or cold weather; and it appears that there is a contrivance almost for the express purpose of removing the superfluous heat. Most probably the evolution of heat is an unavoidable result of increased velocity in the circulation.

Perspiration is the fourth effect of exertion.   By this process the body is relieved from superfluous heat, and superfluous fluid.   It is always refreshing.   It enables the horse to perform his work with less distress ; but when he has little superfluous fluid in him it always produces subsequent exhaustion.   A fat or plump horse may be all the better of a good sweat; he may be fitter for his work next day than if he had not perspired.   A very poor horse can not so well afford such a loss of fluid ; the more he sweats to-day, the less spirit and strength he has to-morrow.   Both, however, are refreshed, though not perhaps in equal degrees, by perspiring at their work.   In both, the perspiration combines with the superfluous heat, and carries it off in vapor.   The evaporation regulates the heat of the surface.   If it were possible to confine the heat which rapid exertion produces, it is probable the horse would soon be fevered.   But it is not possible to do this, for whenever the skin becomes very warm, perspiration follows almost immediately.

Some horsemen, and especially, I believe, post-boys and stage-coachmen, are in the habit of throwing a pailful of cold water over the horse's body in the middle of a long stage on a hot day.   Most people would regard this as a very violent and thoughtless proceeding.   To deluge a horse with cold

26

water, when reeking hot, and perspiring at every pore, appears to be a dangerous practice. I can not speak from very
extensive experience of this, but so far as I have been able to
see, there is no danger in the case, so long as two rules are
observed : the effusion must not be carried so far as to make
the skin perceptibly cold ;—and the horse must be put in motion directly after it is done. One or at most two bucket-
fuls may be dashed over the body, as equally as possible ;
and the horse should immediately resume his journey ; or, if
his journey be over, the water must be scraped off, and the
horse moved about till he be quite dry. The danger lies in
letting him stand till he shivers. With these precautions, I
have never seen the cold effusion do any harm, and I know
well that it is highly refreshing to a heated and travel-worn
horse, *on a hot day*. The water withdraws the redundant
heat, which oppresses the horse, and which he can get quit
of only by a process comparatively slow in its operation and
expensive to the system. The fat, plump horse, having plenty
of superfluous fluid to spare, may not be so much in need of
the cold effusion, but he also is much refreshed by it, particularly after he has already perspired copiously. After the
temperature of the skin is fast sinking to its natural standard,
effusion is both useless and dangerous.

Acceleration of the circulation and of respiration, the generation of heat, and perspiration, are the immediate and most important effects of exertion. But there are other changes,
which can not be distinctly traced, either in number or in
order. The few that can be described do not appear to demand any notice but what they obtain in other parts of this
work. A minute analysis is not necessary, though it might
be interesting, and to the practitioner useful. It may be sufficient to observe in this place, that the nerves, the blood-
vessels, the muscles, tendons, ligaments, and joints, undergo
a slight change of state every time the horse is put to work.
With some of these parts the alteration becomes apparent only
after the change has been produced often, and at short intervals. The change of state, in whatever it may consist, is
beneficial to a horse that has been long idle. By degrees i:
renders all the parts better able to perform their duties. Under proper management the alteration goes on progressively,
until each part and each organ have attained all the improvement of which they are susceptible. When muscular exertion is pushed beyond a certain point, an injurious alteration
takes place in some of the organs connected with motion

The improvement of motive parts is considered in the next section; the deterioration in that which follows it.

PREPARATION FOR FAST WORK.

THE natural powers of the horse, contrasted with those he acquires, are feeble beyond what a stranger can conceive. Some people are prone to talk nonsense about nature. They would have horses placed as nearly as possible in a wild state, or a state of nature, which, I suppose, means the same thing. In the open fields the horse, it is said, has pure air, a whole-some diet, and exercise good for the limbs and the constitu-.ion. God never intended so noble an animal to suffer con-finement in a dark and narrow dungeon, nor to eat the artificial food provided by man. Much more is said; but it is not worth repeating. The truth is, setting argument aside, *we must have service*, even at the hazard of producing diseases that never occur in a state of nature. Before the horse can do all, or half of all that he is capable of doing, he must be completely domesticated. In the artificial management to which he is subjected there are many errors; but instead of condemning the system by wholesale, it were wiser to rectify what is wrong. A horse, kept in a state of nature, would not last half a day in the hunting-field; and at stage-coaching two or three days would kill him.

CONDITIONING, TRAINING, AND SEASONING, as words, have nearly the same meaning. The first is used most in reference to hunters, but occasionally to all kinds of horses; the second is confined almost entirely to racers; and the third to horses employed in public conveyances, mails, stage-coaches, and so forth. They relate solely to the processes and agents by which strength, speed, and endurance, are conferred. The terms have little or nothing to do with the precautionary measures con-sidered in the first section of this chapter; they are limited to the means by which the horse is inured to *severe* exertion. As I proceed I use the words synonymously, and employ *preparation*, or *preparing for work*, with the same meaning.

THE OBJECTS OF TRAINING, whether for the turf, the road, or the field, are the same. They vary in degree only, not in kind. For either of these purposes the horse must have speed, strength, and endurance. This last word is not quite so expressive as I wish. It is intended to signify lasting speed; it relates to the distance; speed is in relation to time; strength, to the weight carried or drawn. In stables, the words *length* and *stoutness* are used for endurance. These three properties are common to all horses, but they exist in various degrees of combination. The age, breed, formation, and condition, exercise great influence upon them.[*] Young horses generally have more speed than stoutness: at, and after maturity, stoutness is in greater perfection than speed. What are termed thorough-bred horses have speed, strength, and endurance, more of each in combination than any other breed. It would require a long chapter to consider all that might be said in connexion with formation; I pass it over, only observing that large, long-striding horses generally have more speed, but less endurance, than lower compact horses. The formation has a great deal to do with strength, and therefore this property is less under the influence of training than the others are. Training does not enable the horse to carry or draw much more than he can naturally, when in good health and spirits; but it enables him to carry a given weight farther and faster. The condition of the horse is the last circumstance I mention, as influencing his working properties. This is a matter of great importance. A horse, say a race-horse, may be of the right age, his pedigree may have no stain, and his formation no fault; he may be in perfect health, sound in wind and limb, but notwithstanding all this, the horse may be in a very bad condition; that is, for running a race. He may have too much carcass, he may have too much flesh about him, he may be short-winded, and his muscles may be unfit for protracted exertion. To put these into that state which experience has proved the best for a particular kind of work, forms the business of training, conditioning, seasoning. Before considering all the agents and processes employed by the trainer, I would make a few remarks upon the size of the belly, the state of the muscles, the state of the breathing, and the quantity of flesh.

Size of the Belly.—Horses that are fed on bulky food, and those that are very fat, have a large belly. In one, its size is produced entirely by the contents of the intestines; they may be laden with grass, hay, straw, or other food, of which much must be eaten to furnish the required amount of nutriment, and there is always a good deal of water along with this coarse food. One dose of physic, or at the most two doses, will empty the bowels. In another case the size of the belly arises from an accumulation of fat inside. This is

[*] There are some others, particularly the temper and the state of the legs.

ᵛemovable only by slow degrees. Purgation, sweating, and other evacuants, take it away. In a third case, the size of the carcass depends partly upon the intestinal contents, and partly upon the accumulation of fat.

When the belly is very large, from either or both of these causes, the horse can not breathe freely. He can not expand the chest, the contents of the belly offer a mechanical obstacle to the elongation of this cavity; and, as a necessary consequence, sufficient air can not be taken in to purify sufficient blood. But the weight of the fat, or of the food, is of itself a great burden, and would tell seriously against the horse in protracted exertion, even though it were placed on his back.

The trainer should know when the carcass is sufficiently lightened. He judges by the horse's wind. When that is equal to the work, further reduction in the size of the belly may not be necessary. Hence, for some kinds of work, it need not be so much lightened as for some others. Without inconvenience the hunter may have a larger belly than the racer, and the stage-coach horse larger than either. Hunters and racers should have a straight carcass, not at all protuberant, and seldom much tucked up; but it is often very difficult or impossible to put a straight carcass upon flat-sided horses.

After the carcass is sufficiently lightened, it is to be kept within the prescribed limits by avoiding idleness and bulky food. The work or exercise must be such as to prevent the re-formation of fat, and the food such as to furnish the required quantity of nourishment without occupying too much room. Fast-working horses are kept on a limited allowance of fodder, and the usual allowance is further reduced on the day preceding extraordinary exertion. This precaution, however is requisite only with great eaters, or gluttons, as they have been termed, employed at hunting or racing.

In former times the grooms had a strange mode of reducing the belly. They bound a strong and very broad roller round it, drew it as tight as a woman's corsets, and compelled the horse to stand in it night and day. This absurd practice is now out of fashion. Those who know their business know that it will not produce the desired effect. But it is not uncommon, even yet, to find a broad surcingle applied as tightly as it can be drawn, for the purpose, as they say, of drawing up the belly. I have seen a good groom do this. It is a mark of ignorance. The roller which was formerly used might possibly have some effect, for it went over the belly;

26*

but the surcingle now used acts altogether upon the ches,
which training ought to expand rather than contract.

State of the Muscles.—Exertion, under certain regulations,
produces a particular state of the muscles, the parts of motion, and of the nerves, the blood, and the blood-vessels, by
which the muscles are supplied. Neither anatomy nor physiology is able to describe the change which those parts undergo in training. The eye, indeed, discovers a difference in
the texture and the color of the muscles. Those which have
been much in use are redder, harder, and tougher, than those
that have had little to do. They contain more blood, and
that blood is of a more decided red color. They are also a
little larger, when compared with a corresponding muscle of
less work. More than this dissection does not reveal. It is
known, without any dissection, that the instruments of motion exist in different states; that in one state their action
is slow and feeble; in another state it is rapid and powerful;
and that in certain states they can maintain their action for a
much longer time than in certain other states.

For practical purposes it is not perhaps of much consequence to learn all the changes which the muscles, the blood,
the blood-vessels, and the nerves, must undergo, before the
horse can possess the condition which his work demands. It
may be enough to know that the condition, in whatever it
may consist, can be conferred only by exertion. There are
numerous auxiliaries, and various modes of giving and of
regulating exertion; but until it has produced the requisite
alteration in the muscles, and their appendages, there can
never be any remarkable degree of speed nor endurance.

State of the Breathing.—I have said that the horse's breathing can not be free so long as a large belly interferes with the
action of the lungs. To lighten a large carcass is to improve
the wind. But I am persuaded that the lungs themselves may
undergo a change particularly favorable to protracted exertion.
Though I can not offer any proof of this, I think the alterations
which take place in other parts of the body make it appear
probable that the lungs also are altered. It is reasonable to
suppose that the tubes which carry the blood, and those which
carry the air, suffer some increase of calibre; and that the
lungs taken altogether, become a little larger. Such an alteration seems necessary to account for the visible change
which takes place in the breathing. As training proceeds,
the horse becomes less and less distressed by exertion,
and ultimately acquires the power of doing that which

would have killed him at the beginning; and the cause of death would have been found in the lungs. I can offer no other proof in favor of this supposition. It will be observed in many parts of this work, that I am compelled to suggest inquiry when it would have been more pleasant to state the result of inquiry already made. But these matters have been so much neglected, that it does not seem to have occurred to anybody that investigation is needful. Our knowledge is incomplete, yet no one speaks as if there were anything to learn. [It is far more complete than our author thought. He had not learned it himself, and commits the error of thinking that no one else had.]

It is well enough known, however, that to improve the wind the horse must have a great deal of exertion. Purging, sweating, and other emaciating processes, remove all obstruction to the lungs; exertion, at such a pace as to quicken the breathing, does the rest. But all horses do not need the same quantity of work to improve their wind. In some it is naturally very good. They have large nostrils, a wide windpipe, and a deep chest. By proper training their breathing becomes remarkably free and easy; hardly any pace or distance produces distress. They go as far and as fast as the legs can carry them. When over-worked it is generally the legs, not the lungs, that fail. There are as many other horses whose wind is bad, never very good by any management. They have small nostrils, and a small chest, neither deep nor wide. In these the wind fails before the legs; work makes the others leg-weary; these it over-marks, producing congestion, or inflammation in the lungs. These horses are never fit for long races.

However good or bad the wind may be before training, it always improves more or less as training proceeds. It is improved at the same time, and by the same means, that power is given to the muscular system. But exertion may be so regulated that the muscular system shall acquire all the energy of which it is capable, and yet the wind may be neglected and defective. Short distances give power and alacrity to the muscles, but long distances are necessary to improve the wind. The horse must go far enough and fast enough to quicken the breathing, but not at any time so far nor so fast as to distress him very much. When the chest is defective, or when there is a strong tendency to the formation and accumulation of fat, the horse may need a great deal of exertion to render his wind fit for his work; and, in either case, he must

have good legs to stand the exertion. When the legs and
the chest are both defective, the horse will turn out a very ordinary animal. He will last longer at slow than at fast work.

Quantity of Flesh.—When the horse goes into preparation
for work he is sometimes lean. He may have been half
starved. He may be so low in flesh that he has neither ability nor inclination to make exertion. To get such a horse
ready for fast-work, we must begin with feeding. He may
require a little medicine, but in general it is sufficient to let
him have plenty of good food, and gentle exercise, enough to
keep him in health. As he takes on flesh his exercise must
increase both in pace and distance. Though not given in
such measure as to keep the horse very lean, it must must be
severe enough to prevent the formation of fat in his belly. To
keep his carcass light and his wind good, he must have an
occasional gallop.

But the horse is rarely very lean when he goes into training. Most generally he is plump, fat, full of flesh, and in
high spirits. In this state he is easily injured by exertion.
He has so much animation that he is willing to do more than
is good for him. The very lean horse seldom has the inclination.

Hunters and racers are idle, or nearly so, for two or three
months before they go into training. During this time they
are so well fed that they acquire much more flesh than they
can safely carry at work. The trainer has to remove a good
deal of this superfluous flesh. Why is it ever put on? I have
elsewhere observed that I think these horses, while idle,
should be fed in such a way that they may not be fat, though
they may be plump and hearty by the time they go into training. But, possibly, there may be something which I have not
considered that may forbid this. I would recommend a trial
of one horse, or two only.

In all horses, not very lean, there are certain juices, solids,
and fluids, which do not contribute in any degree to produce,
or to aid, muscular exertion. Most of the superfluous matter
consists of fat; part lines the belly, part lies in the connex-
ions of the intestines; some lies below the skin, and some
between the muscles, and in the texture of the muscles. Horses that are never accustomed to pass a walk or a slow trot,
carry a great deal of the fat in their belly; others of fast
work carry the largest portion under the skin; it covers the
ribs, where it is carried with least inconvenience. This fat
*is lodg*ed in a tissue, which pervades all parts of the body, as

water lodges in a sponge, only there is no apparent communication between the cells of the tissue, for the fat lies where it is placed, without sinking downward. Fat is the surplus of nutrition. When the food is so abundant as to produce more nutriment than the system needs, the residue is stored away in the form of fat. When the food becomes unequal to the demand, the fat is reconverted into blood, or a nutritious juice, equal to that derived from the food. But as this fat can not be rapidly converted into nutriment, certainly not while the horse is hunting or racing, it had better not be there. It is a useless weight which the horse must carry, and, from its situation, it may embarrass the parts upon which motion depends. Besides the fat, there are probably some watery or serous juices, quite as useless or injurious under exertion. In the stables the superfluous matter is termed *the waste and spare*, and the removal of it is termed, *drawing the horse fine.*

Slow-work horses may carry much superfluous flesh without any inconvenience. Saddle and carriage horses are not supposed to be in good condition unless they be tolerably plump. Mail-horses can not carry much, and it must be all on the outside, not in the belly; hunters carry less, and racers the least of any others. But, for short distances, it is not usual to draw the racer very fine. For a four-mile race, the horse must be drawn as fine as it possible to make him, without exhausting him. It is obvious that the means by which superfluous flesh is removed, will also remove that which is useful, if persisted in beyond a certain point. When carried too far, the horse becomes unwilling to exert himself, dull, feeble, and careless about his food. These symptoms, accompanied by emaciation, show that he is *overtrained.* The trainer is proceeding too fast or too far with his operations. There is no rule to guide him, but the state of the horse. One may be drawn a great deal finer than another. So long as the horse goes cheerfully to his work, and to his food, the trainer may proceed: he may stop so soon as the horse has wind and speed for the distance.

Superfluous flesh is removed partly by sweating, partly by purging, and partly by exertion. When all is taken away that is likely to incommode the horse, further reduction hazards the legs when there is no need to hazard them.

It appears, then, that the trainer may have to lighten the carcass, he may have to put flesh on the horse, or to take it off him; and he always has to give tone to the muscles, and freedom to the wind. Each goes on progressively, and generally at the same time; but the belly is to be reduced to its proper size before all the superfluous flesh is taken away; much of this, if there be much of it, must be removed before power and alacrity can be given to the muscular system. Subsequently, the horse may be drawn finer, if need be, as his wind and speed are under improvement.

It is probable that training produces some alteration in the condition of the blood, the nerves, the blood-vessels, the joints, the tendons, and upon every part connected with motion. The change in these ought to be as permanent as that produced in the muscles; but I can say nothing more about them.

AGENTS OF TRAINING.—The agents and processes employed in preparing the horse for fast-work are, physic, sweating, blood-letting, diuretics, alteratives, diaphoretics, cordials, and exertion. I do not mean that all these are or should be in requisition for every horse, or every kind of fast-work. All, however, are occasionally used, and it is proper to consider all. Without knowing what each can do, and what each can not do, it can not be judiciously employed. I consider their effects in reference to training; but some of them, such as physic and cordials, are often used when the horse is already trained and in work; and to this, or a similar circumstance, I allude in two or three places. Though not strictly connected with the preparation for work, it is right, I think, to say all I have to say about one thing in one place.

PHYSIC.—In the stable this word is entirely confined to purgative medicine.

Uses of.—To a horse going or gone into training, physic may be wanted for one or more of seven purposes. It will diminish the size of the belly; it will rectify a disordered state of the bowels, rousing them from torpor to activity; it will expel worms; it will produce real or comparative emaciation; it will cure plethora; it will prevent plethora; and it will cure swelled legs. Physic will produce other effects; but I here speak of it only in reference to preparation for work, and to the preservation of working condition.

If the horse be newly from grass, one dose will be wanted to empty his bowels. It may be given on the day he is stabled. If lusty, the dose may be strong. If the horse be lean, previously half-starved, or kept on bad food, one, perhaps two doses, may be necessary to empty the bowels, expel

worms, and rouse the digestive apparatus to activity, one or
all. In this case, the horse may as well be stabled for eight
or ten days before his physic be given. It should be mild.
If the horse be fat, lusty, or as stablemen say, full of humors,
foul, or foggy, his flesh soft and flabby, he will require a smart
purgative. If he be very full of flesh, have bad legs, and
be a good feeder, he may need several doses, each as strong
as the horse can safely bear it. His safety is never to be
compromised. There are other means of reducing him, if
physic, in safe doses, will not do it. He may have the first
as soon as his bowels are relaxed by bran mashes. The second is not to be given in less than nine clear days. The
third, if absolutely necessary, is not to be given in less than
fourteen days after the second sets.

Should the horse fall lame, or from any other cause require
to lie idle for several days after his training has considerably
advanced, physic may be necessary to prevent plethora. This
state of the system may also be prevented by reducing the
allowance of food. But racers and hunters can not be starved,
and whatever kind of food they get it must either produce
plethora or a large belly. The physic prevents both. Unless
lameness or swelled legs demand it, the physic need not be
given till the horse has been several days idle. If he must be
out of work for more than two or three weeks, a second dose
may be necessary. But it is only horses of very keen appetite that need physic to prevent plethora. A delicate horse
of light carcass, narrow loins, and irritable temper, rarely requires physic to prevent or to cure plethora, and very seldom
to remove superfluous flesh. They eat sparingly, and the
training exercises reduce them more, and faster, than others
of robust constitution. Between the most delicate and the
most robust there are many others with whom a middle course
of treatment must be adopted with regard to physic, and to
everything else. While those of very strong constitution
may require a full dose, the very delicate may require none.
To some a mild or a half-dose is sufficient ; and to others a
diuretic or an alterative may be useful, when the propriety of
giving even a mild or a half-dose is doubtful.

Horses that have undergone a good deal of exertion, whether in training or in work, often need physic to refresh them.
The legs may be slightly swelled, the horse a little stiff, and
dull. If much emaciated, a mild dose is sufficient ; if lusty
the dose may be strong, particularly if the legs be the worse
of wear.

The Effects of Physic vary with the strength of the dose, the number of doses, and the condition of the horse. One dose, mild or strong, merely empties the bowels; two, three, or a greater number, of mild, perhaps only half-doses, given at proper intervals, rouse the digestive organs to more than ordinary activity, and make the lean horse acquire flesh. But if the doses be given at intervals too short, the bowels become very irritable; they remain relaxed; the evacuations are soft, too pultaceous, and a draught of cold water, or a little fast work, produces actual purgation. In such a case the horse becomes excessively lean and weak, and it is often a long time ere he recovers. He has had physic too frequently, even though each dose were mild.

One strong dose, besides evacuating the bowels, and lightening the belly, produces emaciation. The purgative drug acts first upon the inner surface of the stomach and bowels. It irritates this surface, which pours forth a copious secretion of water-like fluid, for the purpose of diluting and weakening the irritant. The fluid is derived from the blood. When the purgative is so strong as to produce very copious secretion, the loss which the blood suffers in quantity is soon felt all over the body, and an effort is quickly made to supply the place of that which has been lost. Vessels, termed absorbents, commence operations upon the fat, and upon other superfluities. These undergo a change, and acquire a resemblance to blood; they are collected, and poured into the blood-vessels, and fill the place of all the fluid that has been evacuated by the bowels. This absorption of superfluities follows every evacuation, whether it come from the bowels, the skin, or the kidneys; and I need not again advert to it. The horse becomes leaner in order that the blood-vessels may be fuller. The fat is converted into blood, or a fluid like blood; but when there is no fat to remove, or to spare, the absorbents act upon and remove other superfluous fluids and solids, wherever seated. Thus, purging, sweating, and other evacuants, take away fatness, swelled legs, dropsies, tumors, and so forth.

Purgation always produces emaciation, more or less evident according to the violence of the operation. But when one dose succeeds another, before the bowels have quite recovered from the effects of the first, there is danger in the process. Purging proceeds too far; it may be so severe that weeks must elapse ere the horse recover; it may be such as to leave the bowels excessively irritable, easily relaxed: or it may be such as to kill the horse in two or three days. These and some other bad effects of physic, arise either from giving too much physic at one time, or from giving it too often.

In hunting and racing, and even in coaching stables, horses often die under physic. The blame seldom falls upon the medicine, nor upon the man who gives it. The fault is all in the horse's constitution; instead of saying the physic was too strong, the man declares the horse was too weak, as if it were not possible to make the physic strong or weak according to the state of the horse. When the horse dies, however, it is always from an over-dose. He gets too much at once or he gets it too often, or that which he gets is made to work too strongly, for it is possible to make a small dose produce a great effect.

In the stables it is often asserted that physic is dangerous when it does not purge the horse. When not strong enough to purge the horse, the groom says it goes through the body; does not work off, but requires another, to make it work off. This is nonsense. I must have given several thousand half-doses of physic, not intended to produce any purgation, or very little. If any one of these ever did any ill, a full dose would have done a great deal more. But when the groom finds his first dose does not purge any, or not so much as he desires, he is in a hurry to give a second, which, operating with the first, is a pretty sure way to destroy the horse. If one dose do not purge, no second should be given till after four clear days.

Physic in full dose always produces temporary debility, even before purgation begins. It increases as the purging proceeds, and its duration is influenced by many circumstances. The horse is dull, sick, and sometimes a little uneasy while he is purging. He is generally sick before it begins, and while it lasts, but very often he becomes lively and desires food so soon as purgation is established.

After severe purgation the horse is weak for several days; he sweats soon and is easily fatigued. Some recover much sooner than others. To the temporary debility there often succeeds an immediate increase of energy, greater than the horse possessed before, and not altogether dependant upon the loss of superfluous flesh, nor the removal of any apparent evil. Hence physic is frequently given to racers and to hunters, in the middle of their working season, for the purpose as it is termed, of *refreshing* them.

A *Course of Physic* consists of three doses, given at intervals of from 8 to 14 days. Hunters, racers, some carriage,

and other horses, get two courses every year as regularly as
the seasons come round; the racer in autumn after his summer running is over, and in spring after he has lain idle all
winter; the hunter in spring when he goes to grass or loose-
house, and in autumn when in preparation for his winter's
work.   Carriage, and suchlike horses, have their two courses,
simply because spring and autumn are spring and autumn.
This, in reference to ordinary horses, is going much out of
fashion.   A few venerable adherents to the old school, still
remain, but their example is not very pernicious; it is little
followed.

There is no season of the year at which physic is more
necessary than at another.   Horses, indeed, are moulting in
spring and in autumn; but so long as they are in health this
process is not beneficially influenced by physic.   With hunters, the change of food and work alters the case.   They may
need one dose, or three, or more than three, or none.   The
practice of giving a full course to all, without discrimination,
as if there were some magical property in the number three,
is too absurd to merit notice.   Physic is not one of those
simples in which quackery deals.   Its power to do evil is at
least as great as its power to do good.

Composition of Physic.—There are many articles which
purge the horse; but, upon almost every occasion, Barbadoes
aloes is preferred.   It is easily given, and the proper dose is
well known or easily regulated.   It purges with more certainty, and with less danger, than any of the articles which are
sometimes used in its place.   The aloes are powdered, and
formed into a tough, solid mass, soft enough to swallow.   Common or Castile soap is generally used for this purpose.   One
of soap, to two of aloes, is about the proportion.   Other ingredients are sometimes added; but, to produce purgation,
nothing is wanted but the aloes.   On hunting and racing establishments, the head groom usually compounds the physic
himself.   It may be procured ready made, in any strength,
from the veterinarian or the druggist.   A full dose varies from
four drachms to nine   Yearling colts require about 4; ponies
from 5 to 6; saddle, hunting, and draught horses from 7 to 8;
thoroughbreds from 6 to 9.   These last when well prepared
may be purged by six drachms; but when in work they may
require nine.   Horses of narrow chest and light carcass, require less than those of round barrel.

Giving a Ball.—A dose of medicine, whether purgative,
cordial, diuretic, or any other kind, when given in a solid form,

is termed a *ball*. It should be soft and about the size and shape of a pullet's egg. The operator stands before the horse, who is generally unbound, and turned with his head out of the stall, and a halter upon it. An assistant stands on the left side, to steady the horse's head, and keep it from rising out of the operator's reach. Sometimes he holds the mouth open, and grooms generally need such aid. The operator seizes the horse's tongue in his left hand, draws it a little out, and to one side, and places his little finger fast upon the under jaw; with the right hand he carries the ball smartly along the roof of the mouth, and leaves it at the root of the tongue. The· mouth is closed, and the head held, till the ball is seen descending the gullet on the left side. When loath to swallow, a little water may be offered, and it will carry the ball before it.

Some grooms are sad bunglers at this operation. Some can not do it at all; many not without the use of a balling-iron, and none of them can do it handsomely by any means. I have seen the tongue severely injured, half torn out of the horse's mouth; and many horses are so much alarmed and injured by a bad operator, that they become exceedingly troublesome and always shy about having the mouth or head handled.

By keeping the little finger upon the bar' of the mouth, the tongue can never be injured; the hand follows every motion of the head without being dragged by the tongue. By delivering the ball smartly, and without instruments, no pain is produced, and no resistance offered. A hot troublesome horse should be sent to a veterinary surgeon. The probability is that the groom will fail; he may lodge the ball among the teeth, or injure the mouth, and the horse will be pained to no purpose, and taught to resist all operations about his head.

Preparing for Physic.—If a full dose of physic be given when the bowels are costive, it is apt to produce colic and inflammation. The medicine is dissolved in the stomach, passes into the intestines, and mingles with their fluid and semifluid contents; but, as it travels on, it arrives at a point where the contents are solid; the physic is arrested; it lies longer there than at any previous part of its course; its continued presence produces spasmodic and painful contractions of the bowels to force it on. If the intestinal contents be very obstinate, if the obstruction be not dissolved, irritation and inflammation succeed, and the horse's life is in danger. To obviate this, the bowels for one or two days previous are to be gently and uniformly relaxed by giving bran mashes, by withholding

grain, and by stinting the allowance of hay. If the horse
can take exercise, one day is sufficient to prepare him. A
the usual feeding hour, he has a bran mash, warm or cold,
whichever he likes best. He gets water often, and in full
measure, as much as he will take, and, if possible, he should
have walking or trotting exercise, perhaps morning and afternoon. At night. he receives less than the ordinary allowance of hay ; and, if a great eater, a muzzle is put upon him,
that he may not eat the litter after his hay is finished. Few,
however, need to be stinted in their fodder. Most of them
may have the ordinary allowance. Those that will not eat
mashes, nor drink freely, and those that can not take exercise, are the only horses that need to be kept short of fodder.
Early next morning the physic is given on an empty stomach.

Treatment under Physic.—Half an hour, or directly after
physic is given, the horse gets a bran mash ; that eaten, he
goes to walking exercise, for perhaps an hour ; he is watered
when he returns. The water should be tepid, warm as the
horse will take it. He is to get it often, and as much as he
pleases. It should all be warm, that is, it should not be very
cold. Some horses, particularly when under physic, refuse
tepid water. It is often offered too warm. It is better that
he have it cold, than that he have none. But from the time
physic is given till it ceases to operate, all the water should
be warm as the horse will take it, yet not so warm as to make
him refuse it. During the remainder of this day, the horse
has a bran mash as often as he is accustomed to get grain.
Warm are better than cold mashes : if refused they may be
given cold ; if both be refused, dry bran may be tried.
Whether bran be eaten or refused, the horse is to have no
grain. The hay may be sprinkled with plain, or with salt
water. Sometimes a little more exercise is given in the afternoon ; and when the horse is difficult to purge, he is all
the better of more exercise, weather and the legs permitting
it. In wet weather, the horse is not to go out. In cold
weather, he is to be clothed, both in the stable and at exercise. The exercise is given at a walking pace, but in cold
weather part of it may be faster. It should be fast enough to
keep the horse warm, but not so fast as to heat him. Next
morning, about twenty-four hours after the physic has been
given, purging commences. Sometimes it begins sooner. I
have seen physic operate in ten hours, and I have known
thirty hours elapse ere the horse was fairly purged. The
more exercise he takes, and the more water he drinks, the

sooner he is purged. When the dose is strong, exercise must be given with more caution than when it is weak. But too much exercise, particularly beyond a walk, will make even a weak dose over-purge the horse.

If not purging freely next morning, when the stable is opened, the horse may go out and remain for an hour at a walk, with an occasional slow trot. Whenever purgation is fairly established the horse should be brought in, and stand in the stable till his physic *sets*, that is, till it ceases to operate. Some continue the exercise for a good while after the horse is purging; and when very copious purgation is wanted, or when the dose is not very strong, this may be done, the danger of carrying the process beyond the horse's strength being always remembered. A full dose, with proper preparation, and proper treatment, usually continues to operate pretty smartly for twelve hours. All this time the horse gets bran mashes and water as on the preceding day. At night the evacuations should be less fluid, and by next morning they ought to be quite natural. After this the horse returns to his usual diet.

Colic.—If the horse appear in pain, pawing the ground, looking at his flank, rising and lying, or rolling when down, he may have a clyster of warm soapy water, and go to exercise. This sometimes happens before purgation begins. If the pain be very severe, producing perspiration, a cordial ball may be given and more clysters, and exercise, only a walk.

Superpurgation occurs frequently, either from the dose being too strong, or from the horse getting too much exercise. If the physic continue to operate so as to threaten evil, it may be stopped very readily by giving the horse a few oats or beans, one or both. If the horse will not eat, give him a cordial ball; withhold water, and give oatmeal gruel instead; bandage the legs, clothe the body, give a good bed, shut up the stable, and do not take the horse out. In half an hour after giving the cordial, again try the horse with oats or beans. Should these means fail, or should the horse very rapidly become weak, dejected, losing flesh from the back, crest, and thighs, let him have half a pint of mulled port wine, well spiced in as much warm water, and add an ounce of laudanum to it. Repeat this dose every four or five hours till purging stops. It will always succeed, if the horse be not indeed at death's door before the treatment is begun. Bleeding in such a case destroys the horse.

SWEATING.—Every horse must perspire more or less while
27*

undergoing preparation for fast work; but in all racing and
hunting studs there are some horses that require to be purposely sweated. By putting the horse to exertion, under
heavy clothing, the perspiration is excited, and encouraged to
flow in much greater profusion than mere exertion would ever
produce. The object of this is twofold. Sweating removes
superfluous flesh, and it gives freedom of respiration. The
one object may be aimed at more than the other; and the
process of sweating is, or ought to be, regulated accordingly.
If the main object be to remove superfluous flesh, the horse
may be sweated without, or with very little exertion; if the
main object be to improve the wind, the horse must have a
good deal of exertion with less sweating. In both cases the
horse is drawn finer. The fluid which escapes from the skin
is derived from the blood. Copious perspiration is soon followed by absorption. The superfluous fluids and solids are
carried into the circulation, in order to supply the deficiency
which perspiration has produced. Every sweat, if it be carried far enough, draws the horse finer, and such is the result,
whether he get much or little exertion.

I have never met with a stableman who seemed to understand the precise effects of sweating. They confound the
effects of exertion with those of sweating; they proceed as
if they thought the two should be combined. I have more
than once stated that exercise, judiciously managed, gives
power and alacrity to the muscular system, and freedom to
the breathing. I have now to observe that sweating, considered by itself, *does neither*. Copious perspiration can be excited with very little exertion; and, when that is done, the
sweating merely removes superfluous flesh. It removes fat,
or other matters, which encumber the muscles and the lungs;
but it does not improve the functional powers of either. Exertion produces one series of effects, sweating another; and
though both are generally combined, there are cases in which
they may, with advantage, be separated.

Sweating without Exertion.—There is some exertion, but
so little that it is not worth considering. The horse is heav-
ily clothed, saddled, mounted, and taken to the sweating-
ground; here he is ridden at a steady, gentle pace, till he begins to perspire; so soon as the coat is damp, he is ridden at
a smart pace to the stable; the doors and windows are closed;
the horse is stalled with his head out, the saddle is removed,
and more clothing applied. The groom stands by, while an
assistant holds the horse's head. In a few minutes, from eight

to ten, the skin becomes quite wet, perspiration issues from every pore and runs down the legs. The horse's breathing increases, and is often as quick and laborious as if he had just run a race. This arises partly from the heat, and partly from exhaustion. The sudden loss of so much fluid produces a faintness very similar to that which follows a large bleeding; and, without doubt the effect is greater from the heat accumulated on the surface. The time the horse is permitted to sweat in this manner, must be regulated by the groom. It had better be repeated in a few days, than overdone at first. After the first sweat the groom will closely observe its effect, and he will carry the next further, or not so far, according to circumstances. With some the sweating need not stop till the perspiration be dropping fast from the belly, running down the legs, and passing over the hoofs; with some others, upon whom its effect may not yet be known, it will be time to stop when the hair is completely soaked. The groom now and then puts his hand under the clothes, and, passing it along the skin, observes how much fluid be lodged in the hair. If the horse be sufficiently warm when he enters the stable, he may have to sweat from five to fifteen minutes. Few require more than fifteen, and few less than five.

The sweating having been carried to the desired extent, the horse is stripped, the stable boys, usually one, and sometimes two on each side, immediately scrape the horse all over; they make the skin dry, with as much expedition as possible. After scraping the neck, sides, quarters, every place upon which the scraper will operate, the legs and head are sponged. By means of wisps and rubbers the horse is made quite dry; his standing clothes are put on; he gets a quart or two of tepid water, goes out and gets a short gallop; is walked about till quite cool; when he is stabled, dressed, clothed, watered, fed, and left to repose. The first water is tepid, and no more is given than sufficient to make the horse eat. The first food requires to be rather laxative, particularly for round barrelled horses. The sweating produces costiveness, which is obviated by a bran mash: food is given afterward.

If it be desirable that this sweating produce a very decided effect in reducing the horse, his allowance of water for the next twenty-four or thirty-six hours should be moderate. He will be disposed to drink very copiously, but if much be given, it will be rapidly absorbed, and will, in some measure, fill the place of that fluid which perspiration has taken away, and there will be less stimulus for the absorbents to act upon the fat and other superfluities. The water should be tepid, for when cold it increases the horse's desire for it, and enough to make him feed is sufficient.

It is usual to give the horse a short gallop after his sweating, and after he has been dried; when he is able to take the exertion and to suffer so much exhaustion in one day, the practice is unobjectionable; but sweating, whether with or without exertion, does not render a gallop immediately afterward at all necessary. Some gentle exercise, however, is often useful, to prevent perspiration from breaking out after the horse is dressed.

I think this mode of sweating, without exertion, is the best for lusty horses, with defective legs. It is most necessary at the commencement of training, and may be practised two or three days after the first dose of physic sets. It removes so much of the fat that the horse may afterward proceed to exertion, which would have endangered his legs, had it been given before the sweating. This sweating merely removes fat. It confers no energy upon the muscles, nor capacity upon the lungs, beyond that they acquire from having greater freedom of action. This kind of sweating is never necessary for horses already low in flesh; and it need never be repeated while the legs can safely carry the body.

Sweating with Exertion.—It is only in racing and in hunting stables that horses are put through this process. When the training-groom speaks of sweating, he means sweating with exertion. The horse is put through his physic, and prepared for sweating by several days or weeks of walking exercise, varied by an occasional gallop. If the sweating and exertion must go together, it is very necessary to prepare the horse for the process by some gentler exertion, for it is a very severe one. If the horse be very lusty, he goes daily to walking exercise. After a time he is put to a short gallop, varying in speed and distance according to his age. It should at the first two or three trials not exceed half the distance he is to go in his sweat; if he suffer that, without distress, it is gradually lengthened till he is able to go nearly, or quite as far as the sweating distance. If the trial gallop distress him, he returns for a few days to gentler exercise, and the pace and distance are increased more gradually.

Great eaters are muzzled for eight or ten hours before they go to the sweating-ground; some require to be muzzled twelve hours, some six, some not at all; the stomach should not be loaded. In the morning, or when the weather is cold in the forenoon. the horse is clothed in his sweaters, the quantity varying according to the effect desired. A soft porous blanket lies next the skin ; a breast-piece covers the bosom, while the head and neck are enveloped in a hood. Over the blanket, one or two, it may be three or four quarter-pieces are thrown ; and perhaps another hood may be re-quired, the undermost wanting the earlets. These are tied and buckled, with care that no part encumber the action, nor abrade the skin. The legs, the eyes, and windpipe, must be clear ; the breast-piece must not be drawn so tight as to confine the legs or press upon the windpipe. The saddle goes over all. The horse is ridden to some convenient ground, hunters to the field, racers to the course. If the horse's legs be defective, he is mounted by a light weight ; sometimes he is led by a man on another horse. In the first or second sweat it may be proper to forbear riding ; but in general it is not a good practice to lead the horse. He is so little under control that he is very apt to be lamed. Arrived at the sweating-ground, the horse is usually walked round it, just to let him know it, and to give him the use of his legs. The pace increases from a walk to a trot or canter, and from that to a gallop. The length and speed of the gallop must be regulated by the training-groom. Speaking generally, the horse should rarely go at full speed, and not above a few hundred yards at a time. When a cer-tain distance is not aimed at, the gallop should often end so soon as perspiration is fully established, and in no case should the horse proceed at the same pace after he appears the least distressed. As he improves in condition, he goes faster and further before perspiration appears.

In racing-stables the sweats, almost from the beginning, are of a certain length. According to Darvill, " the length for a year-old, is two miles ; for a two-year-old, two miles and a half ; for a three-year-old, three miles, or three and a half ; and for a four-year-old, four miles. In preparing for a four mile race the horse may have to sweat four and a half or five miles."[*]

Though the colt or horse may have to go a certain dis-tance, yet the pace at which he goes must vary with his con-dition. At first, the lusty horse especially should go very slow ; and when the body is loaded and the legs weak, I think the full length should not be tried at first, even though the pace be slow. For hunters the pace and the distance must be limited by the state of the legs, and the freedom of

* Darvill on the English Race-Horse.—Vol. II., p. 270.

the breathing. Excess at the beginning may possibly shorten the time of preparation, but it is much more likely to injure the lungs or the legs.

When pulled up, the horse is walked to his stable. He may stand for a minute to recover his wind. If the sweating-ground be at a considerable distance, the horse is followed there by the groom and his assistants, who dry him in the field. The horse is placed in a sheltered spot, perhaps beside a hedge; his clothes are removed, and he is scraped as dry as possible; fresh clothing is put on, and the horse is ridden smartly home. Subsequently, the treatment is the same as after sweating in the stable. If the stable be near the sweating-ground, the horse had better go there at once. He is in less danger of catching cold.

I need hardly repeat that this process has a double effect, it improves the condition of those parts upon which muscular exertion depends, and it removes superfluous flesh. How far it is proper to aim at both objects by the same process, I leave to the consideration of those who have experience in the practical details of training. I should think it would be safer for the legs of a lusty horse to get rid of great part of the superfluous flesh with as little exertion as possible; to reduce him in the first place by purging and sweating, leaving no more superfluous flesh upon him than what exertion without clothing would remove. Sometimes the trainer unites both modes of sweating. After sending the horse his sweating distance, further perspiration is encouraged in the stable.

The repetition of these sweats must be regulated by the effect produced, and by the effect desired. While the robust glutton may require a sweat once a week, or thrice a fortnight, the delicate abstinent may not need more than one in five or six weeks, or perhaps none at all.

BLEEDING, as an operation preparatory to work, is hardly ever necessary. It is customary, however, in some hunting and in coaching-studs, upon taking the horse from grass. I believe it is nowhere so common as it used to be. It takes the flesh off a horse very rapidly, but it produces great debility. Perhaps the parts which are absorbed after blood-letting, may not be the same parts that sweating and purging remove. It may be that the loss of pure blood may be replaced by the absorption of solids and fluids more necessary to vigor than those solids and fluids of which purging and sweating produce the removal.

DIURETICS are those medicines which increase the flow of urine. They are not of much avail in training. They are useful, however, when there is reason to fear plethora, or when the legs swell, either from rest or from excess of food or excess of work. Nitre, resin, turpentine, soap, and oil of juniper, are all diuretics. For a horse of fifteen or sixteen hands high a diuretic ball may be composed of—nitre, four drachms; resin, three drachms; and oil of juniper, twenty drops; with soft soap sufficient to make a ball of the proper size. From four to eight drachms of nitre, given in a mash, may be sufficient to prevent the plethora which idleness on a working-day might produce, and it is useful when work has excited a little fever, or swelled the legs. No diuretic is to be given within forty-eight hours after, nor before profuse sweating.

ALTERATIVES.—In the stables this term is not applied to any particular drug or prescription. Almost every groom has a recipe of his own, and the effect, when any is produced, must vary according to the articles employed. Taken as a class, the alteratives used in training may be regarded as gentle evacuants, acting upon the secretions of the skin, the bowels, and the kidneys. Nitre, resin, sulphur, balsam of sulphur, Ethiop's mineral, cream of tartar, black antimony, tartar-emetic, calomel, cinnabar, with a host of gums, spices, and herbs, are used individually, or in various combinations. Many inert articles are employed. Very often so little is given, that neither ill nor good follows, and sometimes a dangerous and fatal dose is given through ignorance of its powers.

In former times it seemed to be a rule that the horse should swallow a certain quantity of medicine every year, whether well or ill, poor or fat; and among grooms who pretend to much knowledge, and have a great deal of ignorance, it is still a custom to force drugs upon him, not so much to cure as to prevent. If any evil be threatened, or in existence, it is very right to take measures to prevent or to cure it; but the people I speak of give drugs without seeing any sign that they are wanted. The horse may be as well as they desire him to be, and not exposed to any change of circumstances or treatment that can make him worse, and yet they give some stuffs which they call alteratives.

In training, good grooms do not employ means of this kind without some reason. The horse may not be altogether right, his bowels or his skin may be out of order, his legs liable to swell after work, or frogs to get thrushy in the house. The horse may have a bad appetite, or his appetite may be too good. For these and suchlike matters some medicine which will gently stimulate the secretions of a particular organ may be very useful. An alterative powder in very common use is composed of antimony, nitre, and sulphur, mixed and given in the same doses, and with the precautions, which are mentioned in connexion with grooming, to produce a fine coat. When the skin is rigid, the hair dry—when there any pimples or itchiness upon it—when there is any tendency to swelled legs or thrushes—a few of these powders may be given with benefit, a stronger remedy, such as sweating and purging, being unnecessary or impracticable. When a bad day keeps a hearty eater off his exercise, one or two of them will prevent repletion.

Sometimes the antimony is given alone. Nimrod recommends an ounce every day, for eight days together. The horse should not hunt nor race till a week after the last dose.

CORDIALS.—These medicines are seldom wanted in training. Their principal use is to give the horse an appetite. There are many spare feeders among fast-working horses. They are apt to refuse their food every time they are excited, or exhausted by more than usual work. To such, a cordial is now and then of some service. There is no need for the costly and complicated preparations which are sometimes given.

Take of carraway-seeds	·	·	·	·	·	3 oz.
Anise-seeds,	·	·	·	·	·	3 oz.
Allspice,	·	·	·	·	·	3 oz.
Cloves,	·	·	·	·	·	2 oz.
Gentian root,	·	·	·	·	·	4 oz.

These should all be ground to a fine powder, and beaten into a solid mass with treacle or honey. Divide the whole into twelve balls. One may be given at any time when there is no fever. When the eye and nostrils are red, the mouth and skin hot, they are forbidden.

MUSCULAR EXERTION.—A good deal has been said about exertion in other parts of this work, and it is not necessary to say much here. In preparing for fast work the rule is to proceed from less to more, from a short to a longer distance, from a slow to a faster pace, always by small degrees. In the first week most of the exercise may be given at a walk. This pace has been objected to by Nimrod. He says it injures the legs, and produces spavin. He is in error: there is no pace at which the legs are so safe. When the horse is kept at it for several successive hours, he may be fatigued; but the fatigue falls upon the muscles, not upon the joints nor the tendons. The horse may lie a great deal after much walking exercise, but it rarely makes him lame. Cart-horses often travel ten hours a day, for months together; and though all their work is performed at a walk, they have no spavin till they are overburdened, and not often then.

Walking exercise empties the bowels—gives the horse good use of his limbs—gives him an appetite for food—promotes the secretion of the lungs, the skin, and the bowels—and when much is given, under a good rider, it teaches the horse to walk quickly and gracefully. Even at the beginning, however, all the exercise need not be given at a walk. The horse, whatever be his condition, is always able to take some faster exertion. The walk, the trot, the canter, and the gallop, may alternate one with another, no more of either being exacted than the horse can bear without injury. But when intended to perform his work at any particular pace, at cantering for example, he is to get as much of that as it is safe to give him. A lady's horse would be ill prepared if most of his exertion were a trot. The preparatory exertion should resemble the work as soon and as far as it is safe to give it.

The slow paces make the horse leg-weary. If he lie more than six hours out of the twenty-four, his legs being sound, he is getting too much exercise. Fast paces endanger the lungs of an untrained horse. The rider should know when he has gone as far and as fast as it is safe to go. Existing distress is indicated by signs which do not require much experience to recognise them. They are described in connexion with the accidents of work. The signs which indicate the *approach* of distress are not so well marked, but they are quite visible. The first is rapid and short respiration; the second frequent protrusion of the muzzle, as if the horse wanted more rein; and the third is a deep, prolonged inspiration, something like a sigh, in which the rider feels his legs thrown apart by the expansion of the horse's chest. Quickness of respiration is a necessary consequence of exertion, and it is a symptom of distress only when excessively rapid and short. The protrusion of the muzzle shows that the horse is at nearly all he can do. This is not to be mistaken for the pull of a horse eager to get away; he quickens his pace as he gets his head free. When distress is coming, the head is often darted downward or forward; and though more rein be given, the

28

head still dives, but the horse goes no faster. He need not, in all cases, be pulled up for this; it may be sufficient to slacken the pace for a few hundred yards, to go slower, until he recover a little. The deep sight demands immediate relief; to continue longer at the same pace, even for no more than two hundred yards, is attended with considerable risk. The horse may be fairly over-marked. He may proceed a short distance, but he ought to be held in if possible, or he ought to stand quite still, which is the safer plan, until he recovers his wind. At work, circumstances may demand a continuation of the pace, notwithstanding this sign of distress; but, in training, the deep inspiration should stop it at once.

The severest exertion given to the horse in training is that termed sweating. A certain distance is aimed at; but the groom generally knows pretty well how the horse will bear it before he it is sent to it. He is previously tried in short gallops, which are lengthened by degrees. Horses usually snort, after performing a little smart work; they clear the nostrils by a sudden and forcible expiration. This act does not resemble sneezing nor coughing. The nostrils play to and fro as the air is expelled, and make a peculiar noise, which is well enough expressed by the term *snorting*. It is quite voluntary: sneezing and coughing are not. Many horses do it when starting, but the groom attends to it particularly after a trial gallop. Should the horse clear his nose almost the instant he is pulled up, he has wind enough to go farther and faster in his next gallop; should a minute elapse ere he snorts, still the pace and distance may be increased, but not much. In the next trial, should the horse stand for two minutes without snorting, his gallop has been severe enough for his condition, and it may have been too much so. He does not snort till his breathing is easy; and the more he is unwinded the more time he takes to recover. It seems, however, that some horses do not snort as soon as they recover freedom of breathing. I have watched one for half an hour, after a severe run, without noticing him clear the nostrils; and I have repeatedly observed that, especially after long-continued exertion, the horse does not snort for a good while after his breathing is quite tranquil.

The ground upon which exertion is given is a matter of some consequence. A hard stony surface injures the feet and the legs, and a fall upon it is a serious affair. Deep ground, that *in* which the foot sinks, demands great exertion to get through it, and it hazards the legs, though the rider may have judgment enough to save the lungs. Rough irregular ground gives the legs so many twists, that a fast pace is very apt to produce a sprain. The best is that which resembles a race-course— soft, yet firm.

The kind and degree of exertion must vary with the condition of the horse; the mode of giving it must vary a little according to his disposition. A lazy horse is generally robust, and not much disposed to over-exert himself; he may require a good deal of urging to keep him at the pace, and make him go the distance. He is apt to stop when not inclined to run. If allowed to have his own way a few times at the beginning, it becomes a difficult process to train him, and still more difficult to work him. On the course he may choose to lose a race, and in the field he may fancy he has done enough before he has well begun. A horse of this kind requires to be well mounted. In his training exertion he must be ridden by one who has strength to manage him, and judgment enough to distinguish between laziness and distress.

There are many other horses quite different from this kind. They are timid, easily agitated, easily injured, and very apt to over-exert themselves. The least harsh treatment alarms them; they tremble, the limbs totter, the stride is irregular, unsteady; the horse is so precipitate in his movements that he is often lamed or thrown down. Without whip or spur, such a horse would run till he died. Even a little extra exertion puts him off his feed. These horses are generally less robust than those of phlegmatic temperament: they should seldom carry much weight; yet a thoughtless boy is almost sure to abuse such a horse. He ought to be treated with great gentleness. Some are least alarmed when ridden alone, others when they have companions, which, however, ought not to be sluggards, for a timid horse is in terror when he sees or hears another punished. In general, severe exertion should not always be given on the same ground. After once or twice, the horses get alarmed whenever they arrive there, and know what is coming. But the same place may be used for both the severe and the gentle exertion; and, by stealing slowly away at first, the horse may do his work before he knows that he has begun it. The warning of severe exertion gives him more alarm than the exertion itself.

Indeed all horses should start slowly. A gentle pace prepares the legs, and puts every organ in order for a severe task. It gives the horse time to empty his bowels, and to see the ground, and enables the rider to feel lameness, should there be any not previously observed.

PRESERVATION OF WORKING CONDITION.

The ultimate object of training, seasoning, or conditioning, is to fit the horse for performing his work easily, or at least with as little distress as possible. But it is not enough to give him condition; much must be done to preserve it. The muscles, the lungs, the blood-vessels, the nerves, the blood, every part and every organ connected with motion, undergo a change with almost every change in the treatment of the horse. The racer, it is said, must run upon the day for which he has been trained to run. I can not answer for the truth of this; but most likely it is true, if the horse have previously received all the training he is able to receive. It is very well known that horses which have been trained to extraordinary exertions rapidly lose the power of performing them, unless some means are taken to preserve it.

In the first place, the horse must have constant work. By constant, I do not mean daily work. No horse can race or hunt every day. A certain period of rest must be granted to all. For carriage, cart, and saddle horses, the night's repose is, in general, sufficient to recruit them for next day's labor; but hunters, racers, and many mail and post horses, require a longer interval of repose. They may be out only thrice or twice a week, and some of them not oftener than once or twice a fortnight. Still the work is constant. The time they rest is not, or ought not to be, more than sufficient for restoring such vigor as the work demands.

Agents that injure Condition.—Condition for work may be impaired or entirely destroyed in six ways. Disease, continued pain, idleness, excess of work, excess of food, and deficiency of food, all operate more or less against working condition. There are several other agents by which it may be impaired or destroyed, but those only which I mention seem to deserve particular notice.

Disease of a febrile character, or an inflammation in any of the vital organs, may attack the horse suddenly, and in one hour render him unfit for any work. If it were possible to remove such a disease on the same day, or at least in two or three days, the horse might still retain a portion of the condition he previously possessed. But this is not always *possible.* Between the disease and the cure the horse is much and unavoidably reduced. The debility which a febrile disease of itself produces, is often sufficient to destroy working condition as effectually as if the horse had never had any. Hence racers and hunters are often unfit to come to their work at the expected time. Perhaps influenza, or a similar malady, invades the stable, and for a time suspends all further training, and destroys that which has been given. It is the very same when the horse is at work. An attack of inflammation, or a fever in the middle of winter, throws the hunter out of the field for all the remainder of that season. By or before the time he has recovered, and again been trained, hunting is over.

That which is true of the hunter or racer in this respect, is not less true of other horses. Their work may not require such a long and complicated course of preparation ; but still they must have some. That which served at first may serve now, provided the disease be completely subdued. All diseases and fevers are not alike ; while one may wholly destroy condition, another may only impair it.

PAIN.—While a horse is in constant pain, he is never in excellent condition for work. Very acute pain materially impairs his condition in a couple of days. Many horses are compelled to work when lame, and it is well known that they never carry so much flesh, nor appear so gay, as when sound They are seldom indeed fit to perform full work. In double harness the sound horse generally has more than his share of the draught, and if the lame horse be very willing, he soon wears himself out. But horses are often in pain without being lame. All kinds of abuse and bad management, consisting in cold, comfortless stables, want of grooming, neglect of the proper hours for feeding and watering want of room to lie, disturbed rest from various causes, impair the horse's condition. Harsh usage from bad grooms often destroys the repose and the appetite of nervous horses. Discomfort and terror are actual pain, and though never very acute, yet its constant operation has a sensible influence upon the condition and appearance of the horse. Grease, and sores on the neck, back, or other parts upon which the harness rides, produce a great deal of pain, both in the stable and at work. A large sore on the seat of the collar impairs a horse's condition as effectually as want of food. All kinds of discomfort, annoyance, terror, or ill-usage, are as truly debilitating, when long continued, as the pain of a broken limb, though much less acute.

28*

IDLENESS, whether absolute or comparative, is injurious to working condition. When the horse obtains more rest than his work requires, he is idle.

Absolute Idleness is that in which the horse suffers close confinement in the stable or loose box. He soon becomes weak, fat, short-winded, and stiff. If well fed, he may retain health and spirit for two or three months; but in this time he almost loses the use of his legs, and his skin becomes foul and itchy. Horses that have been long, perhaps several years, in work, with short or no interruptions, become very stiff.

I am unable to say how soon absolute repose will entirely destroy working condition. The time must vary with the horse's employment, and the manner in which he is fed. Those of slow work may suffer confinement for six or eight weeks before they become as feeble as idleness can make them. If half starved, or fed so poorly that the horse loses flesh, less than a month will produce the effect. If fully fed, he accumulates a load of fat, which makes him weaker than idleness with moderate feeding would make him. Fast-workers lose their condition much sooner; one week of superfluous rest sensibly impairs the condition of a hunter; he loses wind, but he is still able for much work. To destroy his condition entirely, he would, in most cases, require about four weeks of close confinement, some would need less, and some would perhaps retain a portion of their condition nearly eight weeks. A great eater degenerates fastest.

Comparative Idleness is that in which the horse gets exercise, or perhaps some work, yet not sufficient to maintain his condition. The owner may not use him oftener than once or twice a fortnight, and he receives exercise from the groom in he intervals. Horses kept for work of this kind rarely have good grooms to look after them. They are generally in the charge of men who seem to think that exercise is of no use but to keep the horse in health. A daily walk, with a smart trot, will keep the horse in condition for moderate work; but if the owner ride or drive fast and far, and at irregular intervals, as much exercise as keeps the horse in health is not sufficient. Every second, third, or fourth day, the exercise should resemble the work. The horse should go nearly or quite as far and as fast as the owner usually rides him. It may be too much to do every day, or every second day; but keeping always within safe bounds, the horse should have *work*, or exercise equal to his work, at regular intervals.

Many people work a horse on Sunday, as if they thought **six** days of idleness should enable him to perform a week's work in one day. When the horse has much to do on Sunday, he should in general do nearly as much on Wednesday, and on other days he may have walking exercise.

EXCESS OF WORK.—A single day of severe exertion may destroy the horse's working condition. His lungs may be injured, a disease may succeed, and require many days to cure it. Between the disease, the cure, and the idleness, the condition may be wholly gone before anything can be done to keep or to restore it. This is termed over-marking, and it is not the excess I here mean.

That to which I allude is not the excess of one day. The horse may perform the work for several days, or even weeks, quite well, yet it may be too much to be done long. One of two things will happen, or both may occur together. The horse will lose flesh, and become weak, or his legs will fail, and he will become lame.

Emaciation, the loss of flesh from excess of work, is easily explained. The work is such as to consume more nutriment than the digestive apparatus can supply. The horse may have as much of the best food as he will eat, yet the power of the stomach and bowels is limited. They can furnish only a certain quantity of nutriment. When the work demands more, it is procured from other parts of the body. The fat, if there be any, is consumed first; it is converted into blood; a little is taken away every day; by-and-by it is all removed, and the horse is lean. Should the demand still continue, other parts are absorbed; the cellular tissue, and ultimately every particle of matter, which the system can spare, is converted into nutriment. When the whole is consumed, the supply must be wholly furnished by the digestive apparatus, and if that were unable to meet the demand at first, it is still less able now. By this time the horse is very-lean, his bones stare through the skin; he is spiritless, stiff, and slow, and his belly is tucked up almost to the backbone. The horse becomes unfit for work. Rest and good food soon restore him, but if work be still exacted, the solids and fluids change, the system falls into decay, and a disease, such as a common cold, or the influenza, from which a horse in ordinary condition would soon recover, produces in this worn-out animal glanders or farcy. Work is sometimes exacted till the horse is ruined, but the owner rarely escapes, for when glanders once appears it seldom stays where it begins.

General Stiffness usually accompanies emaciation. When first taken from the stable, the horse seems to be stiff all over; he obtains greater freedom of motion after he is tolerably well warmed by exertion; but he never has great speed. All old coaching horses are in this state, and all those, whether young or old, who have a deal of hard work, soon become more or less stiff. In racers and hunters, the extent of stride is perceptibly contracted toward the close of their working season. They are termed *stale*, and require some repose, and green food or carrots, and sometimes a little physic, to *refresh* them.

The Legs are often so ill formed, that they fail without any excess of work. But fast paces, long journeys, and heavy weights, ruin the very best. A single journey may produce lameness; it may give the horse spavin or grogginess: or some other lameness may be the result of one day's work. But this is more than excess. The horse may have to perform it twice or thrice in his lifetime, but if it be such as to make him lame, it is too much to form regular work. The excess to which I allude does not produce lameness till after the horse has done the journey several times in succession. When two or three become lame, it is high time to make arrangements for preventing more. The distance may be shortened, the draught or weight lightened, or the place retarded.

The legs often show that the work is in excess, though the horse may not be lame. The fore-legs suffer most, but the hind are not exempt. Where there is much up-hill work, or much galloping, the hind fail as often as the fore. The pasterns become straight; and, in extreme cases, the fetlock-joint is bent forward; this is termed knuckling over. At a later period the knees bend forward. The whole leg is crooked, deformed, tottering. Besides these the legs become tumid, round, puffy. There is a general tumefaction, and the legs are said to be gourdy, fleshy, or stale. The deformity produces unsteadiness of action; the limbs tremble after the least exertion, and the horse is easily thrown to the ground. The tumefaction produces a tendency to cracked heels and to grease.

Very often the back tendons suffer enlargement, which, in some cases, depends entirely upon accumulation of the fluid by which they are lubricated, not upon any enlargement of the tendons themselves. The hock and fetlock joints are always large and puffy. These enlargements are termed wind galls, bog-spavin, and thorough-pin. They are little bags containing joint-oil which prevents friction. Rapid and .asting exertion increases the quantity of this fluid, and dilates the bags which contain it.

The legs of racers and hunters are always more or less the worse of wear toward the close of their working season. If these horses were wanted all the year through, the legs would demand rest, though the ·body might not. Hunters rest all summer, racers all winter, and during repose, their legs regain their original integrity and form.

The legs of horses are very differently constructed. Some are so well formed that they suffer a great deal before they begin to fail ; others are so defective that they will not stand hard work. With racers and hunters much may be done to save them; fermentations, hand-rubbing, and bandages, are of much service after severe work ; but they require too much time and attendance to be employed for inferior horses. In mail and ~coaching studs, horses with bad legs may be put to short stages ; and in many cases it may be proper to let them go to spring grass for four or six weeks ; there the legs may be restored so far as to preserve the horse for a year longer.

It is the fashion at present to dispense with breech-bands or breeching for stage-coach horses ; and where the road is pretty level, or the coach light, they are of little use. But it seems to me they have been too generally discarded. Without breech-bands the whole weight of the coach in going down hill is thrown upon the neck, and from the neck to the fore legs. Hilly ground is destructive to both fore and hind legs ; but the fore ones always fail first. I think breech-bands on the horses that have the worst stage, would make the fore legs last longer.

The Feet are often injured by excess of work. The fore feet are liable to one disease which has been denominated, with as much truth as energy, "the curse of good horses," I mean the navicular disease, or grogginess. It is very common among all kinds of fast-workers. Bad shoeing, neglect of stable cares to preserve the feet, hard roads, and various other agents, have been blamed for producing it. But it seems to me the most common and the most certain cause has been too little considered. Long journeys, at a fast pace, will make almost any horse groggy. Bad shoeing and want of stable care both help, but, I am nearly sure, they *alone* never produce grogginess. The horse must go far and fast ; if his feet be

neglected, or shoeing bad, a slower pace and a shorter distance will do the mischief; but I believe there is nothing in
the world will make a horse groggy, except driving him far
enough and fast enough to alter the synovial secretion of the
navicular joint.   Cart-horses are quite exempt; horses working in the omnibuses about Glasgow, always on the stones,
and often at ten miles an hour, but never more than a mile
without stopping, are nearly exempt.   The horses most liable
are those which work long and fast stages.

I can not pursue the subject in this treatise.   I mention it
as one of the evils of excessive work.   When many horses
become groggy, the stages should be shortened, divided into
two, even though no more than one hour can be allowed for
rest between them.   Founder is sometimes, though very rarely, the result of excessive work; but in most, if not in every
case, there is also some error in feeding or watering in operation at same time.

Though I have spoken individually of the evils arising from
excess of work, it must not be supposed that they always exist
separately.   One horse may merely lose flesh; another may
become stiff; a third stale on his legs; and a fourth may suffer only in his feet.   But it most frequently happens that the
horse is affected in more ways than one.   In general, emaciation, stiffness, and staleness of the legs, go together.

For some kinds of work the horse can be kept in condition
all his life.   But the fastest kinds can be performed only for
a small portion of a lifetime.   Coaching-horses are worn out
in from three to four years.   I have known some last upward
of ten, but these were exceptions.   Hunters and racers would
be done much sooner, were their work as uninterrupted.   The
legs decay, however good the body may remain, and long before old age arrives.   If it be desirable, as in the case of
hunters it is, to preserve the horse till age impairs his powers,
he must be put out of work always before his legs are irrepar-
ably injured, and kept idle, or at some easier work, till they
regain primitive soundness.

Before the close of their working season, hunters and racers
are often sensibly impaired.   Some are stiff, some lean, some
gourdy-legged.   Should any of these signs appear long before the end of the season, it may be necessary to rest the
horse for a while in order to refresh him.   Carrots or green
food may be given with the grain.   Physics or alteratives may
be useful, and directions are given concerning them in another
section.   Exercise should not be neglected, nor given in ex-

cess. From three to six weeks may be required to refresh the horse, but the time varies so much, according to the horse's condition, that it is not possible to state any precise period.

EXCESS OF FOOD.—Horses that are doing full work, as much as they are able to do, can hardly have an excess of food. Some kinds of work, such as that given to mail and stage horses, require an unlimited allowance. If the horse have good legs, or legs equal to the pace, distance, and weight, he can not perform all the work of which he is capable, without as much grain as he will eat. But there are some kinds of work, such as racing and hunting, and especially steeple-chasing, which are so injurious to the legs, that long intervals of repose are necessary; sometimes eight to ten days must elapse before the horse can repeat his task. In this time a great eater will become fat and short-winded upon a full allowance of food, or his skin will itch and rise in pimples. In such a case, bran-mashes, or a few carrots, should be given now and then instead of grain. Alteratives, diuretics, and such like evacuants may be given; but, I think, more economy in the distribution of food would render them less necessary.

DEFICIENCY OF FOOD impairs condition much sooner and more certainly than excess. It produces emaciation and stiffness, dulness and weakness, in less time than excess of work. The food is deficient when the horse loses flesh, and gets less grain than he would eat. The work is in excess when he loses flesh, and has all the grain he will consume.

TREATMENT AFTER WORK.

THIS section treats of the cares and appliances usually or sometimes bestowed upon a horse after severe work. Some of them refer to ordinary work. All horses require water, food, cleaning, and bedding, at the end of their exertions; but some, in addition, have need of cordials, fomentations, bandages, and nursing.

CLEANING.—If possible, the horse is to arrive at his stable cool and dry; when not possible, the first thing to be done is to make him so, and the quicker the better. It is not of importance to clean him thoroughly. When made quite dry and cool, further grooming may be put off till the horse has rested a few hours, or till next morning, if he be much fatigued. The feet being examined, clothes applied, water and grain given, the horse is bedded, and left to repose.   Inferior horses after ordinary work receive no other care.

When the horse comes in very hot, he is, weather permitting, to be walked about till cool ; he is not to enter a warm stable until the breathing be perfectly quiet and the skin dry ; a close stable makes him faint and sick, and encourages further perspiration.   When he comes in wet he is to be dried immediately, or kept in motion till the skin dry of itself. When very tired, the sooner he is stabled the better, but still he must not be left at rest till dry and cool.   When he has been long out, encourage him to urinate before dressing him.

FOMENTING THE LEGS.—I believe this is a useful operation after a day of extraordinary exertion.   It subdues or prevents the tumefaction of the joints and sinews, to which the legs of many horses are very liable.   The water should be as hot as the hand can bear it, yet not hot enough to pain the horse. Clean water is the best fomentation ; salt, sugar of lead, Goulard's extract, soap, and herbs, are sometimes added ; they are perfectly useless, and in large quantities some of them fire the skin.   The legs need not be bathed higher than the knee and the hock-joints.   The water is applied with a sponge, and if possible, there should be a man to each leg.   If there be but one groom, the operation is tedious to a tired horse, and wet warm bandages may be employed as a substitute for fomentation.   That the horse may lie dry, he should be fomented out of the stall, or loose-box, whichever be destined for his repose.   If he flinch as the sponge passes over a particular place, that part is to be examined, lest a thorn be lodged in it.   After the mud is washed off, the hand may be drawn gently up and down the legs in search of thorns.

The fomentation need not be continued above ten minutes. When finished, the legs are to be enveloped in flannel bandages, dry if the legs be sound, or wet if there be any sign of injury or inflammation.

LEG BANDAGES are strips of flannel four to six yards in length, and four or more inches in breadth ; each has strings at one end for tying.   It is coiled up with the strings in the centre ; the groom unrolls it as he wraps up the leg.   Two coils run completely round the pastern, close to the hoof, and the rest is wound round the leg in a spiral form, each coil overlapping another until the leg is bound up to the knee or the hock, where the bandage is secured.   Few horses will attempt to lie when the bandage is carried over these joints. Care must be taken that the bandage presses equally, and not tightly; the strings should admit the finger after tying. The bandages, one to each leg, are used sometimes wet and sometimes dry.

Dry Bandages are necessary only when the legs are wet or cold, or likely to become cold; they confine heat, and absorb moisture. After they have done all they are wanted to do, they should be removed, and the legs hand-rubbed for a little. Some horses will not lie with their legs bandaged. They must be taken off before night, or they should not be put on; the legs may be dried and warmed by hand-rubbing. A dry bandage should always be quite loose, just tight enough to keep its place. When firmly applied, it does not retain the heat so well.

Wet Bandages are of more service than stableman are generally aware of. They retain heat, reduce and prevent swelling, and abate inflammation. When the horse is subject to swelled legs, to tenderness and tumefaction about the joints and sinews after severe work, warm wet bandages help greatly to preserve the legs. If fomentation can be well and quickly performed, it may; if not, it is better not attempted. The bandage may be dipped in warm water, and applied rather more firmly than a dry bandage. The heat and the moisture operating together, produce gentle and continued perspiration. The effect is nearly, or quite the same as if the legs were in a warm poultice. If the horse will lie with them, the bandages may be kept on all night; but they *must be kept wet*. The legs may be dipped into a pail of warm water at shutting up the stables; or the bandages may be so long and thick that they will remain moist till it is time to remove them. A dry bandage to an inflamed leg does more harm than good. It retains the heat without producing the perspiration which abates inflammation. The hind-legs rarely need wet bandages.

WATER.—The tired horse is usually disposed to drink more at one time than is good for him. The water should be tepid, and given every fifteen or twenty minutes, till the horse refuses more. He may have a couple of quarts whenever his work is done. Gruel or hay-tea may be given when the horse needs nourishment, and refuses solid food. He will not take either till it is nearly cold.

FOOD.—Fatigue destroys the appetite of some horses very readily. Carrots, boiled barley, malt, or any article which the horse is known to prefer, may be offered in small quantity. After a severe day, the food should be rather laxative, for hard

29

work constipates the bowels, which is easily obviated by a bran-mash.

Grooms are often in too great a hurry. Though the horse should not eat till he has rested a few hours, he is none the worse. There is no occasion for forcing food upon him, and it is not always necessary to excite the appetite by cordials. Gruel is very good, if the horse will take it himself ; but it is absurd to pour it into a stomach which can not digest it. The very act of forcing it on him is particularly distressing, and it should never be done. I know of no state of the body in which it is ever proper to force food upon the horse.

CORDIALS are sometimes useful after great exhaustion Robust good-tempered horses rarely need them. Timid nervous horses are a good deal agitated by fast work, and in general they remain in a state of fretful excitement for a good while after the work is over. These are much the better of a cordial : a ball, not a drink. Draughts are annoying and disgusting to the horse, though perhaps very palatable to the groom. One ball is sufficient ; it may be given half-an-hour after the horse is dressed. Very often the horse needs nothing but water to give him an appetite.

BEDDING.—A loose box is the best place for a tired horse. It gives him choice of position, and he assumes that which is most favorable to repose. It should be deeply littered over all its length and breadth. When a stall must serve, it should be the widest, the litter deep, and carried back farther than usual.

PULLING OFF THE SHOES.—There are few cases in which it is proper to remove the shoes, merely because the horse has been doing much work. It is not an uncommon practice ; but I believe it has had its origin in a theory or supposition that the shoes act in much the same manner upon the horse's feet that boots act upon those of his rider. The shoes of the horse produce no general compression and no part is relieved from painful pressure by removing them. If the feet be disposed to founder, the soles flat, the shoes may be taken off, but in any other case it is needless. A cold moist stopping is of more use.

THE DAY AFTER WORK should seldom be a day of absolute repose. If the horse be in a loose box, he will have little occasion for exercise, yet a walk of ten or fifteen minutes will do him good. He may be a little stiff, his appetite may be defective, or his legs may be swollen. Walking exercise, particularly in company with a steady companion, is a gentle and safe stimulant. It dissipates dejection and weariness, fines the legs, excites an appetite, empties the bowels, and in some degree removes stiffness. From five to fifteen minutes, morning and afternoon, may be sufficient. The exercise-ground should be soft, the horse lightly clothed, and both body and legs should be kept dry as possible. Unless the bowels be confined, the ordinary food may be given ; carrots or bran-mashes will obviate costiveness. Oatmeal gruel, well made, but quite weak, is the best drink, should the horse crave much water.

If the horse be slightly fevered, his eye red, mouth and skin hot, urine high-colored, bowels out of order, and appetite bad, one or two alteratives may be given. In this case the diet should consist entirely of bran-mashes, carrots, or green food ; and these will give place to the ordinary feeding, *by degrees*, as the horse regains his appetite. If he stand at night, without lying down to rest as usual, the lungs are injured, and the veterinarian should be called immediately.

Subsequently, as the horse recovers, his exercise is in-creased ; and if his work be such as to require four or five olank days, he may have a gallop, or a gentle sweat on the last.

ACCIDENTS OF WORK.

THE accidents of work are very numerous. A full description of each would form a volume as large as this. I select a few from those which occur most frequently, from those which may be prevented, and from those which require immediate attention.

CUTTING.—Young horses, timid horses, and those having ill-made legs, are apt to strike the fetlock-joint with the opposite foot. This is termed cutting, brushing, or interfering.

Fig. 18.

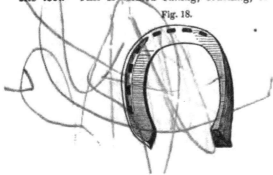

In almost every case, except when the horse is tired, this can be prevented by the shoeing-smith, who may apply a shoe like that represented in Fig. 18. When he can not, or when the fetlock is much swollen, a boot must be worn something like that represented in Fig. 19. It is nothing but a piece of cloth tied over the middle, with its upper half folded over the string. A leather flap is in use; it covers only the inside of the joint, and is secured by a single strap. It is apt to turn round and leave the part undefended.

Speedy cut is an injury of the same kind, and is produced in the same way, only the leg is struck higher up, and when the horse is going fast. The only way of preventing it is to cover the leg with a boot (see Fig. 19), A B or to apply a

FIG. 19.

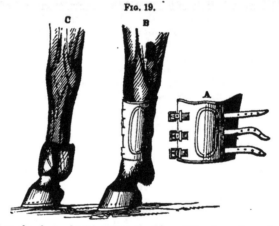

pad to the foot which strikes the leg. The boot does best, when on, the knee-joint must be quite free, and the tendons must have no inconvenient pressure. The pad will not sit on every foot, but it sometimes answers very well. It should be stuffed with horse-hair, and made to go quite round the foot. It is secured by a single strap and buckle, and is about an inch and a half broad.

OVER-REACHING.—The heel and the pastern are sometimes struck by the hind-foot. Most frequently it is the heel, just where the hoof joins the skin. It happens only in fast paces in leaping, or galloping over deep ground. Horses with short backs are most liable. A semicircular wound is made; the skin is raised like a flap, which folds backward and down-

He breathes, sees, hears, swallows, and his blood flows as usual. But the limbs, before and behind, are perfectly motionless and insensible. The horse may be pulled about, rolled over and over, pinched, pricked, and cut, as if he were quite dead. The head, part of the neck, and some of the internal organs alone retain vitality. Looking at the neck as it lies, depression or elevation is sometimes apparent; when not, the seat of injury is shown by raising the head; the neck yields all at one place. When it is clear that the limbs are all quite powerless, the neck fairly broken, recovery is out of the question. The horse may be destroyed. This accident is very rare on the road and on the race-course. It happened, however, on the Paisley course in 1836. The horse tumbled completely over his head, and lay with his tail homeward.

INJURIES OF THE HEAD.—The horse is often stunned from a side or a back fall, or from running against some fixed obstacle. The blow falls with such violence that the brain receives a shock from which it does not immediately recover. The horse lies motionless for three or four minutes; few lie longer without return of sense. Nothing can be done but to remove harness, girths, or whatever may encumber him. He should not be urged to rise, till he is fairly restored to himself. When the skull is fractured, the bones driven into the brain, the horse either dies immediately, or in less than forty-eight hours, never being able to get up. Fracture of the skull is not always indicated by an external mark. But it may be surmised, if the horse be unable to rise, or to stand when raised. Time is to be allowed for him to recover from stunning. Unless death be immediate, the horse always struggles. There is no palsy like that produced by fracture of the neck, or of the back. One or two of the legs, generally two on one side, are powerless when the horse is raised, but in almost every case he can move them while he is lying. When raised it is apparent that he can put only two below him. I have never known a horse recover from an injury of this kind.

BREAKING DOWN.—There are two injuries which go under this name. One is merely a sprain of the back tendons, usually in a fore leg. It may be so slight as to escape notice till the horse be cool; or it may be such as to make him fall very lame in the middle of his work. Pressure on the part injured produces pain. The horse should walk slowly home.

Fig. 21.

unless the horse can be made to alter his pace, by keeping his head well up.

The fore-shoes of clicking horses should be short and having the web broad. When too long, they are apt to be torn off; when too narrow, the hind-foot bruises the sole of the fore one, and may be locked fast between the breaches of the shoe. Hunters, however, must have the web narrow, for a broad shoe makes them slip on tough ground. It must be so narrow that it will not catch the hind foot.

LOSING A SHOE.—When a shoe gets loose on the road, proceed cautiously to the nearest forge. A fast pace will throw the shoe, and break the foot. Should the shoe be hanging off, or twisted across the foot, pull it away entirely, and remove any loose nails that might run into the foot. The loss of a shoe in the hunting field is a sad misfortune. If the ground be soft, and the foot strong, the horse may proceed till the sport be finished, when he may be led home, or to the nearest forge. A hind foot receives less injury than a fore one. Sportsmen sometimes carry a shoe, and set of nails, along with them. The shoe is jointed, that it may fit any of the feet. Mr. W. Percivall has invented a sandal, which promises to be of great use. It is secured by straps, and the rider can adjust it himself. It saves the foot until a shoe can be applied; and, over some pieces of ground, it will carry the horse even at a hunting pace. Mr Percivall has made it patent. It may be procured by sending a paper outline of the horse's foot, to Tate, saddler, Park Street, Grosvenor Square; or to Townes and Son, 141, Cheapside, London. Its cost is half a guinea. The following figures (Fig. 22) represent it on and off the foot.

FALLING.—Horses sometimes fall on the side, sometimes on the head, and sometimes back upon the haunches; but *most* frequently they fall upon their knees. A saddle-horse

Fig. 22.

seldom needs assistance to rise; but if old, stiff, exhausted, lying in an awkward position or upon ice, he may not be able to get up without help, and the rider should know how to afford it. Almost every horse rises with his head first; he begins by throwing out his forelegs, one by one; he can not rise when they are below him; he elevates the head, and then, by a sudden and single effort, he springs to his feet. If assistance be needful, it must be given by supporting the head. Do not stand before the horse, nor on the side to which his feet are lying. Go to the back, seize the reins close to the mouth; when the horse elevates his head, endeavor to keep it up, to render it a fixed point from which the muscles may act in raising the body; while one hand is supporting the head, place the other on the withers or shoulder, and push the horse off you, so as to set the body over the legs. It requires a good deal of practice to become expert in giving this assis tance. Some are so awkward about it that they will have the horse up and down half-a-dozen times, and bruised all over, before they get him on his feet.

In harness, the horse is seldom able to rise till liberated from the shafts or traces. About towns the moment a horse falls, he is surrounded by a crowd of officious assistants, every one giving orders, or doing some mischief. They are very fond of cutting the harness ; and if the owner do not look sharp, he will have traces, pole-piece, and back-bands, cut to shreds before he hears a word about it. The first thing to be done is to secure the horse's head. Keep it down that he may not injure himself, or do further mischief, in fruitless attempts to rise. The next thing to be done, is to unbuckle such parts of the harness as connect the horse with the draught. In double harness, it is generally sufficient to unbuckle the neck strap, which connects pole-piece and traces to the collar. By backing the carriage a few yards, the horse gets room to rise. When lying with his feet inward, his companion should be removed. If the harness do not come separate upon loosing the neck strap, the traces must be taken off the horse, or off the bar. In shafts, the carriage must be put back before the head is freed ; but if there is no weight on the back, and the legs are not entangled, it is enough to support the head, without unyoking the horse. After the horse is up, steady him for a few moments till he collect himself. Examine his knees, legs, haunches, head, and mouth ; see that none of the shoes are torn off. If not disabled, let him start at a gentle pace ; some part may be so painful or benumbed, that a hurried start will produce a second fall.

The Causes of Falling are very numerous. Bad riding, bad shoeing, or neglect of shoeing ; bad roads, over-reaching, cutting, an ill-fitting or ill-placed saddle ; a stone in the foot, and weakness of the horse, are among the most common causes. A bad rider may permit a horse to fall, merely by neglecting to support his head ; he may hurry over roads hardly fit for a walking-pace ; he may lean too much forward ; or he may ride the horse till he can scarcely put one foot before another. Bad shoeing may throw a horse down. By neglecting to shoe at proper times, or to change the mode of shoeing when the work changes, the feet become long, the shoes defective, or perhaps the horse goes to the field with shoes made for the road. There are various other causes which I have no room to describe. Indeed they all belong to horsemanship more than to stable economy.

The horse is sometimes severely injured. Mere abrasions of the head, the haunch, and other parts, need no notice. Among the most common and severe injuries, are those of the knee, the head, the neck, the back, and the legs.

BROKEN KNEES.—The skin may be only ruffled, or the knee may be bared to the bones; in both cases, and in all degrees between these, the slightest and the severest injuries, the horse is said to get a broken knee. The name does not, as a stranger might suppose, indicate fracture of the bones.

If the wound be superficial, the horse may finish his work. A handkerchief may be bound loosely round it merely to exclude air and dirt; but in general no treatment is required till the horse reach home. If the wound be deep, whether large or small externally, it will be prudent to ascertain whether or not it be fairly into the joint, which is little more than half an inch from the surface. Clear away the sand and mud, bend the knee, and examine the interior of the wound. It is sometimes so large that the bare bones can be seen at the bottom of it. When the external orifice is small, and the depth not apparent, the oozing of a whitish glary matter, resembling the white of eggs, is evidence that the joint is open. This fluid is joint oil, and is forced out by bending the knee. If it be clear that the joint has been penetrated, apply a bandage, and take the horse to the nearest stable, and put him immediately under the care of a veterinarian. Apply a poultice till he arrives. If the horse have to go above a mile or two after this accident, the oil will escape, the bones will rub one upon another, intense inflammation will succeed in the course of twenty hours, and ultimately the horse either dies of fever, or he becomes useless. The joint stiffens.

It is not always easy to be sure whether the joint is or is not penetrated. The wound is often in such a state with sand and mud, that the first examination can not be conclusive. When there is any doubt, the horse should, if possible, have the benefit of it. The danger increases with the distance and the pace. If he must go, all that can be done in precaution, is to apply a bandage. A neckcloth or handkerchief will do.

· When valuable horses are travelling, a kind of cap is sometimes applied to each knee. It prevents injury, should the horse fall. It is usually made of cloth, having a circular piece of leather, and a little stuffing opposite the joint. Knee-

into the belly, among the bowels, the horse may go home. When the belly is penetrated, a portion of bowel protrudes. Sometimes it is no larger than an egg. Whether large or little, the horse must not move a yard till something be done to replace the bowel, or to prevent further protrusion. As every motion of the horse tends to force out more of the intestine, he ought in the first place to be twitched. A twitch can be made from whip-cord, and a key or whip-handle will serve to tighten it, if nothing better be at hand. By a little gentle manipulation, the bowel may be replaced, the edges of the wound drawn together, and secured, by pins and tow, or hemp, and a bandage bound round the belly, sustaining a pad over the aperture ; the horse may then be led home, or to the nearest stable, there to remain till a veterinarian arrives. When the gut is wounded, it is not to be replaced till sewed ; none but the surgeon can do that properly. No hair nor the least particle of dust must enter the belly. When the bowel can not, or should not be put in place, a bandage and pad will prevent further escape till assistance is procured.

BLEEDING WOUNDS.—The shoulder and breast are exposed to deep and extensive wounds from shafts, from the pole and the splinter-bar. Until professional assistance can be obtained, all that need be done is to arrest the bleeding, which, however, is seldom very profuse from lacerated wounds. Some blood must escape, and much may be lost before life is endangered ; but if a large stream be running from some particular point, pressure may be applied till the veterinarian arrive. Endeavor to seize the wounded vessel between the finger and thumb, or apply a finger on the origin of the stream. This is better than general pressure, by means of a handkerchief, which fills the wound with blood, and prevents a proper examination by the veterinarian. Bleeding wounds on the legs may be bound by a handkerchief.

CHOKING.—Heavy draught horses, going up hill with much weight behind, sometimes choke in the collar. The collar presses upon the windpipe, and the horse instantly falls; sometimes he staggers for a moment before sinking, but in general there is no warning. Should the fall throw the collar off the windpipe, the horse recovers immediately. The first thing to be done is to free the windpipe, if it be not already free. The collar must be pulled down, or the draught rolled forward, so as to throw the strain from the collar. This must be done quickly ; pressure on the windpipe will produce death in three minutes. Should the driver observe

the horse stagger before he falls, he may keep him on his
feet by pulling him to a side, setting the wheels across the
hill.

When the horse is at a dead pull with his mouth full of
food, he is very easily choked. The accident is very common on canal banks. At certain places the horses are fed,
and often put to draw before the mouth is empty. As the
food goes down the gullet, it is intercepted by the collar, and
the two pressing on the windpipe instantly choke the horse.
He generally falls into the water. Many horses are lost in
this way. The mouth should be quite empty before the
horse is yoked. Before starting, a little water may be given,
which will carry the contents of the mouth before it. No
horse should be put to a hill, or to any dead pull, with food
in his mouth ; and, food or no food, the driver should always
keep his eye on the collar, and his hand at the head, while
the horse is going up a steep hill, with much weight behind
him.

Fast-working horses are liable to what is termed *swooning
in the collar*. The horse staggers, swings from side to side,
lies on the pole, stops and falls or falls running. I know not
whether this arises from pressure on the windpipe, or from
accumulation of blood in the head. It is most common in hot
weather, going up hill ; some are very liable to it. Whenever the horse shows any giddiness, he should be pulled up.
He will recover in a minute. Before proceeding, see that
the windpipe be free, and the bearing-rein slack. Should the
horse fall, remove harness, and assist him to rise, when he
revives. If water be at hand, give two or three quarts, and
start at a gentle pace. It is needless to bleed him at the
mouth. If bloodletting is to do any good, it should be from
the neck after work is over ; but it is rarely necessary. Next
journey, change the horse's place to the other side, to the
lead or to the wheel. Let his head be quite free, and see if
his collar can be improved ; and let him be fed an hour earlier than usual before going to work.

OVER-MARKED.—This word is synonymous with over-
exerted, over-done, over-driven, distressed, and blown. All
are applied, indifferently, to congestion of the lungs, to spasm
of the diaphragm, and to excessive fatigue.

Congestion of the Lungs does not occur all at once. It is
the consequence of keeping the horse too long at a fast pace,
or at the top of his speed. The first symptom is difficult
breathing. It becomes remarkably quick and short ; the nos-

trils are widely dilated; the horse frequently stretches out his head, as if he wanted more rein, yet goes no faster when he gets it; at intervals, short or long, according to the degree of congestion, he makes a deep, rapid inspiration, like a hurried sigh; the rider feels this though he can not hear it; his knees are thrown apart by the expansion of the chest. When these symptoms are apparent, congestion has begun in the lungs. If the horse be now pulled up, or even if his pace be slackened, he recovers his breathing in a little time, varying according to his condition, the depth of his chest, and the degree of congestion. Many horses become sulky and refuse to proceed any further; but the great majority of those employed at fast work can be urged on till they are seriously injured or destroyed. The horse, the camel, and the rein-deer, are, perhaps, the only animals that will kill themselves in the service of man. The dog, the ox, the elephant, and perhaps the ass and mule, disregard the lash when it demands oppressive exertion. But the horse has been so long and so completely subdued, that his obedience seems to have become hereditary.

If urged on after the first symptoms, the breathing becomes more difficult; the deep sigh and the protrusion of the muzzle more frequent. By-and-by the horse falters; his motions are sluggish, irregular, confused; he sinks often on his hind fetlocks, he staggers, reels, makes a running fall, and at last drops, or stands still gasping for breath. For a while before the horse is at his worst, he is so feeble that when put to a ditch or fence he is unable to clear it.

To prevent deadly or dangerous over-marking, the horse ought to be pulled up at the first sign of distress. If in good condition, he may recover his wind in a few seconds; if unprepared for such exertion, or if his chest be small, it may be several minutes ere he revive, and a very little will prevent him from proceeding any further.

When the distress is allowed to become very great, the horse must stop. Slacken the girths immediately, and take off the saddle. This is important: but some grooms have got a foolish notion that it is not right to remove the girths all at once in such a case. They say the wind will burst the horse. There is no need for argument here. I have repeatedly put the matter to experiment, and am perfectly satisfied that it is proper in every case to take the girths away as quickly as possible. Very often the horse recovers immediately, particularly when the girths have been drawn very

tightly, as they mostly always are in hunting and in racing.

Let the horse stand with his head to the wind, take off the
girths, and wait a little. He will get better presently, in five
or ten minutes, and then he may be led home. He must be
placed in a *cold, airy* stable; a warm or close one is very
dangerous. If the breathing does not become easier in eight
or ten minutes, the horse must be bled; but if, in this time,
his breathing become tolerably quiet, bleeding may be delayed till the horse is stabled, and it will then be seen
whether or not the operation is needful. .

Bleeding, when properly managed, gives immediate and
certain relief; but it is folly to bleed from the mouth in a
case of this kind. Open the neck vein, and take away six or
eight quarts of blood, as quickly as possible. As the skin
cools, dry it, and apply clothes. After the bleeding, give six
drachms of the carbonate of ammonia, powdered, and made
into a ball with water and linseed-meal. Give the first three
or four quarts of water quite cold, the rest tepid. Keep the
legs warm, give a bran-mash, and open the stable windows.

Sometimes the horse reaches home before it is apparent
that he is much the worse of his work. Perhaps he is stabled and dressed before it is observed that his breathing is
still quick, that he does not eat, that his eye is red, his crest
sunk, and flank tucked up. Put a finger upon the vein: if it
do not rise, bleeding need not be tried. Give the carbonate
of ammonia, and repeat it in an hour. Should the horse be
no better at the end of that time, it is probable he will then
bleed. The ammonia should make the blood flow. If live-
lier and the breathing easier, bleeding will not be necessary.
Keep the legs and body warm; but give pure and cool air to
breathe. Next day the veterinarian will see whether there be
any danger of inflamed lungs, which is often the result of
congestion.

Spasm of the Diaphragm takes place when the horse is at
work, or it is observed whenever he is pulled up. His flanks
heave rapidly; every fall is a convulsive jerk which shakes
the whole body; a loud noise is heard, as if the heart were
beating violently against the side. The diaphragm seems to
be the seat of intermitting spasm. The action of the heart is
always feeble and indistinct.

This affection is not very common. In a few cases it appears to exist independent of congestion in the lungs, but most
frequently the two are combined. They are produced by the

same causes. If the spasm do not cease in ten or fifteen minutes, give a dose of the carbonate of ammonia; and if the horse is not better in an hour, let him be copiously bled.

Excessive Fatigue is the result of a long rather than of a fast journey. The horse is very dull, his movements slow and stiff; he trips or stumbles at almost every step; when he gets home he eats little or nothing, lies much, is very restless, often changing his position; he drinks freely; sometimes he is a little fevered, the eye red and mouth hot. When there is no fever, the horse may have a cordial ball and his grain. When there is any sign of fever, a ball of the carbonate of ammonia is better; give a bran-mash, plenty of gruel, tepid water, only half grain, a good bed, a quiet stable, and rest for two or three days. On the second day the horse should recover his spirits and appetite. Stiffness remains for a few days longer.

KINDS OF WORK.

POWER AND SPEED bear a certain relation one to another. It has been long and well known that no horse can exert all his speed and all his strength at the same moment; as we increase the pace beyond a certain point, we must reduce the load; that as we reduce the load we may increase the pace; and that as we increase the demand, either for power or for speed, we must shorten the duration of labor. These are general principles, applicable to all kinds of horses, and to all kinds of work, at least to all work that deserves the name of labor.

Various experiments, chiefly in relation to drawing, have been made for the purpose of ascertaining in what degree power and duration decline as the velocity rises. But the strength and the speed vary so much in different horses, and even in the same horse at different times, that an approximation to the relation which one bears to another, is all that can be obtained or expected. The power of a horse is estimated by the load he can draw or carry a given distance in a given time. In drawing it has been stated as equal to a force of 160 pounds, the pace being about $2\frac{1}{2}$ miles per hour. Some experimentalists have rated it at only 112, others so high as 193, the pace being the same. But horses are so different that hardly two experiments can yield precisely the same results. The following table was constructed to show the rate at which power and dura-non decline as the pace is raised ; but it seems of no use except to illustrate the general principle.

Pace in Miles per Hour.	Power exerted in lbs.	Duration of Exertion in Hours.
2	112	10
3	74 two thirds	9
4	56	8
5	44 four fifths	7
6	37 one third	6
7	32	5
8	28	4
9	24 eight ninths	3
10	22 one tenth	2
11	20 four elevenths	1

In the table opposite will be found a statement of work at different paces. The table is not so complete as I wish, but so far as it goes it shows the amount of work actually performed. The weight of the load is stated at the highest, but on many days it may be considerably lighter, especially in stage-coaches.

AUTHORITIES AND REMARKS.	Pace in Miles per Hour.	Distance in Miles.	Number of Stages.	Time of resting between Stages, in Hours.	Weight of Load, Carriage included, in Cwts.	Number of working Hours or Minutes per Day.	Number of Working Days per Week.	Distance in Miles, performed every Week.
Howey's Glasgow and Edinburgh 2-horse wagons, 4 wheels.	2	22	2	8	60	11	6	132
Glasgow and Kilmarnock carriers; 1 horse, 2 wheels.	2¾	22	2	1	22 to 30	8	6	132
Glasgow and Lanark carriers; 1 horse, 2 wheels.	3	27	2	2	34	9	4	108
Howey's Glasgow and Edinburgh vans; 2 horses, 4 wheels.	4	22	2	1½	40	5½	6	132
Glasgow and Paisley coaches; 2 horses, 4 wheels.	8	16	2	1 to 6	32	2	5	80
Glasgow and Edinburgh coaches; 4 horses, 4 wheels.	9	16	2	3	46	1¾	3	48
Ditto, when roads and horses are better than usual.	9	16	2	3	46	1¾	4	64
Glasgow and Edinburgh Day Mail; 4 horses, 4 wheels.	9½	9	1	—	35	57 m.	7	63
Ditto, Night Mail.	10	8½	1	—	30	51 m.	7	59½
Glasgow and London Mail; 4 horses, 4 wheels.	11	8	1	—	30	44 m.	7	56

TRAVELLING.—The preparation for a long journey should consist in training the horse to suffer, with impunity, the influence of those agents and circumstances to which his work will expose him. He should be put into condition for the pace, the distance, and the burden; he should be well inured to the harness, to the weather, bad grooming, indifferent stabling, and irregular feeding hours. Without he be previously accustomed to all that he is likely to meet with in the course of his journey, a cold, a sore back, or a bad appetite, may throw the horse out of work when his place can not be easily supplied.

When there is no time for preparation, the horse may be conditioned on the road, beginning by short stages and proceeding at a gentle pace, and giving additional attention to feeding, watering, stabling, and dressing.

The horse should be shod a few days before starting. If lamed in the operation, the evil will be apparent, and cured in sufficient time to let him proceed.

For a journey of about 300 miles, the horse may travel from 20 to 25 miles every lawful day, resting on Sunday, and doing the work in two stages, when the pace reaches six miles per hour. This work requires a seasoned horse.

HUNTING requires much speed, and more stoutness. The horse must be swift and enduring. The pace seldom exceeds twelve miles per hour, and when quicker, or so quick, the run is short, soon over, or interrupted; yet soft sinking ground, hills, and leaps, make this pace very severe even on the best horses. Good legs are essential only when the weight is heavy, the ground generally deep, or the leaps numerous.

The time required for preparation varies from two to four months. When the horse is neither very fat nor very lean, he may be trained to hunting in three months; or if he has been doing some work for two or three weeks previously, or if he has a deep chest, wide nostrils, and good legs, two months may serve. In that time he may have all the power and speed, and stoutness, his work requires. Even after one month's preparation, he may be fit to enter the field, but when there he must be carefully managed, not tasked very far, nor very fast. His work must be such only as he would receive in training.

The means employed for conditioning hunters, are physic, exertion, sweating, and feeding.

On the day before work, the horse should have exercise sufficient to empty the bowels; if a great eater, he should have no hay before him within eight hours of going to the field; on the working day he should have no water within four hours of going to work, and his grain should be eaten about three hours before he enters the field. When the horse has above five or six miles to go ere he reaches cover, restriction as to fodder and water is less necessary, for the bowels are emptied on the way, the distance being performed at a gentle pace, perhaps at the rate of seven miles per hour.

The number of working days must vary with the condition of the horse in relation to his work. Sometimes he may go out every second day, sometimes twice a week will be sufficiently often, and after a very hard day the horse may not be able to come out again till the sixth or seventh. If he be in good spirits, full of life, and feeding heartily to-day, he may work to-morrow.

While the horse can hunt three days a week, he requires almost no exercise on his blank days; still he should have some, to stretch the legs, create an appetite, and empty the bowels. A walk of half an hour may be sufficient. Such work forbids medicines and sweating. When the work is so severe, or the horse so weak, or his legs so bad that he can not hunt above twice or thrice a fortnight, some alterative or evacuating medicine is usually required in the interval to prevent plethora. To other horses, cordials may be needful to create an appetite, or sweating exertion to keep the lungs in order. In general a stout hunter should have a sweat every third day. Great eaters, with defective legs, may need physic every six or eight weeks, to keep the carcass light, and to prevent plethora. Those who work well and feed well, may require an alterative every time they have to rest more than three days.

RACING requires more speed and less stoutness than hunting requires. The means employed to confer these are the same in both; the racer does not work so often, and, in training, his exercise is not so severe; but sweating and purging are carried farther in the racing than in the hunting stable, particularly with robust horses, near to or at maturity. The preparation, however, varies with the horse's age, the length of his race, the weight he has to carry, the condition of his wind and of his legs; with his disposition to work and to eat, with his temper, and with several other circumstances, all which are well known among practised trainers to require some peculiar treatment. These matters are so well understood by the only people who are interested in them, that it seems unnecessary for me to enter into detail; all that I could say about racing would be of very little use to anybody.

COACHING.—The horses employed in stage-coaches, mails, canal-boats, railways, and other public conveyances, are all prepared for work in nearly the same way; some difference, however, must be made according to the pace and the horse's condition. The proprietor usually allows a certain time to feed and to exercise the horse. It is supposed by a great many, that a new, an unseasoned horse, can not be in condition for work till he has been fed for some days or weeks upon hard food, oats, beans, and hay; some exercise is given, but, in general, I think not enough. They speak and act as if the feeding were the most essential part of the preparation. It is a great deal; but the exercise is quite as important. There is no kind nor quantity of food, that will, by itself, put a horse into condition for fast work. Unless he have exercise, gradually increasing in speed and distance as he can bear it, and increased till it closely resemble the work, the work can not be done easily nor safely.

The ordinary length of a stage is eight miles; but the owner of a large stud should endeavor to have some four-mile stages. At this short distance, unseasoned horses can easily be prepared for the longer stages, and while under preparation they are earning their food.

Some proprietors give physic and some bleed, but unless the horse be lusty, or very large-bellied, or the weather very hot, physic and blood-letting are not imperiously demanded.

In Mr. Lyon's stud the preparation is short and simple. Upon the first day the horse is tried in harness. If very fat, he gets one dose of physic, but in general no medicine is given. The horse is put at once upon working diet; he gets walking and trotting exercise for a week or ten days, and subsequently he goes to the road. In the first fortnight the horse may do only half work, going, perhaps, only half a journey every time he is out, or a whole journey every second or third day. By the end of four or five weeks, the horse is usually ready for full work.

Mr. Fraser, of the Eagle Inn, usually puts each new horse through a course of physic, generally consisting of three doses. He believes that the physic renders the horse less liable to inflammatory complaints; and when he is fat, it certainly does so. Some, however, do not need three doses, and some do not get more than one or two.

The work performed by coach-horses varies from fifty to

eighty miles per week, according to the pace, weight of load, and condition of the road. Four-horse coaches, going at nine miles per hour, and weighing about forty-five hundred weight, usually require a horse for every two miles, counting the distance both ways. A coach running between two places forty miles distant, employs about forty horses to take her away and bring her back.

In some cases the horses work every day, in others only thrice a week, doing, however, double the work every day they are out. When it can be so arranged, it is much better for the horse to do eight miles every day, than to do sixteen every second day.

The work is not always quite regular. An able horse has occasionally, perhaps once or twice a week, to perform a double journey, one of the team being defective, able for only half work, or during a few days unfit for any.

The Glasgow and Paisley Coaches are horsed by Messrs. Lyon and Walker. They run every hour. The distance is very nearly eight miles, which is done in one hour by two horses. When snow lies deep, three and sometimes four are put to the coach. The horses stand for three minutes at half-way. They work five days a week, doing sixteen miles each day. They go and return, resting from one hour to six. This is full work; but in busy times the horses sometimes run a double, or even treble journey, getting some indulgence for a day or two afterward. Defective and unseasoned horses do only half work. They may go out to-day and not return till to-morrow. Some others, very good horses, but easily injured, are so arranged that they shall have a longer time to rest. They usually rest one or two hours after the first stage before commencing the second; but these delicate horses are sent out in the morning, rested all day, and returned at night. Many, with bad wind, bad appetite, or bad legs, are thus kept at full work, who would be knocked up in a week, if required to perform the second stage in an hour after completing the first. Coaching-horses rarely receive any exercise on blank days. They are kept in the stable, well-bedded, and encouraged to lie.

CARTING.—Cart-horses work from eight to ten hours every day, except Sunday. The pace varies from two miles to three and a half per hour. At long distances the draught rarely exceeds thirty hundred weight, cart included. At short distances it ranges from thirty to forty. Twenty-four hundred weight, besides the cart, which weighs seven or eight, is the usual load hereabouts, all placed on two wheels.

The preparation for carting is very simple. The horse is put at once to work; for the first ten or fourteen days he does only half work, afterward he does a little more every day, or every other day, till he is fully conditioned.

PLOUGHING.—" The following has been ascertained to be the quantity of land ploughed, and the ground gone over by a team working nine hours :—

Breadth of furrow Slice.	At 1½ miles per hour.			At 2 miles per hour.		
	Acre.	Rds.	Per.	Acre.	Rds.	Per.
8 inches,	0	3 ·	36	1	1	7
9 "	1	0	14	1	1	33
10 "	1	0	35	1	2	21
11 "	1	1	14	1	3	5

" The distance travelled at the slow pace, was twelve miles, at the quicker it was sixteen miles."*

REPOSE.

IN another place I have stated the immediate effects of muscular exertion. Fatigue, the result of exertion, consists in a particular state of the muscles, the joints, the sinews, and some other parts. Action exhausts the muscles, consumes the blood, the joint-oil, and other fluids connected with motion. Maintained for a certain time, action also inflames the muscles, the sinews, and the joints. During repose, these parts should be partly or entirely restored to that condition which is most favorable to exertion. But if the rest be disturbed, or its proper duration abridged, the consequences are more serious than people generally imagine. The loss of one night's rest renders the horse unfit for work next day. There are many cases, however, in which the horse is almost never permitted to enjoy complete repose. He is frequently compelled to stand when he ought to be lying. The consequences are precisely the same as those arising from excess of work.

The horse does not sleep much, perhaps little more than four or five hours out of the twenty-four. He can rest, however, pretty well when he is standing, and still better when he is lying, though he should not sleep.

By a peculiar arrangement in the horse's limbs, he is able to obtain more rest while standing than any animal I know of; yet, without recubation, his repose is never completed. He may be kept always on his feet, yet he never works so

* Complete Grazier, p. 198.

well, nor lasts so long, as when he lies six or eight hours daily. The legs fail, the horse becomes stiff; his joints and sinews suffer from repeated slight attacks of inflammation, which at last produce lameness. The work is blamed, and very often work is the only cause ; but sometimes it is the want of rest, not excess of work, that does the mischief.

The bed should be well made, the stall sufficiently wide, and the stable quiet. There should be no work going on, nor any person admitted to the stable while the horse is reposing, nor while he is likely to be lying. Two horses should never stand all night in one stall, as often happens at crowded stables. Neither can lie, and that rest which either could take standing, is broken by the other.

Some horses never lie, they sleep standing, or reclining against the travis. A few sink on their knees, and sleep for a few minutes in that position. Some have a stiffness of the back, which renders them unable to rise without assistance, and therefore they forbear to lie, assistance not always coming when they want it. Others have got a fright in a narrow stall, which may have prevented them from rising easily, or at all. This is remembered for ever, and the horse stands always, however wide his stall may be made. Others still, refuse to lie after having been halter-cast and severely injured ; they will not lie while the head is tied.

Some of these horses may, however, be induced to lie. Try a loose box, where the horse will have plenty of room, and need not be tied up. If that can not be procured, put two gangway bales to his stall ; these will confine him to it, and his head may be free. His stall should be wide.

If the horse can not be induced to lie, he may be supported while standing. Place him in slings. This apparatus consists of a broad canvass-belt, which goes under the belly, extending from the points of the elbows to the sheath. At each extremity there is a strong shaft, or staff, to which the suspending ropes are attached, and carried to the roof, or stall-posts. A breast-strap and a breechin are necessary to keep the belt in its place. The horse is not suspended. The belt is fixed close to the belly. When the horse is disposed to rest his legs, he has only to bend them, and the belt receives his body. Whenever he is tired of this support, he again stands on his legs. The breechin should be strong and broad, for many horses throw as much weight upon that as upon the belt. The belt is commonly made out of a canvass sack, stuffed with hay, and stitched like a mattress.

EIGHTH CHAPTER.

MANAGEMENT OF DISEASED AND DEFECTIVE HORSES.

Young Horses are not at full strength till they are nearly five years old. At fast work they require careful shoeing to prevent cutting, careful stable-management to prevent the evils arising from changes of temperature, to which they are more liable than mature horses. They are not fit for full work, but they require good feeding for what they do.

Old Horses, those above ten or twelve, are rarely fit for long stages. They are soon exhausted. They need full feeding ; and some, having bad teeth, need to have much of their food broken or cooked.

Defective Fore Legs last longest in harness, and in the lead ; but when the horse is apt to fall, when he is a notorious stumbler, he is better in the wheel. The other horse helps to keep him on his feet.

Roarers do most work when their work is slow. Some can not go above five miles an hour : and many can not go more than four miles, when the pace is near eight per hour. Some do better on one side of a coach than on another. The head should not be confined by the bearing-rein, and the throat-lash should be loose. Time must be given in up-hill work, otherwise the roarer may choke and fall. He should work with little food in the belly ; the first mile is sometimes the worst with him ; a slower pace for the next half mile enables him to finish the remainder with less distress than when he is pushed from the start.

Chronic Cough, that is, a settled cough, is very common among fast-workers. It is most frequent when the horse is taken from the stable, when he returns to it, and after drinking and feeding. There is no cure. Occasionally a mild dose of physic ; and after severe work, or much exposure in bad weather, cordial balls soften and mitigate the cough. Many horses have it for years without any apparent evil, but it often produces broken wind. Carrots and boiled barley are good. The work should be regular.

Broken-winded horses require regular work, regular feeding, and a rich concentrated diet, consisting of oats, beans, and barley, in large measure, with a limited allowance of fodder. Wheat straw seems better than hay for these horses. From six to eight pounds is sufficient, if the work be fast; when slow, there is less need for restriction; carrots and boiled barley, one or both, may be of use. Bad food seems more injurious to broken-winded than to healthy horses. They drink much water, and before work they should not have so much as they would take. At night no restriction is necessary. Broken-winded horses are rarely fit for more than an eight-mile stage, to which they need an hour. But there are various degrees of the disease, some being much worse than others.

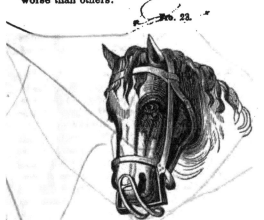

Fig. 23.

Crib-biters are horses who swallow air by a peculiar effort. They seize the manger or any other fixture with the fore teeth, arch the neck, and gulp over a quantity of air, making, at the same time, a grunting kind of noise. Horses often learn this from others: they should stand alone.

When the crib-biter swallows so much air as to enlarge his belly, to incommode his breathing, make him liable to frequent attacks of colic, or keep him lean, a broad strap may

be put on the throat, tight enough to prevent dilatation of the
gullet, yet not to stop the return of blood from the head.

There is a kind of muzzle sometimes used for the purpose
of preventing crib-biting among valuable horses. Its most
essential part is a kind of rack, consisting of two iron spars
jointed at each extremity, and curved to receive the muzzle.
The spars are about three fourths of an inch broad; the space
between them is wide enough to receive the lips, and let
them seize the grain and hay, but so narrow that it will not
admit the teeth. The horse can eat well enough; he can
reach his food with the lips, but he can seize nothing with
his fore teeth. This muzzle is better than a strap, which
disposes the horse to swelling of the head, and is blamed for
producing roaring.

Wind-sucking consists in swallowing air without applying
the teeth to any fixture. The horse presses his lips against
the edge of the manger, having his neck and back arched,
and his feet all gathered together. This habit does not seem
to be so often injurious as crib-biting. It is said that a
muzzle, having three or four short sharp spikes at bottom,
will prevent it. The points run into the lips when the horse
attempts to place them in position for sucking or swallowing
air.

Megrims [*or Epilepsy*].—Some horses are liable to giddiness at work. It is not the same as choking or swooning in
the collar. It seems to be a kind of apoplexy. The horse
drops without the least warning, lies for a few seconds insensible, and then rises somewhat confused. After two or three
attacks, the horse is sure to have more. Saddle-horses are
not exempt. These horses should be kept at slow work in
double harness. Their work and feeding should be always
the same. Excess or deficiency of what they are accustomed to, renders the attacks more frequent. Physic may be
given thrice a year or oftener. The food should never be
constipating. The bearing-rein should always be free. If
the horse be observed to stagger, he should be pulled up, and
allowed to stand two or three minutes. When he falls, he
needs nothing but time to recover his senses.

Blind Horses should not be placed within reach of a mischievous neighbor. They can not defend themselves nor get
out of the way. In harness the wheel suits them better than
the lead. When only one eye is lost, the horse should work
on the side from which he sees

Glandered Horses often work for years after they are in-curably diseased. They require to be well fed, well lodged, and well groomed. So far as my experience has gone, med-icine of all kinds is entirely thrown away upon them.

When the disease appears in a sound stud, the horse should be destroyed, or at least removed without delay. It is possible he may recover; and, if he can be kept where he can do no harm, he may have a trial. If permitted to remain, he is just as likely to give the disease to every horse in the stable, as to get better himself. It is generally supposed that glanders can not be communicated without actual appli-cation of the matter. This is not certain. I am pretty sure that, in some forms, it will spread through the air. It is prudent to suspect and to watch every horse that has breathed under the same roof with a glandered one.

When several are diseased, it may be worth while keeping them. They may be all put to one road, and kept in stables apart from the others; having men, harness, pole, and pole-chains, entirely to themselves. When it can be managed, they should not even enter the stable-yard where there are sound horses, and the men should be carefully excluded from every stable but their own.

When the horses die off, so that sufficient are not left to do the work, their place may be supplied by others, sound, but of little value. In this way, however, the disease is kept up. It is better to destroy the few that remain. Let the stalls, every portion of the stables, from floor to roof, both inclusive, be well washed with soap or sand and water. Let the wood-work be scraped or planed, and ragged portions chipped quite out. If the mangers and racks be of wood, and much wasted, remove them altogether, and replace them by others of iron. After washing, give all the stone or brick a coat of hot lime-water. Till all this is well and completely done, no sound horse should enter the stable; and even after it is done, the stable should stand empty for a week or two.

Sickness.—This word is usually applied to all dangerous or febrile diseases, all in which the horse is dull, pained, and without appetite. The stable-management of these must vary according to the nature of the illness. Directions are given by the medical attendant, as to diet, drink, ventilation, cloth-ing, exercise, and other matters likely to exert any influence upon the disease. In general, bran-mashes, carrots, green food, and hay, form the sick horse's diet; gruel, or tepid water, his drink. Whatever be the surgeon's orders, they

30*

should be strictly obeyed. In many cases a handful of oats
or a bucket of cold water, may keep the horse a week longer
from work, or even kill him.

Bleeding.—After a horse has been bled from the neck, let
his head be tied up for at least three hours, and if there be
no objection, it had better be tied up all night. Never tie it
higher than the manger. If the horse happen to faint, as
some do after a bleeding, he may be choked. The head is
tied high enough, when the horse can not get it lower than
the bottom of the manger. Never remove the pin and tow by
which the vein is secured. They will fall away in a few
days; but though they should remain for eight or ten, they
will do no harm. If removed too soon the vein is apt to in-
flame. It is best to let them remain.

Fomenting.—In fomenting for lameness or an external injury, the groom rarely has enough of water, and he does
not continue the bathing long enough to do any good. If the
leg is to be fomented, get a *pailful* of water as hot as the hand
can bear it; put the horse's foot into it, and with a large
sponge lave the water up as high as the shoulder, and keep
it constantly running down the whole limb. Foment for
about half-an-hour, and keep the water hot by adding more.
If a poultice or wet bandage is to succeed the fomentation,
apply it immediately, before the leg has time to cool.

Poulticing.—Warm poultices are usually composed of bran-
mash, to which it is proper to add turnips, linseed-meal, or
oatmeal porridge; either will do, and one of them is necessary, for bran alone does not retain heat and moisture sufficiently.

Whether applied for sores, bruises, or sprains, the poultice
should be large, moist, and as warm as possible and convenient. It is almost invariably too small; it should cover a
good deal more than the part injured. It should have as much
water as it will hold, and more should be applied every second
or third hour, either by pouring it on the poultice, or by dipping or soaking it. Care must be taken that no part of the
cords or bandages be too tight. They should admit the finger
quite easily after they are all adjusted. When properly applied, and properly attended, a good poultice need not be
changed in less than twenty-four hours. When the horse tears
it off with his teeth he must be tied up; when he paws or
throws it off, he must be shackled.

When too small, a poultice does little good; when too dry,
it confines heat, and increases inflammation; when the strings

are too tight, they stop the circulation of blood, cut the skin, and swell the leg.

Blistering.—Blistering plasters are never applied to horses. We always use an ointment, of which rather more than a half is well rubbed into the part to be blistered, while the remainder is thinly and equally spread over the part that has been rubbed. When there is any danger of the ointment running and acting upon places that should not be blistered, they must be covered with a stiff ointment made of hog's lard and beeswax.

The bedding is to be removed when the leg s blistered. To prevent the horse from slipping upon the stones, they may be covered with a little short litter, sawdust, or bark.

The horse's head must be secured in such a way that he can not reach the blister with his teeth. Put him into a narrow stall, and tie his head firmly to the rack. When a hindleg is blistered, fasten a small bundle of straw to each heelpost: place it high up, opposite the haunch. It keeps the legs off the posts, against which the horse is very apt to rub them.

When the blister has become quite dry, the head may in general be freed, and the horse let down. But sometimes it remains itchy after it is dry, and the horse rubs it. In that case he must be tied up again. If he get very tired, and threaten to go down on his haunches, put the beads on his neck, let go the head, give a good bed, and let the horse rest all day, a man watching him, if the beads are not sufficient to keep away the teeth. At night he may again be tied up, if there be any fear of his rubbing the blister.

When the blister is quite dry, put some sweet oil on it, and repeat it every second day. Without orders from the veterinarian, the blister is not to be washed off, either soon or late. Give it plenty of oil and time, and it will fall off as the new hair grows. By washing, the raw skin is often exposed, the hair torn out, and the horse blemished.

Medical Attendance.

The people who know, or pretend to know, anything about the diseases of horses, may be divided into three classes :—

Owners and their stablemen form one class. They stand at the bottom of the list, having just sufficient knowledge to prove they have any ; that little varies ; but in general it goes no further than to name a few common drugs, and a few common diseases. They know that aloes and resin are two different things; they can tell when a horse has broken wind, when he is a roarer, when a crib-biter, when he is lame, and when he is sick. Some can bleed, give a ball, and put in a rowel. Though they can tell when a horse is ill, yet they can not tell what ails him, unless it be some common affair, such as the influenza, which they may see often. They know when a horse is lame; but they are not very often able to discover where. When they blame the shoulder, it is very likely to be the foot. They can perform a few simple operations, among which bleeding and balling stand foremost; but few can perform these well, simple as they are, and many bungle them most wretchedly. In truth, they know so little, that they can not be depended on. They are just as likely to be wrong as right. But, notwithstanding this, it must be allowed that they know something, although they can not be said to know anything well. They confound one thing with another, like it, but not the same; grease, for instance, with farcy; a common cold with glanders; swelled leg with a sprain; foot lameness with shoulder lameness; and so forth in a hundred other things.

Horse-shoers and village blacksmiths form another class. Some have seen medicines, diseases, and operations, while in the service of a veterinarian, and some have learned a little about them merely by reading books and being consulted by the owner or his groom. Those bred in the country know less than an old stableman; those who have been in the employment of a veterinarian, sometimes know more. The little they learn is learned very slowly, and always imperfectly; but in time, some of them get a name, and subsequently a good deal to do, which teaches them more or less. Their knowledge, at best, resembles that of a nurse employed in an hospital, or about sick persons. Being ignorant of anatomy and physiology, they never improve beyond a certain point, and there are hundreds of things which they can not comprehend nor manage. Operations which require cutting they rarely try, and still more rarely perform as they ought to be performed. Most of them have a few books, of which the bad mislead them, and the good puzzle them.

All boast of practical experience, by which they mean they have seen a great deal. In all ranks, there are men who raise mighty pretensions upon a very slender foundation. Give them a telescope view of the moon, and they instantly become astronomers · show them a few experiments, and they are converted into chymists ; when they have seen a skeleton they have studied anatomy; when they have opened an abscess, or drawn blood, they are good surgeons, having performed many dangerous and difficult operations with great success. To such people is the world indebted for all kinds of quackery, and a good deal of knavery. Their practical experience is but a shadow ; their opinion a guess ; their performance a failure ; and their pretensions to skill, what are they, but the assumptions of ignorance, or the disguises of imposition?

The blacksmith and shoer usually term themselves farriers ; but in most all large towns there are some who take the title of veterinary surgeons, a kind of fraud for which the law has provided no remedy.

Veterinary surgeons form a third, and the only legitimate class of medical attendants on the horse. The term veterinarian came into use when colleges were established in different parts of Europe for improving, or rather for creating the art of treating disease in the lower animals. France founded in 1761 the first school of this kind. There were none in this country till thirty years afterward. At present there are two at London and one at Edinburgh. In each of these schools, the structure and diseases of domestic animals are taught from observations and study of the dead and of the living. The kind of instruction is not quite the same at each school ; but in all, the students have opportunities, many or more, of examining every part of the frame, both in health and in disease, and of watching and treating patients of almost every kind. In one winter, an industrious student will see as much at these places as the people who boast of great experience will see in the whole course of their lives ; and then everything is seen in the right way, the inside as well as the outside. After attending a stated period, the pupils are brought before a Board of Examiners, who ascertain their qualification. If fit to practise, they obtain a certificate, which is termed a diploma ; if not, they are referred to a longer course of study. No one who wants a diploma is a veterinary surgeon. A pretender may assume the name, and among an ignorant people he may carry on the imposition pretty well, and for a good while ; but the day seems to be coming when quackery must expire. The man of education now disdains the proffered services of an empiric for himself, and, erelong, he will take care that his horse or his dog shall not be added to the victims already sacrificed to ignorance.

THE END.

INDEX.

THE END.